Contents

Preface   viii

Réamhrá   xi

Acknowledgements   iv

1. Introduction   1
Materials   6
Tools and equipment   12

2. Creels   17
Technique   35
Mouthwhale   35
Standard creel   37
5 x 4 creel   45
Sligo/Donegal creel   45
Ulster creel   47
Back creel (County Tyrone)   49
Kerry creel   51
Rectangular pardóg (hinged-bottomed creel)   52
Tuam D-shaped pardóg   54
Úimeacha or oval slip-bottomed panniers   57
Aran seaweed creel   59
Crúbóg   62
The crandy   63
Kish   64

3. Potato baskets   67
The skib or ciseog   67
The sciathóg   71
Ulster potato harvesting basket   74
Oak chip potato baskets   77
Technique   80
Skib or ciseog grid base   80
Skib or ciseog, Joyce-country base   84
Sciathóg   86
Variations on the sciathóg   88
Ulster potato harvesting basket   89
Wicklow spale or chip basket   91

4. Wicker currachs 93

Technique 103
The Boyne currach 103

5. Fishing baskets 109

Technique 123
Ribh: Aran logline basket 123
Variation: wooden-backed rib with closed hoop front or head 124
Antrim longline basket 125
Eel trap 125
North Connemara lobster pot 127
Variations of west coast lobster pot 129
Heather lobster pot 131
Straight-sided hazel pot 132
Cork/Kerry bell-shaped lobster pot 133
Dunservick crab pot 137

6. Other traditional baskets 141

Technique 149
Aran cradle 149
Calf muzzle 152
Hand baskets 152
Cradle bird 154
Hazel sheep cribs 154
Wooden sieves 156

7. Straw, rush and grasses 159

Súgán ropes 160
Straw baskets and mats 163
Hen's nests, burden-baskets and chairs 168
Straw hats and costumes 174
Straw collars and harnesses 176
Rough horse-collars of thick *súgán* rope. 180
Rough plaited collars 181
Fancy plaited collars 182
Ox collars 184
Straw and hay packsaddles 185
The *Síogóg, Fóir* or straw rope granary 187
Rush 190
Technique 197
Straddle mat in three-strand plait 197
Hen's nests 199

BASKETMAKING IN IRELAND

Basketmaking in Ireland

Joe Hogan

Wordwell

First published in 2001
Wordwell Ltd
PO Box 69, Bray, Co. Wicklow

Illustrations by Barbara Kelly
Cover design: Rachel Dunne.

ISBN 1 869857 51 8

British Library Cataloguing-in-Publication Data.
A catalogue record for this book is available from the British Library.

This publication has received support from the Heritage Council under the 2001 Publications Grant Scheme.

Typeset in Ireland by Wordwell Ltd.
Repro: Niamh MacKenzie
Editor: Aideen Quigley

Book design: Nick Maxwell.

Coiled straw-work 200
Strawboy costume 202
Rush St Brigid's cross standard pattern 204
Three-legged St Brigid's cross 205
Rush cross using 42 rushes to give a pattern at the centre 205
Eye of God pattern 205
Rush rattle 206

8. Professional basketmaking 209
Technique 226
Underfoot base—round 226
Underfoot base—oval 228
Four-rod pull-down wale 229
French foot 231
Siding using slewing 231
Top wale 232
Borders 232
Handles 233

9. The future 235

Appendices 241
1—Basic techniques 241
2—Notes on curing a rawhide 251
3—Resources 253
4—Heritage collection of baskets 259
5—List of basketmakers working in Ireland about 1945 261

Notes 277

Glossary 285

Bibliography 297

Preface

THE MAIN reason for writing this book was to record the techniques used in making Irish traditional baskets, a task that became more urgent as indigenous baskets, such as creels and lobster pots, began to go out of use. It became apparent that some history of the baskets and their uses would have to be included, because in order to understand these objects, some knowledge of, and respect for the people who made and used them is required. The book is structured so that each chapter contains information that, it is hoped, might be of interest to the reader who has a general interest in traditional crafts; each chapter also has a technique section giving details of how to make many of the baskets described. This technique section is primarily of interest to basketmakers, and I would like to stress that the techniques described here are not the only ways in which these baskets can be made. Working within a craft tradition means having respect for, rather than strict adherence to, the techniques and lore that form that tradition. A tradition that is not changing and renewing itself becomes stagnant and dies, and it is hoped that this book will not only persuade people to re-evaluate our traditional baskets, but might also inspire basketmakers to find new uses for some of the techniques described here.

This sharing of the tradition is also an opportunity to acknowledge the help I got when I was starting out in basketmaking. I was drawn to basketmaking because it offered the promise of a life in the countryside, a consideration that was important to me and my wife, Dolores. The main attraction initially was that one could be involved in the whole process from growing and harvesting the willow to making the basket. We went down to Cork on the understanding that I could get an apprenticeship there, but it turned out that only canework was being taught, so I was forced to learn the basics of willow basketmaking from books. I then heard about Tom and Michael Quinlan from Tallow Hill in County Waterford and, although they couldn't give me an apprenticeship, they gladly gave me much practical advice on basketmaking and willow growing. It can be appreciated from Chapter 8, which deals with professional basketmaking, that the period from 1950 to 1980 was a very difficult time for basketmakers, and it is largely due to the Quinlans and the Shanahan brothers from Carrick-on-Suir that basketmaking survived as a trade in the Republic of Ireland.

When we came to live in Loch Na Fooey in 1978 my reaction on finding that our near neighbour, Tommy Joyce (Tommy Sheáin Tommy), was himself a basketmaker was, of course, one of delight. I knew very little at that time about creels or other indigenous baskets, but with Tommy's gentle instruction I could soon make the creel and the straddle mat. Tommy also told me the Irish names for the weaves, some of which aren't to be found in a dictionary. At that time life here revolved around farming. Most families kept at least one cow, and every spring people cut the turf for next winter's firing by hand with the sleán. They also planted potatoes and oats, the oats being cut with the scythe and stooked before being gathered into a big stack for winter feed for the cattle. If this sounds like a rural idyll, it should also be said that opportunities for employment outside of farming were very limited. Once the young were educated most left to find work elsewhere. Those that stayed found themselves in a declining community with a high number of bachelors. Nonetheless, most people took great pleasure in their work, and a great range of skills were practised inside and outside the home, from making bread to sharpening a scythe or building a stone wall. Baskets were still everyday objects, with creels being used to bring turf home from the less accessible bogs, while the straw straddle mats used with the creels could be made if needed by taking sheaves of oats from the stack and scutching them.

Over a number of years I gradually developed an appreciation for the rich heritage of traditional basketmaking, noticing regional differences in creels and learning about lobster pots and hen's nests. Estyn Evans's pioneering study *Irish Folk Ways* helped in this awareness. I also realised that many old baskets could still be seen in the collections held at the various museums and heritage centres listed in Appendix 3. The largest collections were at the National Museum and at the Ulster Folk and Transport Museum. The collection at the National Museum, which was then held in reserve in Dangan, Co. Offaly, is a tribute to the foresight of people like Muriel Gahan, who was instrumental in arranging for the Homespun Society to donate farm and craft items to the National Museum to form the nucleus of a folk museum, and A.T. Lucas at the museum, as well as Kevin Danaher and Sean O'Sullivan of the Irish Folklore Commission. The co-operation between the two bodies meant that the museum was often informed by the Folklore Commission about traditional craftsmen. This enabled the museum to acquire objects and photographic documentation of these objects being made. Unfortunately, I initially experienced difficulty in getting anything more than very limited access to this collection, but the situation has improved dramatically in the last few years with the appointment of a new keeper of folklife. Also since the opening of the National Folklife Museum at Turlough, Castlebar, Co. Mayo, public access is available to much of the collection. The collection at the Ulster Folk and Transport Museum, although smaller, is well worth seeing, with many of the objects on permanent display. I learned a great deal about traditional baskets from these collections.

In order to be able to properly describe the various traditional baskets, I made a large selection of creels, lobster pots etc., which are explained in detail in the technique sections. This was supplemented by straw-work by Ted Kelly, potato baskets by Alison Fitzgerald and work by other makers in the country tradition such as Pakie O'Toole from Innishturk Island off the Mayo coast. This collection has received an award from the Heritage Council of Ireland, so that it can now become the responsibility of the Irish Basketmaker's Association. The hope is that the collection will be available as a resource to basketmakers interested in examining and making these indigenous baskets as well as being available for display or exhibition if required. While the emphasis in a museum collection is necessarily on the preservation of the objects themselves, the purpose of the Irish Basketmaker's Association Heritage Collection is to preserve the skills and techniques by making the baskets available with a minimum of difficulty.

Finally, I'd like to stress that this book is no substitute for proper training in basketmaking, and the technique sections assume a certain proficiency in the craft (although some basic techniques are explained in Appendix 1). I believe the ideal way to learn basketmaking is in a workshop, where, as well as learning the various weaves, the culture of the workshop is absorbed. This culture is often unconscious but nonetheless of great importance and includes respect for materials and the satisfaction that is the true reward of good work.

Abbreviations used
NMI—National Museum of Irleand
UFTM—Ulster Folk and Transport Museum
DIF, UCD—Department of Irish Folklore, Uinversity College Dublin
NLI—National Library of Ireland
IFC—Irish Folklore Commission

Réamhrá

Is é an príomh réasún atá thaobh thiar de scríobh an leabhair seo ná chun cuntas a choinneáil ar na scileanna a bhíodh in úsáid i ndéantúsaíocht ciseáin thraidisiúnta. De réir mar a bhí soithigh ar nós cléibh agus potaí gliomach ag imeacht as úsáid sea a bhí cúram an fhoilsiúcháin seo ag éirí níos práinní. Tháinig sé chun solais luath go maith go mbeadh sé riachtanach cuid de stair agus úsáid na gciseán a chur san áireamh le cuidiú le meabhair a fháil ar na táirgí ársa sainiúil seo. Chuige sin tá iarracht déanta tuiscint a fháil ar an aire agus an meas a bhí ag ceardaithe ar a gcuid earraí le linn a bheith dá ndéanamh agus dá n-úsáid.

Tá an leabhar leagtha amach sa chaoi go bhfuil eolas i ngach caibideal, tá súil againn, a bheadh úsáideach do léitheoirí le suim ghinearálta i gceardaíocht thraidisiúnta. Freisin tá eolas mion maidir leis na scileanna caoladóireachta riachtanach le cuid de na ciseáin atá faoi chaibideal a dhéanamh. Beidh an pháirt den leabhar atá ag baint le scileanna suimiúil do chaoladóirí, ach ba mhaith liom a threisiú cé go bhfuil déantús na gciseán mínithe ar bhealach amháin anseo, ní gá gur é seo an t-aon bhealach le iad a dhéanamh. Is é mo thuiscint féin ar a bheith ag obair sa cheardaíocht traidisiúnta, go bhfuil sé riachtanach meas agus tuiscint a bheith agat, in ionad cloí go docht le aon scil ar leith, seanchas nó cultúr na ceardaíocha sin. Tá aon traidisiún nach bhfuil ag athrú agus dá athnuachan féin feosaithe nó fiú amháin ag fáil bháis agus chuige sin tá súil go mbeidh tionchar ag an leabhar seo ar dhaoine le áiteamh orthu athmhachnamh a dhéanamh ar an gcaoladóireacht thraidisiúnta maraon le mothú a mhuascailt i gceardaithe chun úsáid nua-aimseartha a bhaint as na scileanna atá mínithe anseo.

Ba mhaith liom an deis seo a ghlacadh agus an traidisiún a roinnt mar admháil ar an gcabhair a fuair mé féin nuair a thosnaigh mé amach ag caoladóireacht ar dtús. Chuir mé suim sa gceird seo mar gur thug sé deis dom cónaí faoin dtuath, rud a bhí tábhachtach do mo bhean chéile Dolores chom maith. Ag an am ba é an príomh-tharraingt go raibh an déantús iomlán, sé sin, cur an bhunábhair, fás, baint agus déanamh na gciseáin. Bhog muid síos go Corcaigh ar an dtuiscint go gcuirfinn isteach mo chuid printíseacht ansin chun an cheird a fhoglaim, ach mar a tharla ní rabhadar ag obair le sail agus mar sin bhí orm na bun scileanna caoladóireachta le sail a fhoglaim as leabhra. Ansin fuair mé tuairisc faoi Tom agus Michael Quinlan as Co. Phort Láirge agus cé nach raibh ar a gcumas printíseacht a thairiscint dom, bhí siad fial flaithiúil lena gcomhairle maidir le fás sail agus scil na caoladóireachta. Déileáileann caibideal 8 le caoladóireacht ghairmiúil ó 1950 go 1980 agus tá sé soiléir go raibh an tréimse seo an-deacair do cheardaithe na linne, agus tá sé beagnach cinnte murach iarrachtaí na Quinlins agus na ndeartháireacha Shanahan as Carraig na Súire gur ar éigin a mhairfeadh ceird na caoladóireachta in aon chor.

Nuair a bhog muid go Loch na Fuaighe le cónaí ann i 1978, nach orm a bhí an-áthas nuair a fuair mé amach gur caoladóir é duine de na comharsain, sé sin Tommy Sheáin Tommy (Tomás Seoighe). Ag an am ní raibh mórán eolais agam ar dhéantús cléibh nó ciseáin dúchasacha eile, ach le lámh chabhrach agus treoir ó Tommy ní raibh sé i bfad go raibh mé i ndon cliabh agus mata srathair a dhéanamh. Roinn Tommy a chuid eolais go fial liom agus thug dom ainmneacha ar na buinní agus na fiocháin éagsúla i gceird na caoladóireachta. Ag an am, is feilméireacht an príomh shlí bheatha a bhí san áit. Bhí bó amháin ar a laghad ag gach clann. San earrach bhaintí an mhóin le sleán i gcóir tine don gheimreadh; bhíodh fataí curtha agus coirce spréite le láí. Sa bhfómhar bhaintí an coirce leis an speal agus dhéantaí stucaí as sar a gcuirtí i gcruach é i gcóir beatha don eallach sa ngeimreadh. Má tá sé seo cosúil le fánaíocht rómánsúil, bíodh sin mar atá ach tá sé tábhachtacht agus fíor le rá freisin nach raibh mórán deiseanna fostaíochta ná aon saothrú eile taobh amuigh den fheilméireacht san gceantar álainn seo. Bhí oideachas ar na daoine óga agus iad ag obair taobh amuigh in áiteacha eile. Bhí an dream a d'fhan sa mbaile idir dhá stól; bhí an pobal ag dul i léig le líon mór baitsiléirí agus easpa daoine óga. Mar sin féin bhí na daoine seo bródúil agus bhaineadar an-taitneamh as a gcuid oibre, obair a raibh líon mhór scileanna riachtanach chun a ngnó taobh istigh agus taobh amuigh den teach a dhéanamh; bíodh sé ag baint le fuinnt aráin, le géarú speile, le tógáil bearna i gclaí nó i mballa cloiche. Bhí na ciseáin mar phríomh uirlis oibre chuile lá, an chiseog leis na fataí a shéalú agus na cléibh le móin a thabhairt amach dena portaigh achrannacha.

Thar roinnt blianta d'éirigh mé geanúil ar an oidhreacht ársa atá ag baint leis an gcaoladóireacht thraidisiúnta, ag tógáil san áireamh difríochtaí i gceantair éagsula, go mór mhór maidir le cléibh agus ag foghlaim le potaí gliomach agus nead circe a dhéanamh. Chuidigh staidéar ceannródaíochta Estyn Evans — *Irish Folk Ways* le mo thuiscint ar an ábhar a fheabhsú go mór. Thuig mé freisin go raibh roinnt mhaith de na sean-chiseáin le feiceáil go fóill i mbailiúcháin seandálaíochta in Iarsmalainn atá liostáilte in aguisín 3. Bhí na bailiucháin is mó in san Iarsmalann Náisiúnta agus san Ulster Folk and Transport Museum. Ag an am sin bhí bailiuchán an Iarsmalann Náisiúnta coinnithe i dtaisce i nDaingean Co. Ua Fháille agus murach gur thuig daoine mar Muriel Gahan ó Chumann na Sníomhadóirí, A.T. Lucas san iarsmalann maraon le Caoimhaoin Ó Danachair agus Seán Ó Suilleabháin as Coimisiún Béaloideas Éireann an tábhacht a bhain leis na gnáth earraí seo, ní bheadh an bailiúchán leath chom mór. Bhí an dearcadh seo fíor fhad-bhreathnaíoch ag an am agus chinntigh an sár chomhoibriú a bhí idir na dreamanna seo gur coinníodh an iarsmalann ar an eolas faoi cheardaithe traidisiúnta go rialta. Thug sé seo an deis don iarsmalann earraí ceardaíochta agus iarsmaí a fháil agus a tharrtháil, agus go minic taifeideadh le pictiúirí, léaráidí agus eolas eile a fháil. Ag an tús ámh, bhí, deachrachtaí agam cead nó mórán eolais a fháil faoin mbailiúchán seo ach le cúpla bliain anuas tá feabhas oll-mhór tagtha ar chúrsaí ó ceapadh stiúrthoir nua seandálaíochta agus oscailt suas an Iarsmalann Náisiúnta Folklife i gCaisleán an Bharraigh, áit go bhfuil cead isteach ag an bpobal ag fur-mhór an bhailiucháin. Cé nach bhfuil an bailiúchán san

Ulster Folk and Transport Museum baileach chomh téagartha, is fiú go mór dul ag breathnú air, agus tá go leor de na hearraí ar taispeáint go seasmach san taispeántas seo. Tá mé féin sásta gur fhoghlaim mise go leor leor faoin gcaoladóireacht thraidisiunta ó bhreathnú agus ó staidéar na mbailiucháin seo.

Le míniú ceart a thabhairt ar an gcaoladóireacht thraidisiúnta, rinne mé líon mór cléibh, potaí gliomach agus rl. Tá siad seo sain-mhínithe san bpáirt den leabhar atá ag baint leis na scileanna. Chun cuidiú leis an léiriú agus an míniú fuair mé go leor cabhair uaidh Ted Kelly — obair as tuí, uaidh Alison Fitzgerald — ciseáin fataí agus uaidh roinnt ceardaithe eile mór-thimpeall na tíre cosúil le Pakie O Toole as Inis Tuirc amach ó chósta Mhuigheo. Tá gradam faighte ag an mbailiúchán seo ón gComhairle Oidhreachta agus anois beidh freagracht as an mbailiúchán á ghlacadh ag Cumann Caoladóirí na hÉireann ortha féin. Is é mo dhóchas go mbeidh an bailiúchán mar áis do chaoladóirí a bhfuil suim acu sa scil, traidisiún, agus an cheardaíocht atá ag baint le déanamh ciseáin dúcasacha, agus go mbeidh siad ar taispeáint don phobal nuair is féidir. Cé go bhfuil an bhéim ar chaomhnú i mbailiúchán an iarsmalainn is é an aidhm atá leis an mbailiúchán úr seo ná an scil agus an cheird a chaomhnú tré na gciseáin éagsula a bheith ar fáil gan mórán deachracht.

Mar fhocal scoir, is mian liom a threisiú nach bhfuil san leabhar seo ach sop in áit na scuaibe i gcomparáid le oiliúint cheart i scil na caoladóireachta. Tá scileanna léirithe ins na caibidil éagsula a bhaineann le teicníc ach atá bunaithe ar an tuiscint go bhfuil bun-scil caoladóireachta ag duine (cé go bhfuil roinnt áirithe bun-scileanna mínithe in aguisín 1). Creidim gur é an siopa oibre an bealach is fearr le scil na caoladóireachta a fhoghlaim, mar chomh maith le foghlaim faoí na buinní agus na fíocháin éagsula, súitear isteach cúltúr agus tradisiún na hoibre trén timpeallacht teagaisc agus go minic tarlaíonn an sú isteach i nganfhíos duit, ach mar sin féin tá sé seo thar a bheith tábhachtach, agus cothaíonn sé ómós don ábhar agus sástacht mar chúiteamh ar dhea-obair.

Acknowledgements

I would first like to thank all of the people over the years who have attended the basketmaking workshops that I've given, and particularly those who have convinced me of the importance of recording the history and techniques of Irish baskets. I would also like to thank the basketmakers who have helped me to develop as a basketmaker — Tom and Mike Quinlan, Joe Shanahan and Tommy Joyce in the early years and, at a later stage, David Drew and Colin Manthorpe. A visit to David and Judy Drew in the mid-1980s was particularly important for me as it helped me to realize that it was possible to make a living as a basketmaker while working to the highest standards.

I would like to thank all those who contributed to the funding of this project. Initial funding for research was crucial, and this was provided by Údarás na Gaeltachta. I would particularly like to thank Bertie Feeney of Údarás, who, as well as helping in many other ways, was largely responsible for the *Réamhra* (the Irish version of the Preface). An award from the School of Irish Studies Foundation enabled me to take some time away from basketmaking to write this book, and I would like to thank Rosemarie Mulcahy of the School of Irish Studies for her help. Thanks are due also to the Heritage Council of Ireland for assisting the publication of this book and for an award towards conserving the Heritage Collection of baskets, in the care of the Irish Basketmakers' Association.

I would like to thank all of the Irish basketmakers who responded to questionnaires and provided photographs. I would especially like to thank Alison Fitzgerald for advice on Ulster creels and potato baskets, Brian Haslett for information on Ulster fishing baskets, Vivienne Mayne for visiting the National Museum collection with me and for various photographs of coracles and other baskets, Vincent McCarron for advice on fishing baskets, for the loan of various baskets and for providing photographs and funding.

Others who helped with research include Paula Cummins, the staff at Mayo Abbey and Meitheal Mara, Clive Ó Gibne, and Críostóir Mac Cartaigh at *Béaloideas* especially for his help with the glossary of Irish terms. Thanks also to staff at the National Museum of Ireland, especially Dr Séamus Mac Philip and Albert Siggins; staff at the Ulster Folk and Transport Museum, especially Megan Mac Manus and Johnathan Bell; Maurice Johnson, Castlecomer, for information about the Castlecomer basketworks; Meg McSpirit Jones for information on the Fermanagh mumming tradition; John Greene of Blindcraft; Geraldine Mitchell for information about Muriel Gahan and for making me aware of Chrissie O'Gorman's survey; Gerry Flynn for information on creels, currachs, folklore and Irish words; Veronica O'Keefe, Sammy Gault and Laurence Hutson.

Thanks are due to all those who allowed photographs to be reproduced and who are credited under the individual photographs. These include the National Museum, the Department of Irish Folklore at UCD, the Ulster Folk and Transport Museum, the Ulster Museum and the National Museums of Scotland. Particular thanks are due to the following people who allowed photographs to be used without reproduction fees: Gráinne Mac Lochlainn at the National Photographic Archive, Dr David Shaw-Smith, Katherine Thompson, Bill Doyle, Roger O'Farrell, Alison Fitzgerald, Vivienne Mayne, Vincent McCarron, Jacqui Hurst, Gerry Flynn, John Fitzgerald, John Gahan, J.E. Manners, Clódhanna Teoranta, Irene Kelly, Lynn Kirkham and all those basketmakers who allowed photographs of their work to be used in Chapter 9. A special thanks to Dolores Hogan, who took all the uncredited photographs.

The drawings, which add so much to the book, are, except where otherwise credited, by Barbara Kelly, and I would especially like to thank Barbara for offering to do them even when it seemed that no fee for doing so would be available. I would also like to thank Alex Bury for preparing a series of creel drawings, which were the basis for many of the drawings in Chapter 2. Drawings of splitting oak and of a shaving horse are based on similar drawings in 'Appalachian White Oak Basketry' by R.N. Law and C.W. Taylor; figs. 3.9 to 3.11 are based on drawings in *Flet Med Pil* by Steen Madsen; figs 3.20, 3.21 and 5.4 are based on drawings by Alison Fitzgerald; figs 7.10 to 7.14 are based on drawings in '*An fhóir*: a straw rope granary' by A.T. Lucas; figs. 7.24 to 7.27 are based on drawings in 'Basketry of the Appalachian Mountains' by Sue Stephenson; figs 7.1, 7.4 and 8.5 are based on drawings by E. Estyn Evans in *Irish folk ways*, and the drawings of wicker doors in Chapter 1 are based on similar drawings in 'Wattle and straw mat doors in Ireland' by A.T. Lucas. I would also like to thank those who allowed drawings to be used: The Royal Society of Antiquaries of Ireland for drawings from 'Making wooden sieves' by A.T. Lucas, The Crafts Council of Ireland for a drawing of an eel trap by Ursula Mattenberger, Alex Bury for a drawing of a creel, and Mrs Evans and Lilliput Press for use of drawings by E. Estyn Evans.

I would like to thank Padraig Hogan and Gerry Flynn, who read large sections of the text and made many valuable observations. Others who read sections of the text included Vivienne Mayne, Vincent McCarron, Linda Scott and David Shaw-Smith. A special thanks to Breda Tully, who typed the manuscript, and to Geraldine Mitchell and Neil Middleton for much helpful advice. Thanks are also due to Nick Maxwell for his decision to publish this book, and to all at Wordwell Publications for their input. Others who helped in various ways included Mary Butcher, Anthony Farrell, Dara Hogan, Ted Kelly, Les Reid, Micheál Ó Conghaile, Micheál de Mórdha, Heather Marshall, Máirín Seoighe and Jim Coyle, Eva Seidenfaden, Bill Sinnott and the late Freda Rountree.

Finally I would like to thank my wife and family for their help with this project, and I would especially like to thank Dolores for her unfailing encouragement and support.

For my Mum and Dad
for all their support during their lives.

1

Introduction

BASKETS have been part of the human story almost from the beginning. Analysis of carved stone figures found in Europe, Russia and Siberia dating from between 20,000 and 30,000 BC (known as the 'Venus figurines') show that people from the early Stone Age (the palaeolithic era) had already mastered the art of weaving plant fibres into cloth, nets and baskets.[1] Fragments of pottery reveal that in some cultures pots were moulded around a basket form, which would have been burnt away in the firing. The earliest evidence of human settlement in Ireland—at sites at Mount Sandel, Co. Derry, and at Lough Boora, Co. Offaly— is thought to date from around 7,000 BC. The site at Mount Sandel suggests that the dwellings of these hunter/forager peoples were tent-shaped huts made from interwoven saplings.

It is believed that Ireland and Britain were joined by a land–bridge until about 9,000 BC so it is probable that many early settlers came across a narrower Irish sea in hide-covered wicker boats. It is possible that some settlers could have travelled up northwards skirting the coastline, possibly via Spain, where a similar tradition of hide-covered boats survives. Certainly references to wicker currachs are frequent in the old Irish mythology where the hero undertakes a currach voyage to a land of youth in the western ocean. It was probably this tradition that inspired the currach voyages of the Irish monks from the sixth century onwards (this is explored more thoroughly in Chapter 4). The use of wickerwork was still common in the sea–going currachs of the west coast up until the 1840s. Hazel ribs are still used in the Sheephaven currach of County Donegal. The framework of the river-going Boyne currach or coracle, which was used for fishing until about 1940, was made entirely of wicker.

Dug-out canoes were also used by our distant ancestors to navigate the inland waterways of Ireland. The flood raft or *cliath thulca* (**Pl. 1.1**), which was used along the Shannon basin until the

1

1920s, is probably of much more recent origin. The one in **Pl. 1.1** was made specially for the National Museum of Ireland and is essentially a floor of reed bound to a wooden frame with a slight wall at the back of interwoven reed. It does not take a lot of imagination to picture an older version of this in which the framework would have been of coppiced rather than sawn wood, with elements of wicker weaving to keep it together, because the Irish word *cliath* implies a woven wicker structure. This flood raft was mainly used to gain access to fields and livestock during the periodic flooding that occurs in the Suck and Shannon river basins.

Wicker was also used for dwellings. There is evidence of post and wattle construction having been used since at least 900 BC. These dwellings were typically circular with double wattle walls and the cavity was stuffed with some insulating material. An excavation at Deer Park Farms, Co. Antrim, an early Christian/early medieval settlement, where a succession of collapsed houses had been preserved through water logging, shows houses made mainly from hazel rods woven around closely-spaced posts with the cavity stuffed with moss, heather or grass-like material. The houses ranged in diameter from 4m to 7m, some having a smaller back house attached. It has been estimated that each house required about 8km of hazel rods, suggesting a well-managed hazel coppice nearby.[2] These houses were sited within circular enclosures, known variously as a rath or *lios*. These enclosures were made of piled earth but often had stone-faced banks. Some wicker dwellings were sited on crannógs, which were artificial or partly artificial islands made in

Pl. 1.1—A flood raft made from timber and reed. The Irish name of this raft, cliath thulca*, suggests that earlier versions were made of wicker and reed. Courtesy NMI.*

Co · DONEGAL.

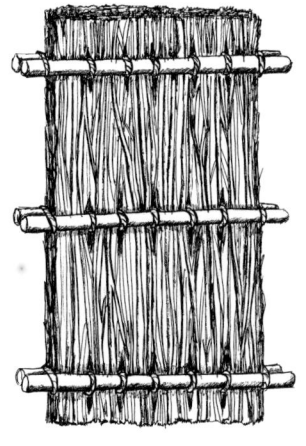

PROOR · CO · KERRY

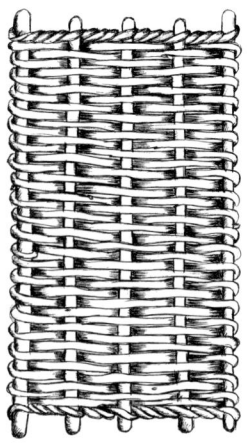

KILMOCOMOGG · CO · CORK.

Fig. 1.1—Wattle doors

lakes with access gained by a narrow causeway or by boat. The rath could be sufficiently large to enclose livestock but the crannóg was smaller, possibly with a defensive purpose.

Wattle and post construction remained a popular method of house-building in Ireland (in common with the rest of Europe) at least until the Middle Ages, and in pre-Norman Ireland it seems to have been the most common method of house-building.[3] Houses of this type, plastered with a mixture of mud and cow-dung, were still common up to 1700, as can be gathered by the passing of an Act of the Irish Parliament in 1705 forbidding the use in wattling the walls of houses or cabins or outbuildings of 'any kind of gad or gads, whth or wyths of oak, ash, birch, hazel or other tree whatsoever'. Even when wattling ceased to be used in housing, doors were still made in this fashion, and in the poorer counties of the west, rod doors were still common in the latter part of the nineteenth century. Different patterns of these doors existed and **Fig. 1.1** shows three different types. These drawings are based on illustrations in A.T. Lucas's 'Wattle and Straw Mat Doors in Ireland'.[4] The examples from County Cork and County Donegal were of wicker, though the uprights (vertical struts) were often of bog fir. Subtle differences exist between the Cork and Donegal examples — the twist of willow at the top and bottom of the County Cork door also appears in the County Cork basket known as a *sciathóg*. Both the Cork and Donegal doors would usually have been hung with a hinge of twisted willow rod, though a twisted rope made from slivers of bog deal was sometimes used. The door from County Kerry is made from birch branches bound together, and it was used as a door for

3

Pl. 1.2—Eel weir of woven hazel, Welch Collection. Courtesy of Ulster Museum.

an outhouse or stable rather than for a house. The wicker door was known in Irish as a *sciath shlatach* (literally a rod shield) in Donegal and as a *scolpán* in Cork and Kerry, though the word *sgurtóg* was also used in Kerry. The stable door was also known as a *scolpán* in these southern counties, but a rougher version made either of furze or heather was known in County Mayo as a *bráca*.

These rod doors were used in conjunction with straw mats (*maoiseógaí*), which were woven in a three-strand plait (described in Chapter 7). The straw mats provided effective draught-proofing for the doors, and Lucas notes that even when the wicker doors were replaced by wooden ones, the use of straw mats persisted for many years.

Wickerwork techniques were also essential for the building of the elaborate eel weir in **Pl. 1.2**. This example, from Toome in County Antrim, was photographed in the early twentieth century. The weaving is of hazel and the amount of work involved suggests that eels were an important part of the local economy at that time. Weirs were placed on a great many Irish rivers, especially from the Middle Ages onwards. Some were made of stone but wattling was also a popular method of construction.

The technique of wattling is known in basketmaking as a stake-and-strand technique, where strands of pliable or semi-pliable material are woven in and out of stakes, and it is this type of weaving that is most common in the Irish tradition. However, the earliest fragments of basketwork found in Ireland are of coilwork. In this technique, the basket is formed by a core that is bound or sewn to form the base and sides of the basket, as for example in the Aran kisheen in **Pl. 7.5** where the coil is of straw sewn with bramble.

Fragments found near Ardagh in County Longford and dated to the fourth or early third millenium BC have a core formed of thin wooden rods bound with strips of some woody plant. More complete fragments from Twyford, north-east of Athlone, Co. Westmeath, show coilwork bags made by joining two discs together.[5]

This style of basketmaking would be associated in more recent times with Africa and the work of the indigenous Indian basketmakers of the American continent.

Fragments of possible wicker (stake-and-strand) baskets dating from about 900 BC were found at Clonfinlough, Co. Offaly, but it is safe to conclude that wicker baskets were in use long before that. The difficulty about stake-and-strand baskets from an archaeological perspective is that the materials they are made from, whether willow or hazel, are relatively short-lived, even when buried underground. Thus a wicker basket that could be strong enough to support the weight of a person or allowed to fall from a height without being damaged may well disappear without trace a few hundred years later. In contrast, a pottery vessel could break within days of being made but the shards will still exist millennia later.

We do not know then with any certainty the shape and pattern of the wicker baskets of a few thousand years ago, though from recent work in the Shannon estuary by the Discovery Programme it does seem that certain basket types are fairly ancient, perhaps as early as 4000 BC. The creel **(Pl. 1.3)**, which is made upside-down by sticking the uprights into the ground and weaving between them with a knot-like weave known as the mouthwale or *buinne béil* (described in Chapter 2), is probably a very old type of basket,

Pl. 1.3—Sos Brothall (a rest in the heat of the day). This photo, taken in Innis Méain, probably in the 1930s, shows two creels, one of which has not yet had the uprights (which were stuck into the ground) trimmed off. The smaller creel is a shoulder creel and the flat basket is a skib (ciseog). *Photo courtesy of Clódhanna Teoranta.*

because it shares the same starting weave as the wicker currachs mentioned earlier. Similarly, the *sciathóg* and *sciath* (described in Chapter 3) may well have been used as shields or breastplates in pre-Christian times and may have gone through many changes and adaptations before their use as potato baskets from the eighteenth century onwards. But we should not assume that the baskets of two or three millennia ago were necessarily more primitive than those of the recent past. Bronze and gold artefacts of the Late Bronze Age (*c.* 1000 BC) show a high degree of workmanship and it is very possible that basketmaking skills were also highly developed. Development in craftwork does not necessarily follow a chronological order; so there is no reason to assume that complex basketry was not in use in Ireland from the Mesolithic on, and that there were also elaborate baskets for somewhat easier use, as suggested by the coilwork bag from Twyford, Co. Westmeath, whose patterns are now lost to us.

Materials

Basketry materials can be conveniently divided into hard and soft. The main hard materials used in Ireland were willow and hazel, though large diameter sections of other timbers such as oak and ash were sometimes used after splitting for specific purposes. Straw was the principal soft material and it was used for a wide variety of baskets as well as for mats and horse-collars. River rush, grasses and field rush were also used. More details of these soft materials are given in Chapter 7.

Hazel was not nearly as widely used as willow for the various wickerwork baskets described in this book, though it was used extensively where it was locally common. It is unlikely that hazel was planted specifically for basketmaking but there is evidence that it was cut regularly in a coppice system in these areas. It is probable that when the wickerwork technique was widely used for housing, the amount of coppiced hazel was far greater, but even in the last forty or fifty years the acreage of coppiced hazel has declined dramatically. The need for the various hazel farm baskets no longer exists and the decline of thatching has affected the making of scollops (thatching spars), which was the main product of these coppices.

Willow was cultivated specially for basketmaking probably for

Pl. 1.4—Harvesting willow using a cutting hook. Photo courtesy of Jacqui Hurst.

many centuries. Willow for basketmaking is easily established by inserting cuttings into clean ground in springtime. The cuttings root easily so that each cutting forms a stool from which rods can be harvested annually. Modern practice is to plant the cuttings in neat rows, the usual spacing being about 2ft (61cm) between rows and about 1ft (30cm) between cuttings. Planting at this density requires about 22,000 cuttings per acre (56,000 per hectare) and the cuttings range from 9" to 18" (23–46cm) in length depending on the softness of the ground. Planting through a black plastic mulch is a widespread practice among contemporary growers, because the plastic suppresses weed growth, ensuring that the willow slips become established without the need for the laborious hand weeding, that was a feature of the initial stages of intensive willow cultivation until relatively recently. The willows are cut with a hook during the winter months when the sap has fallen **(Pl. 1.4)**, though this practice has now been mechanised in many countries. The harvested rods are then graded by putting them butt first into a barrel or similar container and sorting them in increments of 1ft (30cm) **(Pl. 1.5)**. Tom Quinlan from County Waterford described grading willows in the late 1940s into stock twigs (the largest size, which had 200 rods per bundle), barrel twigs (300 per bundle), half-barrel twigs (500), key twigs (1,000) and ferkin twigs (1,500).[6] Rods for sale were always counted in this way but rods for their own use, while sorted in the same way, were bundled without counting. Rods for using with the skin on are known as greens; when allowed to dry they are known as browns. They can be stored in a dry place until needed, then they must be soaked in water for about a week to make them pliable. Rods for stripping must be stood upright in water. This causes them to begin to grow and the rising sap allows them to be peeled easily. In Ireland this was largely done by hand with a willow brake **(Pl. 1.6)**, though this process has been mechanised in most other European countries for many years. Rods that are boiled before peeling are known as buff, because of the golden brown colour given by the tannin in the bark. Whites and buffs need only be soaked for a period of half an hour to a few hours depending on size. They are then mellowed by wrapping the rods in a damp cloth for a few hours or overnight before use. Any white or buff rods that remain unused at the end of the day's work can be dried out and stored away.

Willows for basketmaking can conveniently be divided into four main species, *Salix viminalis* (common osier), *Salix purpurea* (purple osier), *Salix triandra* (almond leaf willow) and *Salix alba* (white willow). Some crosses between these species are also very useful, the most common in this country being *S. rubra*, a cross between *S. purpurea* and *S. viminalis*. *Salix viminalis* is the most vigorous grower and rods can grow up to 10ft (3m) per year. Although not a native willow it has been naturalised here for thousands of years. Because of its quick growth it tends to be fairly pithy and is therefore more brittle than some of the finer varieties. For this reason it is not as suitable for peeling, though some varieties such as 'Green Skin' and 'French Gold' can be peeled. *Salix purpurea* is a woodier, tougher rod than *S. viminalis* and also a lighter yielder, though some varieties may grow up to 8ft (2.4m) in a year. The rods are typically much thinner for their length than other varieties. It is an extremely pliable rod

Pl. 1.5—Grading willow. The harvested willow contains rods of different sizes so the bundles are put into a barrel and sorted into various sizes, usually 1ft (30cm) increments. A bundle of 8ft (2.4m) willow will contain rods greater than 7ft (2.1m) but no taller than 8ft (2.4m). When sorted the willow can be dried and then stored away. The bundles immediately to the right of the barrel are unsorted; those against the railing are sorted.

Pl. 1.6—Stripping willow on a brake.

when green (fresh) or semi-green (part-dried) and some varieties are also suitable for peeling. Varieties popular in this country included 'Irish Black', 'Swallow Tail' or 'Slender Tip' and 'Packing Twine'. *Salix triandra* needs more fertile soils than *S. viminalis* or *S. purpurea* and is also more prone to rusts and insect damage. However, when grown well it gives a good quality rod that is particularly suited to peeling. It only began to be widely grown in this country around 1900, though Mauls and Spaniards were being grown south of Lough Neagh some years before this.[7] Another variety, 'The Barber', was grown in the south-east. *Salix alba*, sometimes in a hybrid form, was widely grown throughout Ireland, and these rods were usually called reds or yellows. *S. rubra* (*S. purpurea* x *S. viminalis*) gives a high-quality rod for brown work, and some varieties, such as 'Mandesley' and 'Harrison's', are also suitable for peeling.

Intensive willow growing as described here was largely centred around the south-eastern shores of Lough Neagh, Co. Limerick, especially along the Shannon and in the fertile river basins of the Suir and the Blackwater and their tributaries in east Munster. It is probable that willow cultivation was well established in these areas for hundreds of years, but with the onset of industrialisation from the nineteenth century onwards, there was a steady increase in the demand for baskets for use in mills and factories. The development of the railways later in the nineteenth century created a demand for various crates, hampers and baskets to be used in the transport of goods. It was a contract from the Railway Company, for example, that led to the setting up of the Shanahan firm in Carrick-on-Suir,

Co. Tipperary, which employed up to sixty people at the height of production in 1914, between basketmakers and rod cutters. Ireland's two major cities, Dublin and Belfast, and many of the larger towns had several basketmaking works at this time. The baskets made by these professional basketmakers were quite standardised, often in response to the demands of a trade or industry, and willow growing developed in the districts already mentioned to provide these basketmakers with the type of rods they needed.

Although professional basketmaking is described in Chapter 8, the main focus of this book is on the indigenous baskets of Ireland. Some of these were made by professional basketmakers but most were made in the countryside, close to where they were to be used, from locally harvested material. Small willow beds known as 'sally gardens' were commonplace throughout the countryside, and in some areas of the west where creels were widely used, most farms had a sally garden. This does not imply that all farmers could make their own creels, but most rural communities had at least one basketmaker who could make the baskets needed in the farm and home. For these men (and they were almost invariably men), basketmaking was a part-time or seasonal occupation practised during the winter and spring. They often did not have large sally gardens of their own but depended on those who wanted baskets from them to supply the rods. The transaction was usually a barter of labour, with the rods often being supplied by the person who wanted the basket.

The bulk of the willow available to these country basketmakers was of the common osier (*Salix viminalis*) family. This was suitable for the rough indigenous farm baskets, but the development of professional basketmaking led to a gradual improvement in the type of rods grown in the areas where willow cultivation was more established. Improved varieties such as *Salix purpurea* (purple osier) began to be widely grown in these areas. These more pliable willows were usually called osiers by basketmakers to distinguish them from the coarser and more vigorous common osier (*S. viminalis*), which continued to be known as sally. Nonetheless, the general term 'sally' tends to be used indiscriminately by most people throughout Ireland to refer to all types of willow grown for basketmaking. In order to avoid confusion, I try to use the word 'willow' rather than sally or osier. However, it should be noted that common osier (*S. viminalis*), or one of its hybrid forms such as *S. rubra*, is the most suitable willow for the rougher baskets such as the creels, while thinner varieties of willow such as *S. purpurea* or *S. triandra* are more suitable for the finer baskets.

Because most of the indigenous baskets were made during the winter, spring and early summer, the rods were usually worked in a semi-green or partially dried state. This was especially true of the creels, which have knots in the weave that tend to minimise the risk of shrinkage. It was generally accepted that willow needed to season for at least eight weeks after cutting to avoid the danger of shrinkage. Working with green rods (immediately after cutting) would result in the rods shrinking in the basket, making it loose and almost worthless. Rural basketmakers would, therefore, try to cut their willow in succession in order to ensure a supply of pliable rods throughout the season. Once the willow had dried for about eight weeks, the basketmaker had a further six weeks to work it before it began to dry out completely. The seasoning time for hazel was shorter; it was considered sufficiently seasoned to be able to work without the danger of shrinkage after about three to four weeks, with a further three to four weeks available to the basketmaker before it dried out. In order to ensure a supply of willow for the early winter, many rural basketmakers were anxious to start cutting in early November. I heard a few of the older generation of these basketmakers refer to the first moon in November as the earliest date that they would start cutting. Even though the leaves were still on the rods, they believed the sap was down by then. Rods cut while the leaf was on them in this way also tended to dry more quickly. With experience in judging the extent to which the willow has dried, good baskets can be made from semi-green willow, particularly if the willow has dried to the extent that slight lines have begun to appear on the bark. Baskets made from semi-green willow should be allowed to dry slowly, ideally for several weeks in an open shed, before being used.

Of course the baskets described in this book can also be made from brown (seasoned) willow. The soaking time for brown willow depends on the hardness of the particular variety of willow and on the temperature of the water. As a rough guide, allow 8ft willow to soak for about seven to eight days in average conditions. Add two or three more days for the very cold water of mid-winter and subtract a day for the warm water of mid-summer. Some varieties take longer than this, for example some *Salix purpureas*. Test the rods in the water to check whether they are pliable, since over-soaking causes skin damage. Once the rods are pliable, take them out of the water and fan out the bundles to allow the surface to dry fully before retying and bringing them into the workshop. If the workshop is at a fairly cool and even temperature, the rods should stay pliable for almost a week. Although many books advise wrapping brown rods in damp sacking, I would not agree with this. I could only imagine doing this if working in a very warm and dry atmosphere, which would not really be suitable for basketmaking. Wrapping the willow in this way usually causes damage to the skin of the willow. Ideally the inside of the willow should be damp, i.e. inside the skin, while the outer surface should be dry. I regularly dry my willow for a few hours after taking it out of the soaking trough before bundling it up again and allowing it to mellow for a day by standing it in a corner of the workshop.

Other material used for basketmaking included young shoots of ash, which were sometimes used for weaving the sides of baskets where ash was locally common. I have also heard of alder and elm shoots being used for weaving. Briar (bramble) was used not only for sewing certain types of straw baskets (as described in Chapter 7) but also for weaving (having first been stripped of its thorns). The buckie briar or wild rose was used mainly for hoops rather than weaving, but other woodland plants such as honeysuckle were used where they were available locally.

Tools and equipment

The basketmaker's needs in this respect are simple and the tool kit of a great many country basketmakers consisted of only a knife. However, a basic tool kit as shown in **Pl. 1.7** consists of a knife, a slip stone, a picking knife, a bodkin, a secateurs, a rapping iron, a greasing horn, a cleave and shaver, some weights and a ruler. A range of hoops in various sizes for gathering the uprights is also very useful, though some makers use a tie instead. Anyone wishing to make square work should also have a screw block, and those wishing to harvest their own willow will also want a hook, though a knife or even a secateurs can be used if harvesting on a small scale. Basketmakers traditonally sat close to the floor on a raised piece of wood called a plank, with the work resting on a lap-board. A soaking trough is also necessary unless there is a suitable place for soaking the willow nearby. A brief description of each item is given below.

*Pl. 1.7—
Basketmaking tools
placed on the lap-
board.*

(a) Knife

This is often referred to as a shop knife to distinguish it from the picking knife. I prefer the blade to have a curve on the top and ideally the steel should be fairly soft so that the blade can be easily sharpened. For this reason I don't like a stainless steel blade. An 'Opinel' knife with a curved blade is very suitable.

(b) Slip stone

I use a medium-grade slip stone for sharpening the knife but any sharpening stone that gives the desired result can be used. The cutting hook also requires frequent sharpening during the harvesting season and the stone is also used for this.

(c) Picking knife

This is used for trimming off the ends of the finished basket and was formerly a very important tool. However, many basketmakers now trim off with the secateurs, using some of the same action one would use with the picking knife. I've allowed my picking knife to go blunt for this reason and I use it instead for kinking the uprights prior to upsetting **(Fig. 3.11)**. A blunt knife is more suitable for this job because it doesn't injure the willow.

(d) Bodkin

This is specialist tool for basketmaking which is especially useful when bordering the basket and putting on handles. When used in

13

this way it is often dipped into the greasing horn. The bodkin is also useful for making split bases (described in Chapter 3).

(e) Secateurs

A secateurs is very useful for cutting base sticks and for use in trimming off the ends of the basket. If used for trimming an anvil (pointed beak), shape is essential. A good secateurs such as a 'Felco No. 2' should last a lifetime and the blade, which can be sharpened with the slip stone, can also be replaced if necessary.

(f) Rapping iron

This can be made by a local blacksmith or purchased, like the other tools, from a specialist supplier. Its function is to beat down the work as required, so it should be smooth and well balanced. Most rapping irons have a hole at the top that can act as a 'commander' for straightening out crooked rods.

(g) Greasing horn

This doesn't have to be a horn, of course; any pot or container can be used and a tin as shown in **Pl. 1.7** has the advantage of being sufficiently stable for the bodkin to be plunged in using only one hand. Tallow was the lubricant most often used in the past, but I use emulsifying ointment, which can be bought in any pharmacy. The emulsifying ointment or tallow should be heated in a pot, and a stiffener used, such as chopped-up sheep's wool or waste hair from a hairdressers. This prevents too much lubricant coming out at a time.

(h) Cleave and shaver

The cleave is used for splitting willow rods into skeins. These are then pulled through the shaver to remove the pith. Where only a few skeins are needed these can be shaved using a knife; a shaver is not necessary for any of the baskets described in the technique section of this book. However, the cleave (or the 'fender' as it was often known in this country) is very useful for splitting large willow sticks to make the ribs for the *sciathóg* (described in Chapter 3).

(h) Weights

These are used to keep the basket steady as it is being made. Low, flat iron weights are best but smooth stones could be used if necessary.

(i) Ruler

A rigid ruler such as a metre stick is best and is essential for professional basketmakers who must work to measure. A flexible tape is not really suitable. Blind basketmakers use a stick notched with grooves or small nails.

(j) Hoops

Hoops ranging in size from the smallest diameter basket to the largest are needed to keep the uprights in position. The hoop should accurately reflect the flow or degree of slope of the basket. Rigid hoops, as described for the *sciathóg* in Chapter 3, are best, and oval hoops should certainly be made in this way to keep their shape. Ties are needed for some of the baskets described in this book and, although this was traditionally done with a rod tie, I suggest using electric wire with a copper core, as it can be re-used indefinitely and is soft enough not to damage the rods.

(k) Screw block

This is essential for square baskets made in the normal manner. It is made from two pieces of heavy, close-grained wood about 3" (75mm) square and about 36" (91cm) long. Holes are bored near both ends to receive coach bolts, fitted if possible with butterfly nuts. Few, if any, country basketmakers had access to a screw block, and the base of the rectangular slip-bottomed creel or *pardóg* (described in Chapter 2) was usually made by sticking the uprights into the ground.

(l) Lap-board.

Professional basketmakers usually used a lap-board in conjunction with a plank, which was essentially a low platform, about 5' 6" x 2' 6" (168cm x 76cm), on which they sat to keep away from the damp floor. If your workshop has a clean, level floor, you can dispense with the plank and just use a low seat about 4" (10cm) high to sit on. A back support can be provided by having a short board at a slight angle from this seat to the wall. Most lap-boards are about 3' x 2' (91cm x 61cm) but the one in **Pl. 1.7** is about 4' x 2' (122cm x 61cm). Usually the board is used at a slight angle. A table and chair may be used instead.

(m) Cutting hook

A cutting hook is a far quicker and more satisfying way of

harvesting willow than a secateurs. This is especially true where the bed is a little weedy, as grasses don't interefere with the cutting. Where the willow has no stock, i.e., several rods growing out from the ground, a large hook such as that used for harvesting thatching reed can be used, but if the willow has a stock or short trunk then a smaller hook such as that shown in **Pl. 1.7** is more useful.

(n) Soaking trough

Many basketmakers use galvanised tanks fitted with inside flanges so that slats of wood can be jammed into position to keep the bundles of willow in the water. Fibreglass or plastic tanks can also be used, but if a permanent trough is being made, then concrete tanks are probably the most durable. Ideally, tanks should have a plug-hole for draining, as the water needs to be changed regularly, perhaps once a month in winter but at least every two weeks in warm weather. The size depends on the scale of work you do, but a trough 9ft (2.7m) long and about 3ft (91cm) wide and 2ft (61cm) deep should be adequate for a professional basketmaker.

2
Creels

IF you pause for a moment and form an image of a basket in your mind, this image will probably reflect the sort of baskets that are common in your area. If you live in Africa or America, this might well be a coiled basket of some kind, but for most people living in Europe this would probably be a stake-and-strand basket, possibly a round basket with carrying handles like a log basket. In the counties along the west coast of Ireland it is likely that the basket that would come to mind would be the creel, known in Irish as *cliabh* (pronounced cleeve), **Pl. 2.1**. The creel was in everyday use for carrying loads of all kinds, not only around the house and farm, but also for carrying seaweed from the shore, turf from the bogs and loads to and from markets.

What distinguishes the creel from ordinary stake-and-strand baskets is that it is made by inserting the stakes into the ground and weaving around the stakes to form the basket. In order to ensure

Pl. 2.1—Donkey with creels, Aran Islands, Co. Galway. Photo courtesy of David Shaw-Smith.

that the weaving cannot slip off the stakes, a special weave known as the mouthwale (*an buinne béil*) is used. This knot-like weave grips around the stakes, giving a binding of rods that acts as the border of the creel. The mouthwale is, as far as I know, unique to Ireland and Scotland, and, as well as being used in the various creels described in this chapter, it was also used to form the gunwale of the Boyne currach, or coracle. When the sides of the creel have been formed, some of the stakes are woven to form a base. The creel is then pulled out of the ground and turned upright. The protruding stakes at the top give the creel a distinctive appearance.

Although often called a donkey creel, there is no doubt that the creel is of very ancient origin and certainly pre-dates the introduction of donkeys to Ireland, which is thought to have been after the Peninsular Wars in Spain and Portugal in the early 1800s. Before this time most of the Irish peasant farmers had either a horse or a pony[1], but the rise in population in pre-Famine Ireland led to a general impoverishment of the peasantry with greater pressure on land, and periodic outbreaks of famine meant that much stock was either slaughtered or sold. Thus we can say with certainty that the creel was a pony creel before it was a donkey creel. The mild Irish climate suited donkeys and they became popular throughout the country. Although they were displaced by the tractor from the 1950s onwards, the decline in the use of donkeys came much later in the hilly and boggy regions of the west. The photo of a team of donkeys going to the bog **(Pl. 2.2)** is fairly recent and the efficiency with which a group of donkeys can move turf over difficult terrain ensures that a few still remain in use.

Many of the creels used with animals were designed so that the

Pl. 2.2—Team of donkeys with creels. Photo courtesy of Bill Doyle.

Pl. 2.3—Boy with donkey and pardógs *(hinged bottomed creels). From the style of* pardóg *it is probable that this photo was taken in west Mayo. Photo from Green Collection, courtesy of UFTM.*

base could open and release the load. This hinged-bottomed creel was known as a *pardóg* (pronounced pardogue), though in parts of north Galway and south Mayo this basket was known as a *lód* (pronounced loadth).[2] Once the sides of the *pardóg* have been completed the uprights are bordered down and a base is made to fit the opening. This base is then secured to the sides of the *pardóg* with twisted rods, and the base is kept closed by means of a stick, which fits into a loop that is usually made from a twisted willow rod **(Pl. 2.3)**.

The creel, depending on its size and design, was often used to carry loads on the back, whereas the *pardóg* was used exclusively as a burden-basket for animals. It was used not only for carrying turf but also for putting out dung on fields. It was critically important when using *pardógs* to release both openings at the same time. The loop into which the closing stick fitted needed to be fairly loose to facilitate this. Almost everyone who used *pardógs* has a story about the time one of the *pardóg* bottoms did not open; the basket would unbalance the straddle of the donkey or pony, sometimes breaking the bellyband and often unsettling the poor animal as well.

The creel was widely used as a human back-basket for carrying all sorts of loads, and many creels were made specifically to be carried by people rather than animals. The back creel (*cliabh droma*) was usually fitted with a rope so that in carrying it both hands were free and the load was well distributed **(Pl. 2.4)**. Once manufactured rope became available, this was usually used to secure the back creel, but before this a rod rope or a *súgán* rope of twisted hay would have been used around which some rags or sacking could be bound to prevent the rope from chaffing. Some enormous loads were carried

19

Pl. 2.4—Aran woman with heavily laden back creel. Note also the small hand basket known as a kisheen. Photo by Thomas Mason, courtesy of NMI.

in this way. Bill Egan from County Offaly speaks of a 10 stone creel being the normal size; this creel would weigh about 65kg when full.[3] It is clear from **Pl. 2.4**, taken by Thomas Mason in the Aran Islands, that women also carried very heavy loads in these back creels.

Such was the amount of back-breaking work that had to be done to survive in the poorer regions of the west of Ireland, until conditions improved in the 1960s, that the creel became a symbol for this hardship. Thus the Connemara author, Pádraig Óg Ó Connaire writes: 'and any girl in the place who was about to go to America it would be said that it was well for her to be leaving the life of hardship, to be leaving the poverty, the contempt and the creel'.[4] Although this implies that emigration was seen as a preferable option to the physically demanding life on the land, the reference is to 'girls', who would generally have had no chance of inheritance. Even at the height of emigration it was usual for at least one family member to remain on the farm. In the history of the Congested Districts Board, which was set up to alleviate the problems caused by the fact that the greatest density of rural population was found in the least fertile parts of the country, no tenants were willing to give up their land in exchange for the opportunity to emigrate. The hardship of the creel wasn't confined to the west of Ireland. **Plate 2.5,** which shows women with back creels loaded down with vegetables, is an urban scene, but, significantly, that photograph was taken at the end of the nineteenth century when such loads were commonplace, whereas the creel was used in poor rural areas throughout Ireland until recent times.

A variation of the back creel was the shoulder creel or the *cliabh ghuailline*. While the back creel was ideal for carrying loads a long distance, the shoulder creel was more suited to short distances, and the fact that the creel was held on the shoulder meant that the load could be emptied quickly. Because of the way the shoulder creel was carried, the handle was shorter than on the back creel and could therefore be easily made from twisted rods.

Like the spade and many other agricultural objects, there were regional variations of the creel and it is often possible to tell the general region of the country that a creel came from simply by looking at it. Even the material from which the creel was made tells us something of its origins. Creels were mostly made from willow (*Salix viminalis*), usually called 'sally' in Ireland, but hazel creels were also made, especially where hazel was locally common, as in the limestone region of the Burren in County Clare and in parts of County Offaly. Whereas the willow rods for creel making would usually be seasoned for about two months before weaving, three to four weeks was sufficient for seasoning hazel. Hazel creels were stronger but were harder and slower to make, because hazel is considerably less flexible and had to be twisted every time it was being woven around a corner to prevent it from cracking or breaking at this point.

A common feature of most creels was an open area, usually about halfway up the creel, variously called the window, the eye, or the gills of the creel and known in Irish as *an t-áis* (pronounced on tawsh). The window is usually put in after the first or second row of weavers. In many willow creels the weaving rods that form the window are first woven into the basket to form a knot, but the window in the hazel creel is invariably formed by sticking the hazel weavers into the body of the creel, as shown in **Fig. 2.12**. This method was also quite commonly used for willow creels.

There is quite a comprehensive selection of creels in the collections at the National Museum of Ireland and the Ulster Folk and Transport Museum, and this, allied to the fact that the creel was

Pl. 2.6—Standard creel with an even number of uprights on the front or longer side. The sides of the creel in this picture are formed by alternating the direction of weave, anti-clockwise and clockwise to give a knot-like effect.

Pl. 2.7—Creel bases. The creel on the left has an uneven number of stakes and thus the rods from the sides must be woven over and under each of the base sticks. In the creel on the right the uprights from the side are woven over two, under two. The creel on top is from County Sligo. Notice how the uprights, which were knocked to form the warp, are woven under each other to give a rope-like effect. Also notice that the warp rods include the corner posts to give a total of six warp rods.

in widespread use in western counties until recently, gives a fairly comprehensive picture of the various creel types. I do not know of any examples of creels from the counties around Dublin or from the fertile regions of south Leinster or east Munster, but it would be a mistake, in my view, to conclude from this that creels were never used in these areas. Rather, it is likely that the creel would once have been widely used in these areas, but improvements in roads and tracks led to the creel being displaced by the cart as, these areas were not only more fertile and level than the more mountainous west but also more prosperous.

The creel often acted as a unit of measure in the area where it was made. Thus a creel of turf or potatoes was a recognisable unit of exchange where goods were being bought or sold. With the development of basketmaking as a profession, baskets that could act as an official measure (e.g. bushel and cran baskets) were developed in England, and these were adopted in Ireland also, especially near the large cities, where commerce in vegetables, potatoes and fruit was an established practice. Baskets such as these gradually replaced the creel in urban areas.

The most common type of creel was the rectangular one. This was the norm not only in the coastal counties of the west but also in those midland counties such as Longford and Offaly where the use of the creel persisted until fairly recently. Most of these rectangular creels had eighteen uprights but since each upright usually consisted of two stakes with three uprights for the corner stakes, the total number of uprights needed was, in fact, forty (**Pl. 2.6**). The presence of an even number of stakes on the longer side of the creel meant that, when making the base, the warp over which the remaining stakes would be woven could be treated as groups of two, and weft stakes could go over two and under two. When the long side had an uneven number of stakes, it meant that the weft stakes had to go over and under one set of stakes at a time, requiring much more elasticity in the rods than in the case of over two, under two (see **Pl. 2.7**, which shows the detail of different creel bases). Creels of this pattern usually had twenty-two stakes, with five stakes between the corner posts on the long side and four uprights on the short side. Since each stake again consisted of two rods with three at the corners, it needed forty-eight rods to stake up this creel (**Pl. 2.8**). These creels were locally common in certain parts of Mayo and Galway.

In areas of the west where seaweed had to be carried frequently, special creels were

Pl. 2.8—Creel with uneven number of stakes on the front (5x4 creel); the base of this creel would be more difficult to weave than the one in Pl. 2.6. Note the turned-in mouthwale in this creel and the randed sides.

Pl. 2.9—Detail of base of seaweed creel.

developed that had a semi-open bottom so that the water from the seaweed could drain through quickly. This creel was made like a *pardóg* in that the stakes were not bent down to form the base. Instead, the base was formed by twisted rods **(Pl. 2.9)**, which were better able to survive the constant wetting and which could be renewed easily without damaging the fabric of the basket. In the Aran Islands, the seaweed creel (*cliabh feamainne*) would have been used with great frequency by the islanders as they sought to transform areas of limestone slab into fertile fields by drawing seaweed from the shore. Sand, which was also used for improving land in Aran, was always drawn by pony or donkey, but seaweed was often carried on the back. Although the main use of seaweed was for manuring land, there was also a thriving kelp industry along the coastline of Ireland about one hundred years ago. This weed was cut in deep water since it was more valuable if free from sand. Men would usually do the cutting and their knives or sickles were often fitted with long handles up to 10ft (3m) long. Women and sometimes children did the gathering. In this case the seaweed creel would probably have been carried on the shoulder and the women carrying the creels would have protected their backs from the wet weed by wearing a goatskin. **Pl. 2.10** shows Micheálín Ó hIarnáin, a basketmaker from Innismór in the Aran Islands, demonstrating how the seaweed creel was carried on the shoulder.

The *pardóg* or hinged-bottomed creel of the west coast is also

Pl. 2.10—Micheálín Phait Bheachlín Ó hIarnáin carrying a shoulder creel or cliabh ghuailline, which he made when he was over 85 years of age. Photo courtesy of Vincent McCarron.

Pl. 2.11—Mike Jack McHale with a pair of pardógs *that he made for use on his farm in north Mayo. The ring or* sloidín *is of iron rather than of twisted willow. Photo courtesy of Gerry Flynn.*

usually rectangular, but, whereas the creel is usually wider at the mouth, it is important for the *pardóg* to be either straight-sided or even a little narrower at the top to facilitate the load falling out. **Pl. 2.11** shows a pair of *pardógs* from County Mayo. The rectangular base was made separately, usually by sticking some stout sticks into the ground and weaving around them. This base was then secured with two 'handle' ties of twisted willow so that it would open quickly and easily and fall entirely free of the basket. In the rectangular *pardóg* the stick used to keep the *pardóg* closed was usually a forked piece of wood known in Irish as the *súdhan* or the *gabhlóg*. The loop into which the piece of wood fitted was known as *an sloidín* and this was usually of twisted willow; the loop for the *pardóg* in **Pl. 2.11** is actually an iron ring.

The National Museum has an example of a semi-circular *pardóg* from near Tuam in County Galway, which they acquired in 1929. This *pardóg* is mostly of hazel and is the only example of this pattern that I have seen. Estyn Evans has an illustration of a semi-circular 'slip-bottomed creel', but this is, in fact, a drawing of the Tuam *pardóg* at the National Museum.[5] A *pardóg* of this type is shown in **Pl. 2.12**. Even in 1929 when the National Museum's *pardóg* was made, this shape was probably no longer common in the Tuam

Pl. 2.12—Semi-circular pardóg *in hazel based on one acquired by the National Museum in the Tuam area of County Galway in 1929.*

Fig. 2.1—Cavan pardóg.

area. Information supplied to the Irish Folklore Commission from Kilbrennan near Tuam in 1934 describes the creels of the area.[6] A hinged-bottomed creel is mentioned but this is rectangular with a border on top. From the description given, this is very similar to the Mayo *pardóg* already described. However, this basket was known in the Tuam area as a *lód múirthin*. This means that it was a creel for bog-mud, which was transported from the bog in these baskets to be mixed with farmyard manure, the mixture then being applied to the crops. Another creel from the area, which had a honeycomb-type open-work base, was known as a *lód móna*, i.e., a *lód* for turf. The fact that the D-shaped hinged-bottomed creel is not mentioned in this description suggests that the one made for the National Museum Collection may have been an older type. We cannot even be fully sure that it was known as a *pardóg*, though I know of no instance where the word *lód* is used to describe any creel that is not rectangular in shape. I feel that it is accurate to refer to the D-shaped hinged-bottomed Tuam creel as a *pardóg*. I think it is also probable that this shape of *pardóg* was once more widespread. Baskets of this shape from County Cavan are also known as *pardógs* **(Fig. 2.1)**, and a similar pair in the National Museum's collection from County Monaghan are described as bardocks, an anglicised form of the word. The Monaghan and Cavan

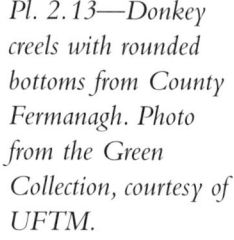

Pl. 2.13—Donkey creels with rounded bottoms from County Fermanagh. Photo from the Green Collection, courtesy of UFTM.

Pl. 2.14—Detail of bases of Fermanagh creels, the creel on the left is of willow, the one on the right is of hazel.

pardógs are made on an entirely different principle to the usual creel practice of sticking the uprights into the ground. Instead they have a ladder-like wooden back, with willow rods woven through the hoops, and with the hinged bottoms made from timber boards.

As we move further north along the west coast to Sligo and Donegal, we find the rectangular creel is still the dominant form, but this version is taller than the creels of the midlands and the west. Another distinctive feature of these creels from the north-west is that the corner posts usually join the other stakes on the long side to form a warp of six groups of stakes rather than the four that would be typical of the western and midland creels. Moreover, the warp stakes are over and under each other, rather than being secured under the bottom wale (**see Pl. 2.7**). The weft stakes are woven over one, under one, rather than following the easier over two, under two patterns described earlier.

Further inland in the north, the rectangular form is softened somewhat so that the sides bulge out from the corners. The bases of these creels are rarely flat but have rounded bottoms, as can be seen in **Pls 2.13 and 2.14**. A further distinguishing feature of these creels is that the uprights are single stakes rather than being doubled, and the butts of the weavers that form the mouthwale are almost invariably turned in rather than being left sticking out as was the usual practice along the west coast. This turning in of the mouthwale was done after the first stroke of normal weaving, and is seen not just on northern creels but also occasionally on the creels of the west, particularly in County Mayo.

The base of this hump-bottomed northern creel is formed by taking each of the stakes on the long side, including the corner post,

Pl. 2.15—Scottish creel, note the rounded bottom similar to the Fermanagh creel. The rods that form the window (an t-áis) were inserted to the left of the upright when making the creel. These rods are always inserted to the right in Irish creels (see Pls. 2.12, 2.17, 2.18, 2.21, 2.26 and 2.27), though this method is also used in Scotland. Photo courtesy of National Museums of Scotland.

and sticking them into the weaving on the other side of the creel, allowing them to form a curve in doing so **(Pl. 2.14)**. Once the stakes on the long side have formed the warp, the stakes on the short side are woven over and under them. It is usually necessary to twist or crank the rods as one would for a handle, so that they will be flexible enough to weave in and out in this way. Because these stakes will not be long enough to fill the base, they are supplemented by sticking other rods down alongside them to complete the base. However, a feature of the base is that these creels, when completed, will have holes on the short side. In shape and construction, these creels are very similar to the Scottish creel shown in **Pl. 2.15**.

Although these hump-bottomed creels may have been sometimes used as back creels, it seems that their primary purpose was for use with a donkey or pony and that the creels for the back were flat-bottomed. The Ulster Folk and Transport Museum has well-made examples of back creels from various parts of Ulster. Many are single-staked and, while more or less rectangular in shape, they usually have an outward bulge on the sides which gives them a slightly oval appearance. They would usually have eighteen stakes with the six stakes on the long side (this includes the corner posts) forming the warp over and under which the other stakes are woven.

They are very similar in appearance to the creels in **Pl. 2.5**.

Among the few examples of creels from south Munster that I have seen are those in **Pl. 2.16**, which shows a donkey laden with creels near Waterville in County Kerry. As can be seen, these are somewhat circular in shape, with eighteen double stakes, and seem to have a knot rather than a mouthwale. The window is formed by sticking the rods into the weaving. In most other creels that I have seen, the weaving on either side of the window is prevented from slipping by a knot of weaving above and below the window. This is absent in these Kerry creels, but I would be very slow to conclude that this was the usual practice in the creel-making of that area. I have sometimes

Pl. 2.16—Donkey with creels near Waterville, Co. Kerry. Photo courtesy of DIF, UCD.

seen knots left out in photos of creels in this area of the west, and it is usually an indication that the technique is forgotten somewhat and might be a sign that creel-making was in decline somewhat by the time the picture was taken. In the Dingle Peninsula in County Kerry and on the Blasket Islands, the donkey burden-basket was known as an *úim* (pronounced oom), but because these baskets were always used as a pair, the plural form *úimeacha* (pronounced oomaka) was more frequently used **(Pl. 2.17)**. These baskets are oval in shape and the base of the basket is made like a frame basket with a hoop of willow being formed to fit the base. Ribs are lashed to this and the base completed by weaving in and out of these ribs.

The Munster back creel is best represented in the National Museum collection by an example from Clonakilty, Co. Cork, and is similar to those of the west of Ireland in being rectangular in shape, but similar to those of the north in having six stakes knocked for the warp. In this base the stakes that form the warp are stuck into the weaving on the opposite side and some of the weavers go over two to provide a rim that protects the base. A back creel from County Tyrone, which is described in the technique section of this chapter, has eighteen single stakes, but many back creels were double staked. This was especially true of creels made to carry the heavy loads described earlier. Back creels from Dunservick in north Antrim had stout double stakes (known locally as the 'stanners') and usually held 10 stone (65kg) of fish — the same size mentioned

Pl. 2.17—Tadgh Ó Conchúir and Seán Pheats Team Ó Cearna with donkeys and panniers (úimeacha) on the Blasket Islands, County Kerry. Photo by George Thompson, courtesy of Katherine Thompson.

earlier by Bill Egan — but 12 stone (78kg) creels were also made there. The height of the Dunservick creel depended on the size of the man for whom it was made. Another type of back creel was the foddering creel **(Pl. 2.18)**. This was used to bring hay to animals who were being out-wintered in fields. Because the loads of hay were light, some foddering creels were quite large. One example in the National Museum collection is over 3ft (91cm) tall and the basket has a large open-work section which is formed by making the window as shown in **Fig. 2.12**, but allowing the new set of weaving rods to be almost vertical. The foddering creel was, therefore, much lighter than the standard creel and, though not as strong, was still adequate for carrying hay. Many back creels were quite small in size and had different names depending on the area. A small creel was known as a 'punther' in west Cork, as a *leath-cliabh* (literally a half-creel) in Aran and as a *cléibhín* (pronounced clayveen) in other parts of the country.

Pl. 2.18—Foddering creel, based on similar creels at Newtowncashel Heritage Centre, Co. Westmeath.

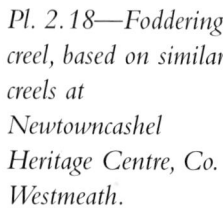

Although willow, and to a lesser extent hazel, was the general material used for creels, dock stems were also used for making creels in the Erris region near Belmullet in north-west Mayo. Docks and heather were used for basketmaking on some of the Scottish islands where willow and hazel was scarce, and this was also true of the Erris region of Mayo, where heather was used for lobster pots (see Chapter 5) and straw was used for back baskets (see Chapter

7). The docken creel was 16" x 13" (41cm x 34cm) at the mouth and had fourteen double uprights, three sets between posts on the long side and two sets between the corners on the short side. The local name for this creel was a *caibín* (pronounced cobeen), and it was mainly used for carrying fish from the currachs. The docks for making the *caibín* were pulled in late summer and allowed to dry in the sun for a few days. They were then worked immediately. The *caibín* was also sometimes made from a plant called a *ceallachóg*, and although I could not find this word in any dictionary I think the plant may be sea-holly, since it is described as having a silvery leaf and growing in sandy soil.[7]

Pl. 2.19—Ciaran Darcy bordering a crandy, photo courtesy of NMI.

Creel techniques were also used in other baskets. In County Meath a potato basket made in this way was known as a *peillic*, while around Hodson Bay near Athlone a circular farm basket made like a creel was called a codger. The *crúbóg* was essentially a low creel that was fitted with two handles on the short side, and an Offaly basket known as the crandy was also made like a low creel. In the crandy, however, the rods that were stuck into the ground were put in deep enough that when the base was completed and the crandy was pulled out of the ground, the protruding stakes were cranked and woven into a trac-type border **(Pl. 2.19)**. The same technique was also used on

Fig. 2.2—Turf creel from County Armagh.

Pl. 2.20—Kish on a slide car. Green Collection, courtesy of UFTM.

another County Offaly basket, a fairly low turf kesh which could be put on a barrow for bringing out turf from the bog. The turf creel in **Fig. 2.2** from County Armagh is designed to be used as a hand-barrow, but the principle of construction is the same as in the creels already described.

The transition from creel to cart can be seen in the kish, a creel-like basket made to fit a slide car, which was used in the Glens of Antrim and in areas of the Sperrin mountains on the borders of Counties Derry and Tyrone at least until the 1930s **(Pl. 2.20)**. Its function was mainly to bring down loads of turf from mountain bogs, but Estyn Evans[8] contends that it was widely used throughout Ireland until the eighteenth century when it began to be replaced by the wheeled cart. A feature of the Irish form of slide car is the provision of wooden shoes or runners that could be replaced when worn out. These are also mentioned by Bill Egan,[9] though he calls them heels, and it seems from his conversation that kishes were used on slide cars in parts of County Offaly, at least until the 1940s. While the Ulster kish had a closed siding, the Offaly kish of which Bill Egan speaks had an opening similar to the creel, but this window had a straw rope woven through it to prevent turf from falling out.

Pl. 2.21—Sligo creel, left, and Kerry creel, right.

Pl. 2.22—Single-staked back creel based on a similar one from County Tyrone in the UFTM. The second and fourth sets of weavers are woven in the opposite direction to the first and third set.

Pl. 2.23—Detail of base of Mayo pardóg.

Pl. 2.24 (left)—Detail of base of Tuam pardóg.

Pl. 2.25 (below)—Detail of bases of úimeacha from County Kerry, based on a pair from Dún Chaoin in the Dingle Peninsula.

Pl. 2.26 (bottom left)—Seaweed creel made by Micheálín Ó hIarnáin.

Pl. 2.27 (bottom right)—Patch Rua finishing seaweed creels, Aran Islands, about 1920. Photo by Thomas Mason, courtesy of DIF, UCD.

TECHNIQUE

Mouthwale

The mouthwale (*buinne béil*) refers to the rope-like weave that is used at the start of the various creels already described. It is used not only for creels but also for the Boyne currach, the kish and other baskets made upside-down in the creel manner. The mouthwale replaces the border and prevents the weaving on the side of the basket from slipping off (**Fig. 2.3**).

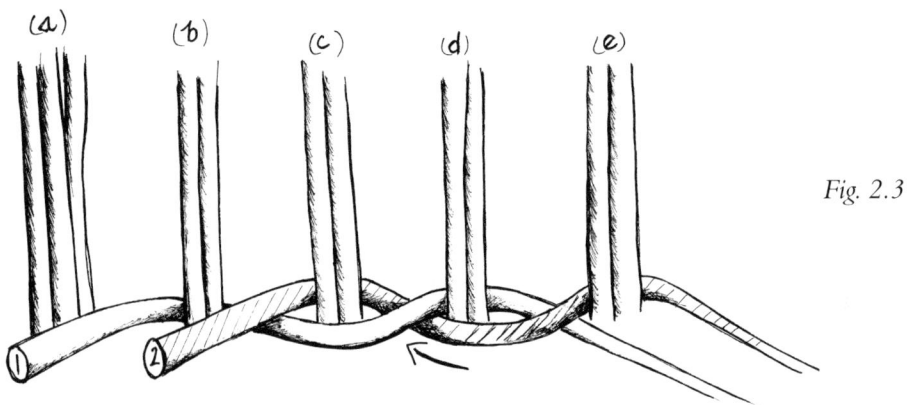

Fig. 2.3

Leaving the butt well out, lay the first rod 1, in front of A, behind B, in front of C, behind D and leave to rest in front of E.

Rod 2 is inserted, butt first, under rod 1 at space CD, behind C and then in front of B where the butt rests. The remainder of rod 2 is taken in front of D, over rod 1, behind E to lie in front of next stake F (**Fig. 2.4**).

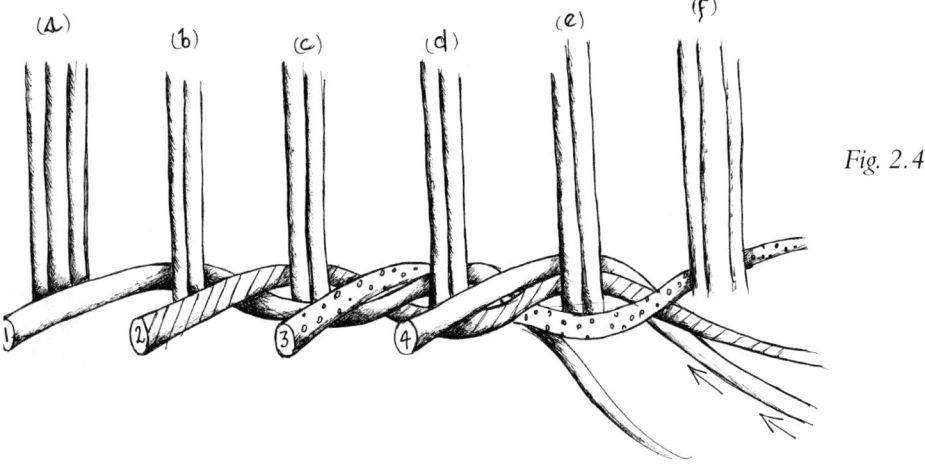

Fig. 2.4

Rod 3 is worked by having butt pushed through at space DE, under rods 1 and 2; butt is then taken behind D to lie in front of C. Remainder of rod 3 is taken in front of E, over rod 2, behind F to rest against next stake G. Rod 4 is treated in the same way by starting at space EF. (**Fig. 2.5**).

Fig. 2.5

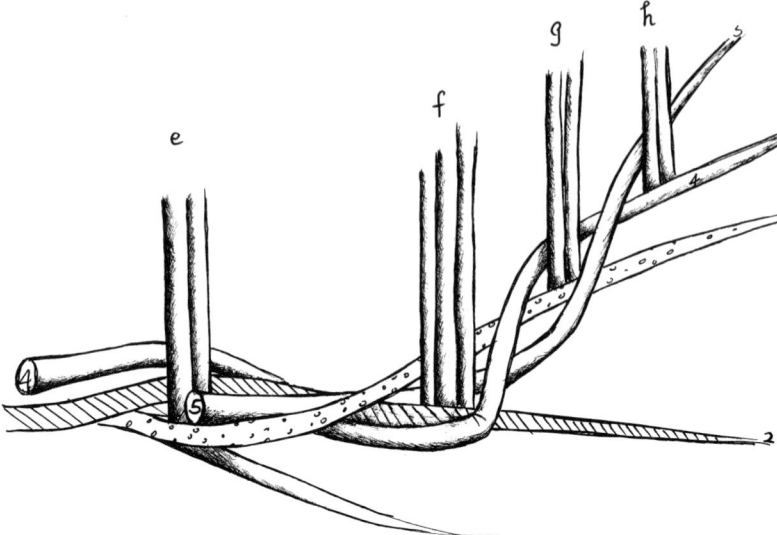

Hold out the corner stake F as you weave around it. Ensure that rod 3 rests against G by holding it there while you weave rod 5 over rod 3, in front of G and behind H to rest in front of I. Continue introducing new weavers until you reach corner post A where you started (**Fig. 2.6**).

When you reach corner post A, thread rod 16 (third-last rod) out under rod 1. Rod 17 is threaded under two rods (1 and 2) and rod 18 is threaded under three rods (1, 2 and 3).

Fig. 2.6

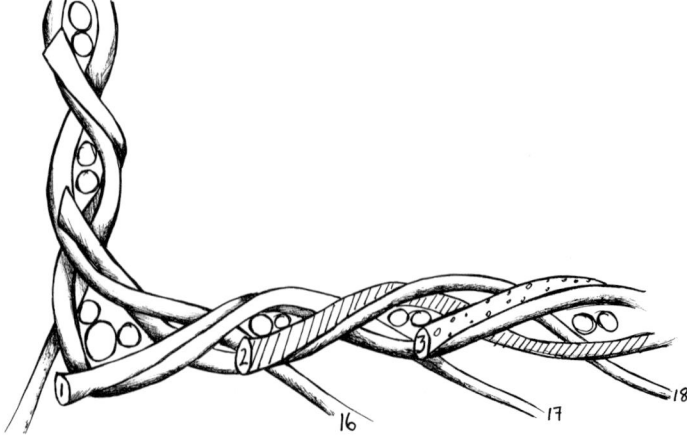

Standard creel

The most common creel is rectangular, with four sets of uprights
between the corner posts on the long
side and three sets of uprights
between the corner posts on the
shorter side. Choose a level site with
soft ground to facilitate inserting the
stakes. Mark out a rectangle 24" x 18"
(61cm x 46cm). This size is suitable
for use as a donkey creel or pony
creel but the standard creel was made
in various sizes, many of them smaller
than the size described here. This was
traditionally done with a rod frame-
work, kept in place by twisted willow staples as shown in **Fig. 2.7**.

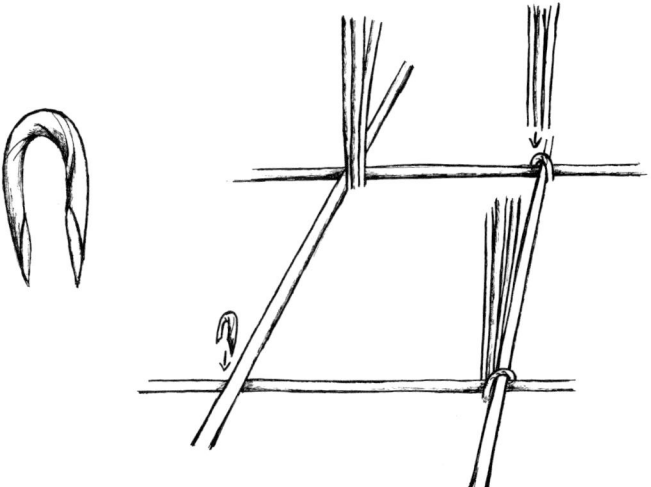

Fig. 2.7

The standard creel requires forty uprights. Thirty-two of these
should be 8–9ft (2.4–2.7m) or about ¾" (20mm) in diameter, and
the remaining eight should be about 7ft (2.1m) or about ½"
(13mm) in diameter. The four thickest rods are put at the corners
and these are supplemented by two of the smaller uprights at each
corner so that each corner post is, in fact, a group of three rods. The
remaining uprights have two stakes per upright. The positioning of
the uprights is shown in **Fig. 2.8**.

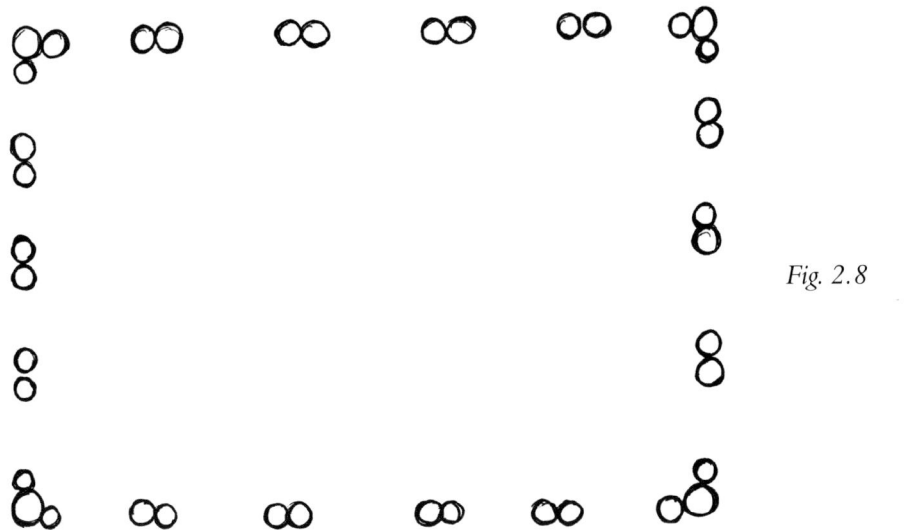

Fig. 2.8

The uprights are then tied to allow the creel to taper inwards while being made (this will be an outward slope when the creel is pulled out of the ground). The corner posts are actually excluded from the tie since they are inclined to slope inwards, or if they are tied, they are tied separately higher up and this tie is removed when the mouthwale has been completed. The uprights in the Aran–style creel are not usually tied since this is a straight–sided creel. For this reason, the Aran creel is not that suitable for making in a wooden template where the stakes can move in the bored holes. The tight grip that the soil has on the uprights facilitates keeping the sides straight. In Aran the three rods that form each corner post are always tied together. This gives the corner post more strength.

Four sets of eighteen weavers (72 rods in all) are needed for the siding of the creel. Two of these sets, for use in the mouthwale and in the window (*an t-áis*), should be about 8ft (2.4m) long, and the other two sets should be somewhat slighter, about 7ft (2.1m) long. If material of this thickness is not available or is considered too difficult to work, lighter material such as 7fts (2.1m) and 6 fts (1.8m) could be used with five sets of weavers instead of four. Eight 7ft (2.1m) rods will be needed for the top knot of the creel.

Take the first set of eighteen 8ft (2.4m) weavers and put on the mouthwale as shown in **Figs 2.3** to **2.6**. In the standard creel the butts of the mouthwale are on the outside of the basket, so trim the butts of the mouthwale to within 1" (25mm) to make it easier to weave the row of French randing which follows the mouthwale, without kinking the weaving rods. For French randing (details in Appendix 1), you will be moving clockwise around the creel.

Having completed the first row of French randing, beat down the weaving. You may now simply French rand to a finish. However, in the strongest of the traditional creels, the weaving consisted of a series of knots. This was achieved by going to the right, moving anti-clockwise around the creel after the initial row of French randing had been completed. When weaving to the right it is necessary to thread the second–last weaver under one rod and the final weaver under two. Then, when the rods are underneath, you French rand, finding your weavers by going to the left, i.e., clockwise around the creel. At the completion of the row of French randing, your weaving rods lie on top so you go to the right again, i.e., anti-clockwise around the creel. Alternate the weaving like this until the rods are used. This will become much clearer once you become familiar with the anti-clockwise weaving, which is used each time a new set of rods is introduced and also when the window is being formed. Therefore, I would advise randing the rods until the pattern of weaving to the right becomes familiar. Apart from its strength, the advantage of the knot-like weave is that it makes it easier to prevent the corner posts from sloping inwards.

Introducing a new set of weavers
Lay rod 1 behind C, then weave in front of D, behind E to rest in front of F. Put rod 2 under rod 1 so that its butt is behind D. Then weave it in front of E, over rod 1, behind F to rest in front of G. Continue introducing rods in this way until you have two weavers left (**Fig. 2.9**).

Fig. 2.9

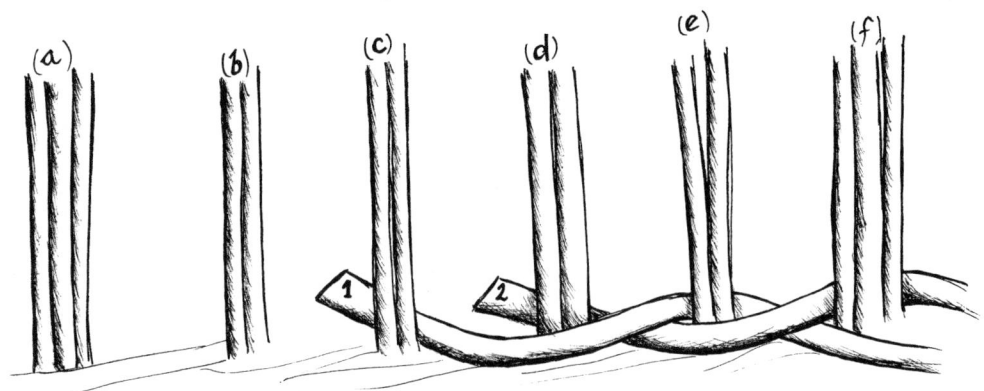

Thread rod 17 under one (rod 1) and rod 18 under two (rods 1 and 2) to finish. Beat down firmly. The rods should now be French randed. Each subsequent set of rods is introduced in the same way but the third set also forms the window (**Fig. 2.10**).

Fig. 2.10

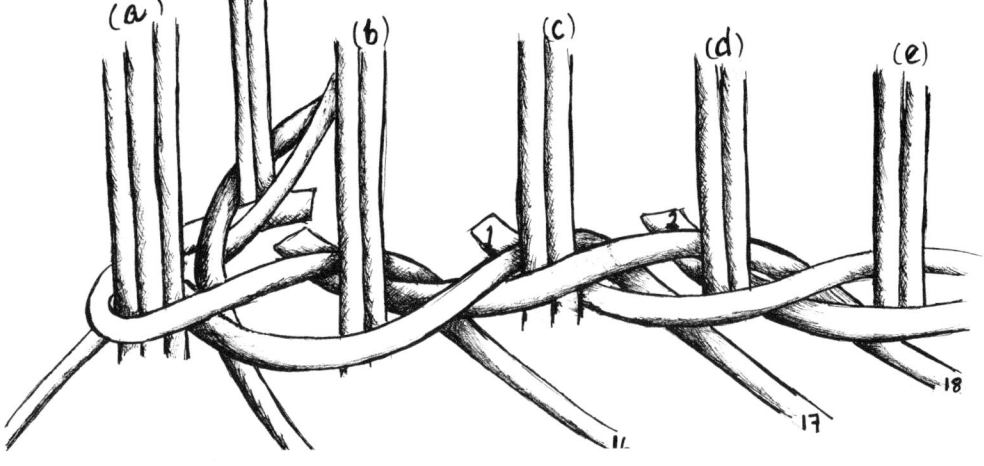

Forming the window

After the third set of rods has been introduced as shown in **Figs 2.9 and 2.10**, the rods are French randed for one round but they are allowed to lie about 3–4" (75–100mm) above the work as shown in **Fig. 2.11**.

Fig. 2.11

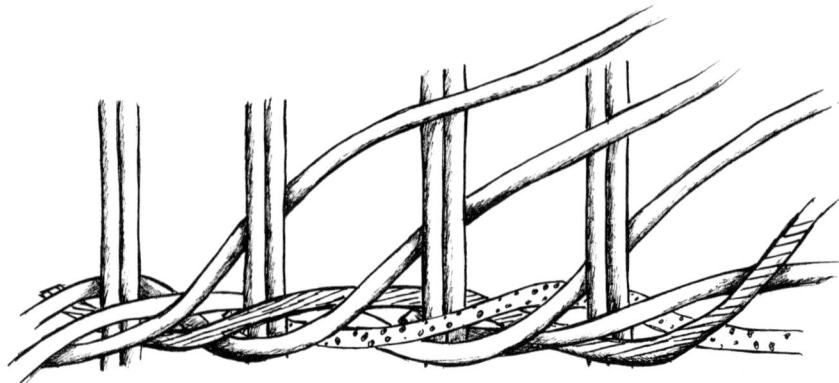

These are then woven by going to the right, i.e., anti-clockwise around the creel in the same manner as when introducing a new set of rods. Remember to thread the ends of rods 17 and 18 under one and two rods respectively **(Fig. 2.10)**.

Fig. 2.12

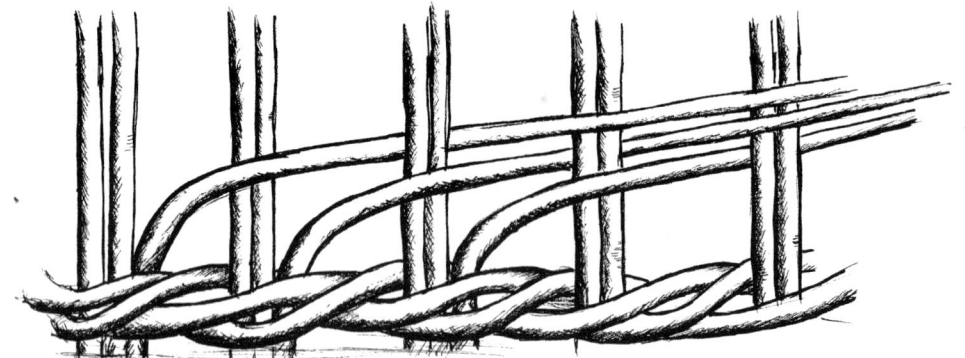

Variations exist for forming the window. That shown in **Fig. 2.12** is almost always used when working with hazel and was also widely used with willow. In this version, the new set of weavers are stuck into the work and allowed to form the window by being French randed. The next round will go in the opposite direction (anti-clockwise around the creel) to form a knot. In most of the creels of the Aran Islands, the rods were stuck into the weave, as shown in **Fig. 2.12**, but each new weaver was introduced by going

40

to the right, i.e., anti-clockwise in front of the next upright but inside the previous weaver before going behind the next upright and out the next space. This row of weaving was then followed by a row of French randing. Sometimes the rods forming the window of the Aran creel were kinked sharply, occasionally all over as in the seaweed creel **(Pl. 2.26)** but more often at the corners **(Pl. 2.27)** rather than being curved as shown in **Fig 2.12**. The weave at the bottom of the window in **Fig. 2.12** is the same as the top knot described in **Figs 2.13 to 2.16**.

The top knot of the creel
When the desired height has been reached (usually after four sets of eighteen rods) and about 15–16" (38–41cm) high, a finishing wale or top knot is put on. In many areas a three-rod wale started with butts is used, but the top knot described here is not only stronger than a three-rod wale; it also agrees better with the other weaving in the creel.

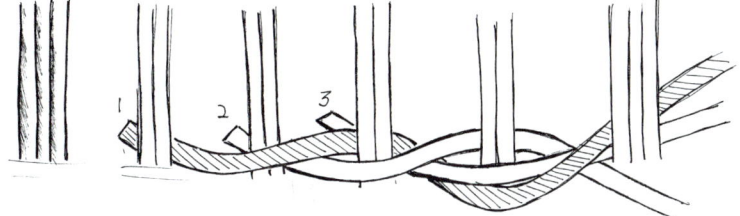

Fig. 2.13

Select four 7ft (2.1m) rods and lay in the first three as if putting on a new set of weavers by going to the right, anti-clockwise around the creel as shown in **Fig. 2.9**. However, when the third rod has been woven, follow it by using rod 1, bringing it in and out of the same spaces as rod 3 as shown in **Fig. 2.13**.

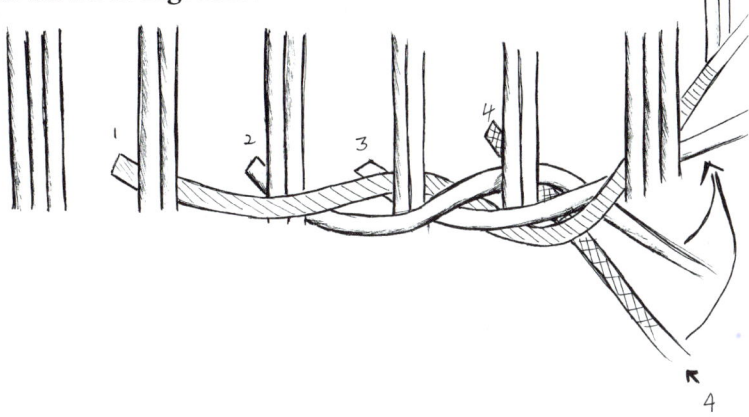

Fig. 2.14

Rod 4 is introduced, as shown in **Fig. 2.14**, and is then followed by rod 2. In this way you get the effect of a knot while weaving with four rods. When the initial weaving rods get thin, they are replaced by adding new rods, butt first, as required. Four additional rods are usually used on the creel, giving a total of eight rods in the top knot. **(Fig. 2.15)**

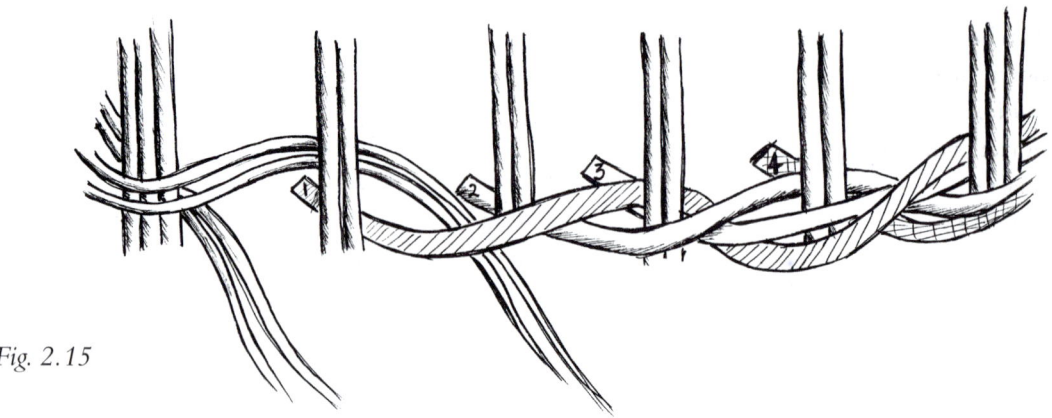

Fig. 2.15

When you reach the place where you started, take both rods AB of the first finishing set in turn out under the initial weaving rod 1. Rods C and D are similarly threaded through in turn under the top knot in the next space, i.e., under rods 1 and 2. **(Fig. 2.16)**

Fig. 2.16

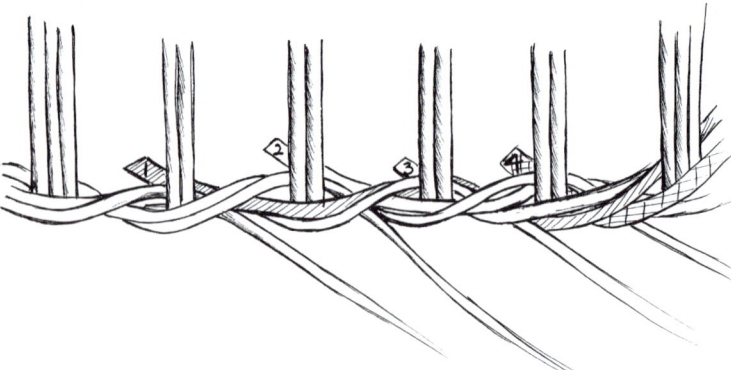

Take rod B of the pair AB and bring out under the top knot in the next vacant space, coming out under three rods as you do so. Rod D is threaded out in the next vacant space, coming out under four rods.

Finishing the creel

When the top knot has been finished and beaten down firmly, the uprights on the long side of the creel are knocked and brought out under the knot, beside the corresponding uprights on the opposite side, as shown in **Fig. 2.17**.

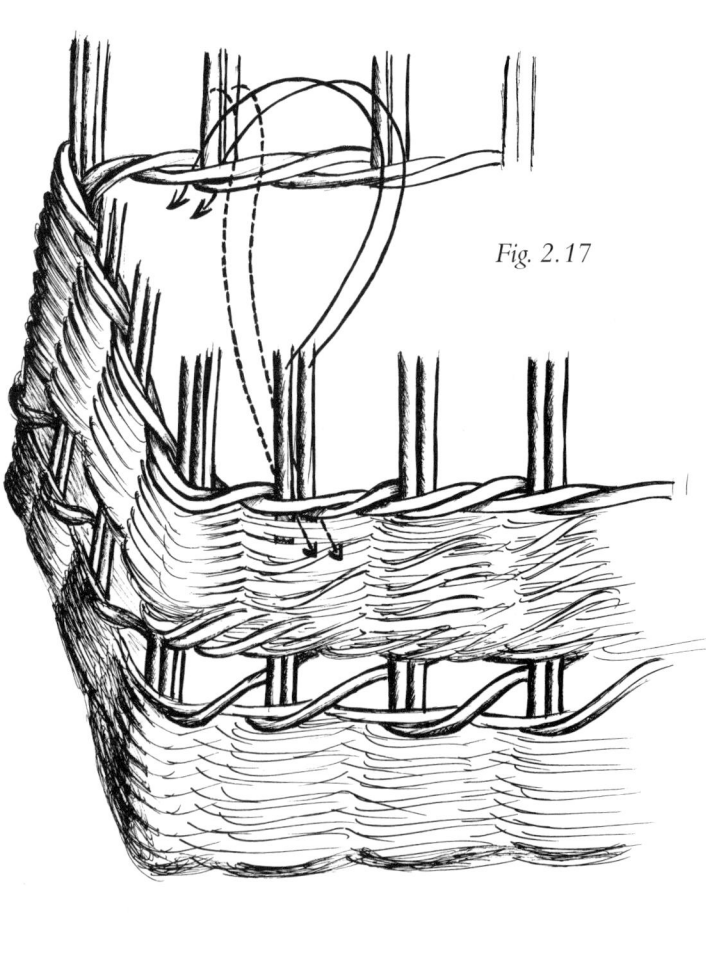

Fig. 2.17

Next knock the stakes on the shorter side of the creel. It is usual to start with the left-hand corner post. The first of the group of three rods that make up this post is taken over two, under two, and out into the open space between the corner post group of uprights and the next group of uprights on the opposite side. Now the first of the group on the right is similarly dealt with, and the uprights are woven alternately until the rods in both corner posts have been knocked down, as shown in **Fig. 2.18**.

At this point go to the other side of the basket and repeat the process. The next uprights from the corner are then taken in turn, over two and under two as before, but these are allowed to divide the uprights on the opposite side as indicated by the arrows in **Fig. 2.18**. The uprights in the middle (of the short side) are the last to be knocked.

Trim off the surplus ends roughly and save the best of these for finishing the filling of

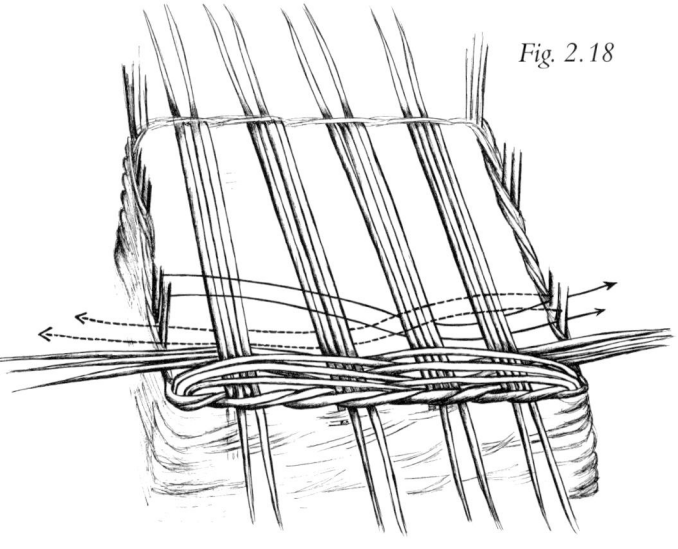

Fig. 2.18

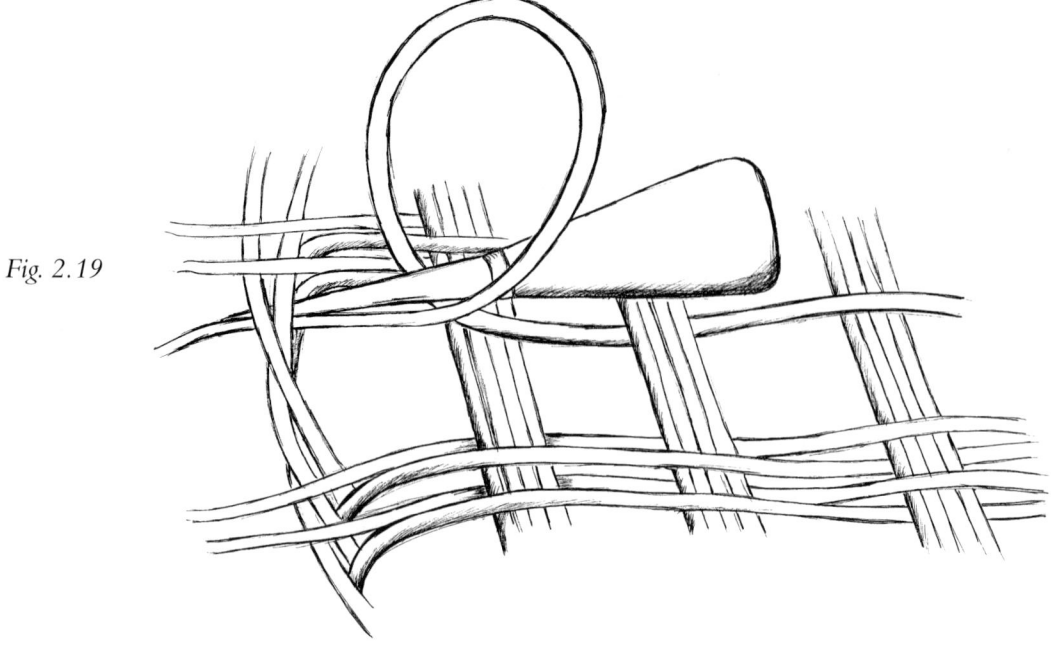

Fig. 2.19

the base. The filling rods go from alternate sides, tip first, under, over, under and over, and are then threaded out under the knot on the opposite side. When you have brought the filling rod out under the knot, it is usually impossible to pull it further, so for this reason it is best to take the filling rods under, over and under, then pull so that the main bulk of the rod has been pulled through, before going over and then out under the knot or wale **(Fig. 2.19)**. Details of other creel bases are given in the descriptions of the respective creels.

When the base has been sufficiently trimmed, all ends are cut flush and the creel is levered out of the ground by putting the hands into the window and lifting up the four corners in turn. The remainder of the trimming can be done once the creel has been pulled out of the ground. The point at which the uprights are trimmed is usually about 3" (75mm) clear of the mouthwale, giving the creel a total height of about 18" (46cm).

If fitting a handle *(iris)*, two stout 8ft/9ft (2.4m/2.7m) rods will be needed and a third rod 7ft (2.1m) long will also be needed. Because of the span of the creel handle it is necessary to twist the rod that forms the handle core; apart from this the handle is similar to that described in the technique section of Chapter 8. The third rod is required because the greater width and height of the creel handle cannot usually be covered satisfactorily with two rods.

5 x 4 creel

In this creel (**Pl. 2.8**) there are five sets of uprights between the corner posts on the longer side of the creel and four on the shorter side. The rods used are somewhat thinner than in the standard creel. This pattern was popular in north Mayo but was also used in other areas, particularly in west Mayo, and in parts of Counties Galway, Sligo and Donegal.

Dimensions are similar to the standard creel, but 48 stakes are needed, four sets of three for the corners and eighteen double stakes. The mouthwale is put on as described for the standard creel, but allow the butts of the mouthwale rods to protrude 5–6" (125–150mm) past the uprights. These should be pressed down when weaving the first row of randing rods and, upon completion of the first row of French randing, these butts are turned into the inside of the basket. Most 5 x 4 creels had a turned-in mouthwale as described here. Because of this, the remainder of the first set of rods was randed rather than knotted, as described for the standard creel. I do not recall ever seeing a turned-in mouthwale combined with a knotted weave on the first set of weaving rods.

The second set of weavers is introduced, as described for a standard creel (**Figs 2.9 and 2.10**), but these are then randed rather than knotted. The window is formed as shown in **Fig. 2.11**. The weaving above the window is often knotted as described for a standard creel. One example of a north Mayo creel that I have seen was made by Anthony 'Soldier' McHale from near Foxford, who used double weaving rods for the window; these would have been thinner than the usual 7–8ft (2.1–2.4m) window rods, probably 6ft (1.8m).

After the top knot is put on, the uprights on the long side are knocked down, giving five sets rather than four as in the standard creel. This means that the rods from the shorter side must go over, under, over, under, over, before going under the top knot and returning to the other side again. This calls for much greater flexibility than required in the standard creel, so lighter and better quality rods are chosen, if available (see **Pl. 2.7**).

Sligo/Donegal creel

The amount of uprights for this creel is almost the same as for a standard creel, though the dimensions are somewhat smaller at 20" x

16" (52cm x 42cm). The only difference is that the uprights are slighter than the 7ft to 8fts (2.1–2.7m) used in the standard creel, and only two rods are used in the corner posts. Thus 36 rods are needed to give eighteen double uprights. The weavers are also slighter, but five sets of eighteen rods are needed because this is a tall creel measuring about 19" (48cm) high without the protruding uprights; two sets of 7ft (2.1m) and three sets of stout 6fts (1.8m) should be adequate for this. This creel usually has a pronounced inward slope, so the uprights are tied lower down than in a standard creel. The corner posts should probably be tied as well, though I still prefer to tie them separately at a higher point than the other uprights.

One set of the 7ft (2.1m) is used for the mouthwale, which is the same as for a standard creel, and the rods are then randed to a finish. The next set of rods, 6fts (1.8m), are introduced with a knot, as described for a standard creel, and then randed to a finish. The window for which 7fts (2.1m) are used is done as described in **Fig. 2.11** and the final two sets of rods are introduced with a knot and then French randed like the other sets.

The creel is topped with a three-rod wale, starting with butts at the middle of the long side. When you come halfway round the creel, join up with three more butts and wale to where you started, at which point the tips of the waling rods are secured by pulling them out under the start of the wale; the first under one, the second under two and the third under three.

The base is different from those already described. All six sets of uprights on the long side are knocked to form a warp, over and under which the stakes from the short side can be woven. When knocking the uprights on the long side they are *not* pulled out under the wale but cross each other instead. To do this, kink any given set of uprights on the long side, bend halfway down, knock its opposite and thread it under the one you have half knocked; then pull both sets of rods by the tips until they are fully knocked. This detail can be seen in **Pl. 2.7**. This method of knocking the uprights is also used in the kish and in the Tyrone back creel. A close look at the creels in **Pl. 4.6**, 'Donegal Natives' from the Lawrence Collection, reveals that the base is of this type. Those creels are as described here except that the window is put in when the second set of rods is introduced rather than at the third set. It can also be seen from **Pl. 4.6** that these creels are used as back creels as well as donkey creels.

Because the corner posts have been knocked already, it is

necessary to insert a rod down at the left-hand corner post to begin the weaving. Select a pliable rod for this, as it must go over at the corner post, then under, over, under, over, under the knocked corner post at the other side before returning over the knocked corner post and then going under, over, under, over and under. It is usual to abandon the rod at this point and to start another one, but if it is sufficiently flexible it can be taken again. The base is closed, proceeding from opposite sides as described for the standard creel and supplementing the stakes on the short sides with extra stakes as needed for weaving the base.

Ulster creel

Although I call this an Ulster creel because it was typically found in Counties Fermanagh, Cavan, Monaghan and south-east Donegal, it was not confined to Ulster; there is an example of a creel of this style in the National Museum collection from County Leitrim, which, although it borders County Fermanagh, is in fact in Connacht.

This creel has only single uprights, so eighteen 8ft to 9ft (2.1m to 2.4m) rods are sufficient. For the Fermanagh-style creel in **Pl. 2.13**, two sets of eighteen 8ft (2.4m) weavers slightly thinner than the uprights are required, but three sets are needed for the deeper styles of creel that were used in some parts of Cavan. The four corner posts are inserted allowing 21" (545mm) between the posts on the long side and 14" (370mm) between the posts on the shorter side. Take a straight upright rod and lay it on the long side *outside* the corner posts. This line will act as a guide for the uprights nearest the corner post, which are put in next, just outside this line. Thus the uprights nearest the corner posts are about 1" (250mm) further out than the corner posts. Once these uprights have been inserted, lay a rod outside these so that the two central posts are set further out again. This gives the long sides a somewhat oval shape. A similar procedure is adopted for the short sides, but once a rod has been laid outside the corner posts, the three uprights between the corner posts are set in a straight line about 1" (250mm) out from the corner posts. The space between the outermost uprights would thus be about 23" (585mm) and 19" (495mm). The uprights on the short side are put in so that they slope outwards; this will give the finished creel a slight bulge at the ends.

The mouthwale is put on as described in **Figs 2.3 to 2.6**, but allow the butts to protrude about 6" (150mm) as this creel has a turned–in mouthwale as described for the 5 x 4 creel. It is therefore necessary to press down the butts that are sticking out when doing the first row of randing in order to prevent unsightly kinks on the weaving rods. The butts are turned in after the first row of randing, whereupon the rods are randed to a finish. Remember to tap down the weaving to close any gaps around the mouthwale.

The next set of rods is the window set. This is introduced by going to the right to make a knot, as described in **Figs 2.9 and 2.10**. The window is of the style shown in **Fig. 2.11**. It is necessary to go to the right again to form a knot on top of the window as already described for a standard creel. This set should bring you to a height of about 9" (230mm). This is the last set that is added for the low Fermanagh-style creel, so we will deal with this style first.

1. Low style (Fermanagh)

Next take some 7ft (2.1m) rods and put on two rows of pairing, joining with butts in hedgerow-style whenever the rods begin to get light. Now take each of the six uprights on the long side and, having allowed it to form a gentle arc or curve, prepare to stick it into the weaving beside the corresponding upright on the other side. It will be necessary to gauge how deeply you can stick the upright into the weave and then cut off the surplus length and point the upright before sticking it. It should usually be possible to get the uprights down deeper than the window on the corresponding side, thus giving the appearance of two stakes along the windows of the long sides. The measurement from the top of curved rods to ground level should be about 14" (37cm).

Starting at the middle of the long side, take two 7fts (2.1m) and chase rand (i.e., starting with the right–hand rod each time, rand one stroke and follow with a stroke of randing with the left–hand rod). When you reach the other side, these rods will be getting thin, so place two new butts on top of these spent ones and chase rand again until you come back to the side you started at. You are now finished weaving around the uprights on the short side. Take one rod and beginning behind the left–hand corner weave in and out, turn at the right–hand corner post. Weave back and forth in this way (pack randing), joining a new butt whenever the weaving rods get thin. When you have woven about 2–3" (50–75mm), incorporate the first of the uprights on the short side into the weaving. If you study **Pl. 2.14** you will notice that in the case of the hazel creel only the relevant upright is used in the weaving, whereas in the willow creel each upright is supplemented by two others. If you supplement the uprights in this way, these rods will be sufficient to finish weaving the base of the creel once you have first randed about 2" (650mm) on either side. In the case of the hazel creel, where only the true upright is used, additional weaving rods are placed as necessary under the curved uprights of the long side that now form the warp. In all cases it will be necessary to twist some of the rods into a rope, as for a handle, in order to weave them in and out without breaking.

2. *Tall style (Cavan)*

For this creel you use a third set of weavers, introduced as usual by going to the right to form a knot, and then simply randed to a finish. Now put on a top knot **(Figs 2.13 and 2.14)** and curve the uprights into an arc as described for the low creel, but in the case of this taller creel the rods being stuck in will not usually reach the window. It is important that both hoop rods are evenly matched.

The filling of the base is as described for the low-style Fermanagh creel but each upright on the short side is always supplemented by two other rods, thus ensuring that the holes in the bottom of the creel are not too large. This taller style of Ulster creel is very similar to a Scottish creel.

Back creel (County Tyrone)

This is a single-staked creel like the Ulster creel described above. The version described here is based on a back creel from County Tyrone in the Ulster Folk and Transport Museum. Such back creels were used throughout the country, and the back creels carried by the vegetable sellers in **Pl. 2.5**, although similar to the one described here, are from County Cork.

You will need eighteen 8fts (2.4m) for uprights, a little more than ½" (13mm) in diameter. Set in the four corner posts allowing about 20" (51cm) between them in length and about 13" (34cm) between them in width. Set the next two rods of the long side at least a rod's width (about 1" or 25mm) out, as described for the Ulster creel, and set the next two uprights (the middle ones) a further rod width out, again as described for the Ulster creel. The first two uprights on the short side are similarly set about 1" (25mm) out and the middle upright is set a further 1" (25mm) out, giving the back creel a somewhat oval shape, with about 22" x 18" (57cm x 45cm) between the posts at their widest extent. This would give the completed creel an external measurement of about 24" (49.5cm). The stakes are tied on top to allow for a good inward curve: the measurement of the creel opening, after the siding has been finished at about 18" (46cm) from ground level, would be 18" x 12" (46cm x 31cm).

Four sets of weaving rods are needed; the opening set is almost as heavy as the uprights, so light 8fts (2.4m) or heavy 7fts (2.1m) would be appropriate for this set. The others need not be as thick; 7fts (2.1m) or even 6fts (1.8m) about ⅜ths" (10mm) thick would be adequate.

The first set of rods is put on with a turned–in mouthwale, so about 6" (150mm) of the butts must be allowed to stick out, as described for the Ulster creel. Presumably, one of the advantages of the turned-in mouthwale is that no rods can catch the person carrying the creel. The back creels of the Cork vegetable sellers **(Pl. 2.5)** do not have a turned-in mouthwale and I have not seen this feature in any creel further south than Mayo. However, in one of the Cork back creels **(Pl. 2.5)**, the butts of the mouthwale rods are caught between the first two rows of randing rather than between the mouthwale and the first row of randing, as would normally be the case; perhaps this was also done to prevent the butts of the mouthwale rods from irritating the carrier of the creel. The Cork back creels have just three sets of weavers, the second and third sets being started with an Irish knot before being randed to a finish. In contrast, the second set of the Tyrone back creel is put on in the opposite direction to the first, with each stroke going from right to left, with the right-hand thumb pinching the rod while the left–hand takes the rod in one space to the left and out the next space.

The knot for starting the second set of rods is thus put on moving clockwise around the creel rather than moving anti-clockwise around the creel as when putting in the ordinary knot. However, the principle of weaving the knot is still the same as that shown in **Figs 2.9 and 2.10**. The randing out of this second set of rods is done by finding each new randing rod to the right, thus moving anti–clockwise around the creel.

The third set of rods is put on with a knot in the normal manner and then French randed, and the fourth set is again put on in the opposite direction as described for the second set. A top knot is put on, and the finished height of the back creel before the base is put on should be about 17" (45cm).

The uprights on the long side are knocked by being interwoven with the corresponding uprights on the opposite side, as described for the Sligo/Donegal creel. The two middle uprights on both long sides are doubled before being crossed over each other, so four extra rods of corresponding strength are needed for this. The base is woven as described for the Sligo/Donegal creel, but the first few weaving rods on either side go over two and behind one in the manner of a three-rod wale, thus giving the creel base a raised surface on the edge to protect the weaving on the base from wear. Back creels from Cork in the National Museum collection also have this feature.

Kerry creel

This creel is based on the creels in **Pl. 2.16**, so the measurements are approximate. The creel is double staked and has sixteen uprights so 32 stakes are required. These should be 8–9ft (2.4–2.7m) and about ⅜" (15mm) in diameter.

The creel is roughly circular in plan with an internal diameter of 21" (535mm). Although there is no long side and short side as in the other creels, care should be taken to ensure that the uprights are placed opposite the corresponding uprights on the other side. This is particularly important in the case of the uprights that will form the warp over which the other uprights will be woven.

The first set of sixteen weavers is started with a mouthwale, as described for a standard creel. Although the creels in **Pl. 2.16** do not seem to have a mouthwale, the general standard of technique in these creels is not very good, so it would be unwise to conclude that the Kerry creel should not get a mouthwale like all other creels. There do not seem to be many examples of fixed-bottomed donkey creels from Kerry in the National Museum collection or in the Ulster Folk and Transport Museum collection. However, Kerry creels in two photos from the Lawrence Collection (Royal 4606 and Royal 4633) seem to be fitted with a mouthwale. Nonetheless, there is a slight question as to whether the mouthwale was used in west Kerry, though it was definitely used in Cork and in Waterford; there are creels with mouthwales from both of these counties in the National Museum collection. The question arises because the hinged-bottomed creels from the Dingle Peninsula, known as *úimeacha* (described later in this chapter), do not have a mouthwale but rather are started with the same weave as the top knot described in **Figs 2.13 and 2.14**. This is the start that also seems to have been used in the Glanmore creels in **Pl. 2.16**. However, I opted for the mouthwale as it is used in all other examples of creels and is far more secure than the top knot.

A second set of sixteen weavers is introduced and then a top knot **(Figs 2.13 and 2.16)** is put on. The window is formed by pointing sixteen weavers, which should be almost as strong as the uprights, and these are stuck in, one to the right of each upright, as shown in **Fig. 2.12**. However, the round to the right, going anti-clockwise around the creel, that follows this stroke in the standard creel to create a knot, is omitted from the Kerry creel. Instead, after one row of 'vertical' French randing, the rods are simply French randed in the normal manner. For this reason, the set of randing rods used for the window must be quite strong so that they will be less inclined to slip down the window. The window opening is about 4" (110mm), and, because the finished height of the creel before the top knot is about 18" (46cm), a fourth set of rods will probably be needed to bring it to the desired height. I used 'cut-off' tops from another creel that were chunky without being long, and simply randed them in without an introductory knot, as I only needed about 2" (50mm) to bring the creel to the desired height. If more height is needed from the fourth set, then they should probably be introduced with a knot in the normal manner.

Put on a top knot **(Figs 2.13 and 2.16)** using eight 7fts (2.1m). Next kink the uprights and cram them down into the weaving beside the upright on the corresponding side. The warp will thus be formed by four sets of four, the ends of which have been crammed down. Because the base is circular, the two curved ends must first be pack randed to bring the weaving to the point where the first upright can be used as a weft rod. This is described in more detail in the technique section dealing with lobster pots in Chapter 5. The uprights that form the weft are woven over two, under two, as described for a standard creel, and the filling is done under, over, under, over, and out under the knot, also as described for the standard creel.

Rectangular *pardóg* (hinged–bottomed creel)

The hinged-bottomed creel was known as a *pardóg* in most areas but, as explained at the beginning of this chapter, it was also known as a *lód* in parts of north Galway and south Mayo. The initial measurement for the *pardóg* rectangle is 24" x 18" (61cm x 46cm). The number of uprights is the same as for the 5 x 4 creel, i.e., five double sets between the corner posts on the long side and four sets on the shorter side, a total of 48. This size is suitable for turf and is similar to the one in **Pl. 2.3**. I got the dimensions and border details from a *pardóg* of this type in the collection of the Ulster Folk and Transport Museum that was made by Mr Sammin from Killadoon, near Louisburgh, Co. Mayo. Not all *pardógs* were bordered; another Mayo *pardóg* in the National Museum collection has the stakes cut off so that it looks like a creel, and the *lód* was never bordered. Dimensions for the *pardóg* with cut-off stakes could be up to 24" x 18" (61cm x 46cm). However, they were often smaller. The *lód* of this area of Joyce Country was about 22" x 16" (56cm x 42cm) and had very little inward flow. As a general principle the hinged–bottomed creels that were not bordered had eighteen sets of stakes like the standard creel, giving a count of 40 in all.

Set the stakes into the ground. For a smaller size allow the stakes to be almost straight up, but for the larger sizes tie the stakes and allow them to flow inwards like the standard creel. This flow will give a wider bottom than top, allowing the load to fall out more easily. Put on the mouthwale and, after the initial row of randing, go to the right (anti-clockwise) around the creel to form a knot. Continue alternating the direction of going round the *pardóg*, randing and then going to the right, as described for the standard creel. The weaving throughout is the same as for the standard creel, the window being formed as described in **Fig. 2.11**, but the gap is somewhat smaller than in the creel; a window of 1–2" (4–5cm) is adequate. Because of this it may take five or even six sets of weavers to bring the *pardóg* to the desired height of about 17" (43cm).

For the *lód* and the unbordered *pardóg*, a top knot (as described in **Figs 2.13 and 2.16)** is put on and the stakes are cut off about 3" (75mm) above the weaving. For the bordered *pardóg* the top knot may be omitted and the stakes kinked down to form a type of trac border. Kink the stakes about 3" (75mm) above the weaving and take each group of stakes in front of two, behind one and out the next space. Drop one of the upright pair at this point and take the other rod into the inside where it is cut resting on the next upright. I prefer to drop the upper of the two rods because the lower one can step over it, thereby locking it in place, when it is being brought to the inside.

The basket is next pulled out of the ground and the rods at the base are trimmed about 1" (4cm) below the mouthwale. Measure the width of the base and make a flat base a little smaller than the opening. For instance, the space between the uprights in the example in **Pl. 2.23** is 17" (445mm), so I set the two stout outer stakes for the base at 16" (425mm) to give a finished base of 16½" (431mm). You could allow a little more tolerance if desired. The outer posts for the base should be stout, about ¾" (20mm) in diameter. I used four double stakes between the outer stakes. Single stakes can be used but it is harder to make the base flat with them. If you have a screw block, use this to make the base. Traditionally it was made in the ground. If making a smaller *pardóg*, three sets of base sticks between the outer base sticks should be enough. The base is woven in the normal manner, i.e., randed with pairing on either end. Instead of a border, a stout willow is kinked at two points and crammed in between the base sticks in the manner of a staple.

Hinges are provided by making twisted single-rod handles, looping one end of the 'handle' under the outer base stick in the same way that a handle would go under the border. Find a forked stick (the *gabhlóg*) and secure the forked end to one of the short sides of the *pardógs* by means of two twisted rods. If the forked stick you chose has further branches up the fork, leave a little of these sticking out as they will prevent the rod tie from running off on this end (see detail, **Pl. 2.23**). Now make a twisted rod noose on the opposite short side to accommodate the other end of the *gabhlóg* or forked stick. Some looseness is required so that the stick can still be released even when the *pardóg* is laden. Usually, the noose is as shown in the detail of the Tuam *pardóg* (**Pl. 2.24**), but this is inclined to turn sideways, so a noose of the type shown in Kerry oval creels (*úimeacha*) (**Pl. 2.25**) is more effective. A handle is fitted on top as described for the creel.

Tuam D-shaped pardóg

This D-shaped *pardóg* (**Pl. 2.12**) is based on the one in the National Museum collection from Tuam in County Galway already described. It is made from hazel. You need sixteen sets of uprights, all doubled except for the two corner posts, each of which is a group of three rods as in the standard creel. This gives a total count of 34 uprights, 30 of which should be ⅝" (15mm) in diameter with the four rods that support the corner posts being a little thinner.

Four sets of sixteen weaving rods are needed. Two of these, the mouthwale and window sets, should be almost as thick as the uprights. The other two sets can be lighter, about ⅜" (10mm) in diameter. There are two top knots in this creel, one before the window and one before the border, so a total of sixteen rods about ⅜" (10mm) will be needed for these.

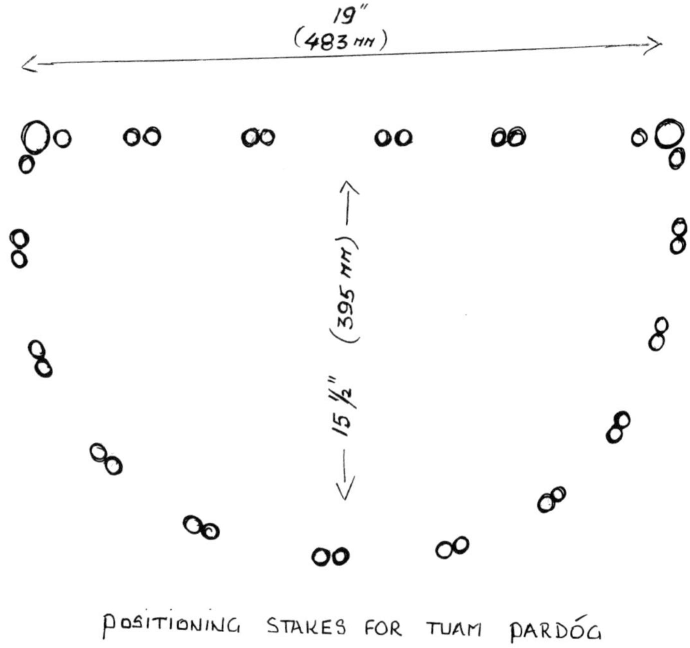

Set the corner posts so that the external measurement is 19" (493mm) along the length and then set four double uprights between them. Mark a point about 15" (395mm) from this line and, forming a slight curve, set four groups of uprights opposite the ones you have put in already. The distribution of the uprights is shown in **Fig. 2.20** and you will gather from it that three more sets of uprights go on each side. Set the uprights straight, as this *pardóg* does not slope in.

Begin the mouthwale along the front curve, as it will be easier to finish there. Remember to twist the hazel weavers each time you go round the corner posts. The rods are randed after the mouthwale. The second set of rods is quite light and brings the height to about 6" (165mm). Put on a top knot. Insert the slyped window rods (a slype is a long angular cut) to the right of the uprights, doing one stroke of randing with them as shown in **Fig. 2.12**. Follow this by a round of weaving to the right (anti-clockwise) to form a knot and then rand these rods to a finish. The last set, which, of course, is introduced with a knot, is quite light. You want a finished height of about 15–16" (395–405mm) including the top knot so that the last set can either be randed or, if this will make the *pardóg* too tall, it can be knotted as described for the standard creel. Finish with eight rods to give a top knot similar to that which preceded the window.

Bordering with hazel is difficult because the fibres of the rods must be twisted at the point where they are to be knocked. Unless

POSITIONING STAKES FOR TUAM PARDÓG

Fig. 2.20

your hands are very strong, this is physically demanding. You could as an alternative twist the entire length of each rod as for a handle, but I would suggest instead twisting the hazel rods at the point where they are to be kinked, using a pliers or even a vice grip. The twist should be in a clockwise direction and each rod should first be twisted before starting the border. Details of the border are shown in **Fig. 2.21**. The first stroke is a simple behind one and out trac border. When this has been done all around, take the lower of the two rods in each space and, going over the border rods in the same space, go behind the next upright and out.

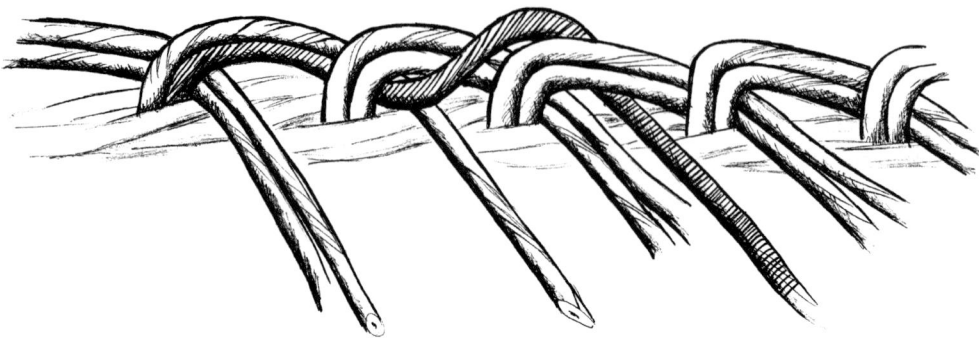

Fig. 2.21

Now shape a thick hazel or willow rod to form the hoop. If willow is being chosen it may be possible to turn the ends of the rods in when cramming the finish of the base. Care must be taken when weaving the base not to allow the weaving to pull this semi-circle inwards. Take three hazel rods about ¾" (20mm) in thickness. Place the first rod so that about 2ft (61cm) of the butt end of the rod is extending past the hoop. Beat the rod at this point with a mallet or a rubber hammer and then you may manage to weave it a bit. The other two rods in the Tuam *pardóg* were simply lashed on, but I found it more suitable to cut a little tongue on each rod in the manner of a French scallom. Rand with willow until the desired height is almost reached. Because of the wide space between stakes, the randing rods should be fairly thick, about 7fts (2.1m), hence the need to be careful that it does not narrow the hoop. To finish, beat the hazel rods and then cram them in alongside the next stake (see detail Pl. 2.24), in a manner similar to that described for the rectangular *pardóg*. If the hazel stakes break, then cram in a willow staple in exactly the way the rectangular *pardóg* base is finished. The base is hinged from the front and **Pl. 2.24** shows details of the closing stick and ties.

Úimeacha or oval slip-bottomed panniers (Dingle Peninsula and Blasket Islands)

Mark an oval in the ground about 18" x 14" (46cm x 37cm). You will need fifteen sets of double uprights about 8ft (2.4m) for each *úim* or pannier. Allow the uprights to slope gently outwards. You are starting at the mouth of the pannier and the base needs to be wider, about 22" x 19" (56cm x 48cm), at a height of 17" (43cm). This pannier is not started with a mouthwale but with a knot, with which the second and subsequent sets of weavers are introduced **(Figs 2.9 and 2.10)**. This is not as strong as the mouthwale and, because I thought one of the panniers in **Pl. 2.17** had two sets of knots, I put on a top knot before the ordinary knot. It makes the top more secure but it is probably not traditional, since the panniers in the National Museum collection rely only on the simple knot to hold the weave. The rods are randed out and each new set is introduced with a knot. The Blasket Islands panniers in **Pl. 2.17** have a window, so if making these put on a top knot after the second set of weavers has been worked out. The window is the variation used in **Fig. 2.12** and the pannier on the right in **Pl. 2.17** has a knot above the window, so for this weave one round to the right as described for the standard creel. The fourth set is introduced with a knot and randed so that the finished height before the top knot is about 16" (41cm). The panniers in **Pl. 2.25**, based on a pair from Dún Chaoin in the Dingle peninsula, are closed so about five sets of rods would be needed to bring these to this height.

The right-hand rod of each pair of uprights is now used to make the border. The first movement is to take each right-hand rod in turn, in front of one and behind one and leave it inside. Once this initial trac has been done, you take each rod in turn to the front and then going under the trac already made, take the rod behind the next upright, i.e., if the rod is lying behind upright A bring it out to the front and under the trac border in the space between A and B and let it rest behind B. This is identical to the first stages of the Aran rope border except that the rods are twisted in the Aran border. The drawings in **Figs 2.22 and 2.23** of the Aran rope border can be used if clarification is needed. If you want to make this border more secure you could take each rod again and follow the sequence in **Fig. 2.25**, Step 3 of the Aran rope border.

Next make an oval hoop that will fit comfortably inside the base of the pannier (the end you have just bordered). If possible, allow the hoop to harden for several days if made from brown willow or hazel, and for several weeks if made from green or semi-green willow. If you cannot allow it to season in this way, take care when weaving that the hoop is not pulled out of shape. As can be seen from **Pl. 2.25**, the pannier base is made like a flat frame basket, i.e., a rough version of the *sciathóg* described in Chapter 3. The base has five ribs, which can either be whole rods or split rods. If split, the rods should be thick ¾"–1" (20–25mm). The central rib is lashed to the frame and the other ribs added as soon as possible. Remember to double around the hoop each time so that the weaving will be level by the time you reach the middle. The base is attached to the pannier by means of a handle-type tie, as described for the rectangular *pardóg*. This ensures that the base will fall easily when the stick closure is released.

The stick used for closing is not forked and should be about 1" (25mm) in thickness. Secure it to the basket by means of a twisted rod, bringing the twisted rod tightly around the stick at least twice so that it will be less inclined to slip off. The rod should be fairly well seasoned for this. Make a noose as seen in **Pl. 2.25** for the other side, allowing sufficient play so that the stick can be pulled out of the noose fairly easily.

Once both panniers have been made they are tied together. First cut two pieces of wood about 1" (25mm) in diameter and about 12–13" (30–33cm) long. Secure each piece in turn to the side of the pannier opposite that which has been used for the hinges and about 3–4" (75–100mm) from the top of the basket. To do this, turn the pannier so that the base is uppermost and force a 7ft rod in beside a stake and down into the weaving. Twist it along its length and bring it around the piece of wood and back into the pannier, around a stake and back out again about twice around the loop you have already made around the stick. In essence, you are making a little handle around the stick. The remainder of the rod is used to repeat the process at the other side of the stick. If preferred you could use two lighter rods to make the two handle-like ties instead of the 7ft (2.1m) rod mentioned here. Next insert two other 7ft (2.1m) rods down through the border beside the two stakes already used when securing the sticks. Twist each rod in turn and bring it down to the stick, circle around the stick twice and bring the remainder of the rod around itself and thread it in about halfway down the basket. Bring it around a stake and then down again, twisting around the rod to give a handle-like effect, before threading the end away near the top of the basket. This detail can be seen fairly clearly in the right-hand pannier in **Pl. 2.25**.

When both sticks have been secured to the panniers in this way, two cross ties are provided using a 7–8ft (2.1–2.4m) rod for each. Secure each rod either by inserting alongside a stake or else by jamming it in behind the wooden hanger and through the basket. Twist the rod as for a handle and bring it around the wooden hanger on the other pannier, allowing a distance of about 8" (20cm) between the pieces of wood. Bring the rod back around itself so that the tie begins to look like a handle. If the ends of the rods already used for tying the pieces of wood on to the panniers are long enough they can be incorporated into the tie, otherwise an additional 6ft (1.8m) rod can be twisted and used to fill up the thickness of the tie.

Aran seaweed creel

The Aran seaweed creel shown in **Pls 2.9, 2.10 and 2.26** was made by Micheálín Ó hIarnáin from Bungowla, Innismór, the largest of the Aran Islands. It measures 18" x 14" (46cm x 37cm) at the base but since this includes the mouthwale the dimensions for the rectangle (see **Fig. 2.5**, standard creel) would be 17" x 13½" (430mm x 343mm). The number of uprights is the same as for the standard creel, eighteen uprights needing forty rods in total. These should be between ⅜" and ½" (10–12mm approximately) in diameter. Four sets of weaving rods are needed, these should be about ⅜" (10mm) in diameter, so a total of seventy-two weaving rods will be needed. You will also need eight rods about ⅜" (10mm) in diameter to put on a top knot before the window is formed.

Put on a mouthwale as described for the standard creel and then rand out the first set. Introduce the second set with a knot and then rand to a finish. Put on a top knot. A close study of **Pl. 2.26** reveals that this window is different to those we have already encountered. This window is formed by sticking in each weaving rod to the right of an upright and then kinking each about 2½" (60mm) above the top knot and weaving each in turn in front, behind and out in the manner of a trac border so that you go to the right to find the next weaver. You will have to thread the last rods in as you would for completing a trac border. When this has been completed, rand the rods to a finish as normal. **Pl. 2.27** shows an Aran Islander called

Patch Rua with what seems to be two seaweed creels. The creel behind him is almost certainly a seaweed creel because it has a rope border. The windows in these do not have the definite kink seen in the creel in **Pl. 2.26** (except perhaps at the corners) but the method of doing the window is similar in that each rod is taken in front of the next upright, *inside* the next weaver before going behind and out. Thus, while it is superficially similar to the window in **Fig. 2.12**, the rods in the Aran window are in fact introduced going to the right, i.e., anti-clockwise around the basket, before being followed by a row of randing to complete the knot.

The last set of rods is knotted by alternating the direction of the weave as described for the siding of the standard creel. This takes the place of a top knot. The creel is about 17" (43cm) high before the border. Twist the right-hand rod of each group of uprights and reduce its length to 24" (61cm) to enable you to do the Aran rope border more easily (**Fig. 2.22**).

Fig. 2.22

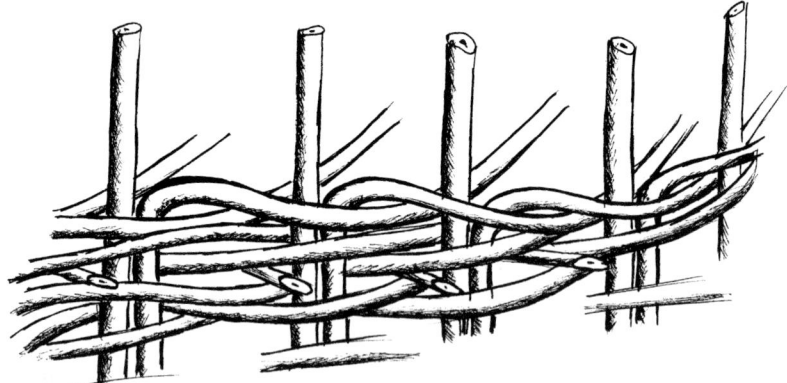

Take the twisted right-hand rod of each group and go in front of one and behind one with it, allowing it to rest on the inside. Since these rods can interfere with the work if left on the inside, you may wish to take the rods out to the outside once the first three rods have been worked. This taking to the outside is the initial movement of **Fig. 2.23**.

Fig. 2.23

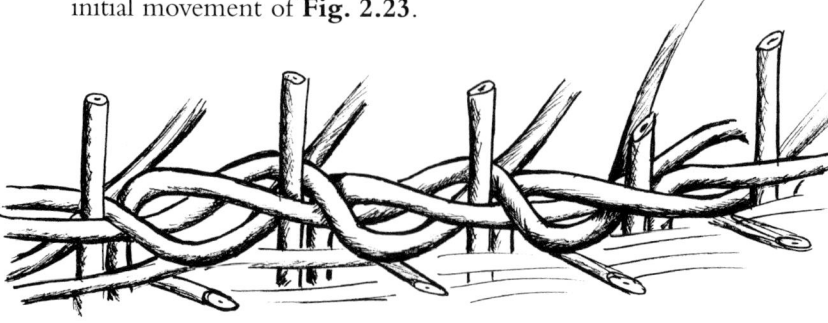

Take the rods to the outside (if you have not already done so) and put them under the border to lie behind the next upright. When three or four of these have been worked you may want to take the rods out to the front again, thereby anticipating the first move in **Fig. 2.24**.

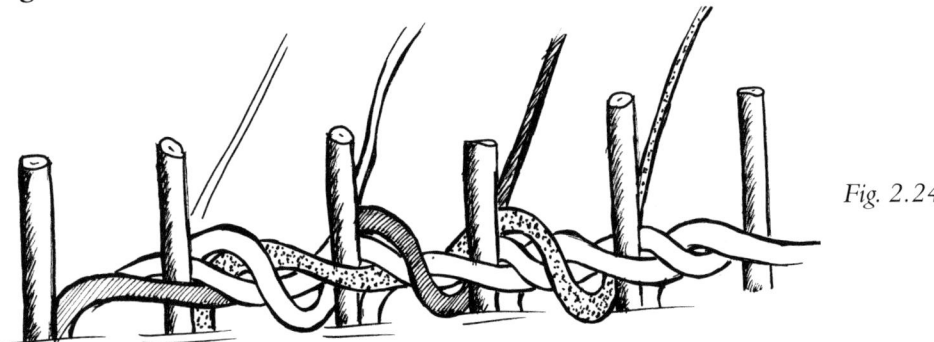

Fig. 2.24

Take each rod to the front (if you have not already done so), pull it tightly and put it under the border to rest behind the next stake **(Fig. 2.25)**.

Take each rod from behind, out the next space bringing it out under all of the border (see **Fig. 2.25**). In some versions (e.g., the Aran cradle) the rod is also taken out under one rod of the weaving on the side of the basket.

In practice, some of these strokes can be taken together but they are shown separately here to enable easier understanding.

The seaweed creel is levered out of the ground and the uprights are cut about 1" (25mm) below the mouthwale. A twisted rod is extended from the middle rod on the short side, over to the middle

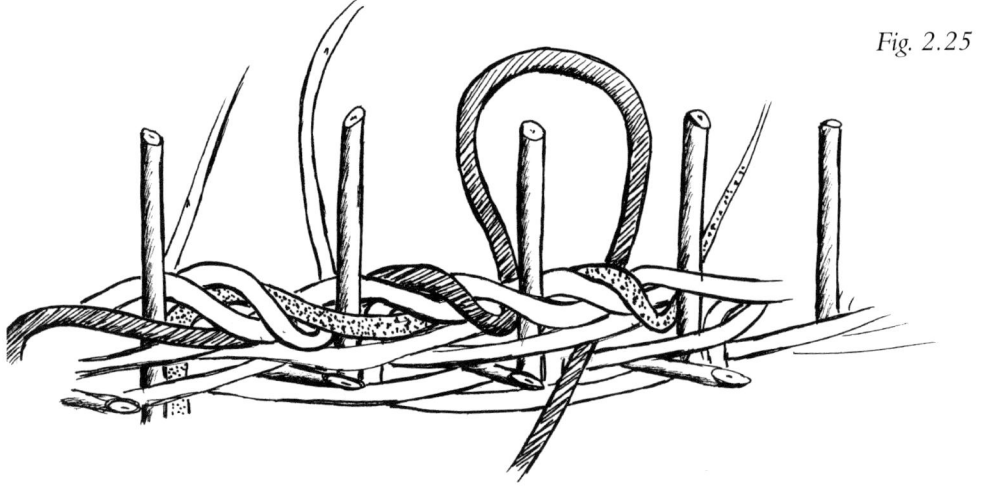

Fig. 2.25

rod on the opposite side, through to the outside of the basket and back, going over and under the rod already extended in the manner of a handle. A further two rods are taken from the long sides in a similar manner, to give six partitioned spaces in all.

The handle is long, about 8" (20cm) out from the basket, to enable the creel to be carried on the shoulder. It is formed by two twisted rods crossing each other before the remainder of the rods are brought back to the side they started from.

Crúbóg

The *crúbóg* (pronounced crewbogue) seems to have been used throughout Ulster, and there are a few examples in the collection at the Ulster Folk and Transport museum, though it is not represented, I think, in the National Museum collection. The measurements in this example are based on a *crúbóg* made by Columbe Campbell of Glenties, Co. Donegal, for the Ulster Folk and Transport Museum. This has a total of 26 uprights ranging in thickness from ⅜"–½" (9–12mm). In this *crúbóg* the uprights are hazel with two sets of 26 willow weaving rods a little thinner than the uprights, but usually the uprights are also of willow.

Set the four corner posts so that the measurement on the long side is 21½" (545mm) and is 19" (480mm) on the short side. Put six uprights between the corner posts on the long side and five between them on the shorter side. Put on a mouthwale with the first set of weavers, allowing 5–6" (125–150mm) to protrude so that a turned-in mouthwale can be put on after the first stroke of randing, as explained for the 5 x 4 creel. The second set is put on with a knot and randed to a finish, which should give a height of about 8" (20cm). No top knot is put on the *crúbóg*. Instead the rods on the long side are kinked and crammed down into the weaving on the opposite side. A total of eight rods on either side are knocked in this way, which means the corner posts are included in these warp rods.

Rods are inserted down beside the stakes and the base is woven going over, under, each warp rod in turn. The stakes are incorporated into the weaving; when you come to them they will need to be twisted in order to enable them to be woven in and out. The base is filled from the ends, leaving the middle until last, in the manner of a creel. The *crúbóg* is fitted with two handles, one on each of the shorter sides. I expected these to be twisted rod handles but instead a very stout rod ¾–1" (18–25mm) is inserted to form a handle core. The span of the handle is three spaces. In the *crúbóg* already mentioned this was secured by a rod inserted beside the core on either side, twisted and then brought around to the other side and back like a partially covered shopping-basket handle. This type of handle was fitted as far as I can recall on all of the *crúbógs* in the Ulster Folk and Transport Museum.

The crandy

Although not strictly a creel, the crandy seems to belong in this chapter since it is made like a creel, but the uprights are stuck about 8" (20cm) into the ground so that they can be used later to form a border. It follows that a soft site with yielding soil is necessary for making the crandy. It seems that the crandy could be round as well as rectangular but this description concentrates on the rectangular crandy.

Mark out a rectangle 20½" x 15½" (52cm x 39cm) as described for the creel. Insert eighteen stout 8ft (2.4m) uprights with four uprights between the corner posts on the long side and three between the corner posts on the short side. A mouthwale **(Figs 2.3 to 2.6)** is put on using eighteen 7 ft (2.1m) weavers, allowing about 6" (150mm) to stick out so that they can be turned in after the first row of randing, as described for the 5 x 4 creel. A further two sets of weavers a little thinner than the first set should be sufficient to bring the crandy to a height of 11" (28cm). These were usually introduced with a knot going to the right as described for the various creels. The top knot was usually omitted on the crandys that I have seen and the base is formed by knocking all of the rods on the long side, including the corner posts, and cramming them in beside the posts on the opposite side. The remaining rods are woven over, under, over, under, over and under, with fillers being used to fill the gaps as described for the creel.

The border is similar to the twisted trac border described in **Fig. 2.21**, but the initial behind one stroke goes *under* the mouthwale. When taken to the front it is brought up over the border and out under the next space as in **Fig. 2.21**. In the photo of Ciaran D'Arcy bordering a crandy **(Pl. 2.19)**, this border seems to be going on in the opposite direction, but the negative may be reversed.

Kish

This kish is similar to the kish in **Pl. 2.20**, but the starting measurements are based on a half kish in the National Museum collection. That kish was made mainly of willow, but Estyn Evans suggests that the kishes of Ulster were made of hazel. I used willow uprights and hazel weavers. The uprights should be at least 1¼" (30mm) in diameter and 24 are required. Stout two- to three-year-old rods will be needed if using willow for the uprights. The 24 weaving rods for the mouthwale should be about ¾" (20mm) in diameter but the 40 rods for randing should be thicker than this, about 1" (25mm) at least. Since it is unlikely that all of your randing rods will be of equal thickness, sort them somewhat so that the thicker material is used higher up in the kish.

Stick the uprights into the ground, sloping slightly outwards, at evenly spaced intervals to give a somewhat rounded square. There are six uprights on each side, so there are no corner posts, but the uprights nearest the corner should be about 30" (76cm) from the corresponding upright on the opposite side, while the measurement at the widest point, from the uprights in the middle to the corresponding uprights on the opposite side, should be 34½" (87cm). Put on the mouthwale as described for the standard creel and then simply rand that set of rods to a finish. Take one of the thinner rods from the randing pile and ensure that it is one of the shortest of the rods. Stick it under at least one line of the weaving so that the butt rests behind an upright and start randing with it. The randing is English randing, which is better known as coil randing in Ireland. When this rod has been used, put the butt of the next weaver behind the next upright to the right and under the rod you have just woven, and weave this rod one space beyond the previous one. Once the first few rods have been woven, you can use thicker hazel. The kish in **Pl. 2.20** is beaten down only while the mouthwale set of weavers is being put on. Thereafter, it relies for its strength on the fact that the weavers are thick and are started by being locked under the previous rod. Hazel rods grip excellently in this way. Two complete rounds of randing should bring the kish to about 22" (56cm), which I would guess is the approximate height of the one in **Pl. 2.20**.

The base is made by knocking the six uprights on each of what will now become the two ends and crossing them under each other as described for the Sligo/Donegal creel. The uprights were taken

Fig. 2.26
(Evans 1957)

over, under, over, under, over, under in the half kish I saw at the
National Museum, but these were of willow and much thinner than
the stakes in **Pl. 2.20**. Despite their being thinner, many of the
original stakes had been broken. It is unlikely that hazel uprights
would be pliable enough to weave in and out in this way, at least
towards the middle of the base, and the option of going over three
and under three in much the same way as the standard creel base
could be taken. Fillers should be of willow, and even with willow
the filling rods will not be easy to pull through due to the greater
tension caused by six warp rods as opposed to four in the standard
creel. The kish base I saw at the National Museum had many
patches where rods weren't pliable enough to go in and out in this
way. The kish is taken out of the ground by putting an iron bar
under each corner in turn and levering upwards. The uprights are
cut with a saw about 3" (70mm) clear of the mouthwale.

The slide car on which the kish was carried is shown in **Fig.
2.26**. The length of the shafts would be about 9' 6" (2.9m) with the
platform beginning about 20" (50cm) from the rear. This
measurement includes the 'shoes' or 'heels' at the back of the car.
The platform could measure from 30–36" (76–91cm) in length. The
width of the slide car at the back was about 36" (91cm) and about
26" (66cm) at the front of the shafts.

3
Potato Baskets

WHEN I look out the window of my workshop, I can see potato ridges on the hillside across the lake. That people found it necessary to make potato beds on steep ground 500 feet above sea-level on a north-facing slope gives an idea of the degree to which the peasant population in pre-Famine Ireland depended on the potato. In many cases potatoes were the only food they had, and this explains why some potato baskets that were made for domestic use now seem so large. The amount of potatoes consumed by each person was much larger than what might now be considered the norm. Even when conditions improved for the rural population towards the latter part of the nineteenth century, the amount of potatoes boiled for a meal included some for the poultry and for the one or two pigs that many small farming households raised.

The skib or *ciseog*

The most common potato basket in use in Ireland was probably the skib or *ciseog*. Although in the last fifty years this type of basket was found mainly along the counties of the western seaboard, there is no doubt that it was once much more widely distributed, with examples from all parts of Ireland being known. The skib was a low, flat, circular basket varying from 18" (46cm) to 30" (76cm) in diameter. The main use of the basket was for straining and then serving potatoes — when the potatoes that had been boiling on the open fire were cooked, the pot containing the boiling water and potatoes was spilled out into the skib. The basket was then brought indoors and where a low table existed it could be placed on this or otherwise on the cooking pot. The family could then sit on low stools or 'creepies' and help themselves to the potatoes. In the nineteenth century at least, it is unlikely that there were enough

Pl. 3.1—An Aran Islander bordering a skib. Photo courtesy of NMI.

stools for everyone in the household so younger members probably sat or knelt on the floor. This absence of tables and furniture meant that frequently the skib was effectively the table, and this also explains why they were so large.[1] Although examples of the flat circular skibs have been found in various parts of Ireland, the pattern of the base shows some variation. Most commonly, the base sticks were spread apart from each other to give a grid-like base **(Pl. 3.1)**. Where this technique was adopted, there were further variations according to the practice in the area, but three base sticks intersecting three base sticks seems to have been the most common pattern. The photograph taken on the Aran Islands by Thomas Mason **(Pl. 3.1)** shows a basketmaker making a skib in this pattern. Examples of skibs from the collection at the National Museum of Ireland show similarly patterned skibs from locations in Counties Cork, Galway and Mayo. In some of the skibs I have seen from Galway and Mayo, the 3 x 3 grid is replaced by a 4 x 4 grid. In the case of the 3 x 3 grid, the basketmaker usually had to add eight extra base sticks, called bi-stakes, about half the length of the original base sticks, but with the 4 x 4 grid, four such bi-stakes would suffice.

Some of these grid-based skibs had an 'inner basket' within the skib. This can be seen in **Pl. 3.2**, which shows examples of different patterns of skibs. This inner basket could have held a jug of buttermilk or whatever fish or meat might be available. It was probably an adaptation of the skib once times improved and a more varied diet than mere potatoes was to be had. Probably the chief advantage of the grid base was that it allowed the basketmaker to start immediately with the pairing weave that makes up the base rather than having to bind the base sticks together as is more usually done. It should also be noted that in the grid base with bi-stakes, the base sticks do not have to be very flexible and it allowed the basketmaker to use poor quality material such as 'Black Sally' (*Salix caprea*), which would be difficult to use in a conventional closed base. I have also heard of basketmakers using rods of hazel, ash, mountain ash and even holly where they did not have enough willow.

In areas with a strong tradition in professional basketmaking, the makers seem to have abandoned the grid base in favour of a closed base. Thus in Letterfrack in Connemara, Co. Galway, where a basketmaking industry had been set up in the late eighteenth century and professional basketmakers had been brought in from France to train the local people,[2] the skibs are of a closed base type. Similarly, in *Irish folk ways* Estyn Evans has an illustration of a skib from County Antrim[3] which shows a closed base, and again I would assume that this is an indication that people had acquired professional basketmaking skills and abandoned the traditonal grid base. The fact that such closed–base skibs functioned effectively as potato strainers seems to disprove the theory that the holes in the base were to allow the water to pass through more quickly. Water will pass through a willow basket fairly quickly unless it is very tightly woven. Moreover, the grid base was the norm amongst country basketmakers, not just for making skibs but also for making circular turf baskets where the relatively open bottom might have been a disadvantage in that it would allow turf dust to leak out. It seems then that the grid base in its various patterns was a more ancient way of opening out a base than was the closed base more generally used by professional basketmakers.

Another interesting variant of a skib base is the type I call a 'Joyce country' base. This is an arbitrary label which refers to the fact that, to the best of my knowledge, the last place this base was made was in Joyce country or *Dúiche Sheoigeach*, an area that includes parts of north-west Galway and south-west Mayo and is so named because many of the people who live in the region have the surname Joyce. I was shown how to make this base by my

Pl. 3.2—Skibs, from left:
(i) 'Joyce country' style base formerly common in east Galway
(ii) Grid style base with added bi-stakes and bands of waling on the base
(iii) Skib with inner basket for holding a bowl of milk or any other accompaniment with the meal.

neighbour, Tommy Joyce, who also showed me how to make the donkey creel. Tommy, one of nature's gentlemen, was a basketmaker in the country tradition, i.e., he worked seasonally at baskets, mostly in late winter and early spring. It would seem that Tommy was the last person in the area at that time (1977) who could make this base. This base also has an openwork section in the middle **(see Pl. 3.2)** so that the centre of the base has four triangles of willow. There seem to be just two examples of this base in the collection at the National Museum and both are from the north-east of County Galway, but it is probable that the distribution of this base would once have been wider.

Even up to the late 1970s skibs were still in daily use in the remote parts of the west of Ireland. After being used they were hung up on a nail outside the front door to dry off. This has given rise to the use of the modern-day skib as a wall hanging which can be taken down and used when needed. Kenny's Bookshop in Galway City has developed this idea by hanging four skibs outside their shop to give a distinctive shopfront.

The skib was almost always made from unpeeled willow but there is no doubt that some were also made from peeled rods. I have been told that these peeled skibs were made in Galway and Mayo for a special occasion such as Christmas. However, Bill Egan, a country basketmaker from County Offaly who had a long conversation about basketmaking and related country matters with J. Delaney of the Folklore Commission in the 1960s, said that in his area such peeled skibs had been used for clothes rather than potatoes.[4] Interestingly, the manner in which the country

Pl. 3.3—Two sciathógs made by Alison Fitgerald; the one on the left has two central ribs, a style that was common throughout the country, the right-hand sciathóg has one central rib with additional ribs being added from the centre. This style was common in the midlands, though the basket made there was flat.

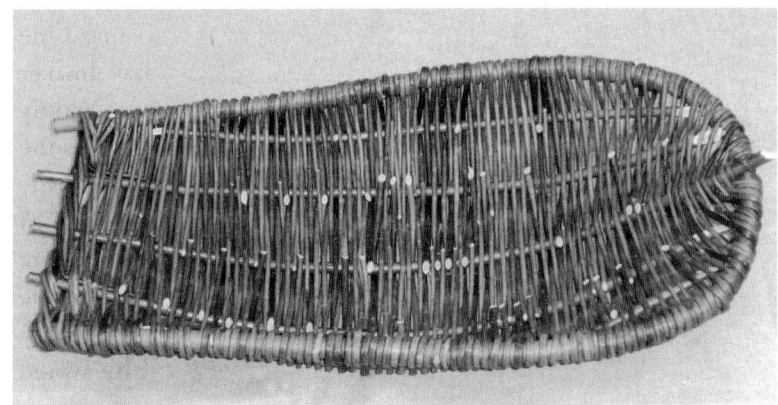

Pl. 3.4—Horseshoe-shaped sciathóg, *west Cork and south Kerry.*

basketmaker obtained his peeled rods was not by pulling them through a willow break in spring when the sap was rising, but rather by curling the freshly cut rods into a pot of water over the fire and taking them out after twenty minutes and rubbing the skins off them.

The *sciathóg*

The skib was not the only basket used for straining and serving potatoes and there are certain areas in Ireland where a frame basket known as the *sciathóg* (pronounced skeeogue) was more widely used **(see Pl. 3.3)**. The *sciathóg* was more widely used in parts of Munster and Ulster and the Midlands and seems to have been known in some form in all parts of Ireland. The *sciathóg* gets its name from the Irish word for a shield, *sciath*, which suggests that larger shallow versions of this basket may originally have been used as breastshields in combat. Thus, the *sciathóg* (literally, little shield) was probably simply adapted for use as a potato strainer. It is usually called a potato teemer in English but is also known as a skib. I have refrained from this usage to avoid confusion between the two types.

The *sciathóg* was constructed by first making a hoop, usually either of buckie briar (wild rose), willow or hazel and then attaching ribs to this hoop. The diameter of the hoop might be as little as 10–12 inches (25–30cm) or up to 18" (46cm), and the basket could be started either with one central rib or two. These ribs could be of split rods or of whole rods **(Pl. 3.3)**. Having secured the central rib or ribs, the basketmaker proceeded to add more ribs as required. The depth of the basket also influenced the number of ribs required — a deep basket of a given diameter needed more ribs than a shallow

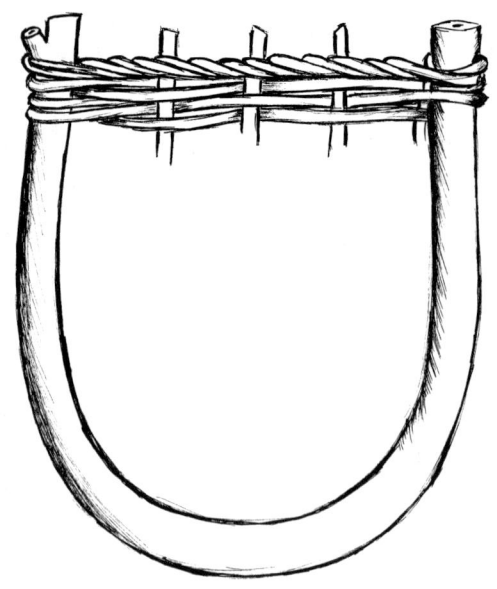

Fig. 3.1—
Horseshoe-shaped
sciathóg.

basket of the same diameter.

The hoop for the *sciathóg* was usually circular but in order to maintain this shape it was necessary to tie a twine or rod tightly from end to end in order to prevent the weaving from forcing the *sciathóg* into an oval shape. This tie could be released once the *sciathóg* had been made. In certain areas, especially in the Munster counties of Cork, Kerry and Waterford, the oval *sciathóg* was the norm, and often this shape was obtained by making a near-circular hoop but omitting the tie at the ends. As the weaving proceeded from either end, the pressure of the weavers forced the hoop into an oval shape.

One regional variation of the *sciathóg* was actually a horseshoe shape **(Pl. 3.4)**. This *sciathóg,* which was popular in parts of west Cork and south Kerry, had the ribs attached to a horseshoe-shaped 'hoop' of willow, and the ribs were first attached to the rounded end. The problem of how to attach the ribs to the open end of the horseshoe hoop was solved by securing them with a row of pairing. The pairing would have further rods added to it to give a bulky, knot-like weave on the open end. There are a few examples of these horseshoe-shaped *sciathóg*s in the National Museum collection, one of which has a lovely detail where a hoop has a forked twig or *gabhlóg* on it. This fork prevents the weaving at the open end from slipping off **(Fig. 3.1)**, and it is a nice example of an imperfection in a rod being used to advantage.

While the *sciathóg* was mainly used as a potato teemer and server, a large version, usually known as a *sciath*, was used for harvesting potatoes. Some versions of the horseshoe-shaped Kerry and Cork *sciathógs* were large enough to harvest potatoes, being up to 90cm long. This was known as a large *sciathóg*, or *sciathóg mór*, to distinguish it from the normal *sciathóg,* which would rarely have been longer than 60cm. Another horseshoe-shaped type was made in east Cork and west Waterford and was called a *sciath*. In this version **(Pl. 3.5)**, the hoop was closed at the straight end so the basket resembled a scuttle.

The *sciath* was usually oval in shape and while in its simplest form it had two grab handles formed by leaving a hole in the weaving in each of the long sides, twisted rod handles were more usual. There were various local names for the *sciath,* such as a scuttle in County Clare and a *birdeog* in County Kerry. Because of the size of the *sciath* it was usually necessary to use two rods to form the hoop, unless a two-year-old willow rod was used. The difference in thickness between the thick and the thin end of a one-year-old rod would have been too great to allow for an effective join in such a large hoop. This problem did not arise when bucky briar (wild rose) was used to form the hoop, because it had the advantage of being almost the same thickness along its length. Bucky briar bends very easily when green and it becomes very hard when dry, so it is less likely to be pulled out of shape than a willow hoop. Hazel was another popular material for making the hoops. I have even heard of cases where the rim of an old bicycle wheel was used as the hoop for a *sciath*. This serves as a reminder that practicality and durability were probably uppermost in most makers' minds and some of them were willing to sacrifice the aesthetic qualities of the basket for the ease of use and strength of a steel bicycle rim.

Pl. 3.5—Scuttle-shaped sciath *from west Waterford made by Tom Quinlan. Photo taken at 'Basketmakers', an exhibition at the Crafts Council of Ireland Gallery in 1994.*

The weaving material for the *sciathóg* and the *sciath* was almost invariably willow that was in a semi-green or partially seasoned state. Because the material for the *sciath* and *sciathóg* has to be fairly pliable, especially when finishing the basket, good quality osiers were used for these baskets whenever possible.

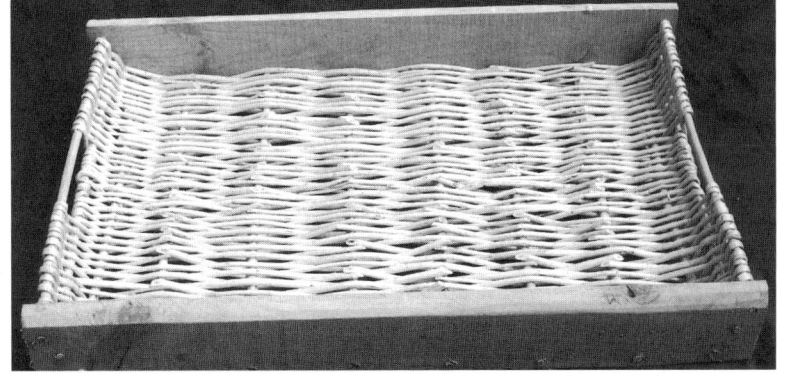

Pl. 3.6—Losset, a Fermanagh-style potato basket.

A basket that developed from the *sciathóg* was the losset (**Pl. 3.6**), from the Irish word *losaid*, meaning a kneading trough or a collapsible table for food. The losset was a white willow basket used in the County Fermanagh area for the same purpose as the *sciathóg*. It had thin wooden boards at either end and these were bored with 8mm holes through which slightly stouter willow sticks were stuck to form the structure, or rib-cage, through which thinner white willow rods were woven. The weaving is simple randing and the losset would have been woven from either end in the manner of a *sciathóg*.

There are examples of the losset in both the National Museum and Ulster Folk and Transport Museum collections, both made by Owen Prunty from County Fermanagh, and it seems clear that the losset was only developed in the twentieth century as a more elaborate potato basket than the *sciathóg*.[5]

Ulster potato harvesting basket

The Ulster potato harvesting basket, while having the same function as the *sciath*, was different in that the ribs were placed across the shorter axis of the frame. Moreover, the central ribs were often made from strips of wood, which gave the baskets a distinctive appearance (**Pl. 3.7**). Each basket measured 22" x 19" (56cm x 48cm) and was about 9" (23cm) deep. This measurement gave the basket a capacity

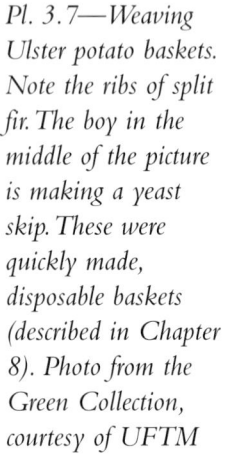

Pl. 3.7—Weaving Ulster potato baskets. Note the ribs of split fir. The boy in the middle of the picture is making a yeast skip. These were quickly made, disposable baskets (described in Chapter 8). Photo from the Green Collection, courtesy of UFTM

Pl. 3.8—A large stack of Ulster potato baskets. Photo from the Bigger Collection, courtesy of the Ulster Museum.

of four stone (25kg approx.), and the fact that the basket could be used as a measure probably contributed to its widespread use.

These baskets were made throughout east Ulster and north Leinster, but especially along the south-eastern shore of Lough Neagh. They were made in large numbers **(Pl. 3.8)** at a number of workshops there, including that of Big Jim Mulholland at Aghagallon on the shores of Lough Neagh in south-west Antrim, an area that had a strong tradition of willow growing and basketmaking. This is one of the few examples where a country basket that would originally have been made by farmers for their own use came to be made professionally in great quantities. They would have been distributed not only in Ulster but further south in Louth, Meath and north Dublin, where commercial potato growing was widespread.

Although Big James Mulholland's workshop possibly had the largest output of these baskets, with up to nine people making them there in the 1920s and 1930s, there were smaller workshops in south-west Antrim, such as those of Willie and James Mulholland at Gawleys Gate. The McAreaveys, Samuel Courtney and the Crossey family are all mentioned in Patrick Smyth's study of basketmaking in south-west County Antrim[6] as having made these potato baskets. More basketmakers worked making these and other baskets for a firm called Judge, based in Belfast.

It is probable that the rims of these Ulster potato baskets were originally made locally from hazel, bucky briar or stout willow. By the early 1920s, however, the hoops that formed the rims of these baskets were being imported from Holland, where they were made

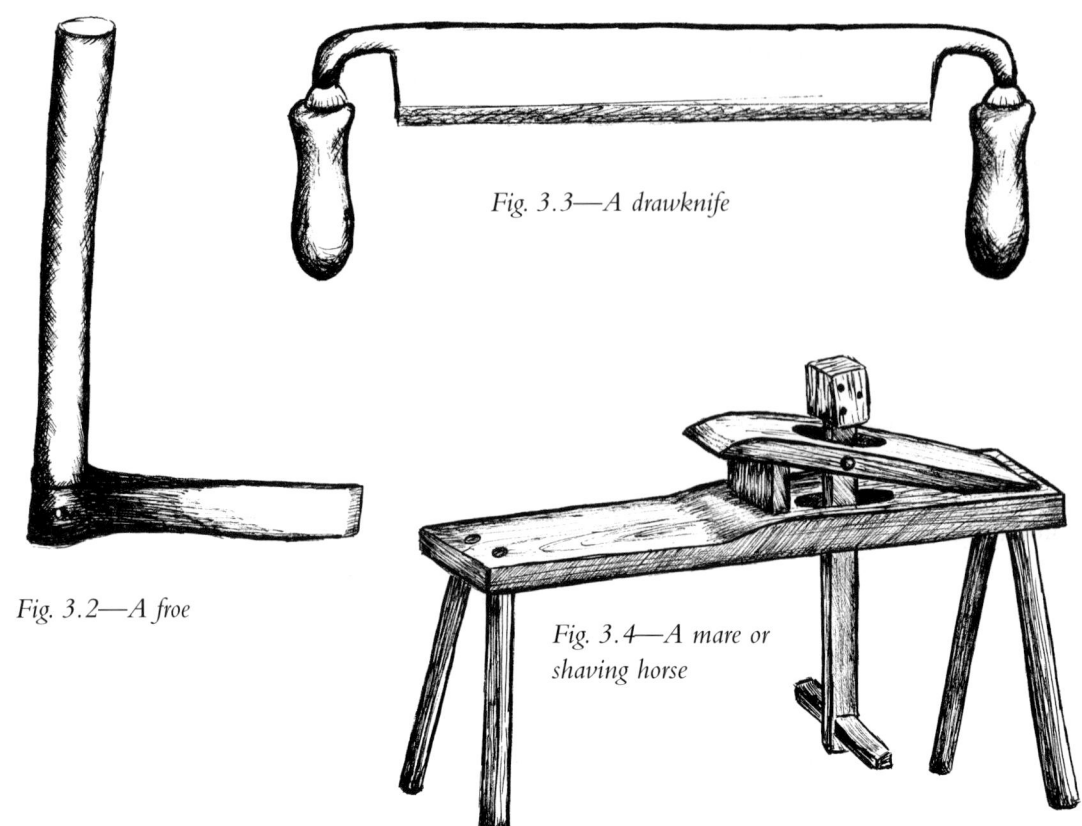

Fig. 3.3—A drawknife

Fig. 3.2—A froe

*Fig. 3.4—A mare or
shaving horse*

from three- or four-year-old split willow. Since these imports
stopped, about 60 years ago, the double hoop has been used
(described in the technique section of this chapter), but this may not
be the original hoop that was used. Alfred Grant is quoted as
follows by Patrick Smyth: 'When the rims couldn't be got any
longer from Holland or anywhere else we were in a fix but we sat
down and worked it out. I had a hand in making the first rim from
two big rods that had been grown locally.'[7]

It is possible that they were simply reinventing the original hoop
that was used before the Dutch imports, but it seems that originally
the hoops were of a single-rod thickness as in the *sciath* used in other
parts of Ireland.

The ribs for the Ulster potato baskets were made from what was
locally referred to as fir, but in fact the wood used seems to have
been Scots pine. The logs would have been cut to size for the ribs,
approximately 30" (76cm) long. These would then have been halved
and quartered using an axe or a hatchet and, once quartered, split

into thinner sections using a type of froe (**Fig. 3.2**). This would have been known locally as a 'lot knife' and would have been made by the local blacksmith. The ribs would have been shaved using a drawknife (**Fig. 3.3**) while the worker sat on a mare (**Fig. 3.4**). Finished ribs would have been about 640mm wide and 30mm thick. With the decline in large-scale production from the 1940s onwards, basketmakers reverted to using willow rods, sometimes doubled, for the ribs, and it is this that is described in the technique section. Not all Ulster potato baskets were of this type. Some had six whole rod ribs, all tied at the start, and another style called a bushel basket was round, with a hoop made from very thick split hazel, and eight ribs of split willow.

Oak chip potato baskets

The oak spale or chip basket (**Pl. 3.9**) was also used for harvesting potatoes. This was made from coppiced oak and it was probably only made in the eastern counties of Ireland where coppiced oak was most readily available. One of the last remaining oak spale basketmakers in the country was Nicholas Hilliard, who lived in Tinakilly in County Wicklow, and who was still making these baskets in the early 1960s (**Pl. 3.10**). This area of Wicklow is an area where oak is relatively abundant.

There are examples of Nicholas Hilliard's baskets in the National Museum collection and also an example of a similarly made basket from County Wexford. These baskets have hazel hoops with ribs and weavers of oak chip or spale. These baskets are very similar to English spale baskets, which have long been made in the district of Cumbria in the English Lake District, an area similarly favoured with coppiced oak woods. Spale baskets also made in other parts of England were variously known as a scuttle, wisket, slop or skip. These baskets were known as chip baskets in County Wicklow.

It is probable that the techniques of spale basketmaking came to Ireland from England, which might account for its distribution along the east coast. There

Pl. 3.9—Wicklow potato harvesting basket of oak 'chip' or spale, made by Nicholas Hilliard. Photo courtesy of NMI.

Pl. 3.10—Nicholas Hilliard weaving an oak 'chip' basket. Photo courtesy of Department of Irish Folklore, UCD.

does not seem to be any tradition of spale work in other parts of Ireland, even where oak woods are prevalent. However, the origin of some of the words used in oak spale basketmaking in Britain are thought to derive from the German. Thus 'pelk', which is the word for the wide oak ribs, is believed to derive from an old German word for cleaving or splitting wood.[8] Other terms such as 'the taws' are thought to be Norse in origin, so spale basketmaking may have been introduced there and possibly also in Ireland by the Vikings.

While spale baskets in England were made from seasoned logs, it seems that fresh logs were used in Ireland. Straight-grained, knot-free oak trees about twenty to thirty years old were best, though younger trees could also be used. These trees were usually found in the understorey of woods, where the competition from other coppiced trees forced them to grow straight, and the fact that there were taller trees above them meant they also grew upright to reach the light. Logs of the desired length, up to 6 feet or 1.8 metres long, were halved and then quartered using a froe or similar device (**Fig. 3.2.**). One of the froes collected by the National Museum from a spale basketmaker is in fact a sawn-off draw knife. If the oak was seasoned, it had to be boiled in a tank, once it had been quartered, before it could be split or riven into thinner pieces.

The hazel rod needed to make the hoop for these baskets could also be of seasoned material, but if so it had to be steamed or boiled to make it pliable enough to form the hoop. Potato baskets that were similar in appearance to the oak spale baskets but that were, in fact, made from split hazel were still being made in Carnew in County Wicklow in the 1960s. It is probable that this method was more widespread at one time, particularly because hazel was common in so many localities throughout Ireland.

Variations, with ribs of split oak but with willow weavers, were also once common in the Wexford area; these baskets were somewhat similar in appearance to the Ulster potato baskets. In many cases these baskets were probably made to a specific size so that they also acted as a measure in the area in which they were used.

Pl. 3.11—Ulster potato basket made by Alison Fitzgerald.

TECHNIQUE

Skib or *ciseog* grid base

To make a grid-base skib of 18" (46cm) diameter, you will first need six base sticks about 24" (61cm) long. These would need to be at least as stout as your little finger, say a minimum of a half-inch or 120mm at the butt. If using commercial willow, such as black maul, this would mean getting your base sticks from 8ft (2.4m) rods, but if using common osier, which is a thicker grower, 7ft (2.1m) rods should be adequate.

Split three of the base sticks and insert the other three base sticks to make a cross. It is best to stagger the butts of the willow so that

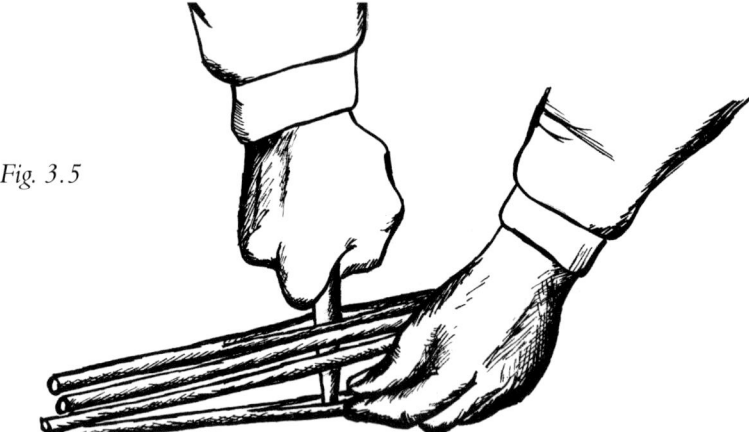

Fig. 3.5

Fig. 3.6

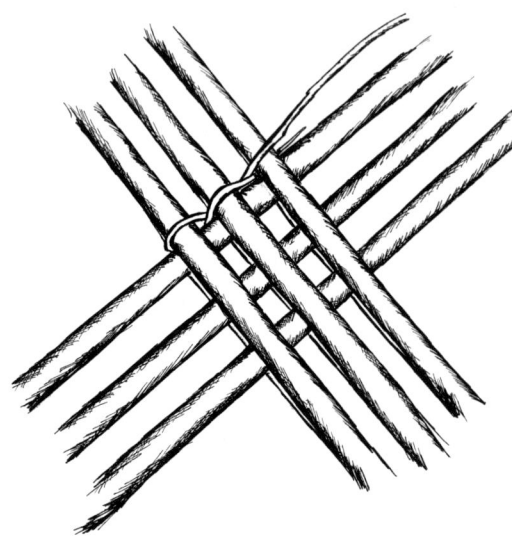

not all of the butts are lying together. Even more importantly, try to split the rods in such a way that the curve of the cross is away from you like an up-turned saucer. It is easiest to split the base sticks with the bodkin **(Fig. 3.5)**, though basketmakers in the country tradition used a knife because they did not usually have a bodkin.

It is important that the three base sticks be split cleanly because they will be exposed, so if the split is uneven and the rod is delicate as a result, discard it. When the cross has been formed, spread the rods apart to form the grid **(Fig. 3.6)**.

Now, take two evenly matched 4ft (1.2m) or 5ft (1.5m) weavers and start pairing by inserting the two tips through the split rods so that they come out in two consecutive gaps. If you have difficulty in keeping the tips anchored, you could instead start with one rod, the tip of which is inserted in the split rod and then randed in an anti-clockwise direction for two or three strokes before being turned back in a clockwise direction again. The second rod is inserted into the space beside it and the pairing can begin. **Fig. 3.6** shows this method of starting the weaving.

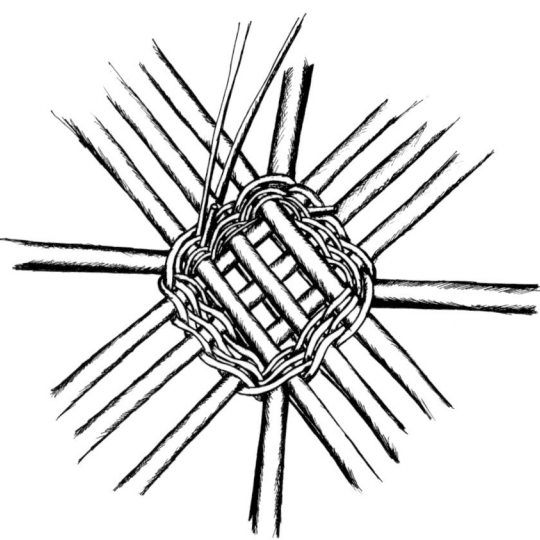

The first join is butt to butt and, once the pairing rods begin to get slender, you can insert the first four bi-stakes. These can be a little thinner than your base sticks and about half as long, i.e., about 11" (28cm). These are slyped on the thinner end and pushed into the weaving and through the split base sticks **(Fig. 3.7)**.

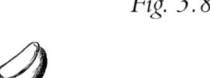

Fig. 3.7

These will then be included in all subsequent rows of pairing. Pairing continues until the required diameter of base is reached, in this case about 16" (41cm). It should be noted that the traditional makers always joined butt to tip, rather than the tip to tip and butt to butt jointing that is more familiar to professional basketmakers. I suspect the reason for this is that while tip to tip, butt to butt jointing requires evenly matched material, the joining of a butt to a spent tip allowed the traditional makers to use all sorts of material that might otherwise go to waste. This would include the cut-offs from the creel and branchy or otherwise inferior material.

Fig. 3.8

When the base is 16" (41cm), the tips of the last two pairing rods are secured by threading them through, and the base is turned upside-down so that the underside is now facing you. The rim is now put on by weaving a three-rod wale over the base sticks (see **Fig. 3.8** where this technique is being used on a Joyce country base).

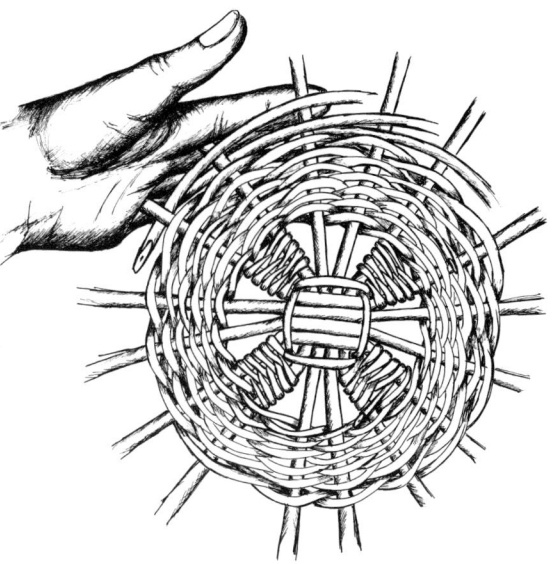

For a basket of this size, the weavers for the three-rod wale need to be 6fts or even light 7fts (1.8–2.1m). This three-rod wale is started by laying three butts behind each of three consecutive base sticks and weaving in the normal way, i.e., in front of two, behind one, starting with the left-hand rod each time. If you have difficulty in keeping the weaving rods in place, slype the butts of the rods and anchor them to the left of each of the base sticks. It is unlikely that your rods will be long enough to form the three-rod wale rim without a join; joins are made by joining the butt of the new rod to the spent rod. This is again a hedgerow–style join, but it works well provided you try to stagger your joins as opposed to grouping them together as you would in professional work. I say that a join will be necessary because the function of the three-rod wale is to provide a rim to protect the base of the basket, and if you work the rods too close to the tip they will not fulfil this function. One round of three-rod wale is sufficient for the rim, so when you reach your starting point you finish by securing each of the weavers in turn, the first under one, the second under two and the third under three.

It is possible to put an additional 'inner rim' on the base by weaving a three-rod wale on the underside of the basket when the base is about 6" (15cm) in diameter. I have seen this on a good number of the old skibs, and it shows that the bases were often made perfectly flat rather than with a slight dome at the centre. They therefore benefited from the protection provided by an 'inner rim'.

When the outer wale is finished, it is usual to cut off the base sticks to facilitate insertion of the uprights, but a careful study of **Pl. 3.1**, showing an Aran Islander making a skib, reveals that he has left the base sticks uncut, presumably to be cut off when the basket is finished. Despite that, I think it is neater to cut them off now.

The rim I have just described is the traditional finish for the base of a skib. However, it does have the disadvantage of leaving the base sticks visible from the side of the basket. Moreover, if the space between the base sticks is fairly wide, it is difficult to put a good tight rim of this sort over them. For this reason, I would usually depart from tradition by putting the rim on the underside of the outstretched uprights. This technique is widely used in Germany, so I call it a German wale, and I have no doubt that it is a superior finish to the traditional three-rod wale. Details of how to put on a German wale are to be found in Appendix 1.

Next select 28 uprights. These uprights are typically 6fts (1.8m) if using *Salix triandra* 'Black Maul', but if using a stouter variety, then

5fts (1.5m) would be adequate. The thickness of the uprights is what matters and 5/16" (7.5mm) is about the right diameter. These are then slyped on the belly (i.e., the underside of the curve) and inserted into the base, with the slype on the underside of the basket. A slype is a basketmaker's term for a long angular cut **(see Fig. 3.9)**. It is important that the uprights penetrate deeply into the base, hence the slype. A simple slype can be done with a single cut towards you, the thumb moving with the knife **(Fig. 3.10)**.

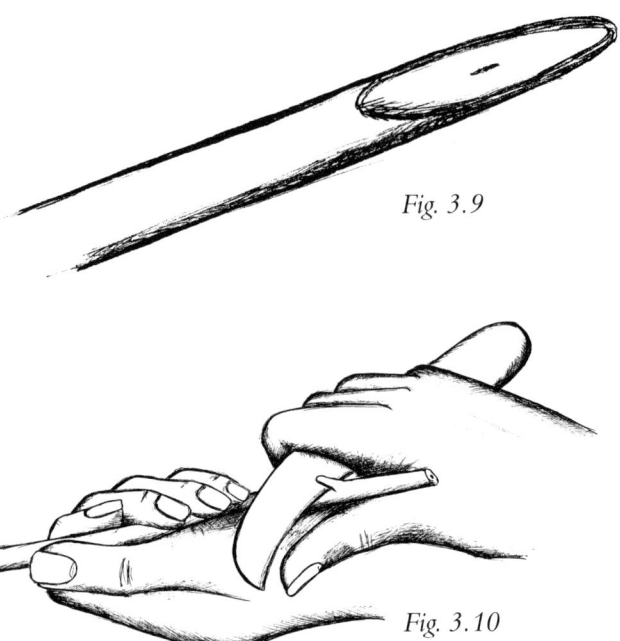

Fig. 3.9

Fig. 3.10

Where the base weaving is tight, a second slype at an angle to the first may be necessary. The 28 uprights are distributed by putting two to each base stick, but the base sticks at north, south, east and west get just one upright. It is important to remember that the number of uprights varied according to their thicknesses — there were no hard and fast rules. Many of the skibs I have seen have only one upright for every base stick. However, the skib will look more circular even if double uprights are used where suitable.

The uprights, once inserted, are kinked with the knife in the normal fashion (**Fig. 3.11**) and may be gathered into a hoop of a similar diameter to the base, now about 17" (43cm).

Traditional basketmakers did not use a hoop but rather a twisted willow tie to secure the uprights. The siding of the basket is simply six rows of three-rod waling using weavers a little thinner than the uprights. I usually start with anchored tips, with 9" (23cm) removed, and then chase the two sets of weavers with butt to butt and tip to tip jointing. However, traditional makers adopted a hedgerow style, using the butts of the rods to start. These were simply laid in behind each of three consecutive uprights and the three-rod waling

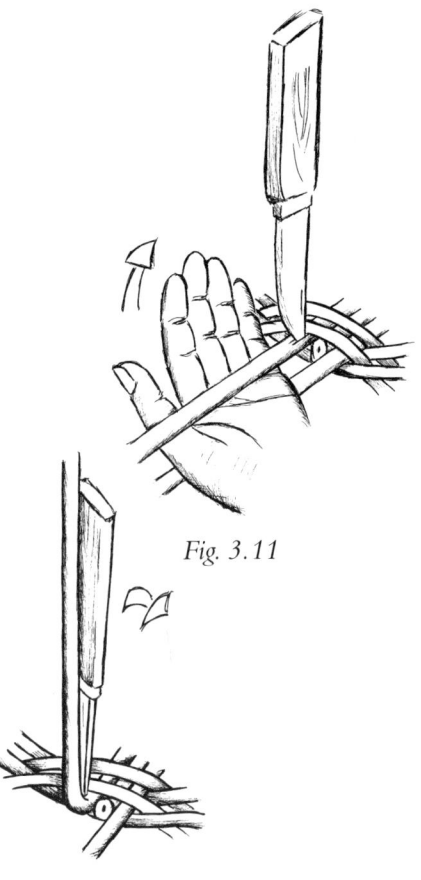

Fig. 3.11

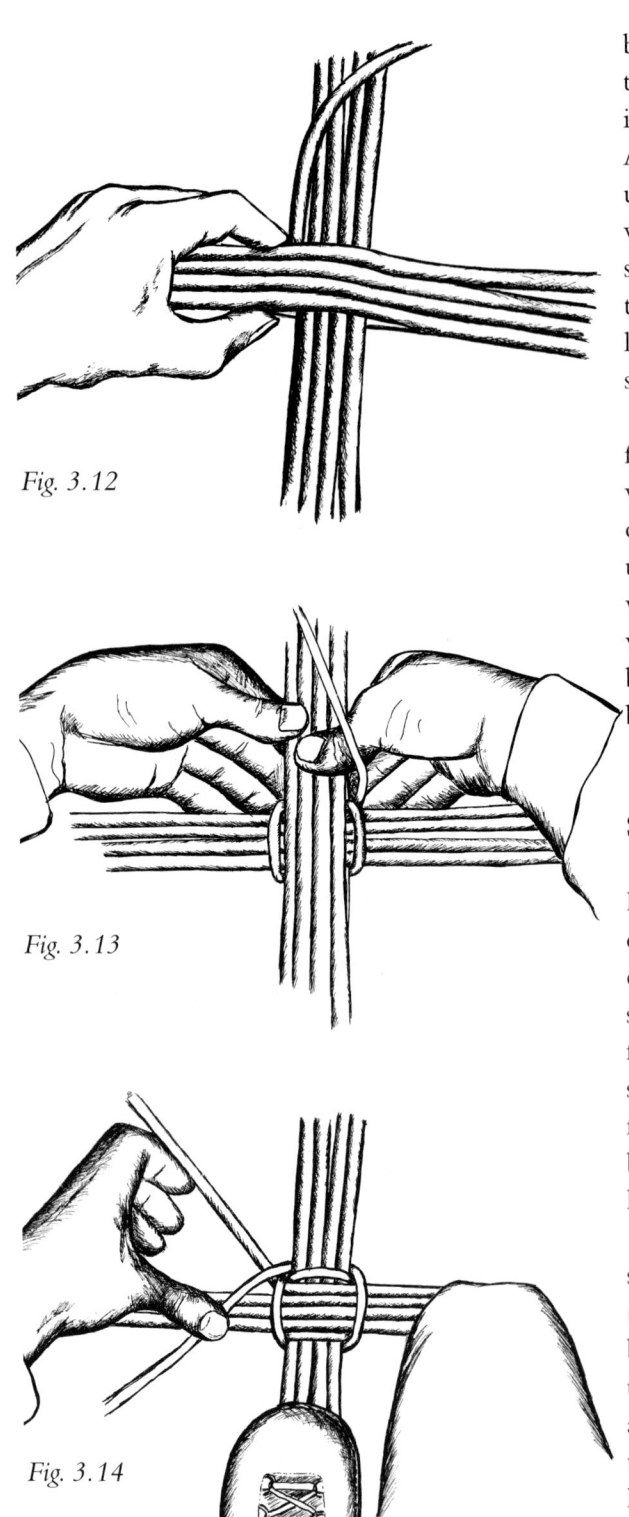

Fig. 3.12

Fig. 3.13

Fig. 3.14

begun. As the weaving rods began to get thin, the spent rods were joined by inserting new rods, butt first, behind it. Again it can be seen that this facilitates using unsorted material, but the weaving will appear more even if the joins are staggered, so it is helpful to begin the three-rod wale with rods of uneven length when weaving in this hedgerow style.

I would complete this skib with a five-pair, behind-two border, details of which can be found in Appendix 1. If only one upright per base stick was used, the space between the uprights would be too far apart for this and it would be necessary to use a behind-one border, such as a four-behind-one border.

Skib or *ciseog*, Joyce country base

For a Joyce country base of similar diameter, it will be necessary to select eight base sticks 22" (56cm) long, the same thickness as for the grid base. Split four and put four base sticks through the split sticks to give a cross of 4 x 4. Of the four you have split, the central ones will be exposed, so it is important that they have been cleanly split.

To open out the base, get one slender 5ft (1.5m) rod and three 4ft (1.2m) rods. Insert the 5ft (1.5m) rod, butt first in the top left-hand corner of the slath (as the base cross is now called), as shown in **Fig. 3.12**. Go over (east), under (south), over and under. Now you have arrived where you started and you reverse direction, as shown in **Fig. 3.13**.

By going over (where you formerly went under), under, over and under, you again arrive at your starting point.

You now open out the nearest spokes at north and west **(Fig. 3.14)** by pack randing in and out between them until you have circled around both base sticks four or five times.

Each of the three lesser rods, 4fts (1.2m) in this case, is similarly used to open out the other diagonals with pack randing (**Fig. 3.15**), each rod being started by inserting the butt into the appropriate split in the slath. With these rods you could go around the base sticks six or seven times, which will leave them higher than the original diagonal you have opened out. This is so that the two rods that start the pairing can be accommodated without too much bulk. This is shown in **Fig. 3.16** where the pack randing has been kept low, as described. The first pairing rod is anchored as shown. You lay it in butt first as if you were going to weave in an anti-clockwise direction, and then immediately turn it around the base

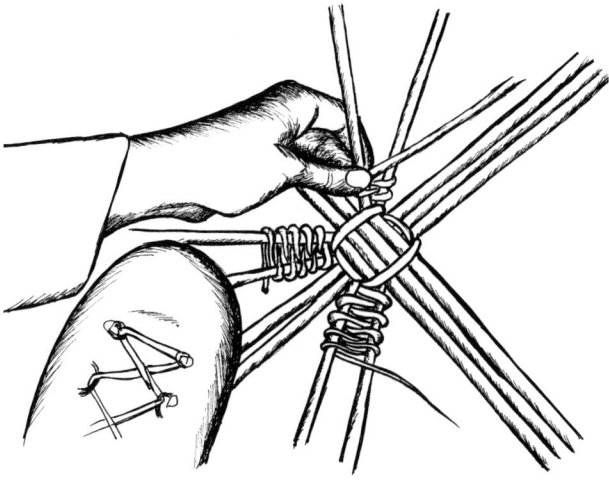

Fig. 3.15

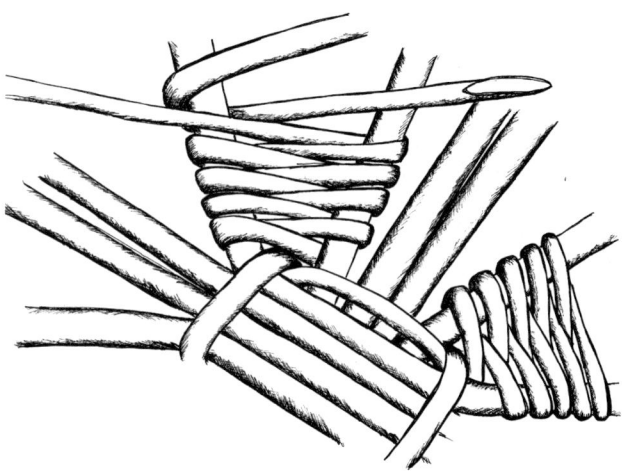

Fig. 3.16

stick so that it is facing clockwise. The second pairing rod is simply placed underneath so that the pairing can begin. Traditionally, jointing would be hedgerow-style with a butt placed under the spent tip as described for the grid base, though I think tip to tip and butt to butt joins give a more even base. I would also prefer to use a lock join when joining butt to butt (see Appendix 1), so that the spent butt and the new butt both rest against a base stick rather than just against each other as is the case in a simple join.

When the base diameter is reached and the rim has been put on **(Fig. 3.8)** 32 uprights of 6ft (1.8m) are inserted and the skib completed in a similar fashion to the grid base skib described earlier.

Sciathóg

First make a hoop about 15" (38cm) in diameter. The ideal material for making the hoop is bucky briar (wild rose). If this can be found growing in woodlands, long lengths without too many thorns should be available. The thorns are simply rubbed off with a thick glove and the hoop is made while the briar is fresh and then allowed to dry. The instructions given here are based on the assumption that bucky briar will not be found too easily and are for a willow hoop, but hazel will give a stronger hoop than willow. Select a stout 8–9ft (2.1–2.4m) willow rod; the diameter at the butt should be about ¾" (18mm) thick. The hoop could be made from green willow but if so it should be left up to dry for several weeks before being used. Even when brown willow is used, it is a good idea to allow the hoop to dry for a few days after it has been made. For a small (15" or 38cm diameter) *sciathóg,* it should be possible to soften the rod for the hoop by pressing the butt against your stomach, but for larger sizes the hoop rod can be bent using a former, as shown in **Fig. 3.17**.

Once the hoop rod has been softened, the inside of the butt is slyped with a long tapering cut. A short slype is also made on the outside at the very butt to further reduce the bulk at the butt of the rod. Offer up the remainder of the rod and make a mark where it needs to be cut, and make another short slype here, again on the inside. For larger hoops it may be necessary to shave the back in this area to facilitate the join.

The join can be held temporarily with two clamps **(Fig. 3.18)** or you can simply hold it with your hand. Traditonally, the join was secured using a thin willow rod or a willow skein and this tie stayed on the hoop and was covered by weavers. Another method, which I first saw used by Alison Fitzgerald, is to tape the join in two or three places — the tape can be removed once the join has been

Fig. 3.17

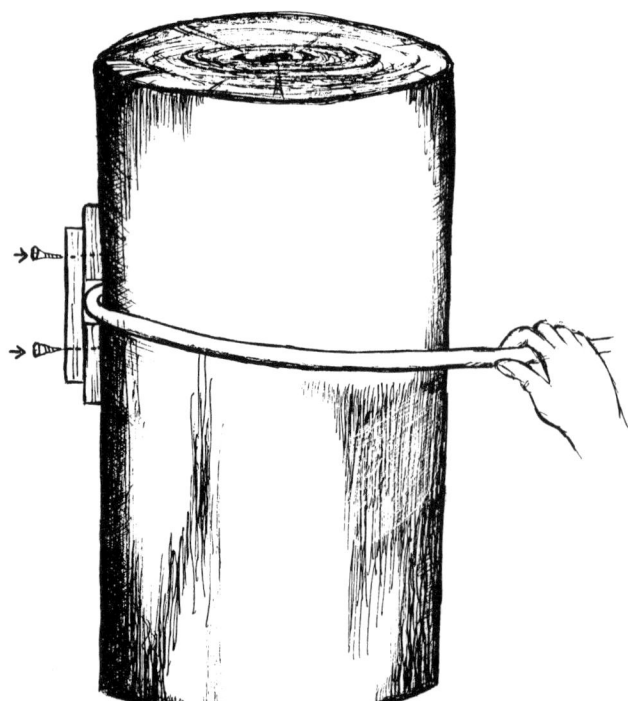

Fig. 3.18

secured by the weaving. This gives a neater finish than when the somewhat bulky rod join is used to secure the hoop.

For the large-size *sciathóg,* the ribs were often of whole rods but for the smaller size, the use of split willow for the ribs will result in a more finely balanced basket. Ideally, the ribs should be made from 8–9ft (2.1–2.4m) rods split with the cleave. If a cleave isn't available then simply split the rods for the ribs by hand using the thumbs to prevent the rods splitting unevenly. The split ribs must then be shaved down with the knife to make them even — it is for this reason that ribs made by splitting a rod in three with the cleave are preferred, since the pith is raised and thus easier to shave. I like to prepare two sets of ribs at a time (twelve ribs from four rods) because they will be better balanced.

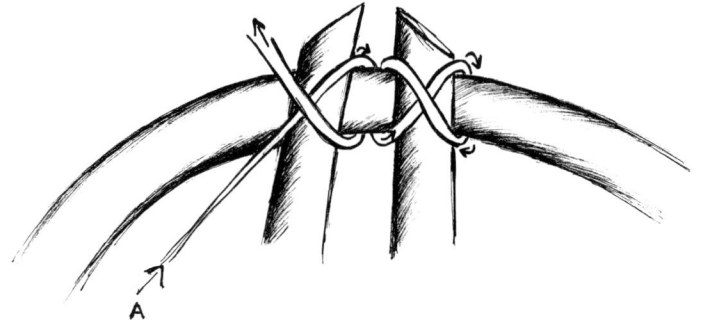

Fig. 3.19

Select a slender 4–5ft (1.2–1.5m) rod and tie the thickest of the prepared ribs to the frame as shown in **Fig. 3.19** using the tip of the rod. Start weaving in and out (in front of one, behind one), taking an extra turn around the hoop each time. Once the first rod has been used, all subsequent rods will be joined butt first. Once two rods have been used on one side, it is usual to secure the ribs to the hoop on the opposite side, weaving out the same amount. It is usually possible to fit the next two ribs at this point. These are added as soon as it is possible to fit them in the space between the rib and the hoop. Weaving from this point on is usually done from the back (from the outside of the *sciathóg*), but with the joins on the inside. Once the six ribs are in place, continue weaving from each side until the *sciathóg* is completed by weaving the last strokes in the middle. In order to keep the *sciathóg* circular it is useful to tie a string from end to end of the hoop in order to prevent the weaving from pulling the hoop into an oval shape. This is especially important if a fresh hoop is being used.

Traditonally these baskets were woven from semi–green rods, and if the rods were a little fresh the weaving of the final rods could be delayed to allow for shrinkage. The rods used could also increase in thickness towards the middle, and the extra turn around the hoop could be omitted if the line of weaving had become straight before the middle point was reached.

Variations on the *sciathóg*

The instructions given above could be modified for a larger–diameter *sciathóg* — up to 20" (50cm) in diameter and with eight rather than six ribs. In this case two–year–old willow could be used for the hoop and for splitting the ribs. A whole–rod *sciathóg* can be made on a similar principle, using two central ribs to start, but one of the baskets in **Pl. 3.3** has a one–rib start and the additional ribs are added each time beside the central rib to give a distinctive appearance to the weaving. There is a similar basket in the National Museum collection from County Longford, which the maker made flat and called a boat skib. In this version, the central rib, known as the main stretcher, was attached to the hoop by cutting tongues on the rod in the manner of a scallom.[9] One–rib starts were also popular in other parts of the country, particularly in counties Cork and Waterford, but here the additional ribs were added between the existing rib(s) and the hoop in a similar manner to the *sciathóg* already described.

The horseshoe–shaped *sciathóg* in **Pl. 3.4** is made by bending a stout hoop in a horseshoe shape. The diameter of the hoop is quite stout; even for the smaller size, which is typically about 12" (30cm) wide and about 20" (50cm) long, the diameter of the hoop at the thick end is about 1" (25mm). A fork on the hoop, as shown in **Fig. 3.1**, is an advantage but not essential. For the smaller version, one central rib about ½– ¾" (12–18mm) is lashed to the curved end of the hoop using the tip of a 5ft (1.5m) rod. All subsequent weavers are joined using the butts, and once three ribs have been introduced, the rods are secured at the open end of the hoop by a row of pairing started by folding a 5ft (1.5m) rod in half around the hoop. More rods are added to the pairing to give a bulky, knot-like weave similar to the top knot on the creel, which is further thickened by allowing the rods to turn back around the hoop and in and out of the pairing until the tips are finally threaded through. Two further ribs are added and the weaving completed in the middle as already described for the *sciathóg mór,* which typically had a total of seven ribs and was around 30" (76cm) long and about 18" (46cm) wide.

The horseshoe-shaped Waterford *sciath* in **Pl. 3.5** has a fixed rod at the wide end and was made by Tom Quinlan of Tallow, Co. Waterford, for the exhibition 'Basketmakers', which was held at the Crafts Council of Ireland Gallery in Dublin in 1994. The end piece could be nailed on or formed by kinking part of the hoop rod to form a back. Dimensions are about 28" (70cm) long, 20" (50cm) wide and 7" (18cm) deep. It has seven ribs.

Ulster potato harvesting basket

Although it is likely that a hazel hoop was originally used for these baskets, details of how to make the double hoop are shown in **Figs 3.20 and 3.21**, based on original sketches by Alison Fitzgerald. The rods for the double hoop, which can be either green or brown, should be stout 8–9 fts (2.4–2.7m) and one can be cut 80" (2020mm) long while the other should be around 60" (1525mm). Bend both sticks into approximate shape and then slype the end of the longer stick on the inside of the curve (belly) for about 7" (18cm), but only as deep as the pith. Put a short slype on the inside (belly) of the shorter stick.

Next get a pliable 5ft weaver and give it a long French-type

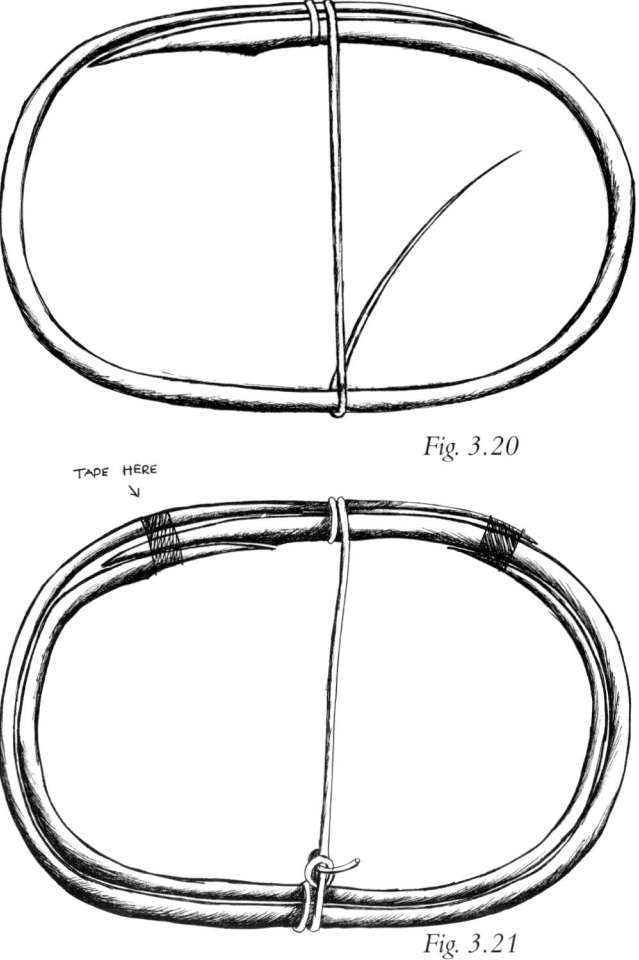

Fig. 3.20

TAPE HERE

Fig. 3.21

scallom (getting thinner towards the butt). Now form the longer stick into an oval hoop with the *thin* end on the outside; hoop dimensions should be about 22" x 19" (56cm x 48cm), as shown in **Fig. 3.20**. Notice that the slype is not in the middle of the oval. Secure this temporarily by locking the scallomed end of the weaver around the join and bringing the weaver around to the other side of the hoop. The shorter stick is then fitted on to the *inside* of the hoop with the slyped butt faces meeting each other; tape them together, including the tip section of the original stick in the taped join. Tie the hoop at the opposite side at the correct width (19"/48cm) and tape the tip ends together as shown in **Fig. 3.21**. The hoop may need to be shaped somewhat before being allowed to set. If green rods have been used, a few weeks should be allowed for drying if possible.

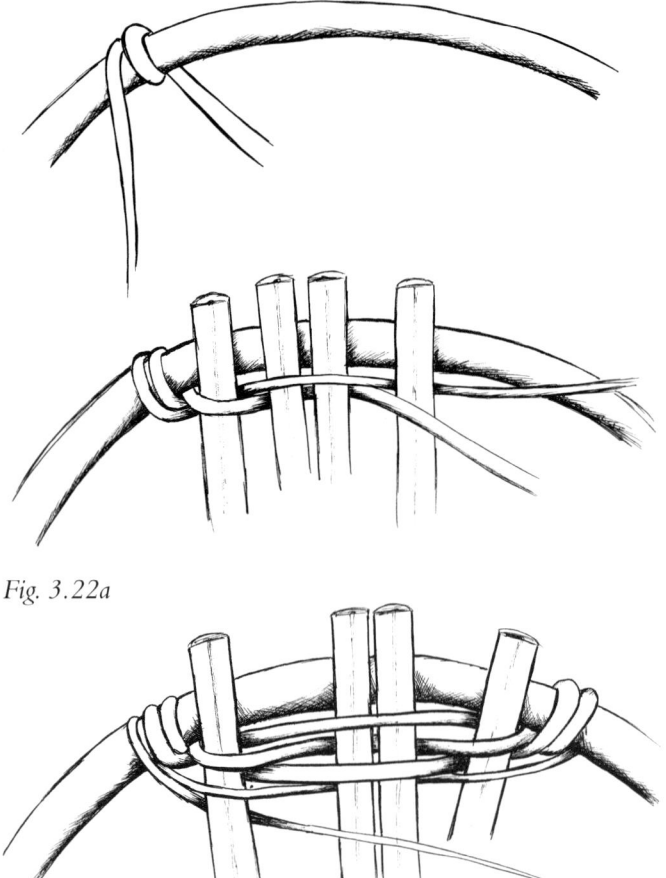

Fig. 3.22a

Fig. 3.22b

The central ribs for the Ulster potato basket are now usually of split willow (**Pl. 3.11**), though as mentioned in the main text wooden slats were formerly used. To make the split willow ribs, split two stout rods in half using the thumbs to control the split. These rods would need to be at least ¾" (18mm) in diameter, and two-year-old rods could be used for this if they are available. Two are used side by side to give a wide central rib with one split rib on either side. These three ribs are lashed to the hoop, as shown in **Fig. 3.22**, and the next two ribs, which need not be split but should be shaved a little at the ends, are introduced immediately so that a total of five ribs protrude above the hoop. The weaving proceeds at a right angle to the hoop to give immediate depth to the basket, with the central ribs going down straight for almost 8" (20cm) before then curving sharply to form the flat bottom. Two additional ribs are introduced on either side of the central ribs as the weaving proceeds to give a total of nine ribs. These last ribs are somewhat slighter than those already in place. The total depth of the basket is about 9" (23cm).

Weaving rods at the start are fairly slender with 4–5fts (1.2–1.5m) being adequate, but the floor of the basket is formed with stouter weavers, about 6–7fts (1.8–2.1m) and up to ½" (12mm) wide at the butts. Moreover, the pattern of weaving on the examples I have seen is not simply joining a butt whenever a rod gets weak; instead, the weakening rod is dropped at the last rib closest to the hoop. Let's assume that this is on the right-hand side. The butt of the next weaving rod is placed at the leftmost rib and woven across towards the right, taking care to ensure that the weave alternates with the previous rod. Either of the two outside ribs can be used, depending on which best suits the weaving pattern while keeping joins on the inside.

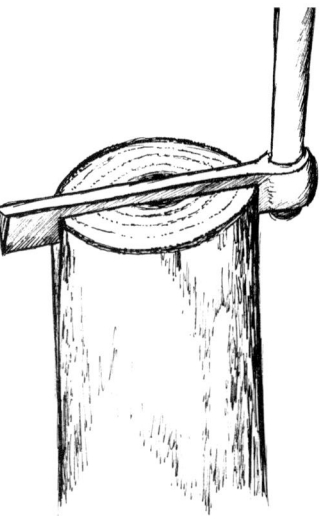

Fig. 3.23

Wicklow spale or chip basket

I haven't made these baskets and the description is based on Chrissie O'Gorman's account of Nicholas Hilliard's work and from information supplied by Owen Jones, an oak spale basketmaker in Cumbria.

The ideal oak saplings, according to Nicholas Hilliard, should be from 4–6" (10–15cm) in diameter and should be clean and straight-grained. Splitting is done with a froe or similar tool and it seems a half draw-knife was what was used by most basketmakers in the Wicklow area. The froe is tapped in to the sapling **(Fig. 2.23)** and the split gradually opened out, while the underneath portion of the sapling is held and balanced with

Fig. 3.24

the other hand. The aim is to divide the sapling as cleanly and as evenly as possible. These halves are then divided so that the original sapling has now been made into quarters or eighths **(Fig. 3.24)**.

Next, the inner heart wood is split from the sap wood **(Fig. 3.25)** and the heart wood is kept for the ribs of the basket. The sap portion is then divided so that the splinters (as the weaving material

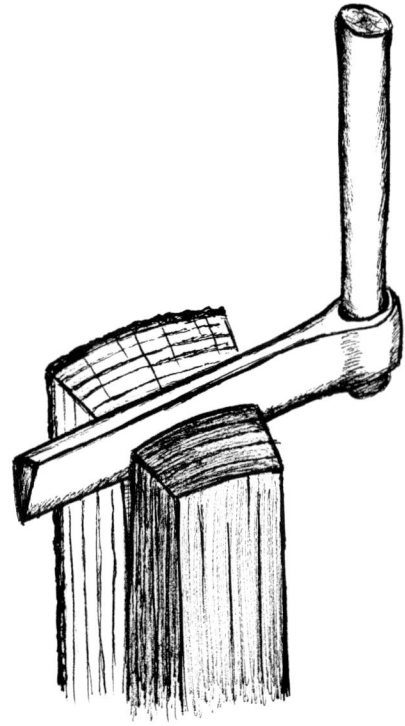

Fig. 3.25

Fig. 3.26

was known) will not be too wide **(Fig. 3.26)**. The splinters are made by starting the cut with the knife; they are then torn away from the sap wood with the hand. The final splinters can be torn away from each other by hand as shown in **Fig. 3.27**. The splinters and the heart ribs are shaved on the draw-horse, the thickness of the ribs being greater than the splinters. The ribs should also be wider than the splinters.

The hazel hoop is made from a stout rod up to 1" (25mm) in diameter — the bulk should be reduced at the butt end by shaving the rod for about 12–15" (30–38cm) along its length before slyping to make the join as described for the *sciathóg*. The join for the hazel hoop was usually secured with clinched wire nails. Hoop measurements should be 21" x 20" (53cm x 51cm) approximately.

The first seven ribs are secured to the hoop using a narrow and thin splinter, as can be seen by carefully studying **Pl. 3.9**. It will be necessary to chamfer the four outer ribs somewhat so that they are a little narrower where they are bound to the hoop. A further two ribs are added as soon as they can be comfortably fitted, and wider weaving splinters can be used thereafter, though the final (middle) weaving splinter in **Pl. 3.9** is a narrow one. Joins are made by allowing the weaving splinters to overlap for a stroke or two. Handles are made using a single twisted willow rod for each handle.

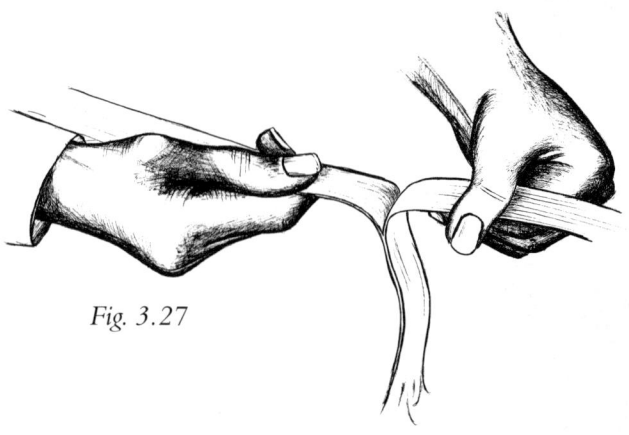

Fig. 3.27

4

Wicker Currachs

THE BOYNE currach shown in **Pl. 4.1** was the only wicker boat that was still in use in Ireland in the twentieth century, although the Sheephaven sea-going currach, shown in **Fig. 4.1**, which is still in use in County Donegal, has hazel ribs stuck into a wooden gunwale. While oars are used with the Sheephaven currach, a paddle is used to propel the Boyne currach. This paddle currach was used on the Boyne River in County Meath for the netting of salmon until the 1940s, when the use of nets for this purpose was made illegal, and the Boyne currach, as a fishing boat, became extinct. Coracle-shaped currachs had also been known on certain other Irish rivers in the past, certainly on the Shannon and the Erne and possibly on the Bann and the Foyle, but by the twentieth century the Boyne was the only Irish river on which they were used. The use of currachs on the Boyne dates back at least to medieval times and we know that upon the dissolution of Mellifont Abbey in 1539 its possessions

Pl. 4.1—A Boyne currach. The currach was propelled by a paddle using a figure of eight stroke. The paddler knelt in the front of the currach; the hay is presumably to make the paddler more comfortable. The person tending the nets sat facing the rear of the currach and the twisted willow ties supported the net. Photo from the Green Collection, courtesy of UFTM.

*Fig. 4.1—
Sheephaven sea-going
currach, which is still
in use in County
Donegal. (Evans
1957.)*

included an annual rent for the use of sixteen of these currachs at Oldbridge.

The Boyne currach is an oval-shaped boat with a framework made of hazel that has been cut and allowed to season for at least a month before being woven. Stout hazel rods are stuck into the ground at a slight outward angle and a special weave known as a mouthwale, also used on the creel, is put on using lighter hazel rods as weavers. The skirting of hazel comes up to about 6" (150cm) and the hazel uprights are then bent over and lashed together to form the bottom of the currach. Although full details of how to make the Boyne currach are given in the technique section of this chapter, it should be noted here that this method of construction is the opposite of that used in making the English and the Welsh wicker coracles. In these, the framework is formed by bending the ribs upwards from the floor of the coracle and tying the ribs to a hoop of hazel which forms the gunwale **(Pl. 4.2)**, whereas the Boyne currach is made upside–down, i.e., the bottom of the currach is formed last. The Boyne currach was made to size so that it could be covered by one large cow or bullock hide. The usual size was either 6' 6" x 4' (198cm x 122cm) or 6' x 4' (183cm x 122cm) and this size was sufficiently large to accommodate two people, one kneeling in front to paddle the currach and the other sitting towards the rear to tend to the nets.[1] An account of fishing at Oldbridge in 1947 shows that the Boyne currach was, in the right hands, ideally suited to its task:

*Pl. 4.2—English
style coracle being
made by Peter
Faulkner. Note the
finished coracle in the
background. Photo
courtesy of Vivienne
Mayne.*

DROGHEDA INDEPENDENT, SATURDAY,   DECEMBER 24, 1938

FORGOTTEN DAYS ☞ No. 25

ONE OF THE MOST VALUABLE AND INTERESTING PHOTOGRAPHS YET REPRODUCED IN OUR SERIES, WHICH IS ATTRACTING MUCH ATTENTION.

It was taken about 45 years ago at Oldbridge on the River Boyne and shows salmon fishers of that district with their coracle (or curragh), a hide-covered boat, which was in use on the upper waters of the Boyne until some few years ago.

In the group are (left to right—James Craven, Maurice Craven, Patrick Coogan and Michael O'Brien. The lady sitting at the tree was a Miss L. Reynolds.

Michael O'Brien was the "only man in Europe who could make a hide-covered coracle." He made one (before his death in 1931) for Dr. Mahr, of the National Museum, and it is at present exhibited in the Museum.

The photograph is so interesting that we are reproducing from "Drogheda and Its Industries" (publish ed in 1932 by Messrs. J. J. and Peter Casey) an article which appeared in it about the hide-covered coracle:—

ONLY MAN IN EUROPE

Who Can Make a Hide-Covered Coracle.

"MICHAEL O'BRIEN, an old man residing in one of the cluster of cottages which forms the remnants of the old village called Oldbridge, near Drogheda, has just discovered that he is the only man in Europe who can make a hide-covered coracle or curragh, and also that the River Boyne, beside which his family have lived for untold generations is the only river in Ireland on which this type of boat is still used. This revelation was made to Mr. O'Brien within the last few weeks when Dr. Mahr, of the National Museum, visited Oldbridge for the purpose of interviewing the person who had kept alive the vanishing art of coracle making, as well as with the intention of having a specimen built for the museum. This was ultimately done by Mr. O'Brien who was assisted by his son and another young man named Philip McCormack, both of whom take a live interest in the old man's unique skill, which they are also anxious to acquire.

"While the coracle was being built, Dr. Mahr and Mr. Francis Stephens, of Trinity College, were both in attend- ance and took photographs at various stages, as well as a film of the entire process, while a detailed description of the work given verbally by Mr. O'Brien was recorded by means of a dictaphone.

"When I interviewed him Mr. O'Brien said he had learned how to make a coracle from his father who had been taught by his grandfather many years ago. "It was made," he said, "simply with hazel rods, willows, and cow-hide, and when finished it was a round-shaped curragh, measuring five feet eight inches in length, and four feet two inches at the widest part." Curraghs had always been used for salmon fishing on the Boyne in his recollection, but they have grown scarcer and scarcer each year, and the fishermen around Oldbridge are the only people now using them on the river, and in fact the only people in Europe to use this peculiar form of fishing craft. He remembered being told by his grand- father that coracles were used on the Boyne since the time when the Cister- cian Monks were in possession of Mellifont Abbey, and he also knew that the cowhide covered curragh had become extinct along the West Coast of Ireland eighty years ago. On some rivers in Wales he believed that hide was still used for covering coracles, but these are a longer type of vessel, more in the style of a canoe.

"Mr. O'Brien feels delighted that his son and the other young man named McCormack are anxious to learn to make coracles and says that they are rapidly acquiring the necessary knowledge and skill which will be the means of preserving this quaint fishing antiquity on our most historic river, the Boyne.

"When I questioned Mr. O'Brien regarding Dr. Mahr's visit to his cottage beside the river at Oldbridge he said: "He came in here with some kind of a machine called a dictaphone and put it on the table. Then when I had told him all about coracles and how to make them he twisted something on the side of the machine, and told me to sit down. In a few seconds the thing began to talk to us, and it told us all I was after saying about the coracle. Then a few days later he brought me up to Dublin and showed me a picture of myself making the coracle from the very beginning to the very end. Bedada, young man," concluded Mr. O'Brien, "you'd want to mind what you'd be saying and doing these days, with all the quare machines that's going."

"Editor's Note.—Since the above was written Michael O'Brien has been gathered to his fathers, but before his death he transmitted the secret of his craft to his son, Michael O'Brien, who is determined to preserve the family tradition in their most unique industry."

Pl. 4.3—Article from The Drogheda Independent, *December 1938. Reproduced courtesy of* Drogheda Independent, Co. Louth.

Every half hour of daylight during the season, the currach makes its brief trip with a draft net around the pool of water where the salmon lie below the weir. Its virtue lies in its lightness and ease of handling — though not for the novice — in the method of paddling over the bows which allows it to keep close to the banks, and especially in the shallow draught which enables it to pass right under the weir without being swept down by the under-current. The paddler kneels in the deep bows and draws the boat along with rapid strokes alternately to left and right. The net-man sits on the thwart facing backwards and plays out the net, the end of which is held by a third man on the bank. Having reached the far end of the weir, the paddler races downstream and returns across the current to join the third man and close the net.[2]

The survival of the Boyne currach until 1947 seemed unlikely in the 1930s, and at that time Michael O'Brien, one of the last of the Boyne currach-makers, was commissioned by the National Museum of Ireland to make one. The making was filmed and is now valuable archive footage. The article and photograph from the *Drogheda Independent* of 1938 **(Pl. 4.3)** give details of this. The belief expressed in the article that Michael O'Brien was the only person in Europe who could make a hide-covered coracle was not strictly true, because hide-covered wicker coracles were being made in Shropshire, a tradition that continues to the present time. Welsh coracles are shorter and smaller than the Boyne currach, however, so it was certainly true that Michael O'Brien was among the last men at that time making the Boyne currach.[3]

There has been a revival of interest in the Boyne currach in recent years. This is largely due to the efforts of Clive Ó Gibne, his wife, Sinéad, and their friends, who were instrumental in holding the first Annual Boyne Currach Regatta in 1998 **(Pl. 4.4)**. Clive, a woodcarver by profession, has learned how to make the Boyne currach and is anxious to develop its potential for leisure use and to gather information locally about its history. This awakening of interest in the wicker currach is not confined to County Meath. Bruce Crawford from County Down and Meitheal Mara in County Cork have also been involved in the making of Boyne-type currachs.

The Boyne currach is a tangible link with the hide-covered sea-going currach that in some form was used around these shores probably even in megalithic times. It is possible that the hide-covered currachs used by the early settlers were paddle boats, but that improvements and refinements were made over time, one of which was the replacement of the paddle by the oar. Whereas in the Boyne currach the gunwale is always formed by the weaving rods, the sea-going currach that was used extensively around Ireland since the first century BC may well have employed gunwales of wood and stout poles to give more rigidity and strength.

We know that the pre-Christian people of Ireland knew how to make large hide-covered boats. Such boats feature in the *iomraimh*, or voyage stories, where heroes of the Celtic world go off on a sea quest or adventure. These stories of the pagan era were part of a vast body of oral tradition, some of which was written down by scribes in monasteries in the Christian era.

The best-known pre-Christian *iomramh* is 'The Voyage of Bran', in which the wanderer sets out with a crew of 27 in a large hide-covered currach. The voyage was inspired by a vision of a beautiful woman who came ashore in a spirit currach. She tells Bran of the delights that await him on an island inhabited only by women, where death never threatens. Bran calls his companions and they build three hide-covered currachs, each large enough for nine people, and set off to seek the beautiful isle. During their voyage

Pl. 4.4—Boyne currach regatta. Photo courtesy of Vivienne Mayne.

they meet the Sea-God, Manaman Mac Lir, and reach the island of women, where they live, time forgotten, in a round of endless pleasure. Eventually, however, some members of the company have a desire to return home to Ireland, but when they return they find their homeland changed and inhabited by strangers. Bran and his companions carve the story of their wanderings on a standing stone in Ogham and sail their currachs back to the island of women. Another *iomramh*, 'The Voyage of Maoldún'[4] is Christian in origin and it describes the many adventures that Maoldún and his companions have in pursuit of enemies. The currachs in this voyage are described as being

Pl. 4.5—Making a sea-going currach for the Colm Cille voyage at Mayo Abbey, Co. Mayo. Photo courtesy of Vivienne Mayne.

three hide currachs, which most commentators interpret as meaning that three hides were needed to cover each currach. Although the stories have many magic elements and would be regarded as fictional by the modern reader, the details of currachs contained in them are certainly credible.

There is other evidence to show that leather-skinned boats with oars and masts were being made well before Christian times. A model of an early Irish currach made from gold sheet was found near Limavaddy in County Derry in 1891 and has been dated to the first century BC. Marks on the hull of the model depict the pressure points of the framework upon the oxhide cover, and the currach is equipped with oars and a sail. Some of the currachs that sailed the seas to the north and east of Ireland up to the fifth century would have been engaged in commerce, but others were undoubtedly manned by pirates from Ireland intent on leading raiding parties for slaves and booty to the coastal areas of Britain. St Patrick, who is largely credited with the successful conversion of the Irish to Christianity early in the fifth century, was first brought to Ireland as a slave from Britain by a raiding party led by Niall of the Nine Hostages.

With Ireland's conversion to Christianity, however, the purpose of the currach journeys changed, and Irish monks sailed northwards, westwards and eastwards to set up monasteries and centres of learning in Cornwall, the Hebrides, the Orkneys, the Shetlands and somewhat later in the Faroe Islands and in Iceland. The purpose of these wanderings does not seem to have been primarily missionary in intent. It seems rather that the monks set off on their wanderings in order to undertake a self-imposed exile, either to gain a greater experience of the presence of God—as hermits have sought throughout the ages—or else as a form of penance for some action that they regretted.

Colm Cille, who sailed from Derry in 563 towards Scotland, where he founded the important monastic settlement of Iona, was motivated by a need to make reparation for his involvement in the battle of Cúil Dreimhe. His currach voyage was re-enacted using a specially built tarred currach in 1963, the 1400th anniversary of Colm Cille's journey to Iona.[5] In 1997, a currach made from hazel ribs and willow weavers was made at Mayo Abbey, Co. Mayo, by a group directed by Peter Faulkner, a coracle-maker from Shropshire, as part of a joint project by the Kilmartin House Trust in Scotland and Mayo Abbey to mark the anniversary of St Colm Cille's death in 597 **(Pl. 4.5)**. Once the body of the boat was made, young ash trees with the perfect form to match pre-determined measurements were shaped with an adze to form a gunwale. Pegs to accommodate oars were made of oak, a young larch tree formed the mast and Douglas Fir was used to form the seats. Hides from eight cows were cured in salts and kept cool and waterlogged until they were measured up against the completed framework and trimmed and sewn together to form the cover (see Appendix 2).

Long strips of hide were made from the off-cuts in order to lash elements of the frame together and to lash the multiple hide cover onto the frame. Once these hides dried, the boat's skin was as tight as a drum. The completed currach sailed from Ballycastle, Co. Antrim, to Erinan, near Kilmartin, Argyll, and onwards from there to Iona, where it was met by the then President of Ireland, Mary Robinson.[6]

The voyage of Brendan the Navigator, which has also recently been re-enacted, was more adventurous than those undertaken by Colm Cille and others, and Brendan seems to have been largely inspired by the *iomraimh* or voyage stories mentioned earlier. It is not possible to prove that Brendan and his crew sailed as far as Newfoundland, as legend has it. Nonetheless, certain aspects of the story described in Brendan's *Navigatio* can be believed even by the sceptical. The arrival of the currach at the Island of Sheep is generally accepted as signifying a landing at the Faroe Islands, since the Faroese name 'Foroyar' means sheep islands. The Island of Smiths, with its inhabitants throwing glowing lumps of slag, is thought to refer to Iceland, where volcanic activity regularly occurred, and the Pillar or Crystal refers to an iceberg.

The *Navigatio* inspired the explorer Tim Severin to try to recreate the legendary voyage and to prove that it was possible for Brendan to have discovered the American continent. After careful research of the *Navigatio* manuscripts, a historically accurate model of the boat described there was made. The currach is described as being ribbed with pliant wood, so it seems that the framework was made from slats of ash rather than from hazel rods. The hides were tanned with oak bark and, having been sewn together with leather cords, the joints were sealed with holly resin, and the entire outer surface of the hide was smeared with fat. The framework for the boat used in Tim Severin's Brendan Voyage was constructed in Crosshaven Boat Yard, Co. Cork, and harness-maker John O'Connell directed the stitching of the 40 hides that covered the boat's framework. Tim Severin and his crew set off from Kerry in May 1976 to sail to the American continent, and the tale of their successful voyage is recounted in Severin's *The Brendan Voyage*.[7]

Pl. 4.6—Donegal Natives. This photo from the Lawrence Collection was taken towards the end of the nineteenth century. Wicker ribs and weavers and currach paddles are all visible. The creels are tall back creels and most have sugán *carrying 'straps'. Photo courtesy of N.L.I. Royal 1409.*

Despite the use of riven timber for the ribs of the Brendan boat, most accounts describe the currachs of that time as having a wicker framework. It seems likely that most of the currachs that were used extensively along the Irish coast, until the gradual adoption of the planked timber boats introduced by the Vikings, used willow or hazel extensively in the framework, though many probably had wooden gunwales. Wicker currachs continued to be used, even after planked boats became well known. An illustration in Samuel Pepys's account of Ireland written in 1670 talks about 'a portable vessel of wicker normally used by the wild Irish', and the account of the retreat of O'Sullivan Beare in 1602 contains a detailed reference to the building of two such boats. O'Sullivan Beare and his party were being pursued by the troops of the Earl of Thomond and were surrounded by the troops on one side and by the river Shannon on the other. Stout osiers were hastily harvested and stuck into the

Pl. 4.7—Detail of Bunbeg paddling currach. Photo courtesy of NMI.

ground and a framework was woven to which stout wooden gunwales were lashed (the normal considerations of allowing the weaving material to season for a few weeks did not apply in this emergency). Twelve horses were killed and their hides were used to cover the currachs, and the party duly escaped across the Shannon.

The sea-going currachs in use along the west coast would almost certainly have been made with wicker ribs — hazel for choice — and hide cover until the middle of the nineteenth century. This hide cover was either seal skin or horse- or cow-hide, and it seems from the references available that the hides were untanned. An account of a funeral procession in the Rosses in County Donegal in the 1750s refers to 60 to 80 currachs covered with seal skin.[8] Currachs covered with horse-hide were in use in Rathlin Island in 1760 and in Erris in County Mayo around 1830. On the Aran Islands in 1853, C.H. Hartshorne saw wicker currachs being covered with cow-hide.[9] Hornell points out that these currachs were much smaller than those we see today:

> In the chaotic centuries that followed the age of the Saints when the flickering light of the old learning came nigh to extinction, curragh navigation suffered eclipse. In size if not in constructional features these craft appear to have degenerated.[10]

He goes on to quote Hartshorne as saying that in 1853 the Aran currach was only about 8ft (2.45m) long with one square end and one pointed end, and was capable of carrying three people. Despite this small size, they were still very manageable on a rough sea. This degeneration mentioned by Hornell might also explain why many of the hide currachs along the west coast seem to have been paddle currachs rather than rowing currachs, which only seem to have fully developed with the introduction of timber and lath construction. But as Estyn Evans notes about the modern currach: 'The method of pivoting the oar on a single tholepin, originally perhaps a strong projecting rib of the curragh frame, rather than in a row lock, suggests that the rowing curragh has native forerunners.'[11] It would be very easy to allow a strong rod to project out of the mouthwale for use as an oarpin, and it is likely that the sea-going currachs mentioned earlier must have had some such feature.

From the middle of the nineteenth century, the hide cover was gradually replaced by tarred canvas or calico, and the hazel framework gave way to wooden laths, which were steamed to facilitate bending, although as mentioned earlier the use of hazel ribs persists in the Sheephaven currach. A close look at **Pl. 4.6** shows that even at the end of the nineteenth century currachs with wicker ribs *and* weavers were still in use. This photograph was taken in Gaothdóir in north-west Donegal and the currach in this picture is a paddling currach of a type more suited for use in sheltered bays than on open sea. This pattern is often referred to as a Bunbeg currach and **Pl. 4.7** gives us a closer look at the wicker framework.

In the Bunbeg currach the wooden gunwale frame was assembled and turned upside-down. Holes were made in it with the help of a red-hot iron, a method often used where no bit and brace or auger was available. The hazel ribs were inserted into these holes and a skirting band of either hazel or willow was woven about 6" or 7" (15–17.5cm) above the gunwale. The skirting band was about 7" (17.5cm) deep. Much of this detail can be observed in **Pl. 4.7**. This method of construction was also described by Lord George Hill around 1840.[12] Once the skirting was put on, the ribs were bent over and bound together in a similar manner to the Boyne currach.

Pl. 4.8—Small pegs in the ground showing position of uprights.

TECHNIQUE

The Boyne currach

The framework of the Boyne currach is made from hazel, which was usually cut immediately after leaf-fall around early December and allowed to season for about a month. You will need 32 clean straight rods about 10ft (300cm) long and about 1" (2.5cm) in diameter for the uprights. A further 60 hazel rods about ¾" (1.8cm) in diameter are needed for the weaving. Ideally, this hazel should be harvested where hazel coppice forms the understorey of woodland and the hazel rods are forced to grow upright towards the light. However, it should be possible to find suitable rods even in an unmanaged hazel wood, as new shoots usually spring up around the base of the old trees. You will also need a handful of 9ft (2.7m) osiers for tying the seat of the coracle and for making the twisted willow ties upon which the net can rest.

Dimensions for the Boyne currach described are 6ft (183cm) by 4ft (122cm). With two pegs and a piece of string, make a compass of the type a gardener might use for marking out a flowerbed. If the string including the pegs measures 2ft (61cm), this will give a semi-circle of 4ft (122cm) diameter. Another semi-circle is marked out 2ft (61cm) away from the first, and both semi-circles are then joined to form an oval shape of 6 ft x 4ft (183cm x 122cm). Thirty uprights are now stuck into the ground pointing slightly outwards. I start with the rod at the head of the oval and ensure that the seven rods that run from head to toe of the currach are in line with each other.

Pl. 4.9—Weaving the mouthwale on the inside of the ellipse. This seems to have been the method used by currach-maker Michael O'Brien, though I advise putting it on from the outside as it is easier that way.

Similarly, the eight rods that go from one side of the currach to the other should be opposite each other in order to facilitate tying them together later. Where the first of these uprights that form the side is put in (the fourth rod down from the head), a second upright is stuck in beside it to give a double upright. **Pl. 4.8** shows small pegs in the ground giving the layout of the currach; these pegs are removed in turn and replaced by an upright.

Pl. 4.10— Mouthwale completed.

When all the uprights have been inserted, a mouthwale (see Chapter 2, **Figs 2.3–2.6**) is put on using the best 30 of the lighter (¾"/18mm diameter) hazel rods. I recently had an opportunity to see a series of photos of Michael O'Brien making a Boyne currach and I noticed he was putting on the mouthwale from the inside of the ellipse. This method is shown in **Pl. 4.9** and it can be seen that the mouthwale looks exactly the same as if it had been put on from the outside in the normal manner. I cannot see any advantage to doing it this way other than, perhaps, making it easier to allow the uprights to slope outwards. I would advise putting the mouthwale on from the outside as one would for a creel. Once the mouthwale has been completed **(Pl. 4.10)**, the rods are simply randed to a finish. If the rods are stout you can use your foot to assist the work, as shown in **Pl. 4.11**.

Pl. 4.11—Using the foot to assist the weaving.

Here is Michael O'Brien's description of what happens next: 'When I have the rim plaited [i.e., the mouthwale], I commence laying eight of the side rods across and goes opposite an' puts the other eight with the points of them at the butts of the one I done first.'[13] I thought this referred to the

Pl. 4.12—Bending over the uprights from either side.

weaving rods, and concluded that it was a form of English or coil randing that was being described, but I now believe that what he is describing here is the uprights being bent to the opposite side. Nevertheless, the height gained by the first row of weavers is not sufficient, so some additional hazel weavers must be used. These appear to have been randed in and out in a fairly haphazard fashion, but the height at the bow-end which contains the extra uprights should be somewhat higher than at the other end. While structurally it would seem to make sense to secure the randing with a row of pairing, this does not seem to have been a consideration, and from Michael O'Brien's description it seems to have been the rods on the floor or bottom of the currach that were most subject to wear.

Once a height of about 5" (12.5cm) has been reached, the eight uprights on either side are bent over and stuck into the ground on the far side to secure them, as shown in **Pl. 4.12**. The seven rods at either end are similarly dealt with, and the two extra rods at either

Pl. 4.13—The currach weighed down with stones.

Pl. 4.14—Tying the ribs with twine.

side of the bow-end also run along the length of the currach, but because they haven't got any rods on the other end to match them, they are single ribs rather than the double ribs used elsewhere. Remember also when bending the seven rods at the bow-end (the end with the extra uprights) to bend them a little higher up than at the stern end, around 20" (51cm) high at the bow and 18" (45.5cm) high at the stern. Once all of the uprights have been secured, put some boards on top — I used a small wooden gate for this — and weigh it down with stones as shown in **Pl. 4.13**. The purpose of this weighing down is to make the floor of the currach as even as possible, so the weight should be distributed evenly to achieve this.

This weight is left on for three days and when removed the uprights are bound together with marling twine at each intersection, using a diamond-shape tie, repeated twice or three times as shown in **Pl. 4.14**. Once tied, the boards and stones are put

Pl. 4.15—Loosening ground around the currach with a spade before pulling it out of the ground.

Pl. 4.16—The currach pulled from the ground.

Pl. 4.17—Clive Ó Gibne holding a Boyne currach with the hide cover on the ground beside him. Photo courtesy of David Shaw-Smith.

on for a further five to seven days and the currach is levered out of the ground, having first been loosened by digging around it with a spade (**Pls 4.15 and 4.16**).

The coracle framework is then trimmed off, though the uprights should not be trimmed flush with the mouthwale, to allow for the possibility of adjusting them further. The hide is soaked for two days in water to make it sufficiently soft to be stretched on over the frame of the currach and is sewn onto the gunwale with strong twine. The hide used for the Boyne currach seems to have been commercially tanned (i.e., oak bark tanned) and was obtained from a local tannery in Drogheda, though it is probable that in former times untanned hides similar to those used in the sea–going currachs were used. It should also be noted that, although the framework may have lasted only three or four years, the same hide cover could be re-used a number of times.

Once the hide has been sewn to the gunwale, long osiers are twisted in the same manner as for making a twisted rod handle, and a twisted cord of willow is put on from side to side towards the back of the currach, roughly where the second-last cross-ribs are. More twisted willow is secured to the back of the currach, and it is twisted around the twisted willow crosspiece to form a support for the nets. This can be seen in **Pl. 4.1**. Next, a seat board of either deal or larch is put on, having first had holes bored in it to accommodate the twisted willow ties by which it is secured; again the detail of this can be seen in **Pl. 4.1**. The size of the board should be about 10" x 1" (25cm x 2.5cm) and of a length to fit comfortably inside the currach.

The maker then sits on the seat and with a wooden mallet hammers down any uprights whose cross members are not connecting well with the hide cover. Any ends now projecting are cut off almost flush with the mouthwale and an extra gunwale is provided by tying straight hazel wands onto the framework to give more rigidity and to prevent the mouthwale from slipping up. Usually two long, straight hazel rods will suffice for this purpose, but more can be used if necessary. The joins overlap in a manner similar to the making of a hoop for a frame basket, and this protective rim is sewn not just to the framework of the currach but also with some stitches to the hide cover. Although this hoop is exposed at the front of the currach, it is covered with canvas or hide from the middle to the rear in order to prevent the net from snarling or catching on it when in use.

5

Fishing Baskets

WITH the notable exception of the quarter cran herring basket, most of the baskets used by fishermen were made not by specialist basketmakers but by the fishermen themselves. The quarter-cran **(Pl. 5.1)** was a fitched basket of stripped willow and kubu cane and had to be made to exact dimensions, because it was an approved government measure. It was always made by professional basketmakers, most notably the Shanahans of Carrick-on-Suir in Ireland, but some were also imported from Scotland and England where large numbers of these crans were used. Most of the imported crans seem to have come from Fraserburgh, one of the largest herring ports in Scotland until the early 1970s.[1] These imported crans were probably made in Yarmouth, England, and sent from there to Scotland before being bought by the firm of Barlows, Dunmore East, Co. Waterford. Herring cran making was specialised, and in Britain was mainly centred around Yarmouth. The fact that

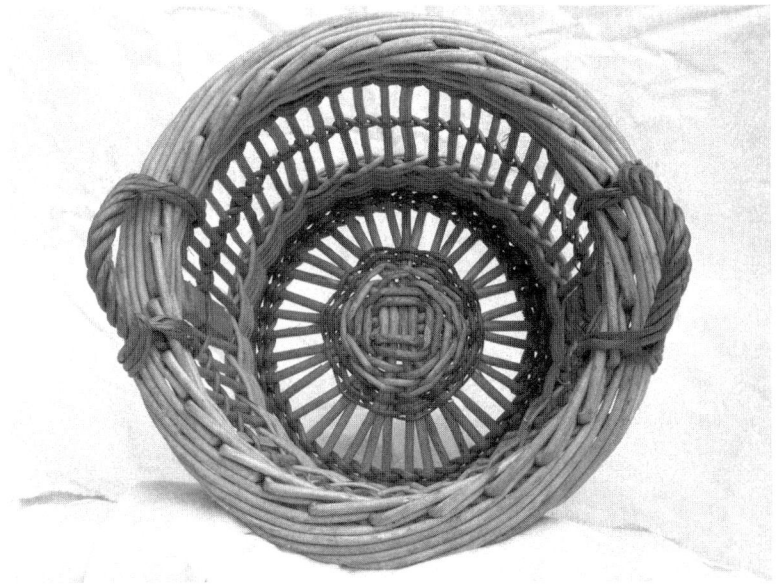

Pl. 5.1—Quarter-cran herring basket, made by Colin Manthorpe, showing detail of base. These baskets were made in vast quantities for the herring industry, where they were used as an official measure.

the basket had to conform to so many separate measurements, not only diameter top and bottom, but also internal diagonal top to bottom, measured in six places, height of bottom dome, etc., meant that it took a lot of practice to perfect.[2] The cane that was used for part of the waling and all of the fitching in these baskets came from the Far East and was once very cheap, because it was used to line the holds of ships and was easy to obtain in the eastern ports of England. It is likely that the Shanahans always had to import this cane from a specialist cane importer in Britain. The quarter cran was a basket of the fishing industry and its use was associated with the marketing of the large quantities of fish landed by the commercial fishing fleets. The catch was usually winched off the trawler in quarter crans so that it was measured for sale in the process of unloading. The baskets might only last a few weeks in constant use, because the repeated wettings caused the basket to swell, making it inaccurate as a measure.

The other fishing baskets described in this chapter were used by small-scale, coastal-dwelling fishermen who used small boats such as currachs and did not go as far out to sea as the commercial fleet. The lobster fishing was done quite close to the shore.

Longline fishermen fished for cod, ling and other white fish using lines that had to be laboriously baited by hand. Each basket held sufficient line for about 180 to 200 hooks. The baiting of the hooks was a task that often fell to women working alone or as helpers **(Pl. 5.2)**. Longline fishermen were noted for their strength and resilience. An account of the longline fishermen of Dunservick in north Antrim by Brian Haslett describes how, having come

Pl. 5.2—Baiting a ribh or long-line basket on the Aran Islands. This laborious task often fell to the women. The man on the right is probably a visitor to the island. Photo., H. Becker, courtesy of NMI.

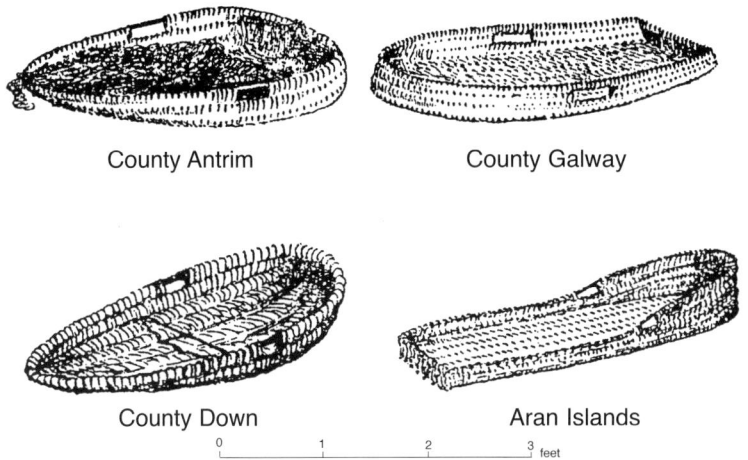

County Antrim

County Galway

County Down

Aran Islands

0   1   2   3 feet

Fig. 5.1—Longline fishing baskets. (Evans 1957)

ashore at the small harbour, they had to carry their catch in loads of more than 1cwt (50kg) at a time up a steep slope to the sheds beside their homes.[3] They carried the fish in double-staked back creels, which they also usually made themselves. It was, however, the toil at sea that made their lives especially tough, and the risks associated with longline fishing demanded fearlessness from those who practised it.

Patterns of longline fishing baskets vary, with a marked difference between the longline baskets of Antrim and Down on the one hand and those of Galway and Clare on the other **(Fig. 5.1)**. The baskets of Down and Antrim are frame baskets made so that one end of the basket is deep and the other shallow, this shape being ideal for arranging the line and hooks separately and so preventing the hooks tangling with the line when it was being played out. Variations exist between the pattern in Down and Antrim, with the Antrim longline baskets being wider and more generously curved at the ribs than the ones from County Down. Both the Down and Antrim patterns are similar to the Scottish sculls (*sguil*), which were used for the same purpose along the west coast of Scotland and the Hebrides. Although the Down longline basket seems to have been extinct for some years, the Antrim longline baskets were being made until around 1990 by Sammy Gault, a fisherman and basketmaker from Dunservick, who also made the distinctive crab pots of the area (described later in this chapter). Because there was a strong tradition of blacksmithing in the area, the hoops for the Antrim longline baskets were often made of iron, thus ensuring that the hoop would last for more than the lifetime of one basket. Sometimes two hazel rods were used for the hoop, with the joins on the long sides of the basket. They were usually made in two sizes, one being about 30" (76cm) long and the other being 36" (91cm) long, and had either nine or seven ribs, depending on the area **(Pl. 5.3)**. If the basket was to be used with heavy line (for catching large fish), then the ribs on either side of the central rib were allowed to curve out more to give a bulge that would enlarge the deep end of the basket, which held the line. Longline baskets similar to the Antrim type were used in County Donegal. **Pl. 7.1** shows a cottage exterior at Rosapeena, County Donegal, with a longline basket of this type and, although the photographer may have gathered the items to compose the shot, it seems safe to assume that the baskets belonged to the local area.

The longline baskets of Aran and the west Clare coast were shallow, flat baskets with a raised open section at one end **(Pls 5.2 and 5.4)**. It was explained to me in the Aran Islands, where this basket was known as a *ribh*, that this shape allowed the *ribh* to be easily stored in the front of the currach. Although some details on making the *ribh* are included in the technique section of this chapter, it should be noted here that there were two basic types, one with a woven back and one where a low board served as the back. I believe the *ribh* with the woven back is the older pattern; the wooden back was probably adopted to save the labour of weaving the back. For the wooden-backed *ribh*, holes were simply bored in the wood and the rods that formed the ribs were stuck into these. The rods at the outer edges needed to be long enough to go past the far end, where they joined with the rods from the other side to form the end hoops of the *ribh*. The longline baskets of the north-

Pl. 5.3—Antrim longline basket. Photo courtesy of Alison Fitzgerald.

west coast of Clare were the same as these wooden-backed *ribhs*, and in the examples that I have seen the outer rods that formed the hoops were often of hazel, reflecting the fact that hazel was readily available in the limestone crags of Aran and the Burren. The outer rods of the *ribh* with the woven back were always of willow, because the rods had to be flexible enough to form a right angle where the back and the sides met. The inner ribs in both types of *ribh* were of willow, because the ends of these rods were twisted to join the projecting hoops at the front of the *ribh*. Usually the end of the *ribh* had an open section, but in some the end is

almost closed **(Pl. 5.4 and Fig. 5.1)**. The longline basket from County Galway in **Fig. 5.1** was similar to the woven-backed *ribh* except that the hoops were not allowed to project upwards as in the woven-backed *ribh*.

Further south, in west Kerry, the longline basket was known as a spillet basket **(Pl. 5.5)**, and it was somewhat similar in shape to the horseshoe-shaped *sciathóg* of west Cork. The outer rim or hoop was made of a number of rods and the spillet basket had a deep section for holding the line, a feature that was also present in the longline baskets of Ulster. It is probable that other types of baskets were used in other areas for longline fishing and there may well have been regional styles of which I am not aware. One photograph I have seen—not now available—shows an oval basket like the oval potato *sciath* described in Chapter 3.[4] This may have been made specifically

Pl. 5.4—Two ribhs/Aran longline baskets. The one on the left has a woven end or back, and is about 32" (81cm) long. The ribh on the right has a wooden back or end and is about 45" (115cm) long. This ribh was made by Vincent McCarron, Bungowla, Aran Islands. Photo courtesy of David Shaw-Smith.

Pl. 5.5—Spillet basket, An Clochán, Castlegregory, Co. Kerry. Photo by C. Ó Danachair in 1947. Courtesy of DIF, UCD.

for longline fishing but I think it is more likely that it was a potato or all-purpose basket being put to this use.

Although lobster pots of hazel, willow or heather have now been replaced everywhere by pots made with nets, such pots were widely used up to the 1950s and 1960s and their use continued in some areas until around 1980. Most fishermen worked about twenty pots, making pots for each season as needed. There was a wide variation in the styles of lobster pots used along the coast. On the Cork and Kerry coast, bell-shaped pots similar to those used in Cornwall and in Brittany were the norm **(Pl. 5.6)**. These pots are elaborate compared to the pots used elsewhere on the west coast. They represent the only example of fitching that I have seen in Irish country baskets. It is possible that these particular pots were made by specialists rather than the lobster fishermen themselves, but I think it is likely that this style of pot and the technique for making it may have been introduced to the south and south-west by fishermen from the south-west of England or Brittany. It seems, according to Tomás Ó Crohan's autobiography, *The Islandman,*[5] that lobster fishing was only introduced to the Blasket Islands from the early 1900s onwards, and if this is true of the rest of the south-west coast, then perhaps this might account for the more elaborate style of pot used in this area.

Further up the west coast along the Clare, Galway and Mayo coasts, lobster pots shaped somewhat like spheres such as those in **Pl. 5.7** predominated. Whereas the lobster pots of Cork and Kerry had to be started on a wooden jig, the west coast lobster pots were started by simply sticking the uprights into the ground. The neck of the pot

Pl. 5.6—Lobster pots at Dún Chaoin, Co. Kerry. Photo by C. Ó Danachair. Courtesy of DIF, UCD.

(*barrach*) was woven, with the maker circling around the uprights (*sáitheáin*). Once the neck was formed, extra uprights were added and all were pulled outwards to form the flat upper part of the pot (*baithis*). While the usual practice was to stick the tips of the uprights into the

ground to form the *baithis*, I have also heard of some makers placing the iron rim of a large cartwheel on the uprights to help keep this section flat. Some makers pulled the neck of the pot from the ground before the *baithis* or flat upper section was fully formed, and held the pot between their knees while weaving to get a curve on the top of the pot. More usually, the *baithis* was woven with the uprights in the ground, and when the neck was levered from the ground the uprights were tied to enable the sides to be formed. The weaving on the sides was pairing or the variant with two sets of double rods, which is used also in finishing the donkey creel. These west coast willow pots were finished in a similar manner to the creel, whereas the pots of Cork and Kerry were finished by slewing some light rods around the base **(Pl. 5.8)**. One photograph of a bell-shaped lobster

Pl. 5.7—Two west coast lobster pots; the larger one is based on a pot by Festy Mortimer from Rosroe near Leenane in north Connemara, the smaller pot was made by Pakie O'Toole from Innisturk Island, Co. Mayo.

Pl. 5.8—Detail of lobster pot bases; the pots at the bottom are Connemara pots in hazel and willow; and the pot at the top is a Kerry/Cork pot.

pot from Cloghane in County Kerry seems to have a base like a creel or west coast lobster pot. Since I believe the design of these bell-shaped pots may have been introduced from Cornwall or Brittany, this would appear to be an example of people adapting a European design to their own needs.[6]

While many of the west coast pots had whole willow uprights, split willow uprights were also common. It seems that whole rods were used for the uprights, but if some rods were too thick to use whole, then they were split in two and used in that form. Pots with some whole uprights and some split uprights were commonplace and this serves as a reminder that often the choice of material available to lobster pot makers was limited. One of the reasons for this was that the common osier (*Salix viminalis*), the sally rod of the donkey creel, was considered too soft to be used for lobster pots. Instead, the lobster pots were made from what was locally called 'Black Sally' (*saileánach*), a hybrid form of *Salix caprea*, which most basketmakers would consider too brittle for using in ordinary basketmaking. This willow was woodier with much less pith than the common osier and would, therefore, be slower to rot in the sea water. It did not grow as large as the common osier, however, so large one-year-old rods were scarce, hence the need to split two-year-old rods for the uprights on occasion.

Pl. 5.9—Hazel lobster pot. This style was used in south Connemara and at one time also on the Aran Islands.

Hazel was also used for lobster pots, particularly on the Aran Islands and on the south Connemara coast. It may also have been used on the north Clare coast, where hazel from the Burren would have been easy to obtain. These hazel pots were almost cylindrical in shape and were much more closely woven than the willow pots already described (**Pl. 5.9**). These pots usually only had fourteen or sixteen uprights, so the space between them was considerably wider than that in the willow pots. The body was paired with hazel, using thin rods for the neck and *baithis* (top) but thicker rods for the side. These closely woven pots were also used to catch a speckled fish (*barrach*) known as a 'gunner' in

Connemara and Donegal and as a rock-fish in Aran (probably wrasse). This use extended the season during which the pots could be used. Normal lobster fishing started in late March and ended around mid-August, but rock-fish or 'gunners' could be fished from early spring to late autumn. When the pots were used for this purpose a boat was unnecessary, as the pots, usually baited with crab meat, were left in likely pools while the tide was out.[7] The base was finished, like the west coast willow pots, in a manner similar to a creel **(Pl. 5.8)**. These hazel pots were noticeably stronger than willow pots. Hazel is stronger and more rigid than willow anyway, but the fact that the hazel pots were closely woven increased their strength further. Such pots were expected to last longer than the willow ones and were particularly suitable in areas where the sea was liable to be rough.

Pl. 5.10—Detail of the finish of a heather lobster pot from north Mayo. A few twigs of heather were used to fill the remainder of the base. Photo courtesy of DIF, UCD.

In west Mayo, heather was widely used for making pots. The windswept Mullet Peninsula in north-west Mayo was not the most favourable location for growing willow, so it is easy to assume that heather was used as a substitute for willow rods. However, further south in Achill, where willow rods were available, pots were also made from heather up to the 1950s at least. Heather had certain advantages over willow, most notably its durability. Two or three seasons at least could be expected from heather pots as against an average of one or two seasons from rod pots. Willow pots also had a distinctive willow aroma, so it was customary to soak them for a week or more in the sea before first use in order to get rid of the smell, which, it was felt, might deter the lobster from entering the pot. I heard one man who used these pots claiming that the heather resembled seaweed in the water and that the lobsters were therefore not suspicious of them.[8] The heather for these pots could be pulled or cut during late summer or autumn and the pots made from it almost immediately, with only a minimal need to season the heather. Although I had been informed that the heather used for these pots was the Mediterranean heather (*Erica mediterranea*), a tall, upright-growing heather locally prevalent around Mallaranny and other areas of west Mayo, I am no longer sure that this was the case. It is possible that the Mediterranean heather was used for the uprights (*sáitheáin*) in some cases, but because it is not nearly as pliable as the common heather (*Calluna vulgaris*), it is unlikely to have been used for weaving. Neither was it necessary for the uprights to be long enough to complete the pot, since in most of the heather pots in the National Museum collection the original uprights were supplemented by having others placed beside them at some point on the side of the pot.

There seem to have been two distinct ways of finishing heather pots. In one, the uprights were continued up the pot until the opening was quite narrow and then crossed across each other and shoved in beside uprights coming up from the opposite side **(Pl. 5.10)**. In all cases where this finish is used, the uprights have to be added to, since the original ones, even if they were long enough, were not strong enough at the end for that finish. The other finish was more like that commonly used on the rod pots, where some of the heather uprights formed a warp over and under which the remaining uprights were woven, so additions to the original uprights were not necessarily needed. This is the type of finish being put on the pot in **Pl. 5.11** by Michael O'Malley, originally from Clare Island but living then at Murrisk near Westport. Perhaps the flatter-bottomed heather pots were typical of the southern part of the Mayo coast, with the rounded bottom being favoured further north. The method of making the heather pots was similar to the making of the west coast willow pots but, whereas the willow uprights were usually stuck into the ground, it was more usual to cut a sod from the ground to start the heather pot. Notes accompanying a heather lobster pot from Doogort in Achill in the National Museum draw attention to three slight depressions on the *baithis* or top of the pot. The function of these depressions (*cosáin iallamuigh*) may have been to make it easier for the lobster to crawl into the pot.[9]

Bait for all of these woven pots was suspended mid-way between the

Pl. 5.11—Michael O'Malley, originally from Clare Island, making a heather lobster pot at Murrisk, Co. Mayo. Photo courtesy of NMI.

Pl. 5.12—Killiney Strands, *a painting by Richard Thomas Moynan, 1894. Reproduced courtesy of AIB Art Collection.*

neck and the side wall of the pot and about halfway down the length of the funnel, or about 4" (10cm) down from the *baithis* or top of the pot. For this reason it was necessary for the top to be fairly closely woven so that there was no possibility of the lobster reaching the bait through the top of the pot. In Connemara the bait was suspended using a little willow rod, but the notes mentioned earlier accompanying the heather pot say that two baits were used and that these were tied in position with a root of bent grass.

There seems to be no record of the use of wicker lobster pots along the east coast or on the north-west coast. Perhaps they were once used in these areas and were replaced by more modern styles of pots, but if the tradition of lobster-pot fishing in these areas is more recent than 1900, then alternatives to wicker pots were already available. The cylindrical pots in the painting of Killiney, County Dublin, in 1894 **(Pl. 5.12)** are often called French pots by lobster fishermen and were used for crayfish. While on the evidence of this painting they were in use on the east coast in the 1890s, a

Pl. 5.13—Heather lobster pots and a cylindrical 'French Pot' at Fallmore, Belmullet, Co. Mayo, in 1935. Photo by A. Campbell. Courtesy of DIF, UCD.*

photograph taken near Belmullet, Co. Mayo, more than forty years later **(Pl. 5.13)** suggests that there the heather lobster pot was still widely used, with the French pot only beginning to gain acceptance.

The other pots in **Pl. 5.12** seem to be hazel whelk pots of a type similar to those that were still in use at Dunservick, Co. Antrim, until the 1970s, but extinct elsewhere. Their inclusion in the painting of Killiney suggests that these pots must have been used along the east coast at the turn of the twentieth century. They were still in use in the south Dublin and Wicklow area around 1947. A countrywide survey of crafts-people conducted during the 1940s by Chrissie O'Gorman describes whelk pots and potato baskets as being the main output of John Marah, a basketmaker from Rathnew, Co. Wicklow.[10] Crab pots are not mentioned for the Wicklow area, but in Dunservick, Co. Antrim, both crab pots and whelk pots were made. The crab pots **(Pl. 5.14)** were similar in shape to the Wicklow whelk pots. However, the Antrim whelk pots, which were known as 'buckie creels' (after the local name for whelk, buckie) were fitted with a little wooden door so that the 'buckies' could be removed by putting one's hand in the opening. Buckie creels were usually more gently sloped than the crab pots and the neck was narrower at 7" (18cm) rather than 8" (20cm) wide as was the case with the neck of the crab pot. All these pots were made by putting stout two- or three-year-old hazel uprights into a wooden jig as shown in **Fig. 5.4**. The jig used in Dunservick was quite elaborate, having an iron or rod hoop at the bottom to help give an accurate slope to the side, but the jig or template used by John Marah in Wicklow was simpler; the base of it was simply a stake

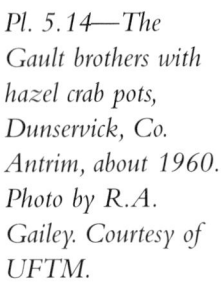

Pl. 5.14—The Gault brothers with hazel crab pots, Dunservick, Co. Antrim, about 1960. Photo by R.A. Gailey. Courtesy of UFTM.

Pl. 5.15—
Fisherman's jetty,
Ballycastle, Co.
Antrim. The baskets
in the picture are
presumably 'buckie
creels' for catching
whelks, because of the
wooden opening. The
one beside the dog
may have been made
by a man called
McCaffrey who,
according to Sammy
Gault, made such
creels for sale in this
area many years ago.
The slope is much
steeper than in the
creels made by
Sammy at
Dunservick less than
ten miles away. The
currach in the
foreground is very
similar to the
Sheephaven currach
of Donegal described
in Chapter 4. The
hazel ribs can be
clearly seen. The
other boats in the
picture are
drontheims, the
typical boat of this
area, and it is hard to
account for the
presence of the
Donegal currach at
Ballycastle. Photo
from the Welch
Collection. Courtesy
of the Ulster
Museum.

driven into the ground. The sides were paired using somewhat thinner hazel, though the siding of the buckie creels was willow. The base was finished by forming a warp of four pairs of rods, over and under which the other rods could be woven in the manner of a creel. More detailed instructions for making these pots are given in the technique section at the end of this chapter.

Presumably the pots shown in **Pl. 5.15**, which shows a fisherman's jetty in Ballycastle, Co. Antrim, are also buckie creels, because they have the characteristic wooden doors. Sammy Gault believes these buckie creels were made by a man called McCaffrey, who was not a fisherman but made creels and other baskets for a living. A close look at the basket beside the dog shows that the opening was formed while the basket was being made rather than having the notch cut out later, and this was apparently a feature of McCaffrey's buckie creels. Much of the hazel for the Dunservick and Ballycastle pots was cut at a large estate near Ballycastle, and Sammy remembers each maker paying the owner two shillings (ten new pence) whenever they went to cut hazel there.[11] John Marah was getting seven shillings and six pence for his pots in 1947.

We have already seen in Chapter 1 that weirs were made of hazel to catch eels, but wicker eel traps were also made. These were laid usually in groups of five or six on the bed of tidal rivers and lifted twice a day for inspection. The uprights that formed the funnel or mouth of the trap were sharply pointed to discourage the eels from escaping. The trap in **Fig. 5.2** is from the Suir area and was made by the Shanahan brothers of Carrick-on-Suir (who were mentioned earlier in this chapter in relation to the herring cran and about whom more information is given in Chapter 8). This trap has a hinged wicker lid for emptying the eels. It was usually baited with sprats. Perhaps there were other types of eel traps in other parts of the country but if so they now seem to have been forgotten.

Weirs were also used for catching salmon, and it is possible that wicker salmon traps were also used for catching salmon in estuaries and tidal rivers. Large salmon traps called putchers, made of hazel uprights and willow weavers, were used in coastal areas of south Wales and the west of England until the latter half of the twentieth century, and recent surveys of the Shannon Estuary have produced strong evidence for medieval fish traps, in particular a large putcher basket, 4.2m in length dating to the 13th century.[12]

Baskets were also made for poaching fish. One such basket was a *starragán*, a poaching basket which could also be used as a back basket and which was eventually deemed illegal to have in one's possession.[13] Most of these poaching baskets were funnel shaped and were made by sticking the uprights into the ground in the manner of a creel.

TECHNIQUE

Ribh: **Aran longline basket**

Select six long rods up to 9ft (2.7m) long and about ¾" (18mm) thick. Make a long slype 6" (15cm) on the back of one rod and on the belly of another, and join them using either a thin rod or skein or alternatively using tape as described in the technique section for the *sciathóg* (see Chapter 3). Repeat this process until you have three sets of joined rods. Lay these on a flat surface, ensuring that the joins are not exactly across from each other, and start pack randing as for a narrow rectangular base, the total width of which would be 3" (9cm). The total length of what will be the shallow end of the *ribh* should be about 19" (48cm). It is easiest to weave 9" (23cm) away from the centre towards one end and then return to the centre and weave towards the other end.

Once this shallow end has been woven, kink these uprights (using the technique shown in **Fig. 3.11)**. This will give a series of three U-shaped hoops extending from the shallow end. The top hoop should extend outwards about 34" (86cm) with an upward tilt, the next about 31" (79cm) and the lowest about 29" (74cm). Each set of hoop rods is joined at the bow end with a temporary rod tie or tape, so that the hoop at the bow end is in each case formed by two rods. The remainder (tip end) of each of the rods that form the hoops are allowed to return towards the back of the *ribh*. It is important that the two rods that form the top hoop are long enough to return at least halfway back towards the shallow end of the *ribh* to give strength to the grab-style handle. The height at the head or hoop end of the *ribh* is about 9–10" (23–25cm), and it is best to use forked sticks taped to the hoops at the head to prevent the weaving from dragging them closer together, as that would result in the head being shallower than the desired height of 9" (23cm).

Now get six 8ft (2.4m) rods about ½–⅝" (15–18mm) thick, and stick the butts through the back of the *ribh* so that they rest between the bottom and the middle struts of the back. The tips of these rods can extend outwards below the lowest hoop at the head of the *ribh*. Start randing using 6fts (1.8m), joining butts every time. Once the weaving has reached about 3" (8cm), prick randing (shoving the butts into the weaving) should be used. Holes should be left for the handle, starting about 19" (48cm) from the base. The handle holes are about 5" (13cm) long. As the base narrows towards the head, the weaving becomes more difficult. Stop when weaving is about 3" (7.5cm) from the bottom hoop. At this stage take one of the outer ribs and twist it along the remainder of its length as you would for a handle, and weave it towards the other side. When you come with this rod to the outer rib on the other side, drop this twisted rod, which is by now almost spent, and take the corresponding rib, twist it and weave as before. Continue twisting ribs and weaving them coarsely until the base has been filled to the bottom hoop. At least one of the central ribs should remain and this is now twisted and turned around the top hoop, returning back to the bottom hoop and being twisted around itself loosely in the manner of a handle, incorporating the middle hoop in the process. It should be long enough to go up twice and down twice, or if the other central rib remains unused, this can be used instead. The aim is to have a chunky, handle-like tie at the top of the *ribh*.

Variation: wooden-backed rib with closed hoop front or head

The wooden-backed *ribh* in **Pl. 5.4** was made by Vincent McCarron of Innismór and is based on one in the Heritage Centre at Innismór, Aran Islands. It is much longer than the *ribh* already described. This one is 47" (119cm) long and about 12" (30cm) high at the head, which is also more closely woven than in the previous *ribh*. First get a back board 18" (46cm) long, 4" (10cm) wide and ¾–1" (18–25mm) thick. Six evenly spaced holes ⅝–¾" (15mm–18mm) are bored in the lower part of the board, the two outside holes being about 1½" (37mm) from the outer edge. Two further holes are drilled about ¾" (18mm) higher up than the first and a little closer to the edge, and finally two holes are bored about ¾–1" (18–25mm) from the top and about 1" (25mm) in from the edge. The ten ¾" (18mm) ribs for this basket are whittled down to fit into the holes. Weaving is as for the *ribh* already described, prick randing being used as soon as possible. The handle is closer to the back of the *ribh*, the handle hole starting after about 15" (38cm). About 18" (46cm) from the head, extra rods are inserted to give three double hoops at the head; weaving then continues and since only four ribs now remain, it is a little easier to weave the base to the close of the first hoop. All four rib rods are twisted and incorporated into the handle-like tie and the space between the bottom and second hoop pack randed with weaving.

Antrim longline basket

The weaving of this basket **(Pl. 5.3)** is similar to a *sciathóg* or any frame basket, so the description will be brief. The version made by Sammy Gault had nine ribs, each almost ¾" (18mm) thick. These are shaved down at the butt end to facilitate the curve and all the butts are at the deeper end of the basket. The hoop was traditionally made of hazel but in more recent years rod iron was used instead. Hoop size is 33" (84cm) long, 21" (53cm) wide at a point 6" (15cm) from the butt end, and 18" (46cm) wide at a point 6" (15cm) from the other end. Because of the size of hoop it would be better to use two hazel rods with two butts joined at one side and the two thinner ends joined at the other. Even if the joins happen where the handle holes are to be, it doesn't matter as this section of the hoop can be bound separately with a rod. The handle holes start about 12" (30m) from the wider (butt) end. The depth of the basket at the deepest point, which is about 9" (23cm) from the butt end, is 7½" (19cm) and the depth where the handle starts is 6¾" (7cm).

Eel trap

These instructions are based on an eel trap made by the Shanahans of Carrick-on-Suir **(Fig. 5.2)**. Put thirteen sharply pointed rods from ⅜–½" (9–12mm) thick, in a circle into the ground or into a suitably deep block of wood. The width of the circle is about 3" (75cm) where the weaving starts, but the rods stick down a further 4½" (12cm) into the block (or the ground) and they will act as a deterrent to the eel escaping. It is also much easier to make this basket with a block of wood and bored holes (½"/12mm), as the block can be

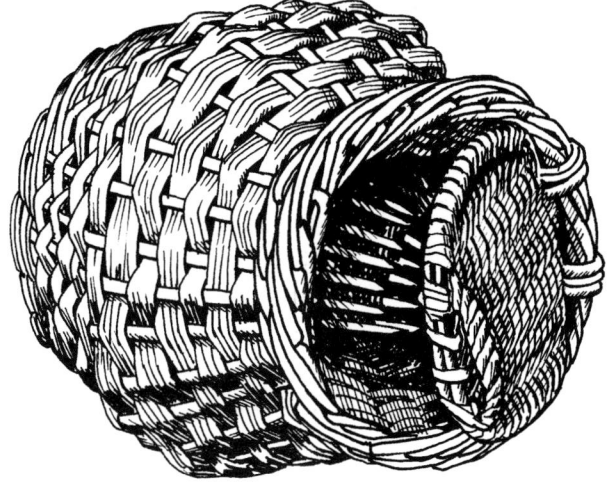

Fig. 5.2 (drawing by Ursula Mattenberger)

moved around, whereas if the ground is used you must do the moving, and since the neck is long and narrow there will be a good deal of circling involved around the neck. If using a block of wood ensure that the holes are bored at a slightly inward angle so that the opening at the slyped butts that project down from the weaving is narrower than where the weaving begins. The funnel or neck is started with pairing using a slender 6ft (1.8m) or 5ft (1.5m) rod folded in half. As you weave you draw the uprights towards you so that the inside of the funnel will widen as you go up. After about four lines of pairing, the weave changes to slewing, using light 4ft (1.2m) rods for a start. The butts of the slewing are left on the outside as you weave, since this will eventually be the inside of the basket.

When the funnel weaving is about 9" (23cm) high, thirteen bi-stakes, similar in thickness to those already used, are inserted and these are opened out using a line or two of pairing before reverting to slewing. Two sets of slewing rods (chasing) will now have to be used as there is an even number of uprights. When the funnel is a little less than 12" (30cm) high and 9" (23.5cm) wide, put on another line of pairing so that the finished dimensions will be as above, and then lever the funnel out of the block (or the ground).

Kink the uprights with a knife and gather them into a 15" (39cm) hoop or use a tie. The siding is started with pairing using one rod folded back on itself, but once a row of pairing has been completed the weave changes to three-rod wale, and three or four rows of this is put on. Select 26 evenly matched randing rods—stout 4fts or cut-off tops from another job would be suitable. The randing rods are chunky but not too long. The randing is French randing, but the second set of randing rods are prick randed (i.e., the butts are pricked in to the right of each upright). The hoop or tie can be removed once the sides have got their shape — a slightly outward angle as can be seen in **Fig. 5.2**. The width of the body of the trap at its widest point, about 8" (20cm) up the side, is about 14–15" (36–38cm). From this point the sides taper inwards gently and a tie (or a narrow hoop) is put on for a while to facilitate this. Once the sides have begun to narrow in, the weave changes to slewing again, using two sets of slewing rods (chasing), because of the even number of uprights.

When the diameter has narrowed to about 10" (255mm), change to pairing. After one row of pairing start pulling the rods sharply towards you, since a fairly sharp outward slope (approx. 30°) is needed to make the collar to accommodate the lid. After about four rows of pairing or whenever a diameter of 11½–12" (29–30cm) has been reached, put on a four-pair, behind two, border. Measure the diameter of the opening after bordering;—it will probably be about 10½–11" (27–28cm)—and make a circular hoop 2.5" (1cm) less than this measurement. Scallom on four rods of light 6ft (1.8m) or heavy 5ft (1.5m) to form the stakes for the lid, and weave with 4ft (1.2m) or similar. When the lid has been almost completed, the stakes are twisted and then turned around the hoop to match the scalloms on the opposite side. The lid is then hinged under the border and a single twisted rod handle is fitted on the other side. The lid should fit tightly, but a pointed stick can be driven in under the handle and the border to keep the lid closed when the basket is being used as a trap.

North Connemara lobster pot

The pot described here is a type I've been making for many years and is based on one I got in the late 1970s from Festy Mortimer, Rossroe, near Leenane, Co. Galway. The pot is usually made from semi-green willow and you will need about 28 uprights, a little less than ¾" (18mm) in diameter. These would usually be found in a bundle of 8fts (2.4m), but the uprights do not have to be that long. You will also need some 5fts (1.5m) for weaving the neck and the start of the flat area on top (*baithis*), and 6fts (1.8m) or light 7fts (2.1m) for the remainder of the weaving.

Find a suitable circular shape about 5½–6" (14–15cm) in diameter and place it on a level grassy site. Slype eight of the uprights and stick them into the ground at regular spacings around the circular shape. Take two rods, either slender 6fts (1.8m) or else 5fts (1.5m), and start pairing with the butts. Once the first round of pairing has been completed bring the pairing *under* the butts of the two rods so that they cannot unravel. Continue pairing, joining butts every time, with joins on the outside (nearest you), since this will be the inside of the neck. The neck should be at least 4" (10cm). Finish by threading the tips out under the pairing.

Slype another eight uprights on the belly and drive them into the neck of the pot so that the slype faces you. Draw a pair of these uprights sharply towards you so that they are almost at a right angle to the neck. Cut 6" (15cm) off the tips and insert each rod separately into the ground to hold the steep angle. If they keep popping up due to stony soil or weak tops, for example, you can simply weigh them down instead. Now draw down the opposite pair in the same way and continue to pull down opposite pairs in this way until all the uprights have been flattened. Select a handful of fine weaving rods and, crouching over the pot, start pairing, opening out the stakes as you go. Keep the first round of pairing close to the neck, ideally less than 1" (2.5cm) out; subsequent rows should also be kept fairly close so that the diameter after three rounds of weaving should not be greater than 10" (255mm). At this point, extra bi-stakes are added and if the weaving is too widely spaced the bi-stakes won't get a firm grip. There is also the very important consideration that if the spacing of the top (*baithis*) is too wide, the lobster may be able to reach the bait without entering the pot. For this reason I prefer to use a form of pairing similar to the top knot of the creel **(see Figs 2.13 to 2.16)**, but in the case of the lobster pot allow the first rods to be used for half of their length before introducing the second rods. In this way you can knot or pair with two sets of two rods and get a very secure and close weave while not having to use very heavy stuff. A close study of **Pl. 5.16** shows that the top of the pot has been woven in this way.

Slype twelve more bi-stakes on the belly and insert them according to your eye to give as even a distribution as possible. Thus, for instance, if you've opened out the pairs hard, you might first insert eight bi-stakes between each of the original pairs and distribute the other four stakes at regular intervals. If on the other hand you've opened them out gently, you might put eight bi-stakes to the left or right of each pair and distribute the remainder. If any space seems wide, feel free to put in an extra upright as seems appropriate. Separate out these new bi-stakes and try to get a fairly even distribution of stakes by the time the top or *baithis* has reached a diameter of 14–15" (36–38cm). This can be seen in **Pl. 5.16**.

Free all the tips of the

Pl. 5.16 Detail of the neck (barrach) *and top* (baithis) *of Connemara lobster pot.*

uprights from the ground and lever the pot gently out of the ground, trim what will be the inside of the pot and trim the uprights that have been in the ground back to within 1½–2" (4–5cm) of the neck. Now place a heavy stone or similar weight on these protruding neck rods and go round and gently kink each upright in turn where it is supported by the weaving. You can use a knife to do this, but if so use your thumb along the belly of the rod to bring back some curvature if the rods are so upright that they will give a very straight-sided pot. Gather the rods up as opposites, north, south, east, west, etc., and tie near the top. Two ties about 15" (38cm) from each other, to give what I call a 'swan's neck', will prevent the uprights from being driven sideways by the weaving.

Once the uprights have been tied, knock the pot on its side and, sitting at about 18" (46cm) from the ground, weave up the sides. If the weaving material is very strong, say stout 7fts (2.1m), then pairing will suffice, but I would prefer slightly lighter weavers, perhaps 6fts (1.8m), and the use of the two rods in the knot-like weave already described. The gap between the rows of weaving on the sides can be up to 2" (5cm) but 1½" (4cm) would be better. The pot is woven to a height of 15–16" (38–41cm) with the upper half of the pot being drawn in somewhat. Two rows of weaving are placed directly on top of each other at the top to give a tight space through which the base rods can be pulled.

The finish is similar to a creel and, since you have plenty of stakes, you can use sixteen rods to form four groups of four warp rods, over and under which the other rods will be woven. Since this pot has a total of 28 uprights, this leaves six on either side, and these can be temporarily tied up out of the way to avoid confusion while the warp rods are being knocked. Now start pack randing, usually at first going over and under the two middle warp rods, but including the other two groups as soon as this becomes possible (**see detail on Pl. 5.8**). When the pack randing becomes level with the first of the remaining uprights, repeat the pack randing on the other side. Knock the uprights over, under, over and under, and use fillers in the same way as described for a creel (**Fig. 2.19**).

Variations of west coast lobster pot

The Connemara pot described above had many variants, depending not just on the region but also on the material available. Some of

Festy Mortimer's Rossroe pots had nine uprights with nine bi-stakes added at the neck, and a further nine or ten added after three rounds of weaving on the top. A pot by Pakie O'Toole from Innisturk, off the Mayo coast **(see Pl. 5.7)**, has eleven uprights around a 5" (13cm) circle, and most of these are of two- to three-year-old 'Black Sally' (*Salix caprea* hybrid) which has been split in two. Apart from reducing the bulk, another advantage of splitting is that it is easier for the split rods to form the angles between the neck and top and the top and sides when split. This is especially true of a brittle willow like *Salix caprea* and its hybrids.

Once the neck has reached 3" (75cm), seven more bi-stakes are added and again most of these are of split two- to three-year-old rods. The rods are drawn out but probably not stuck into the ground as described for the Connemara pot. The pairing is begun by crouching over the pot, but keep the gaps between the rows very close and push the uprights towards the ground as you weave, thus ensuring a gradual curve rather than the sharper angle that occurs after the neck of the Connemara pot. A further nine stakes are added. Most of these are whole rods but the bottom 8" (20cm) approx. of the thicker ones in Pakie's pot have been shaved down; again I presume this is to make it easier to bend them. As already stressed, allow the material to determine the exact number of uprights you use.

When the base is 11–12" (28–30cm), lever the pot out of the ground and gather the uprights into a tie. Again the angle is not as sharp as in the Connemara pot so it is hard to say exactly when the top ends and the sides begin. Sitting on a stool as described for the Connemara pot, continue weaving using the pressure of the knees to draw in the sides. The base should be no wider than 14" (36cm), so if the siding is not underway by this point, kink the remaining uprights gently to make it happen. The pot slopes outwards and is about 17" (43cm) at its widest point, beginning to curve inwards gently towards the finish. The weaving is mainly pairing throughout, but the double pairing weave (top knot) already described is used whenever the weaving material is light.

The base is finished in a similar manner to the Connemara pot, but the four groups of four warp rods are not pulled out under the weaving at the other side. Instead, they are worked under the opposite group as described for the Sligo creel and the kish in Chapter 2. Otherwise the base is the same as for the Connemara pot.

Heather lobster pot

The heather pot in **Pl. 5.11** is made from common heather pulled during the flowering time in late August or early September and allowed to season for a few days before use. Sort the material into thick and thin, and try to put fairly straight and thick material in a separate pile for the uprights. The circle for the funnel is about 5" (13cm), and a sod or scraw can be cut and jammed into a flower pot or a similar container to accept the uprights—an 8" (205mm) pot would be adequate. Select thirteen uprights and insert them around the 5" (13cm) circle. Begin pairing using thin heather and ensure that the butts of the first weavers are caught in the weaving, as described for the Connemara pot. The neck should be about 4" (10cm) high when finished. Next add thirteen bi-stakes. These must be well pointed and I use a bodkin and grease to get them in; another option would be to insert them earlier and allow the pairing of the neck to keep them in place. Crouching over the pot, start the pairing as described for the Connemara and Innisturk pots. The heather pot is similar to the Innisturk pot in that the angle of the top (*baithis*) to the neck is not too pronounced, but the stakes are being constantly pushed downwards as the work proceeds. More bi-stakes are added to bring the number to around 40, though in a basket such as this the exact number is not critical. You may find that if the heather stem branches close to the butt, you will be able to use both stems rather than always introducing a bi-stake.

Once the top is about 11" (28cm), lever it out of the scraw or sod and begin to use the pressure of the knees to form the sides of the pot. It may suit to tie the uprights together, but due to the roughness of the material it is probably easier to rely on the weaving and the use of the knees to form the pot. As with the Innisturk pot, the rows of weaving at the top are very close, but once the siding is underway the space can widen a little. However, the space between the rows, even on the sides, is usually no more than 1–1¼" (25–30mm). The stakes can be supplemented with fresh pieces of heather as required, and as you approach the top of the pot you can allow two uprights to become one, thus reducing the cluster at the top and giving more strength to the group that will form the warp. The warp groups are twisted under their opposite number as described for the Innisturk pot. If the base has narrowed, you can reduce the group of warp rods to three, though I would feel that using four groups is more straightforward. Even if using three groups, the weaving is still over, under, over, and the twig is then pulled out under a convenient piece of weaving. The option of three groups of warp rods seems to be the one being used by Michael O'Malley in **Pl. 5.11**. Twiglets of heather can be used to fill any gaps, and the tips should be twisted to facilitate pulling them through. Where three warp groups have been used it will be necessary to stick every second twig into the body of the pot when filling to keep the weaving in agreement. The finished height for this flat-base type pot would be 14–16" (35–41cm).

The other option for finishing is that shown in **Pl. 5.10**. In this case continue narrowing the body of the pot, allowing single uprights to keep doubling up so that by the time the diameter has been reduced to about 7" (8cm) there are only about twelve to fourteen uprights remaining. These are pulled under each other, but then stout pieces of heather are shoved into the body of the pot on one side and driven through the weaving on the other side. This can be seen clearly in **Pl. 5.10**, but I feel the photograph was taken before the work was complete and that the section of the base closest to the hand holding the pot has yet to be filled. This view is supported by the fact that two heather pots from Achill in the National Museum collection F1947:94 and F1947:95 are both quite filled at the base. This method of finishing will give a taller pot, perhaps about 19" (48cm) high.

Straight-sided hazel pot

Although the pot shown in **Pl 5.9** is of hazel, it could also be made of willow and there are examples of this style of pot in willow as well as in hazel in the National Museum collection. The measurements in this example are based on a hazel pot acquired in the Aran Islands for the National Museum in 1928.

The circle for the neck of the pot is 5" (125mm), and seven stout hazel rods about ⅝" (15mm) are used for initial uprights. The neck is woven using slender (pencil thickness) hazel rods, with the butts being locked in as described for the other pots. Add seven bi-stakes of a similar thickness to the original stakes and draw the hazels out at as hard an angle as possible without breaking them. Crouching over the top, begin pairing the top (*baithis*), keeping the rows of pairing fairly close together. The example from Aran already mentioned had an extra stake added after a few rows of weaving, but

I cannot see any advantage to this and I've left it out. If extra stakes are needed it would be easier to start with eight to give a total of sixteen, though undoubtedly many of the west coast pots did have an odd number of stakes.

When the top is about 14" (36cm), lever the neck out of the ground and, turning it upside-down, put a stone on the protruding uprights at the neck so that the uprights can be gathered up to form the body of the pot. Coax the hazel uprights to bend with your thumb before gathering up. Tie them and begin the siding, keeping the rows of pairing very close to each other. This is necessary anyway for structural strength, but also because these pots were used for catching rock-fish. Because it is not possible to bring the uprights up too sharply, the pot continues to widen outwards from the base so that the diameter 6" (15cm) up from the start of the side is about 21" (51cm). The hazel rods used for the siding can be quite thick, up to ½" (12mm) in diameter. The weaving finishes at a height of 16" (41cm) and the warp is formed with eight rods, four sets of two. Each rod must be twisted sharply before knocking it to form the warp; each rod goes under its opposite number and out under the weaving on the far side; this detail can be seen in **Pl. 5.8**.

Individual fillers of hazel are used, even at this early stage, because the hazel rods would not be pliable enough for the pack randing used in the Connemara willow pot. The other uprights are twisted and knocked and woven over, under, over, under, leaving the middle ones until last as you would for a creel. Fill the spaces with hazel fillers.

Cork/Kerry bell-shaped lobster pot

This pot is very similar to those used in Brittany and in Cornwall, and the tradition of making these pots is still alive in Cornwall, where one maker, George Chambers, has been video-taped making the Cornish version of this pot.[14] This video would be very useful for anyone making this pot and much of the information supplied here was gleaned from it.

You will need a jig or template for this pot. The top of the jig is a 2" (5cm) deep block of timber, which will accommodate a circle of 8" (205mm), so a 10" (255mm) diameter block would be fine. This is bored with twelve evenly spaced 5/8" (15mm) holes to accommodate the standards or uprights. This block is then screwed onto a 36" (91cm) trunk of wood, such as a section of telephone pole; a flat piece of wood could also be nailed to the ground to give stability. Alternatively, the block could be screwed onto a tall fencing post and the pot made outside with the post driven into the ground. The main requirement is that the jig or template is stable and not inclined to topple.

Take twelve uprights about ½" (12mm) in diameter and bend them using a ringer as illustrated in **Fig. 5.3**. This ringer can be simply made by screwing a 4" (10cm) diameter circle of wood and a vertical stick of wood on to a backing board as shown. Now stick these uprights into the template and start the pairing using two slender 6ft (1.8m) rods. Remember to catch the butts in the weaving as described for the other pots. When these rods have run out, start the next set, with butts towards you, opposite the start of the first set. This is more methodical than the pairing joins for the pots already described, where butts are joined whenever tips begin to get thin. Pair in this fashion until the neck is 5" (125mm) high and pull through the tips of the pairing rods to secure them. Slype 30 uprights similar to or a little thinner than the standards and bend them in the ringer **(Fig. 5.3)**. Cut off the tips of these 30 rods so that the rods are now about 46" (117cm) long; the tips can be put to one side for slewing the base. Insert two uprights, one on either side of the standards, using bodkin and grease if necessary. Now insert the other six, one in every second group, so that you have a group of three, a group of four, etc. If you have particular difficulty getting any of these last six in, you could omit a few. George Chambers reckoned twelve sets of three were enough for a pot with an 8" (205mm) diameter neck, but the particular Cornish pot that George makes, the

Fig. 5.3

Porthleven pot, does not flow out as much as the Cork/Kerry pot. However, at least one of the pots I have seen (at the Ulster Folk and Transport Museum) had only 41 rather than 42 uprights coming out of the neck. Now nail twelve staples onto the pole or stake that forms the jig. These staples should be about halfway down (about 18" (46cm) from the block of timber that forms the top of the jig), and short lengths of rope or electric cable should now be tied to each staple. Bring each group of uprights down carefully in turn and tie them to the post using the cable or rope.

Next select two evenly matched 6ft (1.8m) rods and, having slyped them, drive them into the neck of the pot one on either side of one of the original uprights. Bend them about 3" (75mm) up from the top of the neck and start pairing, walking anti-clockwise around the jig and separating each rib or upright as you weave, i.e., take the weaving rod towards you, put the stake in place and then complete the stroke. Once you have used about a third of the initial weavers, supplement them by joining a second rod to each of them. This is done by inserting the butt of the new weaving rod under the rod already there. In the same way, the two weaving rods become three and as the pairing continues around the initial round, a new rod is inserted and a tip is dropped as required. As you return to where you started you widen out to form the next spiral, and, four or five stakes after the starting point, the weave or stitch is changed from pairing to fitching, where the left-hand group will go under, rather than over, the right-hand group.

At this 'turn of the stitch', as it is called by George Chambers, the group of weaving rods has strengthened to four per group, and from now on the group is regularly supplemented (depending on the length of the rods), with each new butt being locked in place. Once the fitching has reached the point where you changed the stroke, spiralling downwards as you go, pause and tie the uprights with a rope, closer to the neck than where you've finished weaving. This allows you to undo all the ties, as the rope will keep the flow of the pot. The Cornish Porthleven pot is straight-sided, so the rope is tightly tied, but the Cork/Kerry pot has more outward flow so the rope should be tied accordingly. On this next round of weaving, extra stakes (called false pitchers in Cornwall) are introduced. These are stuck in, butt first, from underneath to catch in the previous row of weaving and are used wherever the gap between the uprights is becoming a bit wide. Four to six of these additional stakes should be sufficient. Continue weaving until there are three full rows of weaving on the side of the pot. After that, level out more or less below where you changed the weave from pairing to fitching.

Release the pot from the mould by levering out, using a nail bar, for example. Place the pot upside-down on the floor and cut out every fourth rod ½" (1cm) up from the weave. For example, if you have 48 uprights this means removing 12 stakes to leave 12 groups of 3. If you have 46 uprights cut off 11 to give 11 groups, 9 of 3 rods and 2 of 4 rods. Allow the remainder of one of the groups of the fitching rods to lie on the inside of the basket and the other on the outside. Allow the inside set to come out the next space to the left. This is the direction the rods are pointing in already, so this stroke will be put on from right to left, the opposite of the usual practice, because the basket is turned upside-down. Take the outside set and supplement it with two hazel or willow rods about ½" (12mm) in diameter, and put this group of weavers into the space that the other set is coming out of and then out the next (i.e., in front of three uprights and behind three uprights). Now pick up the next set, add two extra weavers to it and weave in the same way. Continue in this way until you have put one stitch or weave into each space, by which time you have returned to where you started this weave.

This time, kink each group of three downwards, cut them off just short of the centre and tie each group, individually, to the neck of the pot as you make the stroke, so that the base of the pot will slope inwards towards the centre. This time you will use a supplementary rod for each individual stake. Thus if you're going over three, use three supplementary rods. For the first round of the base these supplementary rods are introduced behind the vertical stakes (at the side of the pot), giving the pot a firm rim to stand on.

Once the first round of the base has been completed, the supplementary rods are driven butt first into the base in the direction of the stakes and the weaving continues, pressing the stakes *down* with each stroke to give the base a slope towards the centre. As the base narrows it may be necessary to cut more off the stakes and to use your foot to help to press the stakes downwards. The supplementary rods at this stage are simply shoved into the base, and short stumpy willow tips such as those cut off the uprights are ideal for this. As the space narrows further, a nail bar or a similar lever is necessary to work the weavers in and out.

When the space has narrowed to such an extent that it is no longer possible to fit another weave, plait the ends of the two sets of weavers out for a few strokes and get a strong hazel or two-year-old willow stick to jam them into place. The butt of this stick should be up to 1" (25mm) thick and, having pointed it well, it is driven through from the outside, through two or three rows of the base weaving. It is exposed at the middle of the base and traps the ends of the weaving rods underneath, before being driven through another few rows of the weaving to emerge at the opposite side of the base. This can be seen in **Pl. 5.8**. The pot is now complete, but it is a good idea to tie waxed string to the uprights of the neck in three places and to secure this to the first round of weaving on the top of the pot. This is done to prevent the weaving on the neck from slipping off.

Dunservick crab pot

A jig or template is also necessary for this basket and a plan of one similar to that used by Sammy Gault of Dunservick is shown in **Fig. 5.4**. The outer set of eight holes are at a diameter of 8" (205mm) and are used for the crab pot. The inner set of holes are for a 7" (180mm) diameter opening, and these are used for the 'buckie creel'.

The holes drilled should be ¾" (18mm) wide and eight in number for each pot. The material throughout is hazel, with two-to-three year old rods for the standards and one-to-two year old rods for the weavers. Select eight standards about ⅝" (15mm) in diameter and shave them down at the butt end for a length of about 12" (30cm) so that they will be able to curve easily after the neck. Stick them into the holes and start pairing, using light pencil-thickness hazel, catching the butts in the weaving as described for all the other pots. New butts are added as needed, and when the neck is about 4½–5" (11–13cm) thread the tips through.

Select eight more standards similar to those already in place, shave them down and insert them, one for each standard to give a total of sixteen. Bend over the standards carefully and tie to the hoop below to form the shape. For weaving the siding you will be going anti-clockwise around the basket, i.e., when standing facing the basket you will be pairing from left to right. You can separate out the pairs of standards as soon as it is practical to do so, around three rows after starting weaving the sides. Once you have separated the pairs you can begin to use thicker hazel, eventually using hazel of ½" (12mm) and always joining butt first. When you are

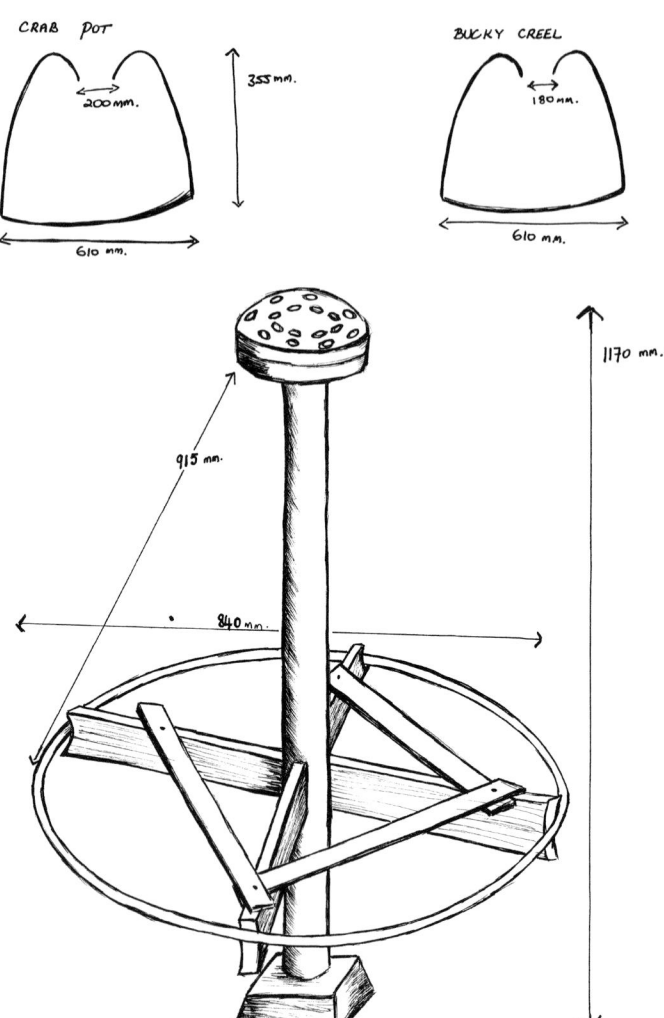

CRAB POT

200mm.

355mm.

610 mm.

BUCKY CREEL

180mm.

610 mm.

1170 mm.

915 mm.

840 mm.

Fig. 5.4—Jig for making crab pots and buckie creels.

introducing a new weaver, especially if it is thick, you can go in front of two uprights with it rather than in front of one for the first stroke. In order not to disrupt the pairing stroke, go back to the upright before where the spent tip is lying when doing this 'in front of two' first stroke. In this way the pairing rod will come out in the correct space.

Once you reach a depth of 14" (355mm), the weaving finishes by securing the ends of the weavers under the previous row of pairing. Four standards from one side and the opposite four from the other side are bent over. It is essential to twist the standard where you intend to bend it down so that it can bend without breaking. Each standard is locked under the other (as described for the kish and the Sligo creel) so that four ribs or warp rods are formed. If the middle standards that you have knocked down prove flexible enough, you could weave their ends under and over the other warp rods to begin the weaving of the base.

Start filling in the base with willow rods from either side until you reach the next standard that is to be knocked down. Twist it where it has to fold down and then weave it over, under, over and under. Repeat with the standard opposite. Now deal with the other three sets of standards in the same way and fill the base with stoutish, about ½–¾" (12–18mm) diameter, willow rods. The willow rod fillers follow the same pattern and the tips are threaded out under a row of pairing to secure them.

The buckie creel is made in the same manner but the inner set of holes on the jig are used to give a 7" (18cm) diameter neck. Because the same hoop is used to tie the uprights, the sides of the buckie creel are more gently angled than that of the crab pot. The door of the buckie creel was formed by cutting away one upright and about 2" (5cm) of weaving, and fitting a little wooden door with two rope hinges on one side and a rope fastening on the other. The pots in **Pl. 5.15** are also presumed to be buckie creels, despite the fact that these are more steep-sided than those made by Sammy Gault. For these, the hole for the door was made during the siding by turning the weaving back on itself to form the opening.

The whelk pots made by John Marah of County Wicklow had seven standards at the start, but nine more were added to give a total of sixteen, the same number as in the Dunservick pot.

6

Other traditional baskets

THERE were, of course, many other country baskets besides those used for fishing and the various creel patterns already described. Baskets were used for many other tasks around the home and farm. Although the creel was the principal basket used for carrying turf, in some districts a specially made turf basket with a border was used for storing turf inside the house. It is possible that this trend may have been influenced by the growth of professional basketmaking in the late nineteenth and early twentieth century, but if so the turf baskets made by country basketmakers were not so finely finished as those of professional makers, with the typical country baskets having fewer but thicker uprights. Techniques were different too. As we will see in Chapter 8, many professional basketmakers used the underfoot base, where the base sticks were lashed together, but this technique was virtually unknown among country basketmakers, who relied upon splitting the base sticks, often using a weaving pattern similar to that described for the potato skibs. Because the

Pl. 6.1—Detail of a foot. Although this foot appears on a professionally made basket, the technique was widely used by country basketmakers.

choice of willow available was usually limited to large stuff suitable for creel making, the uprights of the typical country turf baskets were thick, with one upright per base stick as opposed to two somewhat thinner uprights per base stick favoured by professional basketmakers. Moreover, because of the use of thick uprights, the base often warped, necessitating the use of a foot (a protective border underneath the basket that kept the base from touching the ground). A foot adds enormously to the length of time a basket will last and this technique was kept alive in Ireland by traditional rather than professional basketmakers. **Pl. 6.1** shows detail of a foot.

I have seen a wide assortment of styles of country turf baskets and it seems that, unlike the creel, the style of the turf basket depended more on the individual maker rather than on the region in which it was made. Shapes included barrels and cylinders as well as the more familiar outsloping basket. Some turf baskets were made upside-down in the manner of a creel, but without a mouthwale, and when the base was made and the basket pulled out of the ground, new rods were inserted beside the uprights so that a border could be put on. I have seen hazel baskets made in this way from the Burren district of west Clare. A similar idea occurs in the crandy mentioned in Chapter 2 dealing with creels.

Hand baskets were also widely used and while among professional basketmakers these are usually called shopping baskets, they were generally known as egg baskets in the countryside, or in Irish simply as a *ciseán*. These were usually oval and many of them had a hinged lid with a slit in it through which the handle protruded **(Pl. 6.2).** They were used by farmwives to bring eggs to town and to bring home groceries, which would form part of the payment for the eggs. At first sight, these seem to be very elaborate, but since the delicate eggs were an important element of the rural economy, the extra

Pl. 6.2—A lidded oval hand basket. This style of basket was known as an egg basket. Photo by David Shaw-Smith.

protection provided by the lid was a distinct advantage. It is probable that such baskets were made only by the more specialist makers in the country tradition. In the remoter areas of the west, where the osiers needed for such baskets were unavailable, eggs were brought to market in straw baskets placed in a creel (see Chapter 7). Surplus supplies of home-made butter were also brought for sale to the nearest town, especially in the areas of better land where small-scale dairying was practised. The National Museum collection has a long, low, oval hand basket from County Offaly which was known as a butter basket. Round hand baskets in various patterns were widely used around home and farm. An interesting variant was the Aran

kisheen **(Pl. 6.3).** This was an inward-sloping basket and although a similar shape was made in straw, the straw kisheen was used for the specific purpose of bringing hot food to people working in the fields. A close study of the woman laden with creels in **Pl. 2.4** shows that she also seems to have a willow kisheen in one hand. Examples of the kisheen in the National Museum collection are in pairing weave, though the one in **Pl. 2.4** seems to be waled and of poorer quality than the typical Aran basket.

Pl. 6.3—Aran kisheen in willow. This kisheen is based on a similar one in the National Museum collection, which was made in 1918.

Another distinctive basket from the Aran Islands was a cradle on wooden rockers **(Pl. 6.4).** While the professionally made cradles (as seen in Chapter 8) were usually made from stripped willow and often had plaited borders, the Aran cradle was much rougher looking. The base was made by placing thin wooden slats on an outer frame. Holes were bored in the outer frame to accept stout uprights reminiscent of a creel, and the weaving pattern was also similar to a creel. Once the desired height was reached, a special rope border using one of the uprights was put on. As far as I know, this border was unique to Aran and was also used on the Aran seaweed creel. Details of making the Aran cradle are included in the technique section of this chapter.

In Antrim and perhaps also in other parts of Ulster, an oval basket shaped like a rugby ball was used for holding yarn. Estyn Evans illustrated one from Torr Head in County Antrim which was about 14" (35cm) long.[1] A similar basket was also used in Scotland, where it was known variously as a *murlag*, a *murlainn*, a *ciarachán* or a *creelagh*.[2] These were made on the principle of a frame basket, with oval hoops lashed together to form the initial skeleton for the weaving.

On the Blasket Islands off the south-west coast of Ireland, a multi-purpose frame basket about 30" (76cm) long and 15" (38cm) across was made. Its relatively shallow shape suggests that it might have been useful for longline fishing as well as the many other uses to which it was put. This basket was known as a *birdeog*. The *birdeog* was also used along the Kerry coast, particularly on the Dingle Peninsula. A little further north in County Limerick, Estyn Evans mentions the use of shallow oval baskets for 'hawking' (selling) shellfish or fruit.[3] These may well have been frame baskets also, but I have not been able to get any more information about them. County Limerick had a strong tradition of basketmaking in the nineteenth century according to Rev. J. Hall in his *Tour through Ireland*, published in 1813. He says 'In one house I observed a bed of extremely neat wickerwork, sufficient to contain two grown people, shaped like a cradle; the head jutting out as if it had been one.'[4]

The Limerick area is also the area I associate most with the calf-muzzle **(Pl. 6.5)**. This was a small conical basket about 7" (18cm) deep, which was tied to a calf's muzzle. This was not only to prevent the calf from suckling the cow, since in general in this fertile dairying area the calves were kept separate from the cows; it also prevented the calf from chewing old straw or licking the lead paint that was often used on stables and carts in the early 1900s. These calf muzzles were made by the thousands throughout Munster and possibly in other areas as well, and while they were probably originally made in the locality in which they were used, many were

Pl. 6.4—Aran cradle. Most cradles were made by professional basketmakers, but this Aran cradle was made similarly to a creel.

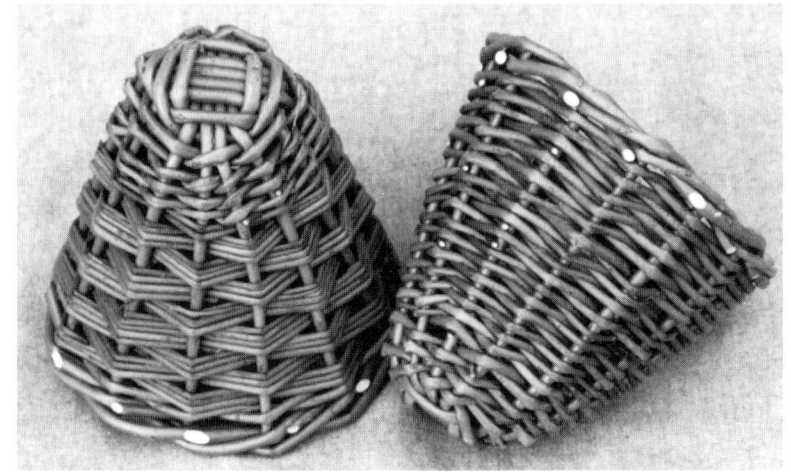

Pl. 6.5—Calf muzzles. The muzzle on the left is slewed and is typical of those made by more specialised makers; the muzzle on the right is paired and this style was more typical of country basketmakers.

also made by professional basketmakers, certainly from the 1940s onwards. The muzzles were called *púicíní* or *púicíns* in County Kerry.

The hazel sheep feeders from County Offaly (**Pls 6.6 and 6.7**) were on a far grander scale than the humble calf muzzle, but again they show that people turned to the available material for a solution to the needs of the farm. It is unlikely that the design of either of these hay feeders is older than 1900, and they were made in response to a need to feed hay to sheep in the fields in winter. Without the feeders, the sheep would have wasted much of the hay by trampling on it. The rectangular feeder in **Pl. 6.6** is from the Kilcormac area of County Offaly and it has a floor suspended about 11" (28cm) above ground level on which the hay could be placed. The eyes or openings immediately above the floor allowed the sheep to put their heads into the feeder, so it was important that the measurement of the eyes, approx. 9" (23cm) high by 5½" (14cm) wide, was sufficiently exact to allow one sheep to feed in each space. The feeder had legs protruding about 4" (10cm) below ground level to enable it to be placed securely into the ground. This also enabled it to be moved from place to place as necessary and to be stored under shelter when not in use. The hazel roof on the Kilcormac shelter probably gave enough protection from the wind and

Pl. 6.6— Rectangular sheep feeder in hazel from the Kilcormac area of County Offaly. Photo courtesy of NMI.

Pl. 6.7—Bill Egan of Clonfinlough, Co. Offaly, putting a sack covering on a circular sheep feeder. A floor of sacking suspended on hazel rods had yet to be fitted when this picture was taken. Photo courtesy of NMI.

rain, but in the round Clonfinlough feeder the hay is kept dry by tying a sack to the top. The Clonfinlough feeder is also less elaborate, with a much more open floor made from just a few rods over which a sack was suspended. Apparently in the original design the floor of the feeder was made entirely of rods but, presumably, because the weaving was fairly rough, it was found that sheep occasionally cut their lips, so a simpler floor using sacking was introduced. Both feeders in **Pls 6.6 and 6.7** were acquired by the National Museum in the 1960s but had, in fact, gone out of use in the 1940s when they were replaced by feeders made from iron. Many of the iron feeders, being far heavier than the hazel ones, had to have wheels added to facilitate moving them. Details of making the sheep feeders are included in the technique section. Hurdles were widely used in Britain to fence sheep in a controlled grazing situation, but there is no reliable record of their use in Ireland. The techniques for hurdle making would certainly have been familiar as can be seen in the wicker doors mentioned earlier. The fact that tillage crops were not widely used for feeding sheep in Ireland would have limited the use of hurdles, but this skill is undergoing a revival here at present, though modern usage of hurdles is mostly for garden screens. Many members of the Irish Coppice Workers Association make hazel hurdles, while most of today's basketmakers occasionally make willow panels and other garden structures.

Another object closely related to baskets was the sieve or riddle **(Pl. 6.8).** Before the widespread introduction of the modern sieve, in which the mesh is created by strips of wire, sieves were usually made from strips of ash, with various sizes of mesh being available according to the use to which the sieve or riddle was being put. The word 'riddle' or *rilleán* was used for wide-meshed sieves in which the mesh was greater than ¼" or 6mm, while the sieve or *criathar* had a finer mesh. The riddle was used for taking straw, stones, grit and other impurities from the grain, while the sieve was used to remove weed seeds and smaller particles of dirt from the riddled grain. Winnowing the chaff from the grain was usually done using a *bodhrán* (goatskin drum) or a specially made skin tray, known in the north-east as a wright. These wrights were used for other carrying tasks as well and were made by stretching a sheepskin (or a goatskin in the case of a *bodhrán*) into a frame of ash or even of bog-fir. Occasionally, sieves were made from these skin wrights by piercing the skin in several places after stretching. In Tory Island, off the Donegal coast, where ash or indeed bog-fir was not readily available, these wrights were bound instead with twisted straw rope (*súgán*).[5] The National Museum has one example of a blind sieve, or *dallán,* where the strips of ash are sufficiently closely placed to allow it to be used for winnowing. Apparently, this pattern was not common however.[6]

Sieve-making as a trade had already died out by 1950, but A.T. Lucas of the National Museum managed to locate two sieve-makers, one in north County Dublin and the other in east Galway, from whom good descriptions of the process of making were obtained, which is the basis for the description of sieve-making in the technique section of this chapter. It should be noted here, however, that after the ash is split the lacing strips are obtained by pounding the split ash until the annual growth rings can be pulled apart by hand. This is the same method used by basketmakers in North America to prepare strips of white and black ash, which are the raw materials for baskets in certain parts of the north-eastern USA.

Pl. 6.8—Sieves made from strips of pounded ash; the sieve on the left is almost finished, the next lacing strips on the sieve on the right would probably run north-west/south-east to counteract the tension of those already put on. Photo taken about 1950, courtesy of NMI.

The 'cradle bird' in **Pl. 6.9** could hardly be described as a basket in the strictest sense of the word, because there is no weaving involved. The cradle bird was used for trapping blackbirds and similar-sized birds for eating, and the trap would drop when the bird alighted on the curved rod. The curved rod was willow but hazel or any straight stiff rods were preferred for the body of the trap. Traditionally these traps were bound with willow rods, but by the 1950s, when the use of these traps was declining, string was often used instead.

Birch-bark baskets, found throughout the Scandinavian countries and even in certain parts of Scotland, do not seem to have been made in Ireland, although it seems there was some knowledge of the use of birch bark in the past. A milk strainer made of birch bark formed into a funnel and filled with straw is mentioned in a seventeenth-century account quoted by the historian E. McLysaght.[7]

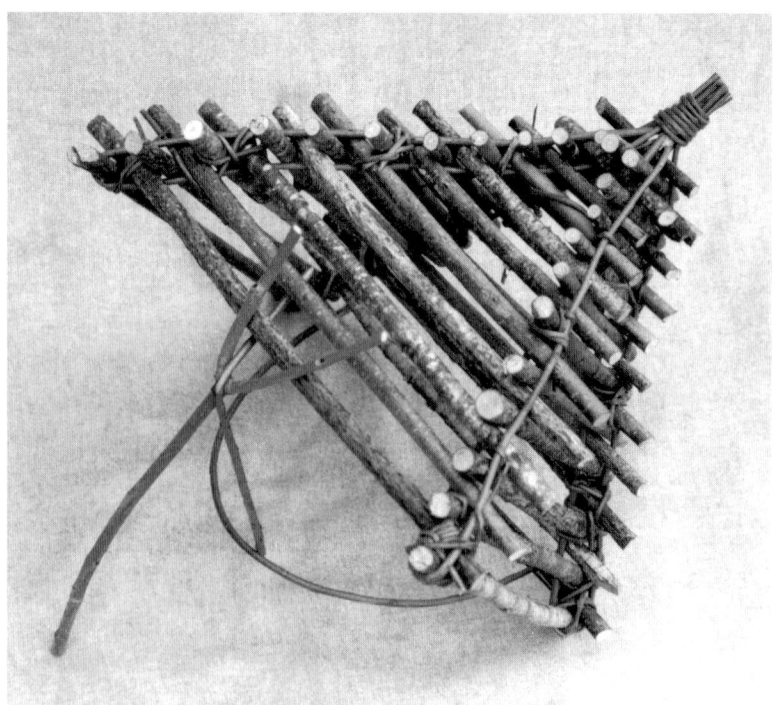

Pl. 6.9—Cradle bird. This trap was used to catch blackbirds to eat. The photo shows the trap set.

TECHNIQUE

Aran Cradle

For the wooden framework you will need two pieces of white deal, 21" (535mm) long of 3" x 2" (75mm x 50mm) and two pieces 35" (890mm) long of 2" x 1½" (50mm x 38mm). The 21" (535mm) lengths act as the rockers, so they need to be shaved down as shown in **Fig. 6.1**. Grooves are also cut in them to accept the 2" x 1½" (50mm x 38mm) lengths of 35" (890mm) wood. Cleats of approx. 1½" x ⅜" (38mm x 9mm) are also needed for the floor of the cradle; eleven of these about 14½" (37mm) long will be needed.

Clamp the wooden framework together using glue, and bore double holes ½" (12mm) wide as shown in **Fig. 6.1.** There are three sets of double holes between the corners on the short sides (front and back) and ten sets of holes between the corners on each of the long sides. This means that a total of 60 stakes about ⅝" (15mm) in diameter are needed. The right-hand stake will form the border (going anti-clockwise around the cradle), so all of the right-hand rods need to be of good quality. The left-hand rods need only be 14" (360mm) long (because they will be cut off), except in the hood area where both rods that make up the stake need to be of good quality.

Select 30 weavers about ½" (12mm) in diameter; these would typically be 7fts (2.1m). Now place the eleven slats between the stakes on the long side. You may need to narrow the ends of these to ensure that they fit. Put on the mouthwale as shown in **Figs 2.3 to 2.6**. In some versions of the cradle, the slats are put in after the

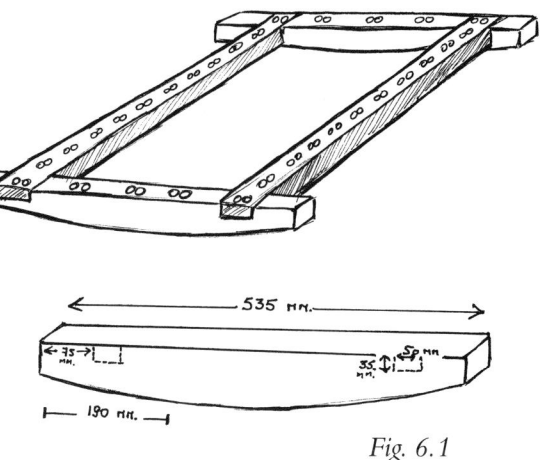

Fig. 6.1

mouthwale, but the version where they are both below the mouthwale seems both neater and stronger to me. After the mouthwale, do one row of randing. Then go to the right again, going anti-clockwise around the cradle, threading through the last two rods; the first of these goes under one and the second and final rod under two. This is more fully explained in the technique section of Chapter 2 dealing with the standard creel. These rods are randed and counter-randed in this way until they have been used out. If in doubt about which direction to go next, remember that when the rods are lying underneath, you have just gone to the right (anti-clockwise), so you are now due to rand. If the rods are lying on top, you have just completed a row of randing (going clockwise around the creel) so you are now due to go to the right.

Once this initial set of rods has been used out, put on a top knot as shown in **Figs 2.13 to 2.16.** Select another 30 weavers, a little lighter than the first set, slype them and insert each one of them to the right of the stakes, as shown in **Fig 2.12** showing the variation for forming the window. However, the weave that follows the insertion of these weavers in Aran is not randing as shown in **Fig 2.12**, but a round going to the right (anti-clockwise around the cradle) with each weaver going in front of the next upright and *inside* the next weaver before going behind and out. A close study of the cradle in **Pl. 6.4** shows that the window is done in the same manner as that shown in **Fig. 2.12**, with a row of randing following the insertion of the stakes. I hadn't noticed by the time I was making the cradle that the Aran 'windows' were done in this way, and the difference is not very noticeable. This set of weaving rods is used in a similar way to the first, going clockwise/anti-clockwise to give a series of knots as described for the first set. The third set of 30 weaving rods should be at least as heavy as the second set in order to bring the cradle up to the desired height before bordering. They are introduced by going to the right, as shown in **Fig 2.9**, and remember to finish as shown in **Fig 2.10**. This set is similarly knotted all the way, as described for the first and second sets. Height before the border should be 10½" (265mm).

Insert a third upright at each of the four corners and also at the uprights where the hood begins, i.e., the fourth upright from the corner post not counting the corner post itself. Twist the right-hand rod of each upright group and, having twisted it, reduce its length to about 24" (610mm) to enable you to do the Aran rope border more easily. Cut the left-hand stakes *except those in the hood area* down to about 3" (75mm), and from this stuff you have cut off, make pegs about 8" (200mm) long. You will want fifteen pegs in all, six for each long side and three for the front. Slype each group of uprights so that you will have two pegs protruding at the finish. Now put on the Aran rope border as described in the technique section of chapter 2, **Figs 2.22 to 2.25**.

As soon as the rope border has been completed, select some pliable 6–7ft (2.1–2.4m) rods for the hood. Starting at the right-hand hood stake (frontal view), take a 6ft (2.1m) weaver, fold it in half and start pairing. Once one or two strokes of pairing have been done, supplement the pairing rods with two other rods so that you will be doing a weave similar to the 'top knot' that you put on before the window **(Figs 2.13 to 2.16)**. This is also the weave described in Chapter 5 for the Connemara willow lobster pot. When you come to the other hood stake, turn and come back, doing a knot-like stroke on the return also. When rounding the outer hood stakes, take each rod separately around; this stroke won't then be knotted and will give a smoother look to the front of the hood.

When a height of about 3½" (90mm) has been reached, stop short of the outer hood stake and turn instead at the next stake nearest the back. This is in order to create a hand hole, which I presume was mainly used for rocking the cradle, though it could also have been used as a handle. Since these stakes consist of only single uprights it is important to go round them gently so that the hood won't be pulled out of shape. When the gap has reached a height of about 4¼" (110mm), go to the outer hood stake again and weave the hood for a further 7" (180mm) to give a total height of 15" (380mm) above the border for the hood.

Kink the stakes on the side of the hood, excluding the corner post. These will form a warp of four groups of stakes; the stake from a given side will be crammed into the weaving on the other side. At the front of the hood each stake consists of two rods, so take both from one side first and stick them down and then repeat for the other side. Don't be tempted to make the cram for these front rods too long, since the space is tight.

To fill the hood, the remaining stakes are woven over, under, over and under, before returning towards the back of the cradle. The stakes will not themselves be enough to fill the hood, so you will need to supplement them by sticking extra rods in beside them to fill the spaces. Filling is done from each side in the manner of a creel, with the middle being left until last. It will probably be necessary to twist all of the stakes other than the corner posts to enable them to be woven in and out; it will certainly be necessary in the case of the middle stake. The extra rods used for filling the hood should be considerably lighter than the hood stakes, with rods similar to those woven in the siding of the hood being adequate. If a pliable variety of rod is chosen for these fillers it should not be necessary to twist them. It is advisable to wrap around the front warp rods an extra turn as required to fill the hood evenly, because the front of the hood is wider than the back.

Calf muzzle

Select six slender 6ft (1.8m) rods and cut off the top 12" (30cm). Lay them, three on top of three, with butts and tips alternating. Get a thinner 6ft (1.8m) rod and a 5ft (1.5m) rod and bind the rods together, as described for the underfoot base in the technique section in Chapter 8 **(Figs 8.1 to 8.3)**, but in this case allow the butt of the initial binding rod to project sufficiently so that it can be used as an extra stake to give an odd number. As soon as the dome has been properly formed gather the rods into a tie or a hoop of about 9" (225mm) diameter. At this point you may abandon the initial weaving rods, or, if they have some strength left, turn them around a stake to allow you to weave from left to right. Joins were traditionally done with butts each time, but when a few rounds of pairing have been done switch to slewing **(Fig. 8.12)**, using 3fts (90cm) or cut-off tops. When the weave reaches 5" (125mm) put on a row of pairing and then a three-behind-one border.

Some basketmakers split the stakes to give twelve uprights and paired the sides, thus eliminating the need for the underfoot base.

Hand baskets

(a) Oval
The oval egg basket **(Pl. 6.2)** has a split rather than an underfoot base, with three longer base sticks about 18" (46cm) long being put through six shorter sticks 13" (33cm) long. Spread of slath is 3½" (9cm) on the inside with the six shorter sticks being doubled; the two in the middle will remain doubled, being treated as one, but

others are separated out once two rounds of binding have been put on. It is outside the scope of this book to give instruction on the making of a split oval base, but it is well described in many of the recommended basketmaking books.[8] Base sticks should be from 7ft (2.1m), and weavers for the base should be 5fts (1.5 m). The finished base should measure 13" x 9" (33cm x 23cm) approximately. Thirty uprights of 6ft (1.8m) are inserted, but these are slyped on the back so that the belly of the rod is allowed to form the curved sides of this basket. The finished height of the basket is about 9" (23cm) and the handle is of the twisted rope type.[9]

The hoop for the lid is made from one rod, which should be about ¾" (18mm) at the butt. Use a scallom to wrap the join and keep the join to the shoulder of the hoop so that it won't interfere with the handle when the lid is being closed. Ideally the hoop should be allowed to harden for a few days before weaving the lid. The lid stakes are scallomed on, using thin (French) scalloms, and a simple two-pair border put on. Allow an opening of 1¼" (30mm) on the lid to accommodate the handle. Rod hinges are fixed on one side and the lid is tied down for a few days to allow it to set properly. In some versions a thin bridge is woven across the basket to fill the space left in the lid for the handle.

All of the 'country' oval baskets I've seen had split oval bases. I recommend using reverse pairing on the base to counteract the tendency of these bases to twist.

(b) Round

The round baskets were also of the split base type and usually had two uprights to each base stick. The Aran kisheen **(Pl. 6.3)**, however, has a base like a 3 x 3 grid base skib, with three bi-stakes added at each space to give a total of twelve extra stakes. The base is paired to 11" (28cm). A three-rod wale is put on over the base sticks, and in the case of the kisheen at the National Museum, over 40 uprights were inserted with doubles at the bi-stake base sticks and singles at most of the others. These uprights were light 5fts (1.5m), but the kisheen in **Pl. 6.3** has fewer uprights, so heavy 5fts (1.5m) or 4fts (1.2m) if using common osier would be more suitable in this case. The uprights are tied to draw them inwards and after three rows of three-rod wale, the weaving changes to pairing, hedgerow-style, i.e., joining with butts every time. A few bands of waling are put on as the siding progresses and the basket is finished with a three-behind-two border. The finished kisheen is about 9" (23cm) high. A slender 7ft (2.1m) rod is stuck into the siding, twisted along its length and brought over and back a few times to form a handle in the style of a single twisted rod handle. The handle is only about 4" (10cm) higher than the basket. Most hand-baskets other than the kisheen were fitted with proper roped handles.

Cradle bird

Select four fairly evenly matched 4ft (1.2m) rods and cut 9" (23cm) off the tips. Fold the rods in half and tie them with a rod so that tips and butts are securely tied. A second tie is added a little lower down. Now draw out the four folded rods so that they form the four angles of a pyramid. The measurement from the lower tie to the ground in the cradle bird in **Pl. 6.9** is about 13" (33cm) but these traps varied in size. Cut four hazel sticks about ¾" (18mm) in diameter and about 13–14" (33–36cm) long. Insert two of these north–south so that they fit inside the folded rod legs; the next two are put east–west in the same way. Four more sticks, a little shorter than the first, are inserted in the same way and the process continues using shorter sticks each time until the structure is tight. The diameter of the rods that form the trap is not critical, and usually slightly lighter sticks are used closer to the top. Any fairly straight wood can be used. The sticks should be bound to the folded rod legs in several places using a twisted rod or string. One of the bottom sticks is split with a knife on each side to allow a thin rod (from 4–5ft, 1.2–1.5m material) to be inserted to form an arc or semi-circle extending about 9" (23cm) into the trap. A forked stick and a bent rod are used to set the trap, as shown in **Pl. 6.9**.

Hazel sheep cribs

(a) Round (Clonfinlough) crib
Hazel that has been cut and allowed to season for about four weeks should be used. About 200 rods will be needed, with 100 of these being ¾" (18mm) in diameter. First make a circle of 4ft (122cm) in the ground using a compass of pegs and twine as described for the coracle in Chapter 4. Insert seventeen of the stoutest hazel rods (¾"/18mm diameter) so that they are equally distributed around the

circle. Then pick out seventeen rods a little thinner than the stakes and put on a mouthwale, as described in **Figs 2.3 to 2.6**. Rand out these rods. Now start English (coil) randing using rods similar to those used for the mouthwale. These rods are stuck under a row of the previous weaving as already described for the kish (technique section, Chapter 2). The weaving continues to a height of about 18" (45cm). In the crib made by Bill Egan for the National Museum, the ends of the last few rods to be English randed are tucked away and then the whole is beaten down, though a line of pairing could be added at this point if desired.

The tips of the rods are now tied firmly and the weaving begun about 10" (255mm) above the previous weaving to create the space for the sheep to feed. A line of pairing could again be used to advantage here. The sides are then English randed using slightly thinner rods for about another 18" (46cm). A few lines of pairing as seen in **Pl. 6.7** are put on nearer the top and the tips of the uprights are cut level. (A sack is used to cover the top to prevent the hay getting wet). The floor is simply four hazel rods driven into the siding at one side (alternate butt and tip) beside four stakes and, having twisted the kinking spot, the ends are crammed down into the work on the opposite side.

The crib should be allowed to stand in the ground for a few days after being made, to allow it to set. These were made in various sizes depending on the number of sheep to be fed, but the space between the uprights was always similar to that in the one described here to allow the sheep to feed safely.

(b) Rectangular (Kilcormac) crib

The uprights for this sheep crib are a little thicker than in the round one described above; 22 uprights up to 1" (25cm) are needed. A look at **Pl. 6.6** shows that one side of the crib is lower and slighter uprights could be used on this side if necessary. Four corner posts are stuck into the ground to give a rectangle 49" x 31½" (125cm x 80cm). Six stakes are put between the corner posts on each of the long sides with three between the corner posts on the short sides. A mouthwale **(Figs 2.3 to 2.6)** is put on using ¾" (18mm) diameter rods, and the sides are randed up to a height of 9" (23cm). The floor is put in using rods driven alongside the stakes on the long side and then crammed down on the opposite side. These form the warp, and lighter hazel rods are woven from either side to form the floor, each rod just doing one journey from one side to the other. Once the floor has been completed, a few more rows of randing are put on and finished with a top knot **(Figs 2.13 to 2.16)**.

The weaving is begun again about 9" (23cm) above this point, using 22 rods ⅝" (15mm) in diameter approx. to put on another mouthwale. The sides are randed for about 8" (20cm) and then the stakes on what will be the higher side of the creel are twisted and woven back towards the side of the crib. This detail can be clearly seen in **Pl. 6.6**. The stakes then form an arch, which is 4ft (122cm) on the higher side. The siding is continued, twisting the hazel to ensure that it doesn't break when being woven around the front of the crib. Willow could be used for weaving the section at the top. This crib is stronger but would still benefit from being allowed to set for a few days before being pulled from the ground. The legs were cut about 3" (8cm) below the ground so that the crib could be driven into the soil when in use.

Wooden sieves

The rim of the sieve is made from clean, knot-free ash about 6–10" (15–25cm) in diameter and about 5½ft (168cm) long. The log needs to be about 4" (10cm) longer than the circumference of the sieve. This log is split into quarters with the axe. Each quarter is split into slivers with an axe or froe and these are then shaved using a draw knife. The shaved sliver, now measuring about 3–4" (75–100mm) wide and about ¼" (6mm) thick, is made into a circle with an overlap of 4" (10cm), and the rim is nailed at the overlap. The diameter of the sieve could be from 17" (43cm) to 21" (53cm).

A briar band of split 'buckie briar' (wild rose) about ¾" (18mm) in diameter is also needed. Wild rose is especially suited as it doesn't taper very much. This wild rose is split in two and shaved down somewhat to form the briar band. The anchoring band shown in **Fig 6.2** is made from some of the thicker pieces split off in the making of the lacing strips.

The lacing strips are made from a split section of the ash log and because these do not have to be very long, the sections of log could be cut in two to enable the splitting to be done more easily. The width of the sections will depend on the type of sieve being made, but for the standard oat riddle shown in **Pl. 6.8** the segments of ash should only be about ¼" (6mm) wide. The process of splitting down the wood is similar to that described in the technique section of

Chapter 3 for the Wicklow spale or chip basket. (**Fig 3.26** shows the splitting process.)

In the case of the chip basket the strips would be about 1¼" (30mm) wide, which is about the width shown in **Fig 3.26**, but for the sieve the wood would have to be divided several more times. The thin segment of wood should then be pounded with the back of an axe or with a mallet on both its thin and wide faces so that the annual growth rings are gradually separated. After pounding, the

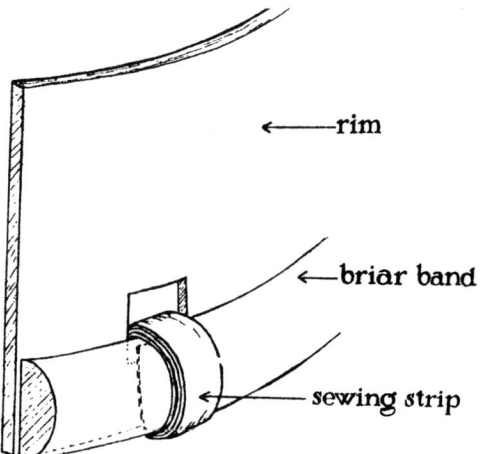

Fig. 6.2 (Lucas 1954.)

section of ash is bent back and forth with the hands, and if necessary a knife can be used to encourage the growth rings to separate from each other. Once this process has been started the strips can be pulled apart by hand. The strips are then shaved to remove the pithy 'rust', using a knife in a manner similar to that used when shaving willow skeins. Finally, the upper face of the strips is shaved using an old knife with a groove of an appropriate width on it so that the edges of the strip will be somewhat rounded in a manner reminiscent of chair-seating cane.

Small holes are made in the rim with an awl or bodkin about ⅝" (15mm) from the lower edge. These holes should be at intervals of ⅜" (9mm) and, once they are made, the briar rim is sewn onto the rim using thin strips of ash similar to the lacing strips. These strips for sewing should be soaked in water for a few minutes before use. The sewing strip is shoved up between the briar band and the rim, brought around the briar band on the outside, through the hole and down on the inside to come out underneath **(Fig 6.2)**. It is brought around twice in this way, and when it enters the hole for the third time it is tucked under the two thicknesses of itself already there and then cut off. This process is repeated for each hole.

The strips for lacing are first soaked in water and the first to be put in are the central ones. The point of a knife is inserted between the rim and briar band to hold them apart and the tip of the lacing strip is put into this so that the strip is about 10" (25cm) above the briar band. The length of ash that is to form the anchoring band is placed against the rim immediately above the briar band, with the lacing strip between it and the rim. The lacing strip is brought around the anchoring band and pushed out between the briar band

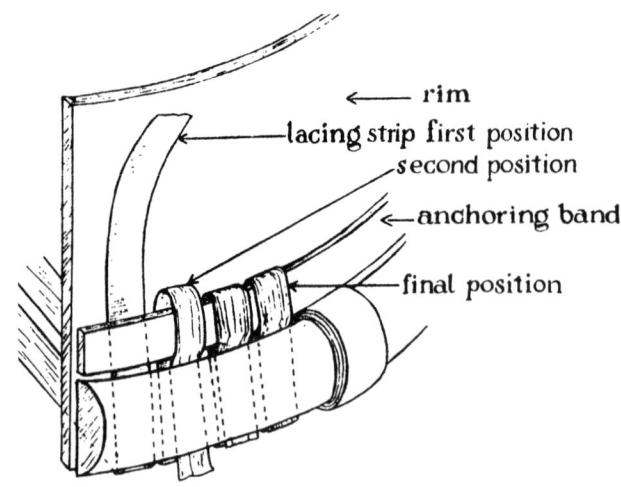

Fig. 6.3 (Lucas 1954.)

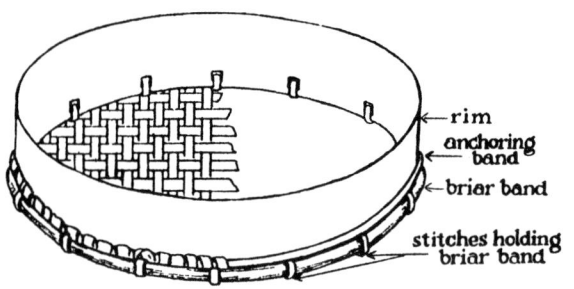

Fig. 6.4 (Lucas 1954.)

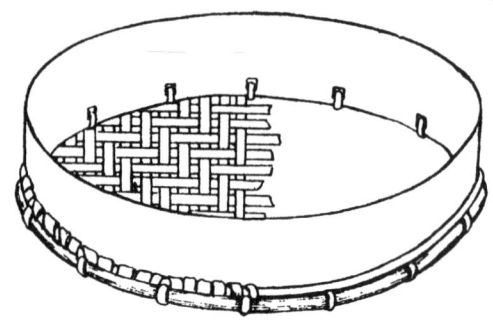

Fig. 6.5 (Lucas 1954.)

and the rim and cut flush. This is shown in **Fig. 6.3**. The other end of the lacing strip is put in on the opposite side in the same way. The next strip is put in a different direction to the first; thus if the first strip is north–south, the next will lie east–west. Others are added in the same way keeping the number being added in one direction (north–south) similar to those being added in the other (east–west). Thus in the part-made sieve in **Pl. 6.8**, the next lacing strips to be put in will balance the eleven or twelve already going across the sieve. Each of these would be worked alternately over under to give the plain weave shown in the almost completed sieve in **Pl. 6.8** and also illustrated in **Fig. 6.4**. As the weaving proceeds, the strips used become shorter and the tension on those already in position increases as each new strip is inserted. Part of the skill in sieve-making lay in allowing just enough slackness in the first strokes, as these would become progressively tighter as the work proceeded.

Some sieves were woven in twill weave as shown in **Fig. 6.5**. There are examples of different types of sieves in the National Museum collection as well as examples of part-made sieves in F 1948 Items 105–123. A sieve in the collection from County Donegal was laced up in a different way and details of this are contained in A.T. Lucas's article (see footnote 6) from which the illustrations used here are also taken.

7
Straw, rush and grasses

STRAW was an abundant material in the Irish countryside at least until the middle of the twentieth century. It was used for thatching roofs, for the making of twisted ropes known as *súgán* and for making a wide variety of baskets. Although thatching is outside the scope of this book,[1] it should be noted that many of the roofs along the Atlantic seaboard had the thatch secured not by the hazel or willow pegs known as scollops but by long *súgán* ropes of twisted straw or grass **(Pl. 7.1)**. Although *súgan* ropes were displaced by manufactured rope once this became widely available, *súgan* ropes swelled with the rain, added weight against the wind and were probably better in storms.

Pl. 7.1—Súgán rope on a thatched roof, County Donegal, c. 1900. Note also the súgán twister or thraw-hook (corr shúgáin) hanging from the eve of the house. The creel on the left may be a pardóg *or hinged-bottomed creel because of the woven base beside it. To the right of the creel is a longline basket similar to the type used in Antrim, so presumably this style was also used in Donegal. Photo from the Welch Collection, courtesy of Ulster Museum.*

159

Súgán ropes

These ropes were made by using rope twisters known as thraw-hooks (*corr shúgáin*). These were formerly made from wood but more recently a piece of bent wire resembling a carpenter's brace has largely replaced the wooden hook (**Fig. 7.1**). Two people are required to make such ropes. One person twists the hook while the other gradually feeds the straw or grass into the rope. As the rope grows, the person who is twisting the thraw hook retreats further and further from the stack of straw or other roping material. When the desired length has been reached the rope is rolled into a ball or clew, which can then be stored until needed. While the clew of *súgán* rope for thatching is usually round, that used for seating is torpedo-shaped and is known as a *miogal* in Irish. Where only a short length of *súgán* rope is needed it is not necessary to use a thraw-hook. Short ropes known as thumb ropes are made by twisting the straw with one's thumb while gradually drawing the rope out of the pile of straw.

Rye and oaten straw were both suitable for *súgán* rope making, but ropes were also made from hay, purple moor grass — usually called sedge in Ireland — bent grass, field rushes, heather, willow bark, horsehair, rawhide and even from strips of bog deal or bog-fir. Hay ropes were softer and stronger than straw ropes and were often used where a straw rope might wear too quickly, such as in horse or donkey harnesses, carrying ropes for creels or for simple burden ropes. A close look at the creels in **Pl. 4.6** shows that these creels are secured on the back in knapsack fashion by *súgán* ropes. Creels were

Fig. 7.1—Thraw hooks

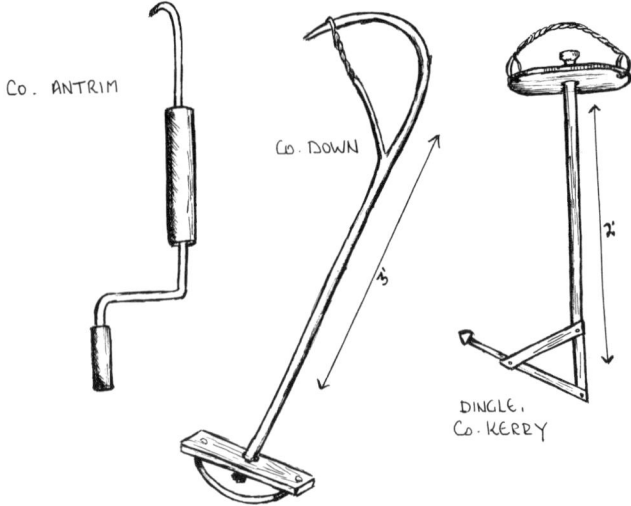

Co. ANTRIM

Co. DOWN

DINGLE, Co. KERRY

also carried by means of a rope across the chest, and this rope was also usually made from hay rather than straw, and wrapped with rags or sacking to make it more comfortable.[2] Burden ropes were used to carry in the harvest where tracks were poor or where there was no tradition of a horse and slide car. Such ropes were also useful for carrying piles of bedding or piles of sedge for thatching. Most burden ropes had a simple eye on one end but some had a piece of wood with a hole bored in it to allow the rope to pass through. Shorter lengths of *súgán* or langles (*lúbacha*) were used

Pl. 7.2—Christie Sullivan seating a súgán chair. Photo courtesy of David Shaw-Smith.

to tether or spancel animals, a practice that was very common in poorer districts in the last century due to a lack of adequate fences. Straw or hay *súgán* was also widely used for chair seating, where it was stretched across the rungs of a chair or stool to form a strong and durable seat **(Pl. 7.2)**. The process of seating is fairly straightforward and is much quicker than seating with rush. **Pl. 7.3** shows the detail of a *súgán* seat: the rope is first stretched from side rail to side rail and then brought from front to back. Allowance has been made in the weaving for the fact that the chair is wider at the front. This style is still popular, but modern *súgán*-style chairs are usually seated with cord or twine in the sea-grass style rather than

Pl. 7.3—Detail of súgán chair seat.

with the original straw or hay *súgán*.

Súgán ropes of willow skin were sometimes used for such seats, especially in areas that had a strong tradition of professional basketmaking — the peeling of willow for so-called 'fancy baskets' meant that a ready supply of willow bark was available. Sedge (purple moor grass) was widely used for rope-making, so much so that the

Pl. 7.4—Making a rope from slivers of bog-fir. Photo courtesy of DIF, UCD.

Irish term for this grass in some districts was literally 'straw for rope-making'.[3] Heather and bent-grass ropes were made using a thraw-hook, but the ropes of bog-fir were always made by hand **(Pl. 7.4)**. For these, thin strips of straight-grained bog-fir are scraped off a log and these are then twisted to form a strong and extremely durable rope. Two or sometimes three of these ropes are twisted together to form a rope that combines strength and elasticity and is also extremely durable even when used outdoors. Bog-fir rope was often stretched across a wooden bed-frame to form a base over which a straw mattress could be laid. Other materials used for rope-making included elm-bark and willow rods, both of which were used to make ropes for plough-traces.

Field rushes for rope-making were cut in late summer or early autumn and were pounded with a wooden mallet or maul and then twisted by hand to get rid of the pith. They were then allowed to dry in the sun; when sufficiently dry these were bundled up and stored in readiness for making *súgán* ropes in the winter.

Thicker ropes of *súgán* were sometimes needed, for example in the *síogóg* or straw granary mentioned later in this chapter. Thick *súgán* ropes were also needed for some styles of horse-collars and for the packsaddle, which is also described later. A thick *súgán* rope was woven through the window of a kish (a large cart basket) in the County Offaly area. Thick *súgán* ropes impregnated with mud or clay plaster and known as *putógs* were sometimes woven between wooden poles to form a straw and post chimney canopy rather than the more usual wicker canopy. This thick *súgán* rope was made by turning a large stick or pole to form the rope, since the thraw-hook would be unable to exert enough force to effect the twist on such thick material.

Straw baskets and mats

The most common technique used in the making of straw baskets and mats was a three-strand plait, where the straw binds the rows of weaving together, and is then plaited into the core of the basket. This technique is in marked contrast to the coiled technique of straw-work that

is so widely practised throughout the rest of Europe, where a core of straw is formed and sewn on to the previous rows using a sewing material such as split bramble. Coilwork may have come northwards to Europe from Africa, where this method is highly developed and where beautiful examples of such work are still very common. Its distribution in Ireland was not so widespread, though it was used throughout Ireland for making beehives **(Pl. 7.5)**. It was also used in the south, midlands and east for making seed-baskets, and a few armchairs in the National Museum collection from the midlands and the south-east were made in this way **(Pl. 7.6)**. There are also good examples of coiled armchairs at the Irish Agricultural Museum in County Wexford. The Aran kisheen **(Pl. 7.7)** is also made using coilwork technique. This basket, made from rye straw and sewn with split bramble, was used for carrying hot food such as boiled potatoes to people working outside in the fields, and there is no doubt that the straw would have acted as an excellent insulator for keeping the food warm. In Aran, a bone pin was used for

Pl. 7.5—Jack Carey from Clonakilty, Co. Cork, splitting blackberry briar to use as sewing material in the making of coiled straw bee-skeps. Note the finished bee-skeps beside him. Photo courtesy of David Shaw-Smith.

Pl. 7.6—Straw seats showing three-strand plait and coilwork. The low seat at the left from Doolin, Co. Clare, is plaited and stuffed with straw or hay. The coilwork chair is from County Wexford. Most coilwork chairs had a timber sub-frame to give stability. The coilwork stool is from County Galway and is also stuffed with straw. Photo courtesy of NMI.

Pl. 7.7—Aran kisheen made from rye straw and blackberry briar. Photo courtesy of NMI.

inserting the split-briar ties. Dr Muriel Gahan, who had a lifelong interest in Irish crafts, suggested that the inward slope of this narrow basket was a response to the terrain of the island, with its network of stone walls that had to be crossed on a journey to the fields, where the contents of a wider basket might be more easily spilled.

While split bramble was the most common material for sewing the coils of straw together, willow skin was also used. J. G. Delaney, a collector with the Irish Folklore Commission, informed the museum: 'Thomas Egan told me of a seed basket for sowing seed broadcast that his father made. It was made of rye straw and sewn with the bark of sally rods, which had been boiled to make peeling of the bark easy. It had two lugs, through which a rope was attached for going around the sower's neck.'[4]

The more common three-strand plait technique was used for a very wide range of baskets such as hen's nests in their various local styles (**Pl. 7.8**). It was also used for mats of different sizes, from the straddle mats that are put on a donkey prior to putting on creels (**Pl. 7.9**) to the straw mattress shown in **Pl. 7.10**. To make a mat, a length of *súgán* rope at least twice the width of the desired mat is required. This

Fig. 7.2—Tates, fletches, sops or wisps.

súgán is then folded in half and the two ropes are plaited across each other in turn with small handfuls of straw (**Fig. 7.2**). These handfuls are known as 'tates' in Ulster, as 'fletches' in County Wexford and as 'sops' or 'wisps' in other parts of the country.

These tates must be made from clean, straight straw, which has not been broken or damaged in any way. Straw that has been hand-scutched (i.e., the seed heads are threshed or beaten over a stone) is ideal, but straw that has been threshed using a flail is also suitable. Even machine-threshed straw could be used, provided the threshing machine was adapted so that the straw itself did not enter the threshing drum, as is done when straw is required for thatching. Oaten straw is the easiest straw for making the three-strand plait type of basket, but rye straw can also be used and, in fact, makes a stronger and more durable mat or basket than oaten straw.

Fig. 7.3—Forming a three-plait.

The thickness of the tates will determine the bulk of the mat; thicker tates will give a thicker plait and thus a thicker mat. When the desired width has been reached, which in the case of a small straddle mat is after seven tates have been inserted, the maker folds the rope over on itself and starts to form a three-plait by incorporating the left and right side of the tate below to combine with the remainder of the rope, as shown in **Fig. 7.3**. It is important to remember that before using a tate one must first insert a fresh tate in the new row, which will provide the plaiting material for the

subsequent row. Whenever the plaiting material begins to run out, the tate below can be incorporated, making the almost spent plait one element of the new triple plait, the other two being provided by the two sides of newly incorporated tate. More detailed instructions for this are given in the technique section of this chapter.

Pl. 7.8—One and two-storey hen's nests made by Ted Kelly, Ballintogher, Co. Sligo, using three-strand plait technique.

The straddle mats were usually hinged together using two or more *súgán* ties as hinges, though sometimes one larger straddle mat was used. In all such cases the straddle mats were secured around the donkey or pony with a rope or 'belly band', which would formerly have been of *súgán* but in more recent times would more likely have been of manufactured rope or of leather. A wooden straddle often formed by a forked piece of wood (*coirb*) is attached

Pl. 7.9—Hinged straddle mats of oaten straw. These were put on the donkey before the creels were loaded on. The straw-work was not always visible however, as it was customary to cover the straddle mats with sacking in many districts (see also Pl. 7.11).

Pl. 7.10—Peter Johnson and Michael Malone of Ballinlassie, Fardrum, Athlone, Co. Westmeath, holding a straw mattress that they made for the National Museum of Ireland in 1967. The process was photographed by Brendan Doyle. Photo courtesy of NMI.

Pl. 7.11—Straddle mat in three-strand plait and wooden crutch (coirb). Photo courtesy of David Shaw-Smith.

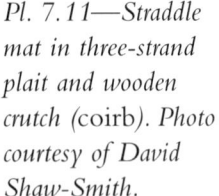

to the straddle and two pegs protrude from the straddle on to which the creels or panniers can be hung **(Pl. 7.11)**, though there were numerous different regional variations of straddle patterns.

The mattress shown in **Pl. 7.10** is essentially a large mat, the principle of construction being exactly the same, except that a thumb-rope or thumb-*súgán* (a *súgán* rope made by hand) was sufficient for the straddle mats. The longer length of *súgán* rope needed for the mattress was more easily made using a thraw-hook. Such a mattress took a considerable amount of time to make, at least a day, and probably used up to 100 sheaves of straw. Some of these mattresses were designed to fold up so that they could be stored under a bed; this seems to have been especially true in Ulster.[5] This meant that mattresses in Ulster were made by joining two halves together in the same manner as the straddle mats. These straw mattresses seem to have been placed onto a base formed by bog-fir ropes being laced from side to side through holes in the framework of the bed to give a mesh-like effect.

The traditional rural houseplan included a bed in the kitchen, often in a specially made jut-out known as an out-shot or *cailleach*, and these beds were usually screened with straw mats.[6]

Mats were made to measure to line the

floor of a cart and these were used, at least in Ulster, when bringing young pigs to market. A small rectangular mat, known locally as a 'wheeze', was used in the Fermanagh area by thatchers to protect their knees. A circular straw mat, or 'head', again of three-plait technique, was made in Armagh for the top of apple barrels to protect the apples.[7]

Mats were also used for covering door openings and windows; the wicker doors mentioned in Chapter 1 were usually used in conjunction with a straw mat. These doors would have been very draughty indeed without a straw mat liner to make them windproof. Estyn Evans suggests that 'wattled houses of the better class may once have been lined with straw mats serving as draught screens and taking the place of the hanging skins, carpets or tapestries of other cultures'.[8]

Smaller mats were used for the window openings in former times when these openings were unlikely to have had glass. Even in the nineteeth century, many travellers commented on the primitive nature of some of the peasant dwellings, so it is likely that not all permanent houses had windows fitted at that time. The tradition of 'booleying' or moving stock to upland or mountain pastures for summer grazing, which was once widely practised throughout Ireland, survived in Donegal and Achill into the middle of the nineteenth century.[9] The booley houses were sometimes built of stone but often they were merely rough sod houses. Because they were only occupied during the summer months, it is likely that straw-mat windows and wicker and straw doors were considered adequate for these. Although these lining mats were usually made in

Pl. 7.12—Window mat in rye straw from the Aran Islands. Although superficially similar to the three-strand plait, the technique used in making this mat is more like coilwork, with each coil or bundle of straw being sewn to the next with straw.

the three-strand plait technique, some used a hybrid technique that, although superficially similar to the three-strand plait, is in fact somewhat akin to coilwork in that the strands of straw are not twisted, but laid down in straight rows, which are secured with ties of straw. A rye straw window mat of this type from the Aran Islands is shown in **Pl. 7.12**, and it is likely that this technique was adopted because it could be done more quickly than the three-strand plait.

Hen's nests, burden-baskets and chairs

Straw hen's nests were made in a wide variety of styles throughout the country. Most were round-roofed baskets with an opening at the front through which the hen could enter. Some of these round nests were tall and conical **(Fig. 7.4)** while others were only a little higher than their width, and almost igloo-like in shape **(Pl. 7.8)**. Some nests were equipped with handles so that they could be hung from pegs in the wall or from the roof timber. This may have been to prevent dogs or even rats from stealing the eggs. Many, however, had no such handles and were simply placed on a shelf some three or four feet (1–1.3m) from the ground. Not all round hen's nests were roofed; some were simply fairly shallow baskets about 10" (25.5cm) deep, which were equipped with a hanger and hung from

the ceiling **(Pl. 7.13)**. Nor were they all round; some were oval with a vertical partition so that two hens could be accommodated at one time, and **Fig. 7.5** shows a rectangular hen's nest with two floors. One hen's nest in the National Museum collection from the Kilmaley region of County Clare has a decorative plait around the opening, a feature that I have not seen on any other nest.

All of these hen's nests served as egg-laying baskets and most had a loose nest of hay or straw placed inside them for greater warmth and comfort. These well-insulated nests were so popular with hens that they would often wait to use one rather than lay elsewhere.[10] As anyone who has kept free-range hens can confirm, one of the difficulties can be preventing such hens wandering off and laying their eggs in secret places, so the hen's nests were a great help in solving this problem. Eggs replaced flax after the Famine to pay the rent. Fowl were complementary to small-scale pig production since they picked up all the minute waste of the farm. Prices for livestock crashed in the 1920s and 1930s, and eggs provided a vital cash income at this time. I remember my father telling me that in those years his mother often earned more from her flock of hens than his father did from livestock. Many small farms then had twenty or thirty laying hens as well as various other types of poultry, so it would not have been unusual to see six or more hen's nests around the farm. Though they may appear picturesque to us now, they were eminently practical then.

An unusual style of hen's nest in the National Musem collection comes from the Dunkellin area of east Galway. This style has a wicker door and may have been used to train a wandering hen to the nest. Another possibility is that the door was for the protection of a clutching hen, i.e., a hen sitting on a clutch of hatching eggs, though such hens were often accommodated by providing them with a creel lined with hay or straw.

Hen's nests are usually started in a similar fashion

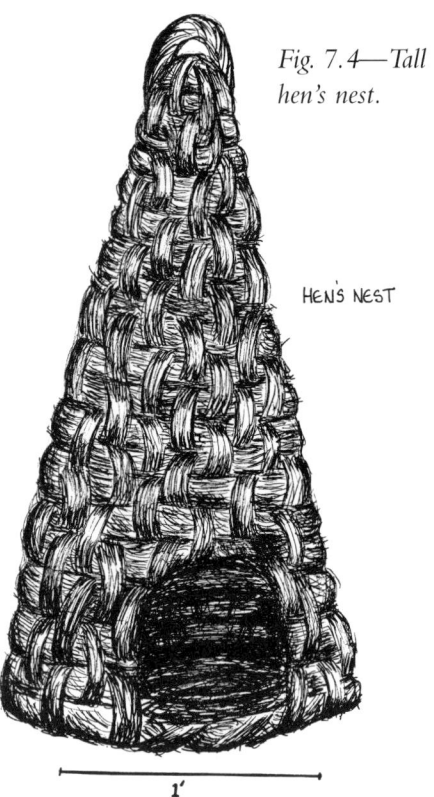

Fig. 7.4—Tall hen's nest.

HEN'S NEST

1'

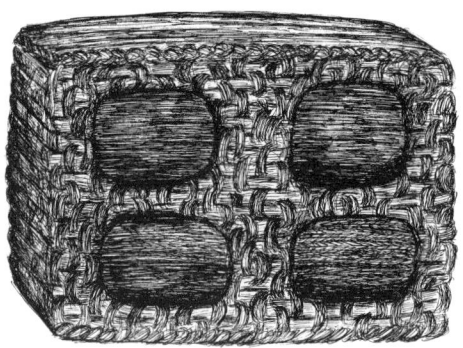

Fig. 7.5—Rectangular hen's nest.

Pl. 7.14—Side view of base of hen's nest showing protruding tates of straw. A new tate is just being added at this point. Photo courtesy of David Shaw-Smith.

to a mat or straddle with a thumb rope of *súgán* being folded over and a two-plait begun. Four or five tates of straw are inserted at the intersection as already described for the straddle **(Fig. 7.2)**. For the nest this rope with protruding tates is then rolled up to form the inner core of the basket or nest **(Pl. 7.14)**, with the base being made on its side and further tates being added as the circle widens. A small hen's nest of about 13" (33cm) diameter would require about twelve tates, but a large nest of 20" (51cm) diameter would require at least eighteen tates.

Another basket which was made in a similar way to a hen's nest was a pigeon's nest. This was a basket of about 10" (25cm) diameter with low sides of about 4" (10cm), though up to 6" (15cm) high at one point **(Fig. 7.6)**. These baskets were hung in stables and out-houses in Counties Down, Armagh and Tyrone. The County Museum in Armagh has one such nest, which was made and donated by Peter Hagan of Legaroe, Co. Tyrone.

I learned to make a hen's nest from John Michael Larkin of Ballinakill near Woodford in east Galway about 1979, and he called the hen's nest a *siomnóg*. In the Erris area of north-west Mayo, the nest was known as a *peillic* and in County Clare it was called a *siantán*. Ted Kelly, Ireland's foremost maker of plaited straw-work, says that in his part of County Sligo the hen's nest was simply called a *ciseán* (anglicised as kissaun), the Irish word for a basket. Interestingly, Ted starts his nests and stools by simply folding a tate or handful of straw across itself and inserting a larger handful of straw, which would be of sufficient bulk for four or five tates. The three-plait is begun immediately and the plaiting is augmented by dividing the thick central tate into four or five lesser ones as the weaving proceeds; further details of this are given in the technique section.

The chair in **Pl. 7.15** is also made in the three-plait method and this method of construction was

Fig. 7.6—Pigeon's nest

far more popular for chairs and stools than the coilwork technique used to make the chair in **Pl. 7.6**. Low stools of straw, which might nowadays be regarded as footstools, were more common than chairs. These stools were usually called 'bosses' and were regarded as being perfectly adequate at least for the young able-bodied members of the family. They were easier to store away than the straw armchairs. These stools were in effect round three-plait weave-baskets that, when made, were stuffed full of hay to prevent the seat from sagging. In modern examples that I have seen, this stuffing is kept in by tying a lattice of binder twine across the mouth of the basket so that it won't spill out on the floor when the basket is turned

upside-down to become a seat. It is likely that this criss–cross tying was formerly done with *súgán* rope. The chair was made in the same way as the boss or stool and when turned upright extra tates were poked through the sides and the back to allow the remainder of the chair to be woven. The boss features in William Carleton's story about hedge-schools in the early 1800s:

> along the walls on the ground is a series of round stones, some of them capped with a straw collar or hassock on which the boys sit; others have bosses and many of them have hobs – a light but compact kind of boggy substance found in the mountains.[11]

The fact that Carleton does not need to explain the boss to his readers suggests that these straw stools were then commonplace. I have already referred in Chapter 2 to the lack of furniture in many peasant houses in pre-Famine Ireland. The scarcity of wooden furniture or even of wood to make furniture in the poorest districts makes it easier to understand the popularity of straw furnishings, because they could be made by people themselves, without tools, from the material at hand.

Another item associated with the hedge-school was the suggan, or dunce's muff. This was a collar worn around the neck by

Pl. 7.15— Conchubhar Pheadair Ó Síocháin, Oileáin Chléire, Co. Cork, with a straw armchair in three-strand plait. At his feet is a long mat, which may be a straddle mat for using with creels, though because of its length it might also have been used for carrying sacks on a donkey or pony. Photo taken around 1930, courtesy of DIF, UCD.

inattentive pupils at a hedge-school, apparently for up to two hours. It would have been itchy and uncomfortable on the neck and would probably have been regarded as a deterrent to inattention in the future.

Straw was also used for burden baskets. The straw *tiachóg* (pronounced cheeakogue) in **Pl. 7.16** was acquired by A.T. Lucas, then Director of the National Museum, in 1955 at Portacloy, Co. Mayo. I had never heard of such a basket from any of the straw-workers that I have met, nor had I come across any reference to it in anything I had read. Indeed, until I found the photograph of the straw *tiachóg* in the National Museum collection, I believed that Ireland, unlike Scotland, had no examples of straw burden-baskets. It is unlikely that such baskets were

Pl. 7.16—Straw tiachóg from Portacloy, Co. Mayo. This straw burden-basket was made for the National Museum of Ireland in 1955, but the baskets had gone out of use in the area many years earlier. Photo courtesy of NMI.

common here, the creel being the popular burden-basket in Ireland. In Scotland, however, the kishie, a straw burden-basket using a twining technique, was widely used especially on the outer islands where willows were fairly scarce. The Portacloy area in north Mayo is close to the Mullet Peninsula, an exposed area where willows were not so readily available due to lack of shelter. It is also in the Mullet area that heather lobster pots and creels from docks were

Pl. 7.17—Straw shopping or egg basket made in three-strand plait. The tates or fletches of straw used for this basket are much thinner than those used for the hen's nests or straddle mats. This basket is at Newtowncashel Heritage Centre, Co. Westmeath. Photo courtesy of Vivienne Mayne.

used. Perhaps the survival of the straw *tiachóg* here until the 1950s is due to the fact that the choice of other materials was not as great in the area. Indeed the straw *tiachóg* was not in general use even in 1955 when the museum acquired the one in **Pl. 7.16**. The museum notes written by Dr. Lucas state that it was made by Thomas Burns of Portacloy, 'under the direction of' Michael Garvin, who was then aged 92 and who remembered these baskets in use. This implies that they had gone out of use in this area sometime previously. They were mainly used for carrying potatoes and corn. When used for carrying corn into the house for drying on a rack over the fire, the full straw *tiachóg* was often left beside the fire so that the corn could get a preliminary drying while still in it. The rush *tiachóg*, a bag-like basket made from field rush, which is described later in this chapter, was also made in this area. The relative isolation of the area probably contributed to the fact that traditional skills survived there when they had become extinct elsewhere.

Undoubtedly, the three-plait technique was also used to make other baskets. K.M. Harris reports that seed-sowing baskets in various parts of Ulster were made using the plaited technique,[12] though in the midlands, south and east, where straw seed-sowing baskets were also used, these seem to have been made from coilwork.[13] Many small baskets, for storing eggs for example, were made in the plaited techniques, and the work could be made slighter and less bulky.

Pl. 7.18—Straw cradle made by Ted Kelly. This cradle is on display at Riverstown Heritage Centre, Co. Sligo. Photo courtesy of David Shaw-Smith.

While most of these baskets were probably round, **Pl. 7.17** shows a nice oval basket about 11" (28cm) long from Newtowncashel Heritage Centre, Co. Longford. The plaiting technique was also employed to make the cradle in **Pl. 7.18**.

Straw hats and costumes

Straw hats and costumes were worn by revellers at various festivals and celebrations. Strawboys dressed in tall conical hats and in straw costumes similar to the one in **Pl. 7.19** would attend a wedding as uninvited guests. These were young men from the surrounding area who, because they were dressed in this fashion, were allowed in and entertained at the house dance that usually followed a country wedding. The leader of the strawboys claimed the right to dance with the bride. The tall conical hats ensured that the strawboys were well disguised and that the other guests could not be sure of their identity. In County Fermanagh, it was customary for the strawboys, if they had been hospitably received, to burn their costumes in front of the bride and groom to bring good luck to the newlyweds. If, however, they were dissatisfied, they hung their costumes up in a tree so that all might see the meanness of the newly married couple.[14]

Disguise was also an important element in the mumming or Christmas rhyming that was practised throughout the twelve days of Christmas. At its most elaborate, this involved the mumming group going around from house to house to perform a medieval-style drama, which was spoken in verse. This tradition was strongest in Ulster and still survives in County Fermanagh, where the play may last for about a quarter of an hour, and the cast of characters includes Captain Mummer, Jack Straw, Prince George and the Doctor. Each member of the group, other than the Doctor, relies on a tall straw hat to conceal his identity, and much of the fun for the onlookers lies in trying to guess the identity of each member of the troupe. The money collected at the end of the twelve days of Christmas was spent on a dance or *céilí* where there would be drink and

Pl. 7.19—Straw costume, Co. Fermanagh. These costumes were used by strawboys at wedding as well as by Christmas rhymers and mummers. The vertical elements were often plaited to give a more elaborate mask or hat. Photo courtesy of UFTM.

tobacco for the men and tea with bread and jam for the women. Halfway through the night each character would fetch any part of his costume that was made of straw and this was piled high in a nearby field and set alight.[15] The cast of characters of the Fermanagh mumming play are preserved in beautiful miniature dolls made by Meg McSpirit Jones, Mullinastea, Co. Fermanagh, which can be seen at the National Museum, Collins Barracks. An account of a mumming troupe from County Tyrone calls them Christmas Rymers and describes them as follows:

> They wore high straw helmets, their faces being blackened, and peeping out through the straw which partly hid their faces. Coats of straw encased their bodies like coats of mail … Straw encased their legs too, and partly covered their leggings or strong boots.[16]

Fig. 7.7—Whelper's suit from County Roscommon. This is a drawing of a suit made from rye straw in the National Museum collection.

Further south, the Christmas mumming activity was concentrated on St Stephen's Day, 26 December, when a wren was killed and carried around the countryside from house to house by a procession of youths and young men formally dressed in straw costumes or with blackened faces. The group usually had music and songs, often accompanied by percussion from the *bodhrán* (goatskin drum). They called on each house to give them the money to bury the wren or, failing that, to give drinks or refreshments to the troupe. Estyn Evans believes that: 'The wren boy processions, despite their English rhymes, appear to be a degeneration of more elaborate performances of native origin.'[17] This view is supported by the fact that in Irish-speaking areas, the wren boy rhymes are in Irish.

Halloween, or *Samhain*, was another time when straw costumes were worn, and the many games and amusements involving apples, nuts, etc., are probably survivors of an older pre-Christian festival. Halloween caps of plaited straw or woven rushes were made in certain parts of the country, at least until the early part of the twentieth century.[18] Some straw costumes were quite elaborately made, the whelper's suit in **Fig. 7.7** being a good example.

On St Brigid's Eve, 31 January, people dressed in straw costumes (biddies or biddy-boys), and carried a straw doll known as a *brídeog* from house to house in honour of the saint. This practice was especially common in the south-western counties of Cork and Kerry. Remnants of such practices exist in other areas. In the Blue Stack Mountains of County Donegal, Robert Bernen describes how his neighbour, Peadar Nohar More, a person whom he describes as faithful to old traditions, 'brings in Brigid' each St Brigid's Day (1 February). [19] Undoubtedly, it is rush rather than straw that is most associated with St Brigid's Day, and this will be discussed in the later part of this chapter dealing with rush. However, in Tory Island, Co. Donegal, a protective charm, known as the *Bratóg Bhríde* (St Brigid's sheet or cloak), was made of oaten straw. It was worn by the fishermen of Tory as a protection against storms. [20]

Harvest knots were formed from newly ripe straw and were exchanged as love tokens in the past, though more recently this symbolic meaning was lost and they were simply worn as decorations. The young women's harvest knots had the ears of corn left on, making them more decorative than those of the young men. Harvest knots were also made from flax, particularly in Ulster, where flax was more widely grown than in other parts of Ireland, although flax was widely grown in other parts of Ireland up to the nineteenth century.

A corn dolly was sometimes made for decorating the stack of corn in autumn. This was often made from the last sheaf of corn. This sheaf, known variously as the *cailleach* or the hare, was the subject of ritual cutting when the harvesting of the corn involved most of the community in the saving of the harvest. Sometimes hooks would be thrown, usually by the young men, at the last standing sheaf and the person who succeeded in cutting it was expected to be the first to marry. [21] Where corn dollies were made, they do not seem to have been nearly as elaborate as those in Britain, where corn dollies of great skill and intricacy were made.

Straw collars and harnesses

The earliest information about the type of harnesses used in ploughing in Ireland is a reference by William Lithgow, who, in Ulster in 1619, saw ploughs being pulled by horses, of which he says: 'wanting garnishing [lacking harness], they are only fastened with straw or wooden ropes to their bare rumps'.[22] This is a reference to the then common practice in Ireland of 'ploughing by the tail'. In this arrangement a group of horses, which seems to have been usually four but could number up to six, walked abreast with ropes of twisted rods (gads) or of *súgán* securing the plough to their tails. This practice was explained by another writer, Thomas Dineley, who said that if the plough met an obstacle it was far easier to stop the horses walking abreast than if they had been tackled singly or in pairs in a long line.[23] The fact that the ropes were attached to the tails meant that the horses immediately felt the obstruction and stopped. This practice, condemned by many observers as primitive and cruel, explains why collars, so necessary for providing traction when horses plough in a line, were not used for ploughing in Ireland at that time. Indeed, the practice of ploughing with horses was only introduced in Ireland from the twelfth century onwards. Ploughing up to that time had been done by teams of eight oxen, and while the old Irish Brehon Laws mention the use of straw and withy ropes for tethering livestock, no details are available of how these oxen were yoked for ploughing.

We have no information on whether straw collars were in use for other purposes when Lithgow was writing, around 1620. Collars would still have been necessary for cartwork, and where tracks were unsuitable for wheel carts it is possible that slide cars, for which collars would also have been necessary, were used. Perhaps most loads at this time were carried using the packsaddles of straw or hay described later in this chapter.

More orthodox methods of ploughing were gradually adopted from the eighteenth century onwards, and it is not surprising that straw was used for making the collars, since it was already in widespread use for saddles. A city by-law was passed in Dublin near the end of the seventeenth century forbidding people to ride with straw saddles or stirrups, a practice that seems to have been widespread at the time. A traveller from Dublin to Dundalk in 1729 described meeting over two hundred horsemen, only seventeen of whom had leather saddles; the others had saddles and harnesses of straw.[24] It is likely that these saddles were made on the same principle as the straw mats described earlier, and although I know of no photographs or sketches of them, such saddles were still in use in 1860 near Diamond Mountain, now the site of Connemara National Park.[25]

Pl. 7.20—Slide car in use at the Glens of Antrim. Note the 'rough' straw collar, straw straddle mat and súgán rope harness. Photo from the Welch Collection, courtesy of the Ulster Museum.

Straw horse-collars were to be found throughout the country from 1800 onwards, and while they were dismissed by some observers because they weren't leather, others realised that they fulfilled the same function as leather collars and did so far more cheaply. However, in 1827, the Irish diarist, Amhlaoibh Ó Súilleabháin, writing about the region of Callan in County Kilkenny, laments the replacement of the Irish *súgán* collar by the English leather collar. Writing about the harness-maker *Súgán* Keogh, he comments:

Pl. 7.21—Mick and John McHugh, Co. Donegal, holding a 'rough' horse-collar made from súgán rope. Photo courtesy of UFTM.

> His trade is gone; for the foreign soogawn [leather collar] has replaced the Irish one, during the last twenty years. The Irish collar was made as follows—a straw rope was twisted and turned round on itself in the shape of an O, and withings of woven briar were attached as a front to it. Then it was simply pushed down over the horse's head wherever he was going to do some work. To this collar were fixed suitable hames, by means of a loop above and a breast withe, gad brollaigh, underneath.[26]

This is in the prosperous county of Kilkenny, however, and it seems that straw collars were still in widespread use especially in the west and north of the country. A German visitor writing in 1842 observed:

In other countries, straw ropes are also occasionally used, but I never before saw an entire harness of plaited straw; and what is more remarkable is, that it was not a mere makeshift, or the whim of an individual, but the general custom throughout the whole west of Ireland.[27]

Nor was the use of these collars confined to the west. **Pl. 7.20**, a photograph taken in the early 1900s, shows a horse and slide car in the Glens of Antrim, where the harness is entirely of straw. Straw collars were sufficiently common in Ulster up to the 1950s that Estyn Evans wrote in 1957:

> Straw collars — made entirely of straw and not merely straw stuffed — have so recently gone out of use that I have seen several decayed specimens on hill farms in the North, and the art of making them is not forgotten.[28]

Pl. 7.22—Rough plaited straw horse-collar. Photo courtesy of UFTM.

Fortunately, the museums acted before the art of making collars was forgotten, and throughout the 1950s and 1960s both the National Museum of Ireland and the Ulster Folk and Transport Museum obtained various examples of straw collars and harnesses. Even as late as 1980, the Ulster Folk and Transport Museum obtained a newly made horse-collar from north Donegal.

Straw collars can be divided into two classes, rough and fancy. Rough collars seem to have been more generally used. Not all so-called rough collars are the same; there are two basic types: (a) rough collars that are formed by using a thick *súgán* rope, such as the collars shown in **Pls. 7.20 and 7.21**, and (b) rough plaited collars similar to that shown in **Pl. 7.22**. Fancy collars were plaited also but were made from straight straw rather than the twisted *súgán* and were more time-consuming to make. A completed example of a fancy horse-collar, as well as the straw plait prior to sewing the plait together to form the collar, can be seen in **Pl. 7.23**. All of these collars were usually made from oat straw.

Rough horse-collars of thick *súgán* rope.

To make the collar, a thick *súgán* rope must first be made. Because of the thickness of rope needed, the thraw-hook or twister mentioned earlier (under the *súgán* heading) is not sufficiently strong and instead a strong stick about a yard or a metre long and at least 1" (2.5cm) in diameter is used. A thumb-rope of straw is wrapped around the stick and then the rope is formed by one person twisting the stick while the other adds the straw, adding it evenly to ensure the thickness of the rope remains constant. About 13 yards (12m) of rope are needed, and one end of the rope is formed into the shape of the collar and held there. The remainder of the rope is turned in and out of this closed collar to give the twisted ply effect seen in **Pl. 7.21**. The collar is completed by tying a knot on top. The collar in **Pl. 7.21** was made by Mick McHugh and Patrick Brogan, both from near Hornhead, Dunfanaghy, Co. Donegal, and Mick McHugh also made a hames for the collar. These are different to the hames used on a leather collar. As Jonathan Bell, a curator with the Ulster Folk and Transport Museum, explains:

> In most leather harnesses, hames are made of wood and metal bound together at one end to make a distinctive lyre shape. The hames Mr McHugh made were much simpler but equally effective; two flat pieces of wood curved on the inside to follow the shape of the horse's neck. These pieces of wood were simply joined by string.[29]

Because of the use of flat pieces of wood for the hames, it was not necessary to provide a groove in the collar to accommodate the hames. The collar in use on the Glens of Antrim slide car **(Pl. 7.20)** is made in a similar fashion to the one just described, and a close look at the photograph reveals that the hames on the collar is also made of flat pieces of wood.

This type of horse-collar was the simplest and quickest to make, which suggests that it was once widely distributed. It seems to be the type described in the account quoted earlier from County Kilkenny and may also be the type of collar described in County Kerry more than a century later. An 83-year-old man from Ballincollig, Co. Kerry, told a collector with the Irish Folklore Commission in 1951 that the only type of collar used on plough horses in his youth was one of straw or hay rope, of a type he called a *braighdeán shúgáin*.[30] This method of making a collar with thick *súgán* rope was also used to form the core of the packsaddle and the ox-collar (mentioned later in this chapter).

Rough plaited collars

These collars **(Pl. 7.22)** were plaited using the three-plait technique described for the hen's nests. However, no tates are added; instead the plaiting is done by starting with three thumb-ropes of *súgán* and plaiting with these. It would theoretically be possible to make these collars with long lengths of *súgán* that had been twisted on a thraw-hook and plaiting with these, but, because of the lengths needed, these *súgán* ropes would be very much inclined to get repeatedly tangled up during the plaiting process. I think it is more likely then that the plaiting was done with shorter lengths of *súgán* rope made by hand, which would have been added to as the need arose. It is relatively easy to add on to *súgán* ropes in this way (like splicing rope) and the plaiting process itself would consolidate the join. Plaiting proceeded until a length of plait about 10m to 13m long was formed. This plait was looped around four or five times to form the collar, and the plaits were then sewn together using a packing needle and twine.

The edges of these plaits, usually about five, formed the face of the collar, and a separate plait was placed flat on to the face of the collar and sewn on to form the groove on which the hames could rest. The hames for this collar was similar to the hames used with the conventional leather collar, and they could rest against the raised surface provided by the extra row of plait.

The collar in **Pl. 7.24** is made in exactly the same fashion as just

Pl. 7.24—Plaited horse-collar of field rush. Photo courtesy of NMI.

described, but the material in this case is not straw but field rush (*Juncus effusus*), which, after cutting, was steeped in water for a day or two and then pounded with a stick or club, a process known as 'melling'.

The groove for the hames in these collars, though usually formed by a flat piece of plait, could also be made in other ways. In one example at the Ulster Folk and Transport Museum, the groove is formed by a two-ply of thin *súgán*. Another collar, made by James Hughes of Knocvanny, Tuam, Co. Galway, has the groove formed by an oval of *súgán*, which forms a core around which a rope of *súgán* is tightly twisted (**Fig. 7.8**).

Most of these collars are about 27" (69cm) long and from 17–21" (43–53cm) in maximum width, with the opening being about 17" (43cm) long and up to 12" (30cm) in width. Collars for donkeys were made in the same way but the dimensions would have been smaller, about 20" (51cm) in maximum length and 16" (40cm) in maximum width being appropriate external dimensions.

Fancy plaited collars

These collars (**Pl. 7.23**) were plaited with three separate strands or groups of straw, each group consisting of about six to ten stems of straw, but this straw was not twisted as was done for the rough plaited collar. Instead, plaiting was begun with three wisps of straight, untwisted straw, which were constantly renewed by gradually inserting other straws into the plait. If too many straws were introduced together, the plaiting became lumpy and uneven. Mr Patrick McMenamin of County Tyrone, who made a collar of this sort for the Ulster Folk and Transport Museum in 1976, commented that if the straw was cut by a scythe or a sickle, rather than by machine, it was easier to introduce it into the plait, because this type of straw had angular, uneven ends rather than the flat, straight ends that result from machine cutting.[31] He also chose brown oat straw to work with, saying that white oat straw was more brittle and thus more difficult to plait.

Once about 12m of straw plait had been made, one end of the plait was curved into shape to form the inner edge of the collar. The next round of plait was placed outside this one and both were sewn together with a packing needle and twine, in the manner described for the rough plaited collar. However, because the plait in the fancy collar was finer and thinner, it usually took more layers of plait to build up the collar to the required size, with six to ten rows being needed. An important point made by Patrick McMenamin was that the second and subsequent rows needed to step out a bit from the first one in order to enable the collar to slope out slightly. These fancy collars were usually lined with pads of horsehair covered with a strong cotton fabric, known as ticking, and it is possible that the stepping out was done to facilitate this. A flat plait was sewn onto the face of the collar in the same manner as described for the rough plaited collar to form a groove into which the hames could fit. After trimming off all protruding bits of straw, Patrick McMenamin singed away remaining ends using a burning twist of paper.

Although Mr McMenamin seems to have had no tools other than a knife, a scissors and a packing needle, John Feeney of Larganboy, Co. Mayo, who is pictured holding a fancy plaited collar in **Pl. 7.23**, also used a small wooden mallet for hammering the needle through the straw and a pincers to help in pulling it out. The collar he is holding in the photo was made in 1960 when John Feeney was 76 years old; he had been making and selling collars in

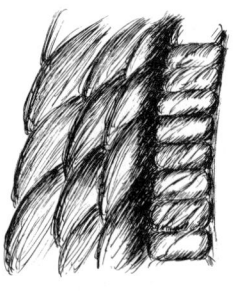

HORSE COLLAR, KNOCKVANNY TUAM. Co GALWAY.

Fig. 7.8—Horse collar.

the area for the previous 50 years.

Fancy collars took considerably longer to make than rough collars, but it is likely that they were not always subjected to the same amount of rough wear either. Patrick McMenamin estimated that his fancy collar would last about twenty years, which is considerably longer than the two- or three-year lifespan that Bernard Gillen estimated for his rough plaited collar pictured in **Pl. 7.24**. Even allowing for the finer workmanship in the fancy collar, which would result in the plaits being tighter and less likely to unravel, this discrepancy seems too great, and I believe Jonathan Bell is correct when he suggests that part of the reason for this is that fancy collars, because of the work involved in making them, were more carefully looked after and less frequently used than rough collars.[32] This is also borne out by John Feeney, who estimated the working life of his fancy collars at about five years.[33] Because his collars were commercially made they were probably not as carefully looked after.

It seems likely that much of the fancy style of straw harness was reserved for special occasions when its decorative qualities could be appreciated. The set of straw donkey harnesses in **Pl. 7.25** is beautifully made and includes very fine detail in the plait of the bridle and plaited rings. Such finely worked straw would not last long in an everyday work situation and this set of harnesses was almost certainly intended for decorative use. Jonathan Bell quoted Mr F. Mullen, a saddler from Draperstown, Co. Derry, as remembering seeing such straw harnesses only on fair days when horses wore straw collars decked with ribbons as decoration.[34]

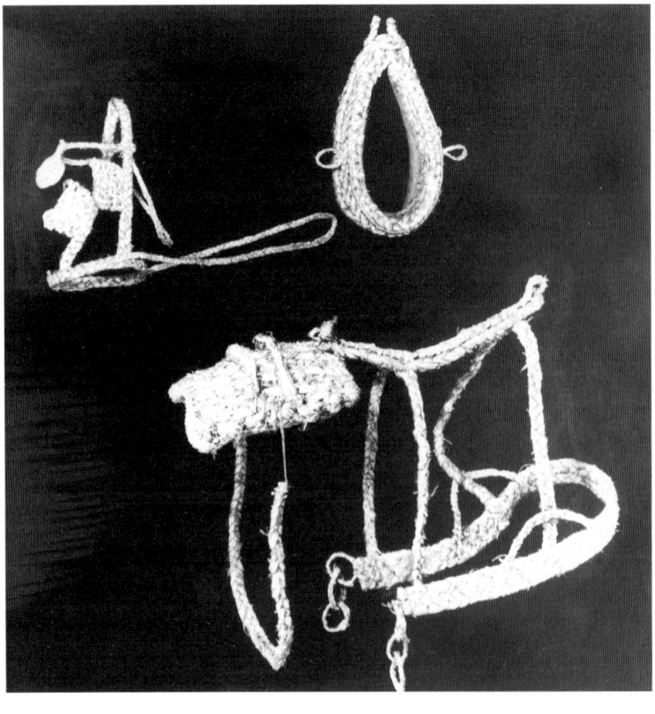

Pl. 7.25—Complete set of fancy plaited donkey harnesses from County Mayo, now in the collection of the Ulster Folk and Transport Museum. Photo courtesy of UFTM.

Ox-collars

Oxen for ploughing were, as I have mentioned, largely replaced by horses from the twelfth century onwards, and from the seventeenth century the use of oxen was almost wholly confined to the large estates of the landed gentry. County Kildare proved an exception, however, where Arthur Young, writing in 1776, noted:

> Tillage is done with both horses and oxen, and which is extraordinary, the latter are used by common farmers as well as gentlemen.[35]

The use of oxen in Kildare and on prosperous estates in other counties continued until the second half of the nineteenth century, and in one large estate in County Meath oxen for ploughing were used until 1907. Thomas Oonan of

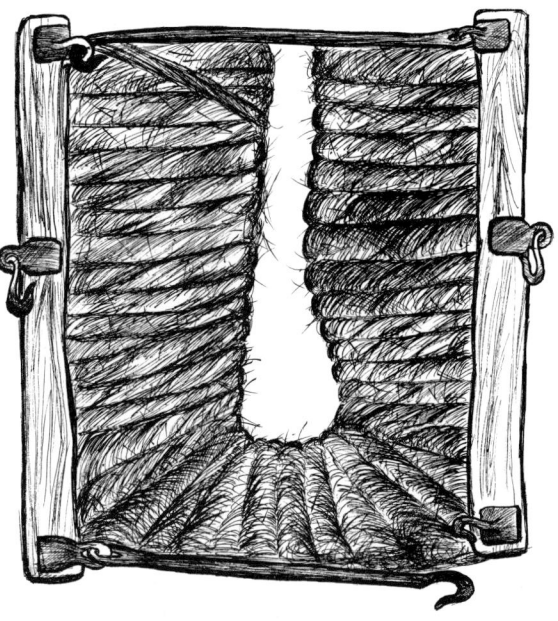

Fig. 7.9—Ox-collar.

Julianstown, Co. Meath, worked with oxen on the Ballygarth Estate in his youth, and he made two ox-collars for the National Museum around 1950, even though such collars were well extinct by then. Unlike the straw horse-collar, which, being closed, was pushed down over the horse's head, the ox-collar was U-shaped, because the ox horns would have prevented a closed collar being pushed over the head. The foundation for the ox-collar is a thick *súgán* rope of straw or hay around which a thinner *súgán* rope is tightly bound **(Fig. 7.9)**. Because the collar is not closed, the structure is strengthened by attaching the collar to a wooden frame, which also acts as the hames.

Straw and hay packsaddles

These saddles were made of either hay or straw and were used throughout the country where sacks were being carried by horse or pony, although there is evidence that they were also used as saddles for people.[36] Their main use, however, was as packsaddles and when in use they were held in place on the horse's back by a rope bellyband. The packsaddle in **Pl. 7.26** is from the Ravensdale area of County Louth and it was used for carrying turf from the mountain bog in Ravensdale for sale in Dundalk. The turf was packed in large canvas sacks, each of which weighed up to 3½ cwt

or 170kg. A full sack was balanced across the horse's back on the saddle, which held the sack on the horse's back and prevented the sack rubbing on the horse's skin. The reason for the extra thickness at the closed end of the pad was to prevent the sack from slipping forward onto the neck of the horse when descending on the slope.

The local name for the saddle in the County Louth area was a 'panel', and it seems this name may have also been used in some Ulster counties. The panel, excluding the crupper rope (which secures the panel around the horse's tail), is 37" (94cm) long. The crupper rope is about 19½" (50cm) long in total, and is a thin *súgán* rope wrapped in sacking. The panel is thickest at the closed end, where it is about 5½" (14cm) in diameter, tapering gradually towards the crupper end where the diameter is about 3"(8cm). The core of the panel was a thick core of straw or hay, twisted with a stick in the manner described for a thick *súgán* rope. This rope was thickest at the section destined to be the closed end of the panel. A thin *súgán* rope was wrapped tightly around the core, going all around the core for the most part, but the turns at the closed end of the

Pl. 7.26—Hay packsaddle from Anaverna, Ravensdale, Co. Louth, where these were locally known as 'panels'. Photo courtesy of UFTM.

packsaddle where the curve was greatest sometimes went through the core, rather than all around it, in order for the *súgán* wrapping to lie neatly on the panel. The panel was also braced with one or more ties of *súgán* to prevent it from going out of shape.

The National Museum has examples of these packsaddles from counties Sligo, Mayo and Cavan, as well as from County Louth. Dr Lucas believed that they were once in widespread use throughout Ireland:

> The further back in time we go, the greater must have been the necessity for some such contrivance since the fewer wheeled vehicles there were for the transport of goods and the greater the

reliance on pack animals for that task. It would seem then that the panel is one of a kind, formerly in use over the whole country.[37]

The *síogóg, fóir* or straw rope granary

The *síogóg* or *fóir* was a cylinder made of thick *súgán* ropes and was used for storing grain. It was used up until the 1950s in west Cork, though one instance of its use in the neighbouring region of Kerry was known. It was known as a *síogóg* or a *fóir*, depending on the region of west Cork, and it was known as a sop in Kerry.[38]

The *síogóg* was started by putting a foundation of dry branches and twigs, furze bushes, etc., on a dry site in the farmyard. The foundation was about 6ft (1.8m) wide and 1ft (30cm) thick. This foundation was covered with a layer of straw, which was firmed to make it level, and this in turn was covered by a layer of pulled straw, which formed an effective seal through which the grain would not escape **(Fig. 7.10)**. In some districts, a sheet made from old meal bags was used instead of the pulled straw to prevent the grain from falling through to the foundation.

Next, a stout *súgán* rope about 6" (15cm) thick was made, using a thick stick to do the twisting, with one person judging carefully the amount of straw to allow into the rope in order to keep the diameter of the rope consistent. The rope could be twisted hard to give a firm rope, or less tension could be applied to give a softer rope; this tended to depend on the region. Soft ropes tended to bed into each other well, providing a good seal between each ring of *súgán*. They might not, however, be quite as strong, structurally, as a harder rope. Where the rope was twisted hard it was necessary to line the inside of the *síogóg* to prevent grain from slipping out between the rows of *súgán*. The rope for each ring needed to be about 20ft (6m) long, and was allowed to taper off into thin tails a few feet (50–70cm) long. When the first length had been twisted, it was laid on the foundation

Fig. 7.10—Bed of gorse and straw.

Fig. 7.11—Finishing off the row.

in as perfect a circle as possible, and one end was secured by driving a wooden peg into the ground through the loop left by the twisting stick. The other end was brought a few times round the rope so that the rope lay in a continuous ring. A second length of rope was prepared and was secured to the first by passing its end a few times under the first ring. This should be done away from the join in the first ring so that the structure of the *síogóg* is secure. The rope was then brought around to fit snugly on top of the first ring and the end was brought past where the second ring started, and tucked under itself a few times. This technique was followed in the placing of all the rings so that each ring was started by securing it to the one below it, and each was finished by being secured under the early part of itself **(Fig. 7.11)**.

When three rings had been placed, the threshed oats were emptied, one sack at a time, into the centre of the foundation until it formed a heap. This was dragged towards the outer edges of the *síogóg* or *fóir*. In some districts, especially where the *síogóg* rope was twisted tightly, a lining of pulled straw was placed inside the *súgán* rings and the loose oats were scooped against this lining, locally known as the fencing, to keep it in place **(Fig. 7.12)**.

Fig. 7.12—Three layers of sugán *partially filled with grain.*

The makers proceeded to add the fourth and subsequent rings and the person filling the grain added it at a rate that allowed the two people making the body of the *síogóg* to have the rings in place and to have sufficient time to put in the lining of pulled straw. As the height of the *síogóg* grew, a chair or a step was necessary to facilitate the spilling in of the grain. When the second-last ring had been put on, the handle of a fork was inserted into the grain close to the wall of the *síogóg* in order to allow the walls to slope outwards. A good deal of force

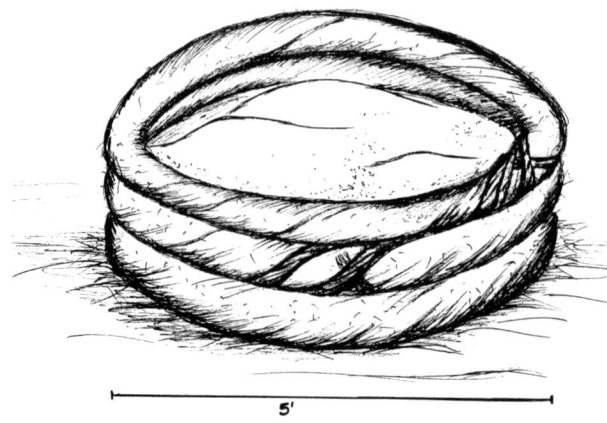

5'

was used in the levering out, as Dr Lucas comments: 'It is a measure of the strength of the ropes and the soundness of the tyings that they can withstand the strain without breakage or damage.'[39]

Once a satisfactory slope had been achieved, the final ring was put on and the grain was filled level with the top ring and allowed to slope upwards towards the centre. Loose straw was then thrown up onto the grain and tapped down. Then a thatch of pulled straw was put on, the lowest bundles of which projected beyond the uppermost ring of the *síogóg* for about 1ft (30cm) to form an eave. More loose straw was piled on top of this thatch and this also helped to stabilise it. More thatch was placed on top again, and this process of adding loose straw and then a layer of thatch was continued until the desired height and slope had been achieved **(Fig. 7.13)**. The cap was then raked down and tied with two long *súgan* ropes, which passed over the top at right angles to each other and were secured to the base of the *síogóg*. It was allowed to settle for two or three weeks, during which time the cap sank and lost pitch. The ropes were then removed and more straw was added to the cap and raked down to provide a steep, waterproof surface. In some districts, an outer thatch of field rush was added. Four quarter-ropes were tied on as before, but these were reinforced with a number of horizontal ropes, which were tied on the quarter ropes and circled round the cap. The quarter ropes were secured by hanging stones on them to allow for any further slight settling **(Fig. 7.14)**.

There were slight regional differences throughout west Cork in the making of these granaries. In the townland of Garrynapeaka, where the granary was known as a *fóir*, the sides sloped outwards towards mid-height and then sloped inwards again. This slight barrel shape was also the norm near Macroom, where the granary was known as a *fóirín,* (or little *fóir)*. In the district around Dunmanway, where the granary was known as a *doimhineóg*, the sides were straight.

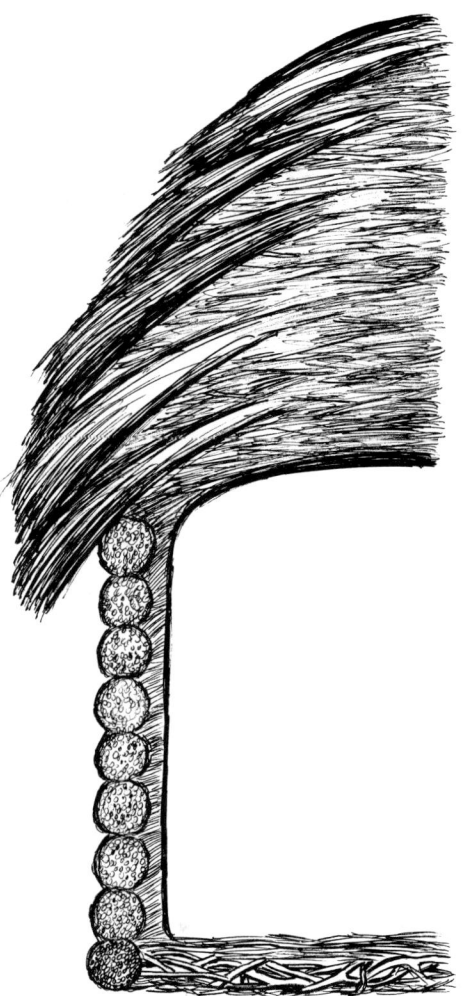

Fig. 7.13—Cross-section and roof detail of síogóg.

Fig. 7.14—Síogóg.

Small quantities of grain could be removed from the *síogóg* by slightly lifting the cap under the eave and scooping the grain out over the top ring. This could be repeated at different spots around the eave. For large quantities, however, the granary had to be opened. When the grain was lowered to the level of a ring this was taken off and shaken. The *síogóg* could be recapped once the required amount of grain had been withdrawn. The granary kept the grain perfectly dry throughout the winter and, although the *síogóg* could be built in half a day, each was capable of holding three to four tons (3000–4000kg) of grain.

Dr Lucas believed that the *síogóg* was formerly in use in other parts of Ireland. Ireland was a corn-exporting country in the seventeenth and eighteenth centuries and yet barns for storing this grain were almost entirely absent. Thus he concludes: 'We must regard the west Cork examples as the last survivors of a thing which was once in widespread use over the greater part of the country.'[40]

Among the evidence he cites to support his contention is a wash drawing of a fort near Kinsale in Thomas Phillips's *Military Survey of Ireland* in 1685, which seems to contain partially dismantled granaries similar to the *síogóg* just described. This account of the *síogóg* is based on Dr Lucas's paper, '*An Fhóir*: a straw rope granary', which should be read by anyone who wants further information about these granaries.

Rush

When basketmakers speak of rush, they usually mean bulrush (*Scirpus lacustris*), which grows in slow-moving rivers and also along the margins of lakes. It can grow to heights of nine or ten feet (3m). The rushes are usually cut in early July and if the weather is favourable they are dried outdoors for about two weeks before being bundled and stored in a dry place. It is important that the rushes are not exposed to too much rain while drying, as this is inclined to discolour the surface of the rush and make it spotty. If broken weather occurs during the drying process, the rushes can be brought into an airy shed to dry partially until drying can be finished in the sun. Once dried, the rushes will keep for a number of years if stored in a dry, dark place; light causes the colour to fade.

Rushes for working are sprayed thoroughly with water — a hose or watering can is ideal for the job — and then mellowed by being wrapped in a damp cloth for a few hours. As with stripped willows, it is best to prepare only as much as can be worked in a day. Rushes can be used to make mats, hats and baskets, and it is also possible to seat chairs with them.

Although it is safe to assume that bulrush has been used in Ireland for centuries, very little information is available about when and where it was used. We do know that rushes have been extensively harvested in the past for chair seating and also for caulking barrels, but the tradition of making baskets from rush seems to have died out in most areas by the early twentieth century, though doubtless it was still practised by a few people where the rush was readily available.

Credit for the revival of interest in rush baskets must largely go to the United Irishwomen (renamed the Irish Countrywomen's Association in 1935) and especially to Livie Hughes, who learned rush basketmaking after seeing a rush basket in a Belfast shop.[41] She began harvesting rush in Fethard, Co. Tipperary, and by the 1930s rushwork classes had been organised in many parts of the country. Rushwork sales grew through The Country Shop, which had been set up by Muriel Gahan in 1930 to provide a market for the work of rural crafts-people. The Country Shop was to prove important not only to rush-workers but also to professional basketmakers, as will be seen in the next chapter. Muriel Gahan decided to set up The Country Shop in 1930 after a visit to a skilled weaver called Patrick Madden in County Mayo, who, despite being such a good craftsman, lived in very poor social conditions.[42] By the 1950s rush baskets accounted for a significant part of the turnover of The Country Shop, largely as a result of the rushwork courses. Throughout the 1960s and 1970s rush baskets were made in large numbers. In Strokestown, Co. Roscommon, a co-operative called Slieve Bawn was formed, which had great success throughout the 1970s selling rushwork on the home and export markets. The co-

Pl. 7.27—Rush hand basket made by Mary Landy, Co. Carlow. This basket was awarded the California gold medal at the RDS National Crafts Competition around 1980.

operative has since ceased trading, though one founder member, Patricia O'Flaherty, still makes rush-work commercially.

Returns from rush-work are poorer than willow-work, and most people who make rush baskets for sale in Ireland do so as a part-time activity, more for pleasure than for profit. I have been told by most rush-workers that the payment they get does not reflect the time spent making the items, though this would probably not be true of St Brigid's crosses. **Pl. 7.28** shows commercially made rush baskets of a high standard. The design of most of them is relatively straightforward in that undue complications in shaping as well as time-consuming features such as ties and fastenings are avoided. This allows them to be made relatively quickly, but if rush-work of this high standard is to remain available then prices currently paid will have to improve dramatically. While it is heartening to see rush-workers refusing to drop standards, poor prices make this attitude harder to maintain and also act as a deterrent to younger workers learning the skill. The rush-work in **Pls 7.27** and **7.29** is beautifully made but work like this would probably be impossible to make commercially at present. The masks in **Pl. 7.30** represent a new use for rush and straw in this country.

Pl. 7.28— Commercially made rush baskets. The rectangular letter tray was made by Patty O'Flaherty, Strokestown, Co. Roscommon. All other baskets made by Pearl Sheehan, Kilcolgan, Co. Galway.

The other type of rush used in Ireland was the field rush (*Juncus Sp*). Although field rush would normally be dismissed as a basketry material, it was widely used in rural Ireland in the past, particularly for making St Brigid's crosses and also for making small ephemeral objects as the rush rattle and the butterfly cage shown in **Fig. 7.15**. It is likely that such toys were fashioned for and often by children. The rush rattle was usually provided with two hazelnuts. The butterfly cage was sometimes left open on one side and had a dock leaf as a hinged door. Most of these objects are, in the words of Estyn Evans, 'the products of the infinite leisure of long summer days of cattle tending in field, bog or mountain'. [43]

However, field rush was also used for more lasting objects. We have already seen that pounded rushes were used to make the horse-collar in **Pl. 7.24**, as well as for the making of ropes. Pounded rushes were also used for making baskets, as in the case of the rush *tiachóg*. This was a rushwork bag made from a number of strips of rush plait-work, which were then sewn together with rushes edge to edge.

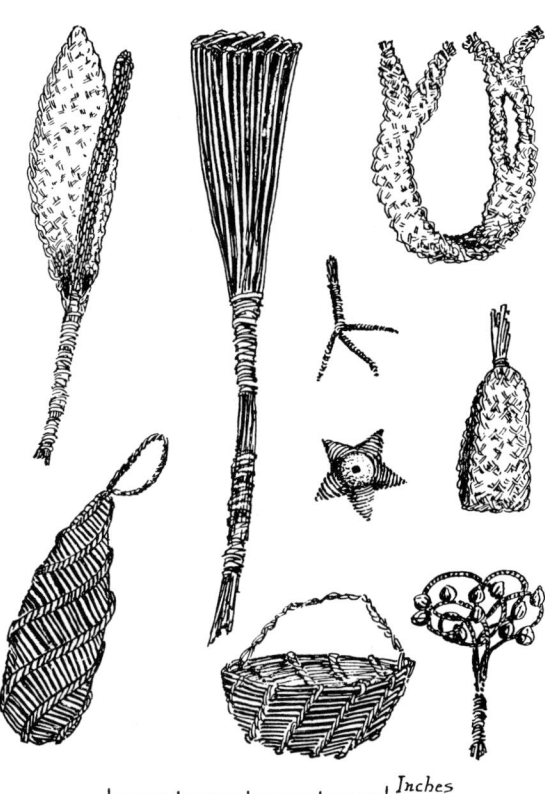

Fig. 7.15—Rush, grass and straw work (Evans 1957).

The National Museum obtained a rush *tiachóg* in 1956 **(Fig. 7.16)** from the townland of Srahataggle in the Erris area of north-west Mayo, not far from where they obtained the straw *tiachóg* mentioned earlier **(Pl. 7.16)**. At that stage, the rush *tiachóg* was already extinct but was made with the help of the older people in the area. The rush *tiachóg* in question was about 19½" (50cm) high, 19½" (50cm) wide across the bottom and 10½" (27cm) wide at the mouth. The strips of plait needed to be twice the height of the *tiachóg* so that each strip was long enough to run from the top at one side to the top at the other side. The *tiachóg* did not have a separate bottom; each strip of plait was long enough to form sides and bottom. In fact, the strips of plait needed to be longer than twice the height of the *tiachóg*. This was to allow for a fold on top of the

tiachóg, which, when folded over and sewn, held a running string made from a hard plait of rushes, by means of which the mouth of the *tiachóg* could be closed. The base of the *tiachóg*, known as the *tóin druidte*, was strengthened by having a band wrapped around the plait where it folded to form the base. Although the example obtained by the National Museum was not perfectly made, it remains the only example of this type of basket. Detail of the method of plaiting is shown in **Fig. 7.17**. Each section of the *tiachóg* has 23 rushes and each section is sewn to the next with thread or twisted rush.

Another type of field rush *tiachóg* was made by making a very long strip of plait and then coiling it around in the shape of a cylindrical container, the edges of which were sewn together with thread. The base of this *tiachóg* was a separate piece sewn onto the base of the hollow cylinder, but even in 1956 no definite information was available about how this base was made. Both types of *tiachóg* were used inside the house. One type was hung on the wall to hold articles of clothing; the other type was lined with cloth and used for holding meal or salt.

The other main use for field rush was in the

Pl. 7.29—Rush shoulder bag by Irene Kelly, Co. Wexford. Photo courtesy of Irene Kelly.

Fig. 7.16—Rush tiachóg.

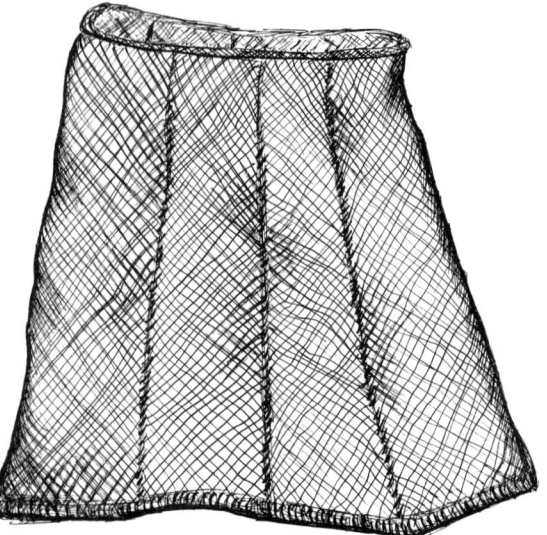

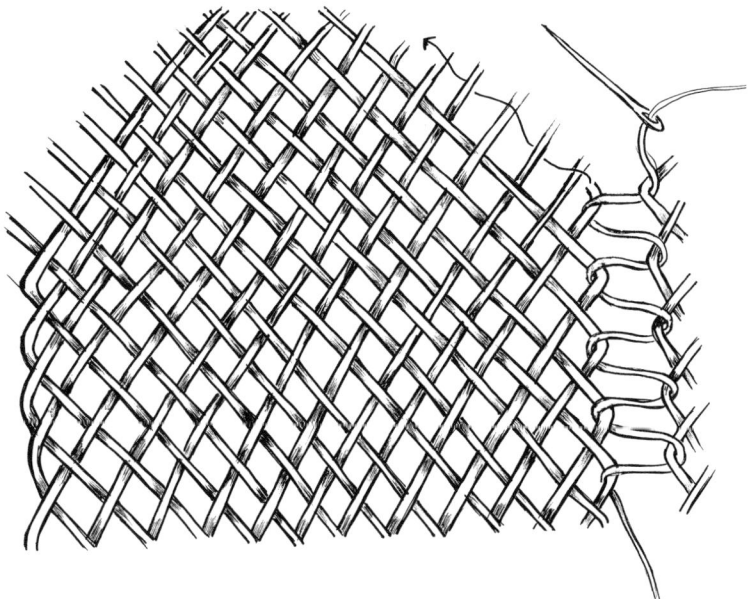

Fig. 7.17—Detail of sewing in rush tiachóg.

making of St Brigid's crosses. The feast of St Brigid on the 1 February marked the beginning of spring. This date was significant even before the introduction of Christianity to Ireland. Ancient custom decreed that no work involving the turning of wheels, the grinding of corn or the spinning of wool was done on that day. On the eve of the feast, rushes were harvested for use in the making of the crosses on the following day. Estyn Evans comments:

Pl. 7.30—Masks by Lynn Kirkham, Greenmantle, Templemore, Co. Tipperary. The mask on the left is made from straw, the centre one from willow and the right-hand mask is made from rush. Photo courtesy of Lyn Kirkham.

On that day rushes are fashioned into protective charms known as Briget's Crosses, a name which illustrates how the Church has won over pagan symbols, for the 'crosses' take the form of either swastikas or lozenges, and comparative evidence suggests that they are suns or eyes.[44]

Of the St Brigid's crosses shown in **Pl. 7.31**, it can be seen that the God's eye is not really a cross at all, and Estyn Evans points out that this symbol existed as a charm in diverse cultures, not only in Europe but also in Africa, Tibet, Indonesia, Melanesia, Polynesia, Australia and the American continent, where charms of this design were made by Californian Indians and the Huichols of Mexico. Whatever their origins, these crosses were believed to protect both the house and livestock from harm, fire and evil spirits. The crosses were hung above the door of the house and the byre or out-house, and Evans remarks that the three-legged cross in **Pl. 7.31**, which he compares to a Celtic triskele, was reserved for use in the byre. Usually crosses were left in place until the following year, when they were replaced by freshly made crosses, though Estyn Evans remarked that he often saw old crosses piled in the under-thatch: 'the decaying accumulation of annual offerings'.[45]

In some areas it was customary to take the old cross from the house to the byre and simply make a fresh cross for the house, but this may have been an indication that the custom was already in decline.

Pl. 7.31—St Brigid's crosses in different patterns made from field rush: left, cross using 42 rushes; centre top, three-legged cross; centre bottom, four-legged cross which is the most usual pattern; and right, a 'God's eye' on a willow framework.

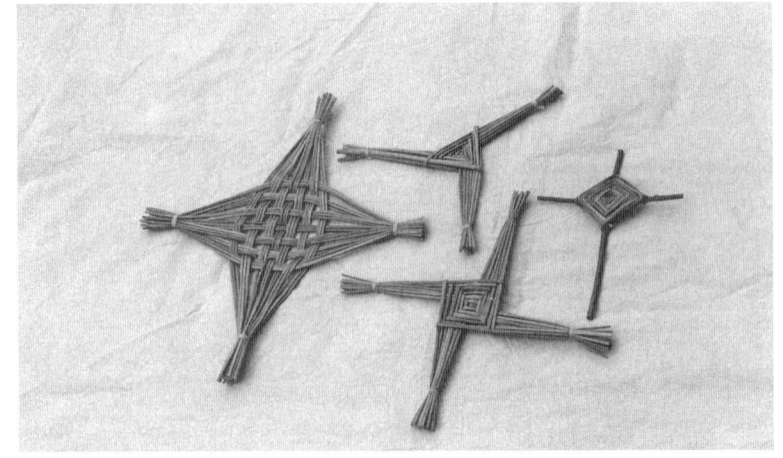

TECHNIQUE

Straddle mat in three-strand plait

As observed in the main text, clean, undamaged oaten straw that has been scutched is ideal for this. An alternative to scutching is to cut off the seed heads. Make a thumb rope of *súgán* by pulling four or five stems of straw halfway out of the sheaf and begin to twist them clockwise with your thumb. Gradually add more stems of straw by allowing two or three at a time to be drawn into the rope whenever it seems to be getting thin. Continue twisting until you have a rope of about 45–50" (115–127cm) in length. Prepare some tates by taking about ten stems of straw for each and laying them to one side. These can be piled at right angles to each other so that up to twenty tates can be prepared at a time. Fold the *súgán* rope in half and insert the first tate in the

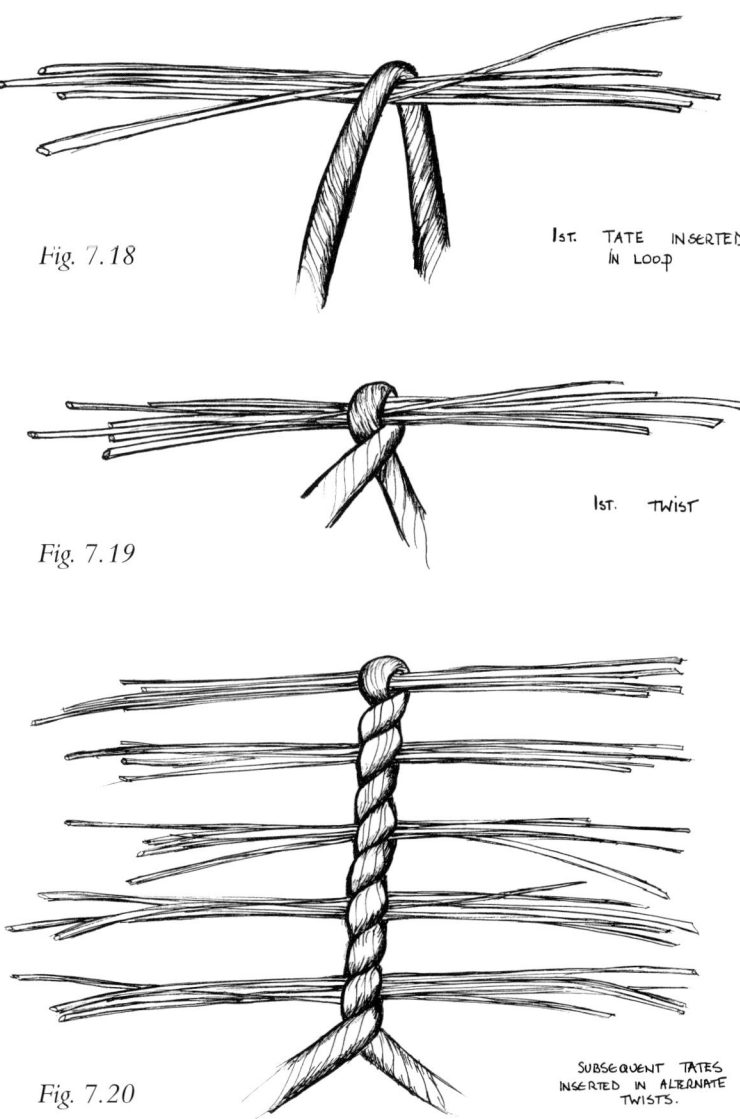

Fig. 7.18

1ST. TATE INSERTED IN LOOP

Fig. 7.19

1ST. TWIST

Fig. 7.20

SUBSEQUENT TATES INSERTED IN ALTERNATE TWISTS.

loop as shown in **Fig. 7.18**. Give a twist to the *súgán* rope as shown in **Fig. 7.19**. Repeat the process of twisting the right-hand part of the rope over the left-hand part, and after this second twist insert a tate into the intersection. Subsequent tates are inserted in alternate twists as shown in **Fig. 7.20**.

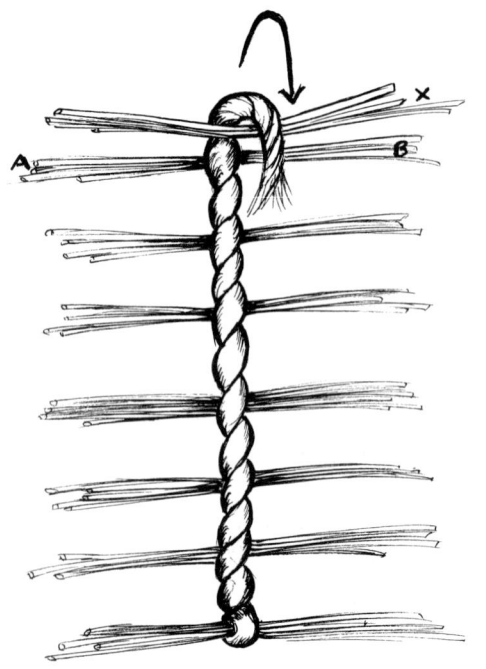

For a straddle mat 19" (48cm) wide, seven tates should be sufficient. When you have inserted and secured these, fold the rope over on itself and insert a new tate, X, in this loop **(Fig. 7.21)**. Now take the right-hand part of the underneath tate (B) and bring it to the left to begin the plait. Next take the left-hand part (A) of the underneath tate to the right as shown in **Fig. 7.22**. The third element of the plait is the end of the *súgán* rope, which is used next. Plait with these three elements for a few strokes until the next tate (C/D) is below you. Insert a new tate under the plait and incorporate tate C/D by taking the right-hand part C to the left and then bringing the left-hand part D to the right. The third element now is the almost spent plait and this is used next. Since this is bulky, some of its bulk can be lessened by taking strands of it into the other two elements. If it is short it can be lengthened by incorporating a few long strands into it from the other two elements.

The weaving proceeds in this way until the mat is the desired width. These straddle mats are almost square, so a length of about 18–20" (45–50cm) would be appropriate. There is no need to add tates for the last row of plaiting. Because the function of the tates you add is to provide plaiting material for the next row, this is not necessary on the last row. The final plait is worked in and out of the mat a few times to secure it. To complete the straddle mat, a second small mat is made to match the first and these are joined together by poking *súgán* ropes inside the first row of the mat on both sides. Large mats such as the mattress in **Pl. 7.10** are made in the same way, but the *súgán* rope is longer, a greater number of tates is needed for the width and the tates should be thicker to give the bulk needed for the mattress.

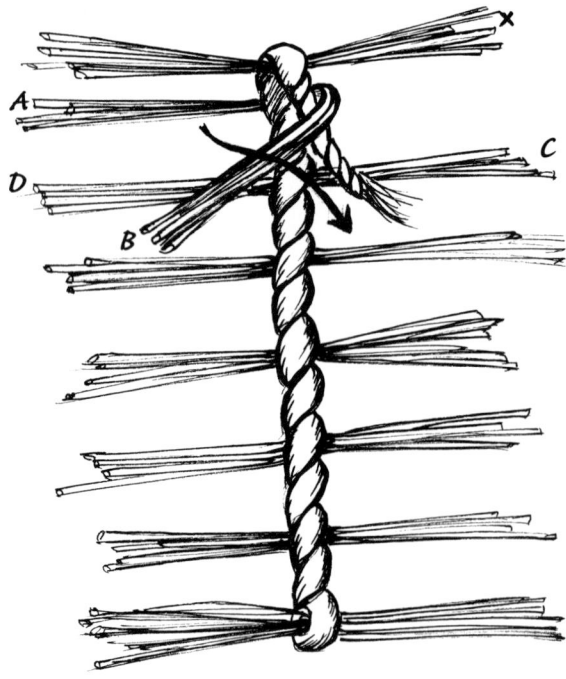

Fig. 7.22

198

Hen's nests

The start is similar to the straddle but the thumb rope can be shortened. (It is possible to make the start by folding a very long tate of straw over itself if such a long straw is available). Proceed exactly as with the straddle until five tates have been inserted as shown in **Fig. 7.20**. Now begin to roll this up as shown in **Fig. 7.23**. The roll-up is consolidated by taking the first tate in the roll-up and beginning to plait with its right and left parts, with the third element of the plait being the remainder of the thumb-rope. The base is worked on its side like this throughout, with a new tate being placed in under the row of plaiting to provide for future plaiting material each time a fresh tate is incorporated into the plaiting. As the base begins to widen, extra tates will be required. These can be poked in under the previous row as the need arises, or some tates of double thickness can be laid in to be divided in two the next time they are to be used. A nest with a base 13" (33cm) wide would need twelve to fourteen tates. You keep plaiting the core until the next tate becomes available underneath, so if you have too few tates this is indicated by the plaited core running out before a fresh tate becomes available to add to the plait.

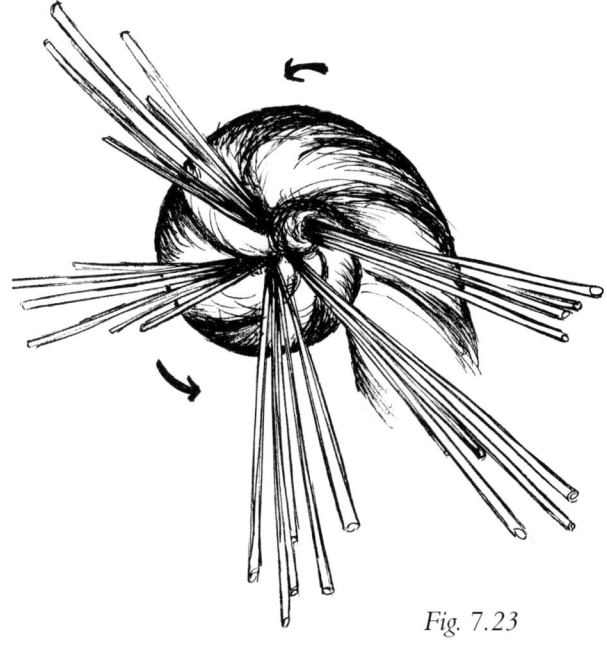

Fig. 7.23

When the base is large enough, the plait continues by stepping up onto the base to form the side. The base is placed flat once the sides are started. It can be brought to the edge of a table if required so that the tates that are facing down from the base can be grasped easily for incorporation into the plait. Thus in the base the plait is on its edge and in the side the plait is flat. The opening can be started immediately, as in the nest in **Fig. 7.4**, or one or two rows of plait can be put on before the opening as in the nests in **Pl. 7.8**. To create the opening the plait simply turns back on itself — if tates have been added under the opening during the previous row they can simply be pulled out again. The opening may have three or four turns at its side depending on how high an opening is required. The opening is closed by simply continuing the plait across to form the 'lintel'. Tates can be put under the 'lintel' during the next round of plaiting as needed, to provide enough material for the plaiting. After the 'lintel', the nest usually begins to close in fairly quickly, so the number of tates is *gradually* reduced by occasionally omitting the tate that is to be put in for the next row. By the top of the round nest in **Pl. 7.8**, for example, only three tates are left, and when the opening at the top is about 3" (7.5cm) the plait is continued until the straw has run out. The end of the plait is tied securely with twine to prevent it unravelling and this plait is then shoved into the hole at the top of the nest. This is pulled into the nest by putting your hand into the opening to grab the end and, having pulled it in, it is shoved out through an opening made near the top of the nest. The end is pulled to the outside before being pushed through to the inside for a final time to finish the nest. Stray straws are clipped with a scissors and a hanger of *súgán* provided if required.

Coiled straw-work

Whereas most of the straw-work in Ireland was of the three-strand plait type, coilwork was used, as we have seen, for chairs, the Aran kisheen, seed-sowing baskets and for bee-skeps. Rye straw was used for the Aran kisheen, but it appears that wheat was the material used in the midlands, south and east. Again the straw should ideally be cut with a scythe and the seed heads are usually cut off. Where wheat is used, winter wheat is preferred since it is harder and tougher than spring wheat.

The traditional material for sewing the coils together was split bramble, or briar as it was usually referred to in Ireland. Briar growing in woodland where it has to reach for the light is best. In these conditions the briar tends to have good length and few thorns. Any thorns on the briar are removed with a knife or a gloved hand. The briar may be split in half or quartered depending on its thickness and the pith shaved off with a knife. These briar skeins can be soaked to make them pliable if they dry out. Lapping cane is used instead of split briar in most commercially made straw coilwork. Tools needed other than the knife are a piece of cow horn, to shape the coils of straw and keep them a standard width, and an awl or bodkin. The traditional awl apparently came from the hind leg of a

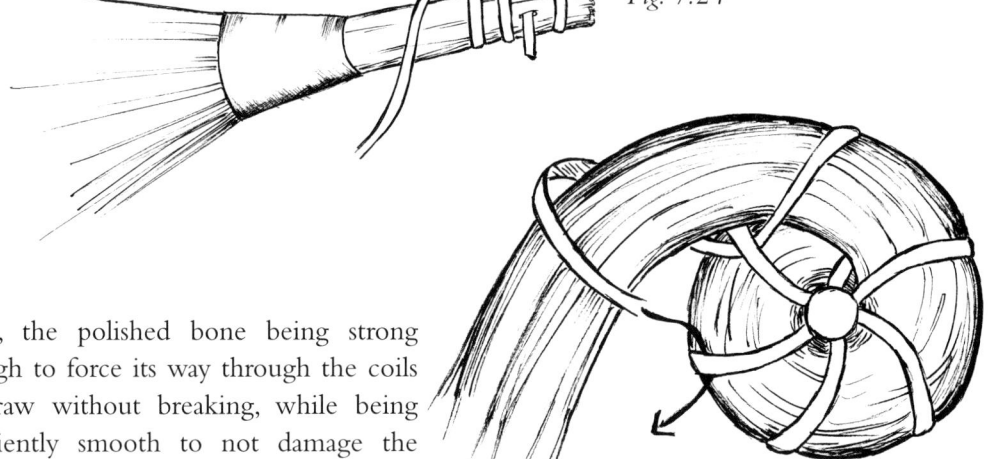

Fig. 7.24

Fig. 7.25

horse, the polished bone being strong enough to force its way through the coils of straw without breaking, while being sufficiently smooth to not damage the straw. The awl should be a thin, smooth, flat strip about ⅜" (10mm) wide, tapered bluntly at one end. The neck of a bottle or a funnel shape made from cardboard could replace the cow horn. The diameter at the mouth of the horn would be about ¾" (15mm), but might be a little thinner than this for the Aran kisheen.

Fig. 7.26

A core of straw is prepared and the horn slipped over it. The binding material is anchored into the core as shown in **Fig. 7.24** and the core is built into a circle and sewn as shown in **Fig. 7.25**. The new stitch is caught under the stitch of the previous row (see **Fig. 7.25**, and detail **Fig. 7.26**). New straw is added, a few stems at a time, at the wider side of the horn or funnel. This should be done in small amounts frequently to keep the core even. As the base widens, a greater number of stitches is needed to keep the work tight, and extra stitches are placed as needed between two stitches on the inside row. Thus the base in **Fig. 7.27** has five stitches at the middle and nine by the time the fourth coil has been reached.

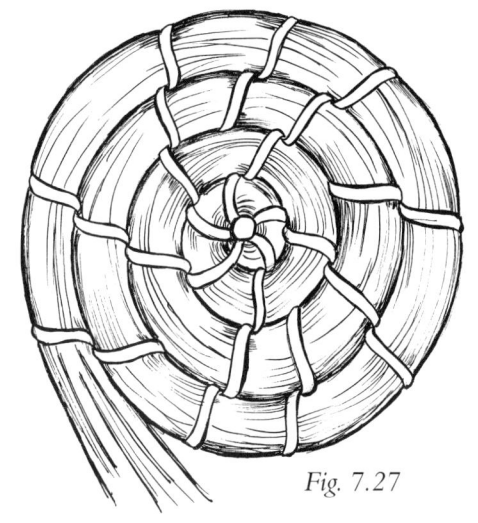

Fig. 7.27

The side is formed by allowing the coil to ascend gradually onto the base and the side is finished by allowing the core to get gradually thinner by feeding fewer and fewer stems of straw into it. The top row is stitched closely to prevent it from unravelling. The length of bramble must be joined frequently. Different methods of securing the new length of binding exist. In the Aran kisheen the join is formed by turning the binding back to secure it under the previous stitch. A careful look at **Pl. 7.7** shows several joins on the side facing the photographer; some can be seen left of centre, sixth row from the top upwards. The tapering coil to finish the basket at the top and the ascending coil at the bottom to start the sides can easily be seen in **Pl. 7.7** also. The kisheen also has a foot — a coil sewn below the base to protect it.

Strawboy costume

Oaten straw is the easiest to use for making these masks. Rye straw can also be used and although it is a little stiffer it is also longer so it is more suitable if a long skirt is required. The whelper's suit in **Fig. 7.7** is made from spring-sown rye straw; winter-grown rye straw is more like wheat in working quality and is not flexible enough for straw costumes.

Prepare several tates of straw as described for the hen's nest. Now take one other tate, slightly thicker than the rest and hold it horizontally (i.e., east–west). Take the first of the prepared tates and bind it onto the horizontal tate about 6" (15cm) away from the butt of the tate as shown in **Fig. 7.28**. Ideally the butt of the folded-over tate should be long enough to be caught by the next two tates to be folded over, but unless the straw is long this will not be possible unless you are content with a mini-skirt! Otherwise, allow the folded-over butt to be caught by the next tate and give a little twist so that the butt becomes integrated

Fig. 7.28

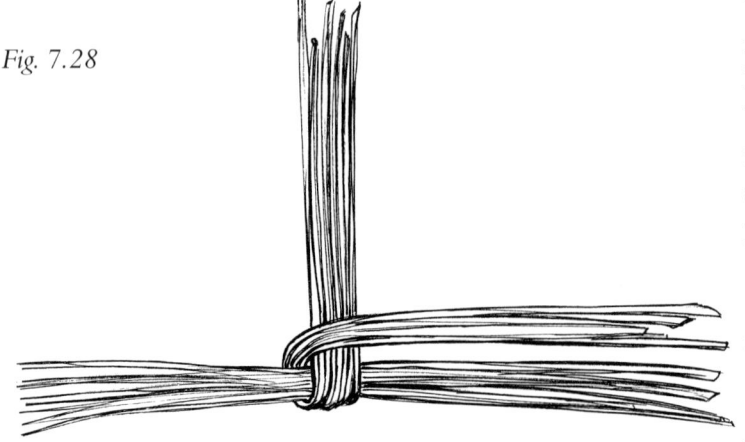

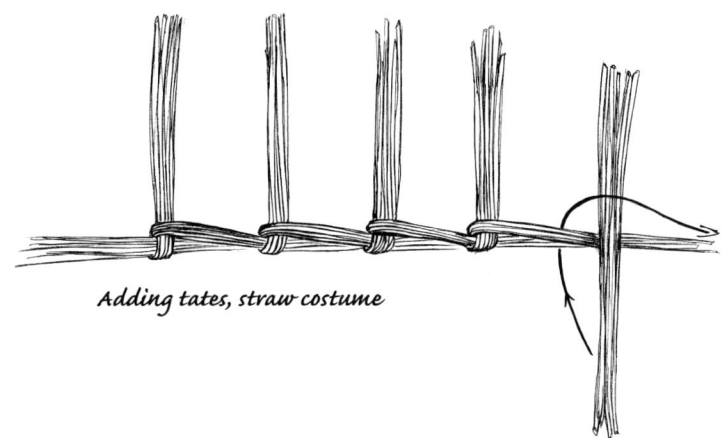

Adding tates, straw costume

Fig. 7.29

with the core. (The movement of securing the tates is very similar to the scallom used by willow basketmakers to secure uprights to a hoop except that here the scallom is taken to the right.) Join the remaining tates in the same way; **Fig. 7.29** shows a few tates folded over in this fashion. For headgear continue until the band measures about 28–30" (70–75cm) and tie it together. This is usually done with twine, but a thin *súgán* rope could also be used. The end of the last tate should be worked under the initial one if possible. It is also possible to plait a head band of the correct size first and then to 'scallom' the tates onto this. Once the tates have all been attached to the bottom ring the tops are gathered in sharply and tied on top. If the tates are plaited before being tied at the top this creates a more decorative effect, but the tates in the headgear in **Pl. 7.19** have not been plaited but simply tied on top. This tie can be string or thin *súgán* rope. Two horns have been formed on the one being worn in **Pl. 7.19**. These are made by simply dividing the straw at the top in half and then plaiting each half in three-strand plait for a few strokes and tying again. A plaited crown can be put on top of the mask instead of the horns shown in **Pl. 7.19**.

To make a skirt, continue adding tates until the total length is about the same as the waist measurement of the person who is to wear it. Tie the last tate to the band with twine. Note that the original horizontal tate does *not* have to be as long as the waist measurement of the skirt. The butts of the tates being bound onto the band increase the length of the band each time so that a skirt of any width can be made starting with a short horizontal tate. The skirt is secured by means of a rope or twine attached to both ends of the band and tied like an apron. *Súgán* rope could be used to make this more unobtrusive. The ends of the tates are clipped with a scissors to give the skirt an even hem. Leggings can be made to complete the costume using the same method, and some costumes also included a cape or a cloak to complete the disguise.

Rush St Brigid's cross standard pattern

The rushes for this cross do not have to be full length. Pieces of rush about 16" (40cm) are long enough. Although they were originally made from field rush (*Juncus Sp.*), bulrush (*Scirpus lacustris*) is now widely used. Place a rush so that it is lying north–south. Fold another rush across this so that it lies at east as shown in **Fig. 7.30**. Turn the structure anti-clockwise so that this folded rush lies pointing north. Fold another rush across this so that the new rush lies east, as shown in **Fig. 7.31**. Move anti-clockwise so that the newly introduced folded rush lies at north, and repeat. Continue in

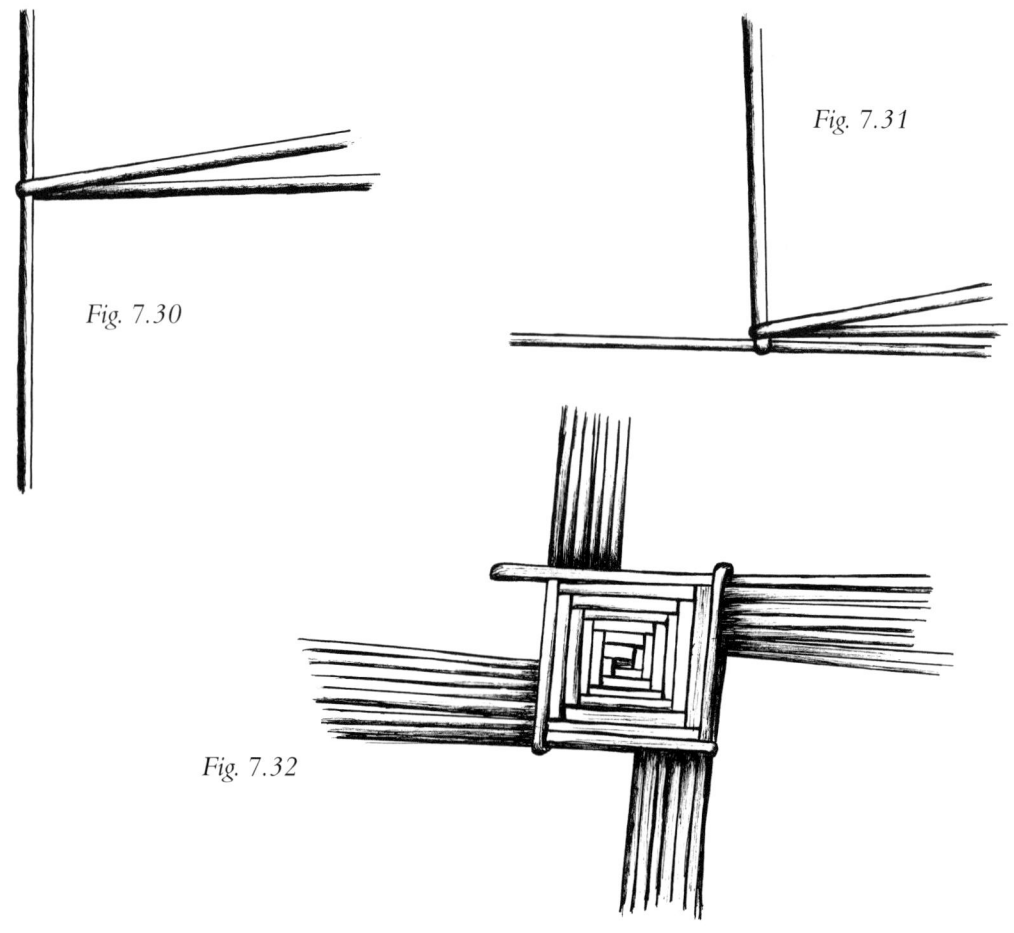

Fig. 7.31

Fig. 7.30

Fig. 7.32

this way until you have a large enough cross. To finish, loosen the folded rush at east so that the ends of the last rush being folded can be caught by it **(Fig. 7.32)**. Tighten the last rush and tie a knot 4" (10cm) from the outer edge of the centre of the cross. Cut off the surplus ends about 1" (25mm) from the knots.

Three-legged St Brigid's cross

Start in the same way as with the four-legged cross by folding a rush across a vertical rush **(Fig. 7.30)**. Now fold the vertical north/south rush over to give a second leg. The third leg is formed by folding a rush against the second leg you have just formed. Build up to the desired size and finish by catching in the last rush as described for the standard St Brigid's cross.

Rush cross using 42 rushes to give a pattern at the centre

Take 42 rushes and cut off surplus tips so that each rush is about 18" (45cm). Tie them in fourteen groups of three. In each group of three, alternate butt and tip so that each one has two butts and one tip at one end, and two tips and one butt at the other end. Lay seven of the groups of three vertically (north–south) and kneel on them or place a block or similar weight on top of them. Take one of the remaining groups and weave it west to east under, over, under, over, under, over, under and leave it. The next rush group starts over, under, over, under, over, under, over and is left; third starts under, etc.; fourth starts over, etc.; fifth starts under, etc.; sixth starts over, etc.; seventh starts under, etc. Allow the groups to curve out a little. Tie the four ends about 3.5" (9cm) from the edge of the weave and cut off surplus rush ends as for other crosses.

Eye of God pattern

Get two pieces of willow or other wood, about pencil thickness. Cut one 10" (25cm) and one 6" (15cm). Cut a little notch in both where they intersect to form a cross. If necessary, you could put a light panel pin or tack to hold the cross together. Begin the Eye of

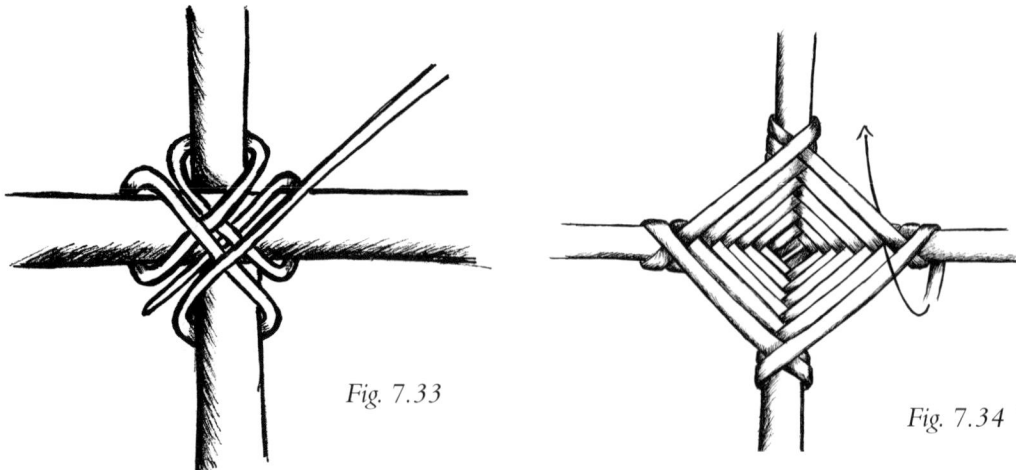

Fig. 7.33

Fig. 7.34

God with a long rush as shown in **Fig. 7.33**; this is usually started with the butt of the rush. When the rush begins to get thin lay the butt of a new rush beside it and weave both together for a few strokes. Join repeatedly if necessary. Finish by tucking the rush under the previous row of weaving as shown in **Fig. 7.34**. This can be repeated to make the finish more secure. More elaborate crosses can be made by having up to three more God's Eyes on a long vertical stick with two more on the horizontal stick in addition to the central God's Eye.

Rush rattle

The rush rattle in **Fig. 7.15** seems to be started with the tips. In order to learn the basic five-strand plait, it is probably easier to start with the butts. Tape five butts of evenly matched rush together.

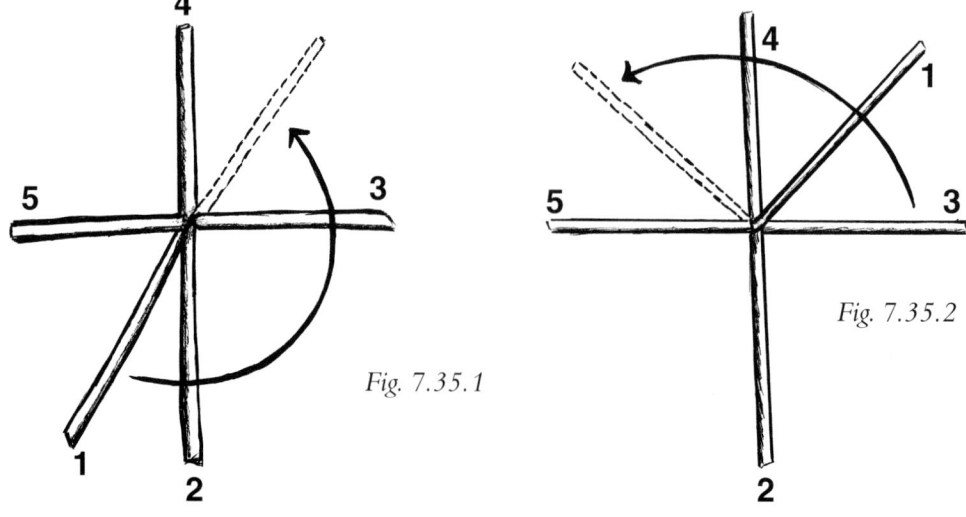

Fig. 7.35.1

Fig. 7.35.2

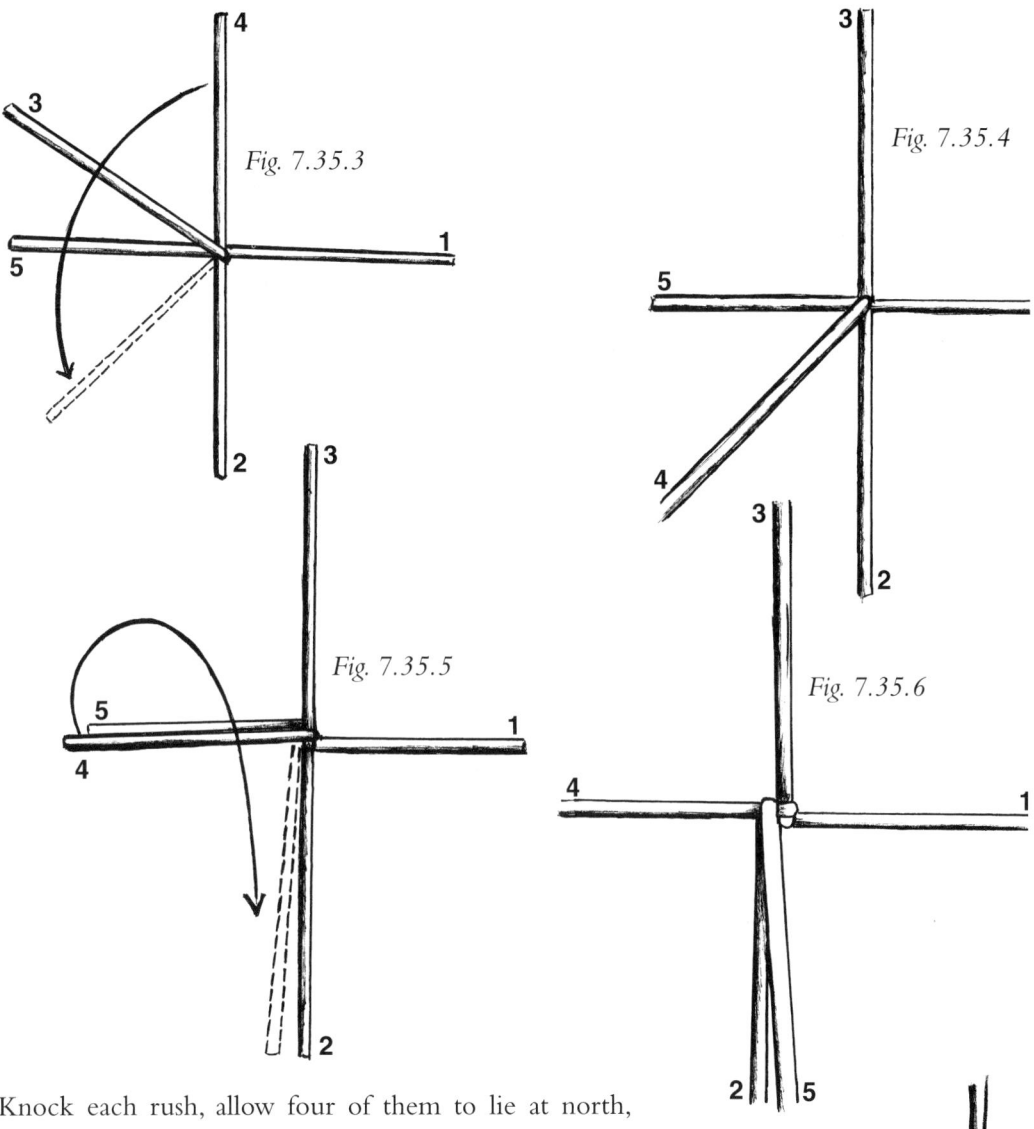

Fig. 7.35.3

Fig. 7.35.4

Fig. 7.35.5

Fig. 7.35.6

Fig. 7.35.7

Knock each rush, allow four of them to lie at north, south, east and west and the fifth between any two of them. In this example, the extra rush 1 lies between south 2 and west 5. Fold no. 1 over so that it lies between no. 3 and no. 4 **(Fig. 7.35.1)**. You are going anti-clockwise to make this movement. Fold no. 3 across so that it lies between no. 4 and no. 5 **(Fig. 7.35.2)**. Fold no. 4 across so that it lies between no. 5 and no. 2 **(Fig. 7.35.3)**. This movement is shown completed in **Fig. 7.35.4**. Move no. 4 over beside no. 5 and then fold no. 5 over no. 4 to lie beside no. 2. This movement is shown in **Fig. 7.35.5** and completed in **Fig. 7.35.6**.

Thereafter move the structure with two rushes lying at six o'clock, a quarter turn clockwise so that the two now lie at nine o'clock. Bring the underneath one of these two rushes to six o'clock, move a quarter clockwise and repeat. It is helpful to hold your thumbnail on the uppermost of the two rushes at nine o'clock to ensure that the lower one folds over it neatly without exerting too much force on it. Keep up this process until the body of the rattle is wide enough, usually before half the length of the rush has been used. Narrow the body of the rattle by taking the active rush inside the square as shown in **Fig. 7.35.7**. The final ends are tucked under a few previous strokes to anchor them. You may need a bodkin or awl to open a space for them.

8

Professional basketmaking

MOST of the baskets that we have looked at up to now were usually made by part-time basketmakers. Most districts had someone who could make creels and the rougher baskets needed for farm and fishing use. Even where there might not have been a good creel-maker in a district, itinerant basketmakers travelled from place to place to make baskets. Most makers of farming baskets were essentially seasonal workers, usually working with half-fresh willow from late autumn until late spring. With the growth of towns and cities, the need arose to transport food, fuel and other goods from the countryside, and there was a more constant demand for baskets to hold these goods. Disposable packaging has become so common and so problematic that it is easy to forget just how recent it is. Until

Pl. 8.1—Baskets that were made by professional basketmakers in use in the fishing industry, Co. Cork. Photo from the Lawrence Collection. Courtesy of the NLI. Royal 2668.

FISH CURING. KINSALE. Co. CORK. 2668 W.L.

well into the twentieth century, cardboard and plywood were very rare, and plastic, despite its ubiquity, is more recent still. In almost all of the cases where goods are packed in plastic or cardboard, this need was formerly met by a basket.

During the last half of the nineteenth century and the earlier years of the twentieth century, when professional basketmaking throughout Europe was at its height, enormous quantities of baskets were made. Baskets were used to transport, sell and measure vegetables and fish **(Pl. 8.1)**. In the home, baskets were in use for laundry, for general storage, for shopping and as cradles and chairs. Baskets were widely used in woollen mills and factories. The linen factories of Northern Ireland used rectangular baskets for storage and transport. In the pre-motoring era, large skips or hampers were used to transport the goods of commercial travellers by train, who upon arrival in a town would hire a horse and float to take the hampers containing their goods around the town. Parcels sent through the postal service were delivered by a tricycle which had a large hamper encased in the steel frame. Deliveries from the butcher and the baker were similarly delivered by bicycle and basket. Stone spirit jars were covered with basketwork to protect them, and bushel and half-bushel baskets were used in markets as measures, thus avoiding the need for weighing. These do not, however, seem to have been as widely used in Ireland as in Britain. In Ireland, on the evidence of photographs of markets in Cork and Galway, creels (see Chapter 2) were also common in urban settings. This is also apparent from **Pl. 2.5** (Chapter 2), but the arm or shopping basket in that photo was certainly the work of a professional basketmaker (see detail in **Pl. 8.2**). The yearly output of these arm baskets from the typical workshop was enormous, because they were used not only for shopping and selling produce but also for a wide range of other uses. Roughly made baskets known

Pl. 8.2—Detail of shopping basket, also seen in Pl. 2.5. This slewed shopper was certainly made by a professional basketmaker. Photo from the Lawrence Collection, courtesy of the NLI. Royal 2704.

Pl. 8.3—A young woman making a yeast skip. Thousands of these roughly made, disposable baskets were made for the transportation of yeast, until the introduction of cardboard boxes ended the demand for this basket. Note the pile of skips in the background (with bundles of rods) and the Ulster potato baskets to the right. Photo from the Bigger Collection, courtesy of the Ulster Museum.

as skips **(Pl. 8.3)** were the basketry equivalent to cardboard boxes and they were made in the thousands as cheap and efficient transport containers. At the other end of the scale, professional basketmakers also made the wicker trunks that were the suitcases of the day for those who could afford to go off on holidays. Even the reticules in which the affluent ladies of the early 1900s carried their personal belongings were elaborate creations of fine basketwork. The photograph of a Cork market in 1900 **(Pl. 8.4)** gives some idea of how commonplace baskets were at that time. Now, however, it is difficult to get much information about the number of people who

Pl. 8.4—Baskets for sale at Cork City around 1900. Note the two styles of cradles, numerous arm/shopping baskets and a bird cage hanging on the wall. The pile of baskets to the right of the bird cage includes rectangular baskets with curved lids. Photo from the Lawrence Collection, courtesy of the N.L.I. Royal 2677.

worked in the industry at the start of the twentieth century, so few are the traces of their work that remain. The remarks of Alastair Heseltine in relation to professional basketmaking in Britain could equally apply to Ireland:

> The number of craftsmen employed and the output of their labours must have been immense, but such are the temporary nature of willow and the humble status of the basketmaker that the evidence of the scale of production has all but disappeared.[1]

The reference to the temporary nature of willow may seem puzzling at first, particularly when you consider that a well-made willow basket is very strong and durable. However, most of these baskets were worked hard, often carrying enormous loads, and because they were not regarded as having any intrinsic value they were usually used until they broke. Moreover, when a willow basket was stored or left for a while it was very important to protect it from the threat of woodworm, a precaution that was rarely taken. Although technically a hardwood, willow is of a relatively soft nature, and is readily attacked by woodworm. This fact, combined with the lack of importance attached to the objects themselves, means that old examples of the work of professional basketmakers are relatively rare. The fact that such baskets were so commonplace also meant that museums were not very interested in them.

Unlike the seasonal makers of the creels, professional basketmakers worked full-time to satisfy a constant demand, and so had to soak their willow to make it pliable. Clusters of basketmakers occurred in areas that were particularly favourable to willow growing, most notably close to the slow-moving rivers of Munster — the Shannon, the Suir, the Blackwater and the Bride, among others — and on the south-eastern shore of Lough Neagh in Ulster. These are all areas where a tradition of willow growing survived until recently, or still continues on a much-reduced scale. Professional basketmaking was not confined to these areas, however, and we know that there were professional basketmakers scattered throughout the country in the 1800s and 1900s. The census of Ireland for the year 1841 lists 770 adult males and 59 adult females employed in basketmaking. With the growth of professional basketmaking, willow growing and processing also developed. While many basketmakers grew and harvested their own willow, there were also specialist willow growers who could supply willows to basketmakers with insufficient supplies of their own. Professional basketmaking also created a demand for stripped (white) willow, as the old varieties of common osier (*Salix viminalis*) were not as suitable for this. Throughout the 1800s in Britain growers began to plant new varieties from the *Salix purpurea* and *Salix triandra* families. William Scaling published pamphlets on willow growing in Britain in the mid-1800s, as did Krabe in Germany in 1886, but the degree to which such improved varieties were planted in Ireland was limited. Certainly in the willow growing regions of Lough Neagh and south-east Munster, improved varieties of willow suitable for peeling were planted, but the extent to which they were adopted elsewhere may have depended on whether peeled rods were required. Thus in many areas where baskets were chiefly made from unpeeled rods, old varieties of common osier predominated, and even a great deal of the output of peeled willow was similarly supplied by common osier.

By 1885 there were nine firms of basketmakers listed for the city of Dublin (these are shown in **Table A**), and it is likely that there were also a lot of individual makers who were not listed. In 1910 the figure is still nine, though the names have changed. Although no listings are given in these early Thom's Directories for towns or cities outside Dublin, we know that there were basketmaking firms in Belfast in the early years of the twentieth century. It is also likely that there were many basketmakers in various locations throughout the country at that time even if there are no written records of their existence.

One nineteenth-century basket workshop of which some history is known is the basketmaking 'factory' in Letterfrack, Connemara, Co. Galway. This was started sometime during the Famine (1845–1851) by James and Mary Ellis, members of the Society of Friends (Quakers) who tried to alleviate the distress caused by the appalling social conditions by providing sustainable employment, mainly in agriculture and related projects. It was re-established in 1888 by another English Quaker, Sophia Sturge.[2] She first came to Ireland in 1887 but spent the intervening year learning about basketmaking and willow growing not only in England but also at the basketmaking village of Origny-en-Thièrach in France. She started classes in basketmaking in 1888 and in the following year further training was provided by a basketmaker from Origny. Willows were planted and, although a boiler was purchased for making buff,[3] the main output of the factory seems to have been in

*Table A.
Basketmakers in
Dublin listed in
Thom's Directory
of 1885 and
1910.*

1885
Carnegie, R., Bride St.
Dea, L., Fishamble St.
Killeen, A., King St., North.
O'Reilly, John, 25 Moore St.
Preston, Owen, Christchurch Place and East Arran St.
Richmond National Institute for the Blind, Sackville St.
St Joseph's Catholic Male Blind Asylum, Drumcondra.
Sheehan, Michael J., 1–7 Fishamble St.
Smith, George & Co., 10 Castle St.

1910
Cunningham, E., 2 Usher's Quay.
Holahan, Hugh & Co., 16 Usher's Quay.
Horey, T,. 24 Arran St., East.
O'Connor, M., 50 Capel St.
Richmond National Institute for the Blind, 41 Sackville St.,
Upper.
Skelly, J., 66 Arran St., East.
Smith, George and Co., 24 Merchant's Quay.
Soldiers and Sailors Help Society, 66 Lower Mount St.

white willow with many baskets having elaborate designs. Furniture was also made — I repaired two fitched white willow chairs in the early 1980s that had been made in the Letterfrack factory some 80 years previously. The factory was supported by the Congested Districts Board, and a report for the Board by W.J.D. Walker in 1897 emphasised the value of the employment provided to the local area. At that time there were twelve 'boys' working at the factory but it is clear that some of these 'boys' must have been over twenty years of age. Sophie Sturge returned to England in 1896, and when the Congested Districts Board withdrew the subsidy in 1905 the factory closed shortly afterwards.

Another basket factory operated from Castlecomer, Co. Kilkenny. This was set up at the beginning of the twentieth century by Richard Wandesforde of Castlecomer House, and there was a large willow plantation on the estate. Output seems to have been exclusively in processed willow, mainly white, and the factory diversified into making prams that were very elaborately crafted in white willow. The publicity material of the company shows a group of eleven people all stripping willow by hand at willow brakes with a similar group inside making the wicker pram bodies, but the factory declined thereafter and ceased trading long before the death of Richard Wandesforde in 1956.

Although such social experiments are interesting, there is no doubt that most baskets were made in smaller workshops where the owner was himself a basketmaker (the industry at this time was predominantly male). One such workshop, which survived until the 1980s, was that of the Shanahans of Carrick-on-Suir, Co. Tipperary. This business was set up in 1888 by John Shanahan and, while the basis of the business in the early years was the making of large numbers of potato-harvesting baskets, the Shanahans expanded into making rectangular skips, which were supplied to the railway companies in Ireland and even in Britain. These skips were used to transport fowl supplied by the producers to the railway car dining trade and should not be confused with the skips in **Pl. 8.3**. The word 'skip', or 'skep', was widely used as a term for a basket and could have a different meaning depending on the region of the country. The Shanahans also made the type of skips in **Pl. 8.3**, though they called them yeast baskets because they were mainly used by bakeries and breweries to transport yeast. Output from Shanahans of these yeast baskets reached up to 1200 per week at one point and, by 1914, up to 60 people were employed in the firm, including basketmakers, apprentices and rod cutters. The period from 1900 to 1920 seems to have been the boom years for basketmaking, not only for the Shanahans but throughout Ireland and in many other European countries. Thereafter, basketmaking began to decline, with cardboard increasingly displacing baskets in the industrial area, which would have been the largest market for baskets at that time.

Despite this apparent decline, Thom's Directory for 1930, which also listed basketmaking outside of Dublin by this time, has fourteen entries for the capital for 1930 **(Table B)** compared to nine for 1910. However, without information about the size of the firms and the number employed by them, it is difficult to say whether there were more people employed in basketmaking in 1930 than there were twenty years earlier.

The other difficulty is that the Directory for any given year does not give an accurate picture of those involved in basketmaking. We can be definite that there were a far greater number of people involved in the basketmaking profession than the list suggests. For instance, the entry for Belfast in 1930 records only five

Table B.
Basketmakers
throughout Ireland
listed in Thom's
Directory 1930.

Dublin
Arigho, J. and Son Ltd, 15 & 16 Christchurch Place.
Cunningham, E., 3 High St.
Hicken and Co., Usher's Place
Horely, T., 27 Arran St., East.
Linnane, J., 49 Capel St.
Maguire and Gatchell Ltd, 7, 9 and 10 Dawson St.
O'Connor, M., 50 Capel St.
Phelan and Co. Ltd, South Brown St.
Richmond National Institute for the Blind, 41 O'Connell St., Upper.
Ryan, Mrs Jane (Hampers), 25 Charlemont St.
St Joseph's Catholic Male Blind Asylum, Drumcondra.
Skelly, J., 66 Arran St., East.
Smith, George and Co., 24 Merchant's Quay.
Soldiers and Sailors Help Society, 26 Frederick St.

Belfast
Clarke, William, 34 West St., Belfast.
Erskine and Sons Ltd, Ann St., Belfast.
McGrath, W.J. and Son, 30 Shankill Rd., Belfast.
Ulster Ex-Servicemen's Association, Factory 15, Rugby Parade, Belfast.
Workshops for the Blind, 28 Royal Ave., Belfast.

Skibbereen, Co. Cork
Collins, J., Charagh, Skibbereen.
Kearney, T., Church Cross, Skibbereen.
Sullivan, P., Windmill, Skibbereen.

Carrick-on-Suir, Co. Tipperary
Galvin, Joseph E., Carrick Beg.
Shanahan & Sons., Chapel St., Carrick-on-Suir.

Drogheda, Co. Louth
Donegan & Co., Drogheda.

Bandon, Co. Cork
Boyle, H., Bandon

basketmaking firms and does not include the firm of Miss Judge at Middlepath St. We know from Patrick Smyth's book about basketmaking in the Lough Neagh area that Judge's sold enormous quantities of yeast baskets and that many of these were out-sourced from the area of Lough Neagh around south-west Antrim.[4] The firm of Big James Mulholland (Aghagallon), mentioned earlier in the context of potato baskets, was also still thriving in 1930 and had an average workforce of 30 for most of the period between the end of World War One in 1918 and the outbreak of World War Two in 1939. There was also a large number of other workshops in the general area of south-west Antrim, which had been a traditional willow growing area since at least the early 1800s and probably long before that. Isaac Mulholland from Upper Ballinderry had a substantial basketworks during the 1920s and 1930s. Samuel Courtney of Aghadalgon employed six or eight basketmakers during this period and Sam McAreavey, also of Aghadalgon, had a few people employed making baskets around this time. There were numerous other small workshops in the area run by the Brankins, Crosseys, Grants and Laverys, among others. While most of these workshops principally made potato baskets and yeast skips, some workshops, notably the Crosseys, specialised in fine basketware (usually called fancywork).

As was the case in the Republic of Ireland, demand for yeast skips in Northern Ireland also declined during the 1930s, and the closure of the Avoniel Distillery marked the beginning of the end of the trade there. Yeast skips made in the south-west Antrim area were also exported to Scotland, but with the advent of war it became impossible to get space for them on ships. The war did, however, bring about a demand for airborne panniers — lidded rectangular baskets that were used by the RAF to drop supplies from aeroplanes. A factory for making these panniers was based in Deerpark and this provided alternative employment for those basketmakers skilled enough to make them. One such basketmaker was James Mulholland of Moss Road, Aghagallon (no relation to Big James Mulholland mentioned earlier). After the war, James worked as a self-employed basketmaker making various types of baskets including log baskets and cradles **(see Pls. 8.5 and 8.6)**.

Similarly, there were a lot of basketmakers in the south-east Munster area who are not listed in Thom's Directory. A notable example would be the Quinlans of Tallow Hill, a family that had a continuous involvement in basketmaking for about 300 years until

Pl. 8.5—James Mulholland making a cradle. Photo courtesy of Alison Fitzgerald.

Tom's death in 1995. This tradition may indeed continue, because Tom's daughter, Veronica O'Keeffe, is still involved in basketmaking on a part-time basis. Tom and his brother Michael made a wide range of baskets and wicker furniture from their workshop in Tallow Hill **(Pls 8.7 and 8.8)**. Although the Quinlans never had the big contracts that the Shanahans had enjoyed in the early years of the twentieth century, they nonetheless had a steady trade making a wide range of baskets, including shopping baskets, log baskets, cradles, linen baskets and wicker furniture. They also made the traditional potato *sciath*s of the area, but demand for these declined from the 1940s onwards so that fine basketware (fancy work) became the mainstay of their business. They had lean years, particularly in the 1960s and the early 1970s, when the first stirrings of a new-found prosperity in Ireland meant that many traditional crafts became unfashionable. I remember Tom Quinlan telling me about going to Cork City with samples of his work at the height of

Pl. 8.6—Two cradles typical of the Ulster type with lower hoods than those in Pl. 8.4. Both of these low-hooded cradles have uprights scallomed onto a frame, a detail that can be seen clearly in Pl. 8.5. Photo courtesy of Alison Fitzgerald.

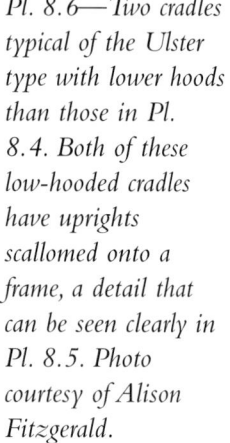

Pl. 8.7—Tom (standing) and Michael Quinlan from Tallow Hill in County Waterford pictured in their workshop around 1980. Photo courtesy of Roger O'Farrell, Foto Press.

the formica boom and finding that no one wanted to see baskets. What particularly struck him was that some shopkeepers did not even want to know the price of his work. Baskets were, for a great many people, out of fashion. As Tom said to me, 'You could hardly give them away never mind sell them.' Despite this discouragement, Tom kept a great affection for the trade and both he and his brother

Pl. 8.8.—Tom Quinlan making a willow armchair. Photo courtesy of J. E. Manners and Veronica O'Keeffe.

Michael were always helpful to any aspiring basketmakers who visited them when interest in basketmaking revived from the late 1970s onwards. Moreover, they continued to use a large proportion of their own willow, and, because a lot of the demand at the time was for baskets made from processed willow, this meant not merely harvesting but also peeling a large amount of willow each year.

It is in the context of the difficulty of selling basketwork and especially of finding new markets that the importance of The Country Shop to many craftspeople can be understood. From the time it was set up in 1930 until its closure in 1978, rod and rush baskets were always sold there, along with a broad range of traditional Irish craftwork. Many of The Country Shop's suppliers had been 'discovered' during a survey of craftsworkers by Chrissie O'Gorman during the 1940s when, at the

Pl. 8.9—Interior of The Country Shop, Dublin, in 1933. This shop, which was set up by Muriel Gahan in 1932, was a significant outlet from traditional craft work. This photo includes a súgán chair (right), a plaited straw chair, a rush log basket and a coiled bee-skep (centre) and willow baskets on the left of picture. Photo courtesy of John Gahan.

behest of Muriel Gahan, she toured the country by train and bicycle to find the remaining traditional craftspeople at work.[5] The aim of the survey was that The Country Shop would help such craftspeople by selling their work and also by promoting them through helping to organise demonstrations of their work at the RDS Spring Show. The survey gave a lot of detail about those working in basketmaking in the 1940s (see Appendix 5). The Country Shop was started in response to the poor social conditions in which many craftspeople worked, and sought from the outset not only to sell traditional crafts but also to make the public aware of their importance and thus guarantee their survival. Its founder, Muriel Gahan, was interested in handcrafts (she later became a founder member of the Crafts Council of Ireland), and from the outset the workmanship at The Country Shop and the standard of display was high **(Pl. 8.9)**. Early suppliers of basketwork included Patrick O'Connor from Nenagh, who first demonstrated basketmaking at the RDS in 1930 when he was just seventeen years of age and did so subsequently on a number of occasions until he gave up basketmaking in 1950 **(Pl. 8.10)**.[6] Other suppliers of basketwork to The Country Shop included Patrick Quinlan, up until his death in 1952, and Nicholas Hilliard, the maker of potato 'chip' baskets shown in **Pl. 3.10**. Around 1960 John McGrory from Monaghan and Mr Grimes from Baltray had joined the Quinlan brothers as suppliers of baskets to The Country Shop, and sales of both rod and rush baskets remained high throughout the 1960s and early 1970s.

The situation elsewhere was not so bright. From the 1960s onwards, cheap imported basketware began to displace Irish baskets in shops. By the late 1970s, when wicker furniture had become fashionable and shopping baskets and cradles were also becoming popular, it was almost impossible to buy an Irish basket in any of the shops specialising in basketware. These shops sourced their baskets from Poland and other eastern European countries where labour rates were cheaper. Only a few speciality shops stocked Irish baskets. As well as The Country Shop another significant buyer of basketwork at the time was the Kilkenny Design Centre, which stocked the work of the Shanahans. In general, however, basketmakers had to find their own markets and were under great pressure to compete on price with imported basketware. This had implications for the design and quality of the work produced; the buying public, unfamiliar with the fact that baskets should be strong and durable, demanded above all that they be cheap. Durability was not uppermost on the minds of those designing the baskets being imported into Ireland from eastern Europe at that time. Log baskets generally had weak spindly uprights, and shopping baskets were made of such slight material that they had to be heavily varnished to lend them some strength. One popular design of wicker chair from Poland had the seat tied in afterwards rather than having the seat integrated in the making. It was sometimes only when baskets like these needed repair that people located an Irish basketmaker. The difficulty faced by Irish basketmakers at that time in getting a fair return for their work, and making to a reasonable standard should not be underestimated. Imports continue to be a problem for basketmakers in Ireland, and I will return to that topic in the next chapter.

Pl. 8.10—Patrick O'Connor, Nenagh, Co. Tipperary, demonstrating basketmaking at the RDS Dublin. Photo courtesy of Irish Times Ltd.

The decline in the number of people employed in basketmaking had started long before the 1960s and 1970s. While the demand for baskets for industrial use fell in the 1930s, yeast skips continued to be made up until the 1950s, but the demand for baskets in agriculture also lessened sharply after World War Two with the introduction of wire baskets for the harvesting of potatoes. Some of these wire baskets mimicked traditional styles. I remember seeing a photograph of the poet Patrick Kavanagh posing in his native County Monaghan with a potato basket and, although it was shaped like the Ulster potato basket, it was made entirely of wire. These were apparently manufactured nearby in County Louth and they largely displaced the traditional willow potato-harvesting baskets before they themselves became obsolete due to the increased mechanisation of potato harvesting. Nonetheless, there were still sizeable numbers of people employed in basketmaking around 1950, as can be seen from **Table C**, which includes only those listed as basketmakers in Thom's Directory of 1950. Basketmakers not included in **Table C** but known to be working around 1945 are included in Appendix 5, and it must be stressed that this is still only a partial picture.

Despite the information contained in Chrissie O'Gorman's survey (Appendix 5), it would probably be impossible to gather information about the exact number of people working in the basket trade even as recently as 1950, so rapidly did the trade decline after that. By 1976, when I became interested in basketmaking, I was aware of only Blindcraft in Dublin and Cork, the Shanahans of Carrick-on-Suir, John Delaney in Limerick, and the Quinlans in Tallow Hill being involved in basketmaking as a profession. I did not know about James Mulholland of Aghagallon, Co. Antrim, and, although he stopped working as a basketmaker around 1969, he was back working at the trade by 1977 and continues to do so to this day. I am sure there may have been a few other basketmakers scattered around the country making baskets at that time. Certainly, Bill Sinnott of Clonduff, Portlaoise, was occasionally making baskets then. Bill was typical of many basketmakers in having had plenty of work making potato baskets, shopping baskets, etc., during the 1950s but when trade declined he continued to make a few baskets each year to keep his hand in, even when no longer employed as a basketmaker.

The Shanahans managed to remain working full time at baskets even during the time of least demand in the late 1960s. Joe and Mikie Shanahan were grandsons of John Shanahan, who set up the

Asylum for the Industrious Blind, Infirmary Road, Cork.
Belmore Industries Ltd, Lower Lodge Ave., Belfast.
Boyle, W., Bandon, Co. Cork.
Clarke, William, 8/10 Brown St., Belfast.
Collins, J., Charagh, Skibbereen, Co.Cork.
Erskine and Sons Ltd, Ann St., Belfast.
Glennon, James and Son, Hamilton St., Belfast.
Hicken, Albert, Usher's Place, Dublin.
Irish Cottage Industries Ltd, 6 Dawson St., Dublin.
Judge, J., 16 Kirkliston Pk., Belfast.
Judge, William, 2 Smithfield Market, Belfast.
Kearney, T., Church Cross, Skibbereen, Co. Cork.
Linnane, J.H. and Co. Ltd, 49 Capel St., Dublin.
O'Connor, M., 50 Capel St., Dublin.
Phelan & Co. Ltd, South Brown St., Dublin.
Richmond National Institution for the Blind, 41, Upper O'Connell St., Dublin.
St Joseph's Catholic Male Blind Asylum, Drumcondra, Dublin.
Shanahan, John & Sons, Chapel St., Carrick-on-Suir, Co. Tipperary.
Skelly, J., 66 East Arran St., Dublin.
Smith, George and Co., 24 Merchants Quay, Dublin.
Soldiers and Sailors Help Society, 26 Frederick St., South, Dublin.

Table C. Basketmakers throughout Ireland listed in Thom's Directory of 1950.

business, and while all of John Shanahan's sons were involved in the business, Joe and Mikie were the only members of the next generation to be involved **(Pl. 8.11)**. The Shanahans were one of the few firms in Ireland to have made the quarter cran herring basket, which was used by the fishing industry until the 1960s. With the decline in demand, the Shanahans enlisted the help of Córas Tráchtála, the Irish Export Board, who put them in contact with the Irish Pavillion in New York, through whom they were able to develop a valuable export market for their baskets in the USA. This led to Joe taking part in a promotion at Bloomingdale's Store in New York in the early 1980s.

Joe and Mikie also featured in the documentary series *Hands*, which was commissioned by RTE (the Irish national television station) from David Shaw-Smith. Programmes such as these helped people to be more appreciative of crafts generally and also helped to further promote sales of the Shanahans' baskets. At a time when marketing was largely ignored by most craftspeople, the Shanahans

Pl. 8.11—Mikie (left) and Joe Shanahan pictured outside their workshop. The basket at front left is a slewed log basket, the two fitched (openwork) baskets to the left of Mikie are herring crans and the wicker armchair is of a style popular in the 1960s and 70s. Photo courtesy of NMI.

also published their own brochure to publicise their work **(Pl. 8.12)**. As a new generation became interested in basketmaking, Joe and Mikie found that people were looking for apprenticeships, and while they were hesitant at first, believing that basketmaking as a trade had little future, they subsequently trained a number of apprentices, some of whom, like the Kelly sisters of County Wexford, are now working full-time as basketmakers. Mikie Shanahan died in 1983, but Joe continued to run the business, sometimes with the help of apprentices, until his own death in 1992.

Institutes for the Blind have been involved in basketmaking since the latter half of the nineteenth century. They began with two centres in Dublin. By 1930 the workshops for the blind at Royal Avenue, Belfast, were also making baskets, and by 1940 a workshop for blind basketmakers had also started in Cork. By the early 1960s only the Board for the Employment of the Blind at Baggot Street, Dublin, and the blind workshops at Infirmary Road, Cork, were still involved in basketmaking. The workshops at Baggot Street made a large number of rectangular hampers at this time, with cradles, log baskets and linen baskets also being produced. Willows for the hampers and cradles were sourced from Somerset in Britain, but much of the material for the log baskets and other brown-work came from local sources, including Eddie Carry, a willow grower in

Guaranteed Irish

**SHANAHAN
WILLOW CRAFT**

Chapel Street
Carrick-on-Suir.
Co. Tipperary
Ireland
Carrick-on-Suir 307

Pl. 8.12—Brochure issued by the Shanahans, Carrick-on-Suir, Co. Tipperary. Items shown are herring cran (top left), slewed oval shopper (top right) and bottom from left, rectangular picnic basket, armchair and small dog basket.

County Meath. The Dublin workshops also produced willow hurdles in great quantities and the rods for these, which did not have to be of such good quality, were sourced from Fethard in County Tipperary. The Dublin workshops moved to Rathmines around the mid–1960s and at this time there were about 60 people employed. Not all of them were employed in making baskets. The blind workshops also did a good trade in French cane and sea–grass chair seating, so a good proportion of the workforce were employed at this. The Rathmines workshops of Blindcraft, as they were now called, were beside a laundry and the warm water from there was often used in the soaking of willow. Blindcraft moved from Rathmines to Inchicore in the 1990s and it still continues to employ three people in basketmaking, mainly making cradles and linen baskets, and a further three people making chair seating. The workshops in Cork closed around 1980, though one worker from there continued with some chair seating at another location until the mid–1990s. Although there has been an awakening of interest in basketmaking among the general public in Ireland since 1990 onwards, it seems unlikely that Blindcraft's involvement in basketmaking will expand again. A wider range of career choices for the visually impaired is currently available, and keyboard skills, in an era of information technology, are proving more attractive and lucrative than basketmaking.

Although the story of professional basketmaking from the 1950s onwards was one of decline, this changed from about 1980 onwards when a growing number of people got interested in basketmaking as a possible profession, and it is this development that is explored in the next chapter.

TECHNIQUE

One of the factors indicating that a basket was made by a professional is an underfoot base. Not all professional basketmakers used them, but if there was an underfoot base on the basket then it was almost certainly made by a professional basketmaker, because part-time basketmakers in the country tradition did not use this technique. Other techniques that were almost exclusively used by professional basketmakers included the four-rod pull-down wale at the upsett (the start of the sides of the basket) and the use of slewing (weaving with a few rods at a time) on the siding.

Underfoot base—round

For this example let us suppose that we are making the base for a round log basket. Cut six base sticks about 17" (43cm) from prepared 8fts (2.4m) for a 13" (33cm) base. The base sticks should be cut from the thickest of these 8fts (2.4m). If you have difficulty making the base you may slype each of these base sticks on the belly, in which case you make the base with the slype side uppermost towards you. Select one long slender 7ft (2.1m) and one slender 6ft (1.8m) for 'tying the slath', as the process of starting the base is usually called. Slype the thinner slath rod, in this case the 6ft (1.8m), and dip the slyped butt in grease to make it easier to insert it later on. Lay three of the base sticks north–south, with belly uppermost.

Fig. 8.1

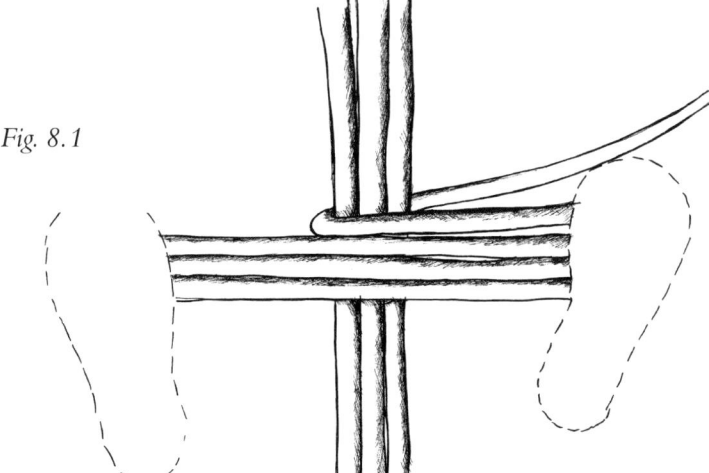

Lay the remaining three west–east (belly uppermost) and stand on them. Take the 7ft (2.1m) slath rod and fold it so that the butt joins the group at east, under your foot, as shown in **Fig. 8.1**.

You will probably have to give the slath rod one sharp twist to ensure that it folds over without breaking. Take the remainder of the slath rod and start the binding with it by going over (to south), under (to west), over (to north), and under (to east).

Now insert the second slath rod as shown in **Fig. 8.2** and begin binding with it (over to east, under to south, over to west, under to north). For each stroke with this rod the original slath rod follows it so that you reach the corner between north and west where pairing begins. Kneel down but keep the base under the left foot.

Fig. 8.3 shows the pairing begun. Where four base sticks are present at north, open out the base sticks as doubles first. Where three are present you may still open out the base sticks as doubles or open them out singly as shown in **Fig. 8.3**. Pairing continues with the base under the left foot with the base sticks being pulled towards you as you work to create a domed base. For the first few joins 5fts (1.5m) will be adequate. Join by adding new tips to the slath rods when there is about 10" (25cm) left on their length. Work the tips of the new rods and the original slath rods together for a stroke or two so that the new rods will be secure by the time the tips of the slath rods are spent.

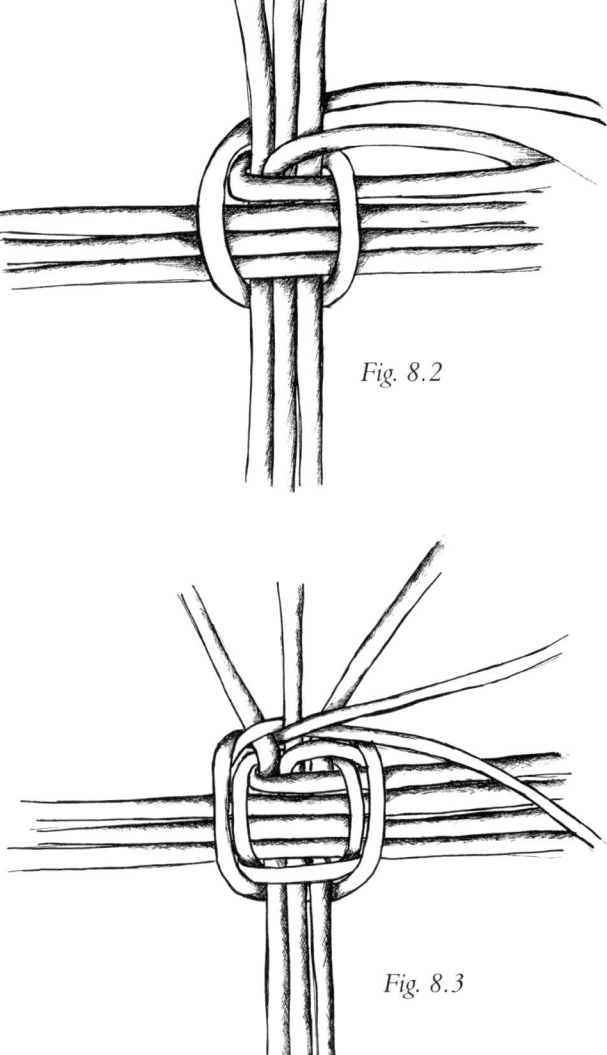

Fig. 8.2

Fig. 8.3

Subsequent joins are usually done butt to butt and tip to tip, but only the tips are worked together after joining. Joins for the butts may be simple joins initially, but as the space between the base sticks widens, lock joins (see pairing in Appendix 1) are more secure. In this example there are thirteen base sticks, enough for 26 stakes or 25 if slewing the side. If only 24 stakes are required, the extra base stick formed by the butt of the heavier slath rod can be cut off once the binding of the slath has been completed. The base is finished by securing the tips of the last two pairing rods inside the previous row of pairing. It is best to finish while the tips are still fairly strong.

Underfoot base—oval

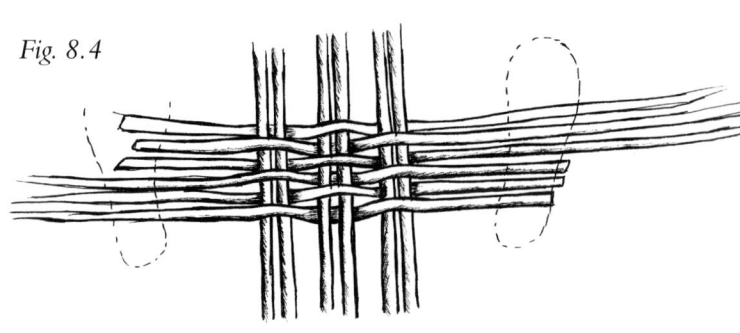

Fig. 8.4

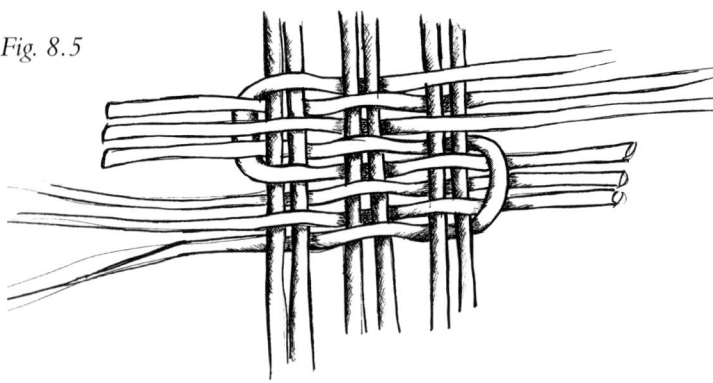

Fig. 8.5

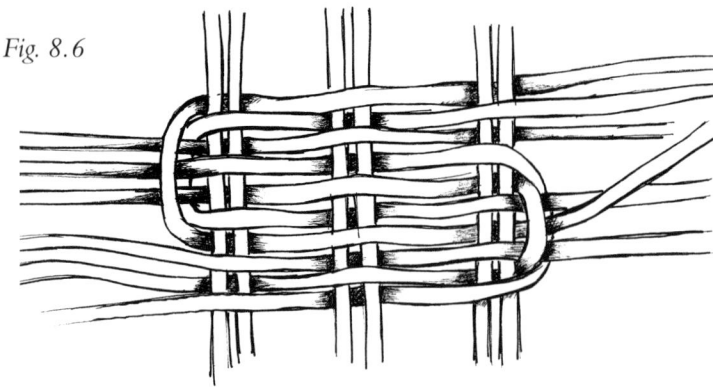

Fig. 8.6

This oval version of the underfoot base was the one most widely used by professional basketmakers in Ireland. As is the case with the underfoot round, the curvature of the base is drawn towards you as you work. Thus it is the underside of the base that faces you as you work.

First place left foot on the butt end of three long rods. Insert pairs of base sticks by lifting up the tips of the rods in sequence as shown in **Fig. 8.4**.

The number of pairs of cross sticks depends on the spread of slath required. For example, in a shopping basket base, as shown in **Fig. 8.4**, a spread of slath of about 6" (15cm) with three pairs of cross sticks would be appropriate, but for a cradle the spread of slath might be around 16" (40cm), with up to seven pairs of base sticks being used. Next add the other three long rods as shown in **Fig. 8.4**.

Start by weaving with the first rod from each group of three long rods as shown in **Fig. 8.5** (these are the long rods closest to the centre). These are woven only as far as the last pair of crossways base sticks at the other end of the slath and dropped.

Take the next two long rods and weave them similarly as shown in **Fig. 8.6**. The third rod is taken next, but in order to create tension in the binding this is usually taken inside the previous two on its first stroke (see detail **Fig.8.7**).

When this third binding rod has reached the end of the slath it is dropped like the others were, and the first is taken again and randed around the end of the oval, opening out the base sticks as it is woven. Each rod is similarly chase randed as shown in **Fig. 8.8**.

When the original rods have run out, lay in two new randing rods at both sides and chase rand them. The last four or eight rods are usually paired to make the ending of the base more secure. Large oval bases are often slewed, the odd number for slewing being arrived at by splitting up a pair of cross sticks on one side into singles. I am indebted to Barbara Kelly for help with this, as I do a different version of the oval underfoot base.

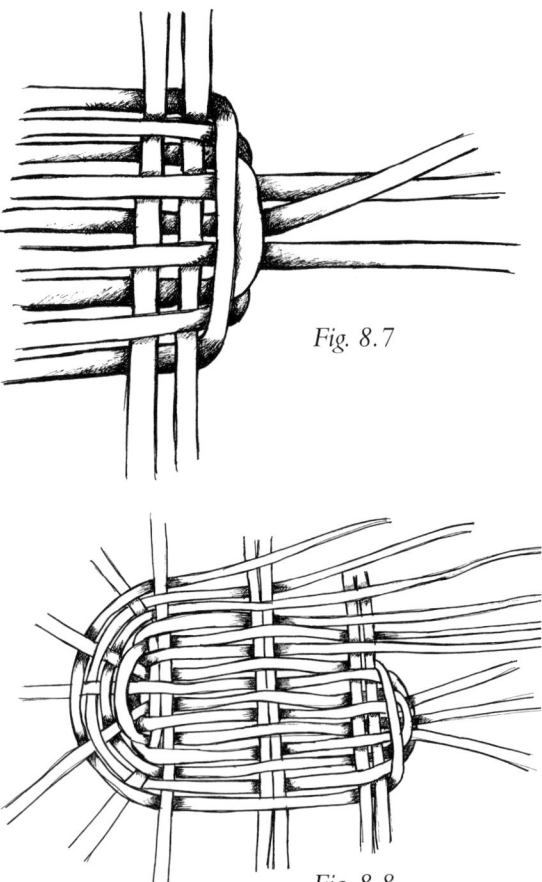

Fig. 8.7

Fig. 8.8

Four-rod pull-down wale

Although not as extensively used in Ireland as in Britain, this technique was still very popular among professional basketmakers in Ireland. I have never seen it used by traditional country basketmakers; they used a three-rod wale over the base sticks **(Fig. 3.8)** or a foot in the case of heavy-duty work.

Once the uprights have been pricked up and gathered into a hoop, the basket is knocked on its side to begin the four-rod pull-down wale. The kinked uprights are tapped in flush to the side of the base with the rapping iron. If using 8ft (2.4m) uprights, as for a log basket, the rods for the pull-down wale should be heavyish — 6ft (1.8m) or light 7ft (2.1m). Eight evenly matched waling rods are selected and four of these are pointed and inserted butt first to the right of four consecutive uprights. Because this is a four-rod wale,

Fig. 8.9

the movement is in front of three, behind one, but every second stroke is pulled down hard between the upright and the base stick, in this way forming a protective rim for the basket to sit on **(Fig. 8.9)**. Stop waling before getting halfway round the basket and start a second set of waling directly opposite the first. When this second set

Fig. 8.10

WALING

reaches the point at which the first set started, one of the four rods is cut off and the remaining three climb up to form a three-rod wale on the side of the basket. The same procedure is followed on the other side, and then the basket is placed upright on the lap-board and a weight is placed on the base to prevent the basket slipping off the lap-board. When the first sets of waling rods have been used to within 12" (30cm) of their tips, six new rods are selected and, having

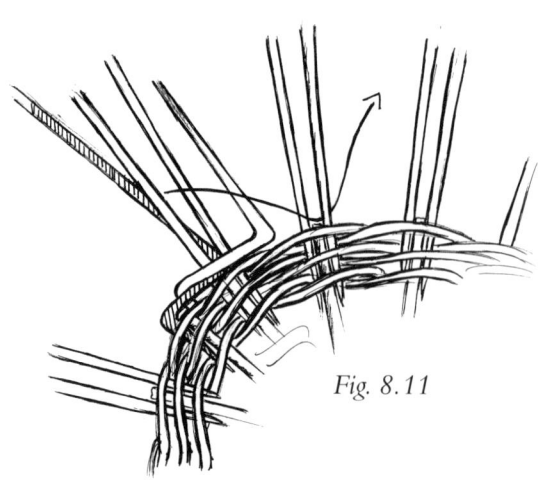

Fig. 8.11

cut about 12" (30cm) off the tips of these, they are joined tip to tip as shown in **Fig. 8.10**. A further six waling rods are needed to complete the upsett (as the bottom rounds of waling are called), each set of three chasing the other around until the tips are arrived at again.

A variation of the four-rod pull-down wale involves starting with the four waling rods to the left of each upright. If using this variation it is best to start the wale at the right-hand rod of a pair of uprights.

French foot

Another fairly popular method of providing a protective rim for the base of the basket involved taking each outstretched upright in front of two (facing the underside of the basket) before kinking and gathering into the hoop **(Fig. 8.11)**. This method was used fairly extensively by the Shanahans, who called it a French foot.

Siding using slewing

Although randing (See Appendix 1 for technique details) was widely used in professional work, slewing was more popular, especially for larger work such as log baskets, because the siding up could be done more quickly this way. Baskets for slewing are usually designed with an odd number of stakes, so that one of the base sticks has only one upright inserted beside it rather than the usual pair. The slewing for a log basket would be about 5ft (1.5cm), but if any cut-off tops are available these can be used up also. Starting with the shortest material, the first rod is woven in and out for about one third of its length, a second rod is added on top and weaving proceeds again for a few strokes so that the third rod can be added. Each time a rod is used up the spent butt is laid inside **(Fig. 8.12)**. The chief difficulty in slewing is preventing the slew from driving the uprights in unwanted directions. It is most important to hold the slew firmly against the upright with the left-hand thumb while supporting the upright at the back with two or three fingers. Although **Fig. 8.12** shows a three-rod slew, four- or five-rod slews were common. The greater the number of rods in the slew, the more difficult it becomes to control the shape, so it is best to familiarise yourself with slewing by using a small number of rods at first.

Fig. 8.12

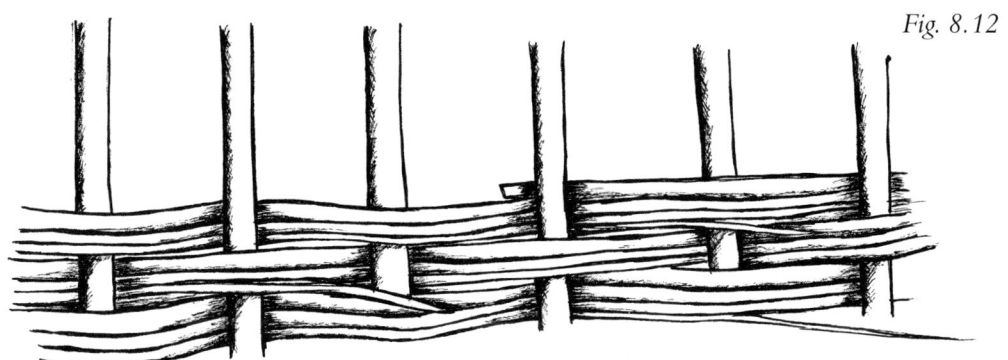

Slewing needs to be beaten down frequently to keep the weave tight. This is done by banging the top of the slew repeatedly with the side of the left hand as the work proceeds, though light taps with the iron can be used if preferred. One of the vegetable sellers in **Pl. 2.5** has a professionally made, slewed shopping basket on her arm.

Another form of slewing, which did not need an uneven number of rods, was French slewing. This is the same technique as French randing except that multiple rods are used. Thus when the first set of randing rods has been laid down and it is the turn of the first randing rod to be woven again, a second set of rods is added on top of the previous set. A third or fourth set can similarly be added. The rods for French slewing must be graded first, selecting three or four sets at a time as appropriate, of which the shortest should be used first.

Top wale

Some professional baskets had no top wale (fruit sieves, for instance) and others had a three-rod wale. Some, however, had a special top wale using four rods, each going in front of two, behind two. This wale was started with tips and, because the wale exerted equal pressure on the front and back, it was possible to wale with strong rods as thick or thicker than the uprights. This wale is almost invariably used where the sides of the basket have been fitched, as for example in the herring cran.

Borders

The five-behind-two border as detailed in Appendix 1 was probably the most widely used border in professional work in Ireland in the twentieth century. Sometimes a six- or seven-pair border was used, as in the herring cran, the fruit sieves and other baskets made for hard use. The six-pair border is similar to the five-pair, except that six uprights are kinked and knocked in turn before the border sequence begins. Moreover, because of the greater width of the border, more flow must be allowed, so the first few strokes must be more loosely worked. Many professional workers used pegs to keep the first strokes shoved out to the desired width.

Handles

Professional baskets were characterised by well-made double-rod handles that used two long rods. The handle described here is suitable for a log basket. Standing with one foot inside the basket, insert two slyped 8ft (2.4m) rods down through the border into the siding. These are usually inserted three spaces apart about 6" (15cm) from each other. The left-hand rod

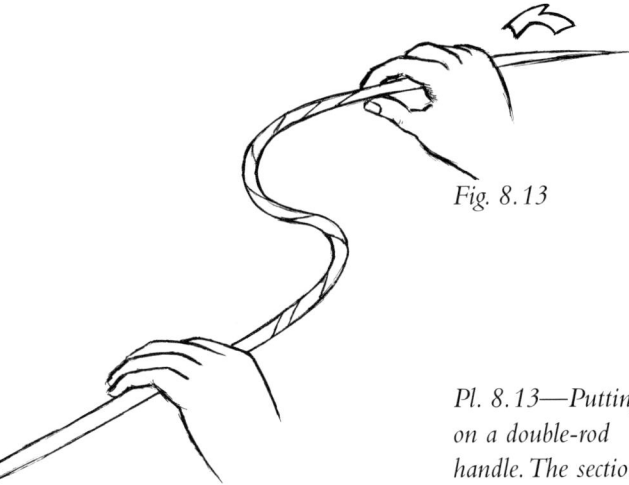

Fig. 8.13

looking from *inside* the basket forms the handle bow, so it can be a little thicker and longer than the other rod. Put the bodkin outside the right-hand handle rod and under the border and the top wale. Pull the tip of the left-hand rod through carefully to form a handle bow about 2–3" (5–7.5cm) above the border. Release this rod and twist the right hand rod by cranking it from the tip as shown in **Fig. 8.13**. Although difficult to do at first, this twisting becomes routine

Pl. 8.13—Putting on a double-rod handle. The section of the rod that forms the core is left untwisted and the other rod is twisted around it. The remainder of the rod forming the handle core is then twisted to complete the handle.

with practice. Remember that the left hand encourages the twist rather than having a rigid grip on the rod. This twisted rod is then brought around the handle bow 2½ times (some call this three) and is pulled under the border from the outside **(Pl. 8.13)**. The rod then returns, keeping close to the previous twists, for 2½ times turns and goes under the border from the outside and returns one more time to finish at the left of the handle. The remainder of the handle bow rod is now twisted and brought around the handle bow in the same way, usually needing three journeys to fully cover the handle bow. The tips of both rods are threaded through under the border for a secure finish. If the number of turns around the handle bow is increased by one more to 3½, it will not be necessary to do three journeys with the second handle rod, and shorter handle rods may also be used; it is this version which is shown in Pl. 8.13.

9
The future

Two of the professional basketmakers I mentioned in the last chapter, Tom Quinlan of Tallow Hill and Joe Shanahon of Carrick-on-Suir, both told me that they had believed in the early 1970s that basketmaking as a trade was finished and that they were among the last of their profession. While probably not consciously bearers of tradition, there had been a degree of regret in the recognition that the trade of basketmaking in this country, in which both families had been involved for three generations, would probably end with them. There weren't any hopeful signs on the horizon. Although baskets had begun to be fashionable again from the mid-1970s onwards, this demand was largely met by imported basketware. Wages were still too low to make basketmaking seem like a worthwhile trade. The renewed interest in basketmaking as a profession, which gradually became apparent from the late 1970s and early 1980s onwards, probably took both men by surprise. Many of the people who became interested in basketmaking at that time were attracted to it because it seemed to offer the possibility of

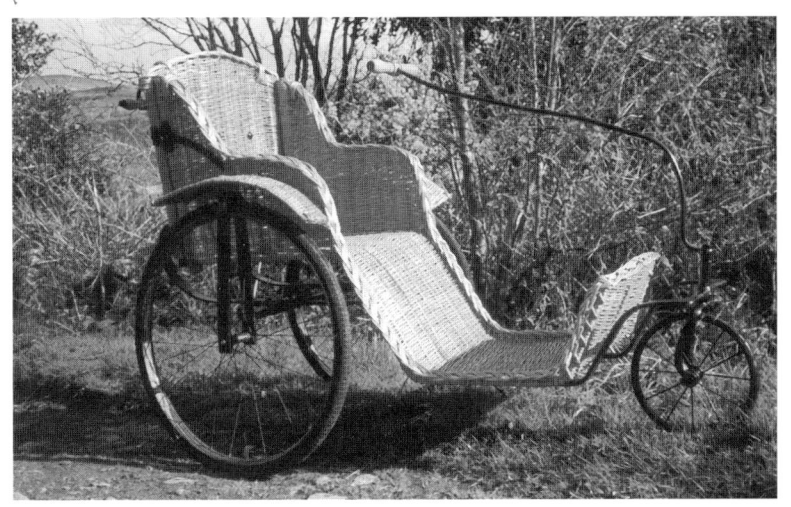

Pl. 9.1—
Nineteenth-century
Dublin bath chair
restored by Katrin
Schwartz. Photo
courtesy of Katrin
Schwartz.

235

sustainable and satisfying work rather than for any sound financial reasons. They were choosing to make baskets because it interested them, and most had no family ties to the trade. Many were from other parts of Europe, and some had a certain disenchantment with a materialistic culture that did not value personal fulfilment or meaningful work. The old crafts and agricultural skills that survived in Ireland were valued more highly by these immigrants than by the majority of Irish people at that time.

An interest in willow growing also fuelled an interest in basketmaking. Because the Quinlans harvested their own willows they were able to offer advice on this as well. They were helpful in getting a few of the County Cork basketmakers started in the trade, and as I have acknowledged in the Preface, I found the Quinlans invaluable in the first year or two that I was making baskets. In Northern Ireland, Alison Fitzgerald found herself living beside the willow beds of the Loughgall Horticultural Research Station and, having had her interest awakened, she got started with the help of basketmakers James Mulholland and the Crosseys.

Pl. 9.2—Willow mask made by James Mulholland for the Armagh Rhymers. Photo courtesy of John Fitzgerald.

A more structured way of learning basketmaking was provided by a series of small training programmes in Joe Shanahan's workshop in Carrick-on-Suir. These were funded by the ANCO training authority and each programme lasted about six months. Amongst those who attended this programme was Irene Kelly-Stafford, who subsequently taught her sister, Barbara, and they now run a basketmaking business together in County Wexford. Irene also taught Gráinne Uí Maitiú, a cousin of Joe Shanahan's, to make baskets.

Most of these basketmakers were working individually and while most would meet other basketmakers occasionally, especially those in their own area, the formation of the Irish Basketmakers Association in 1994 facilitated greater contact between basketmakers. The Association now has a membership of almost one hundred people and is open to all who are interested in basketmaking, regardless of whether they make baskets. In that year also, the then Exhibitions Officer at the Crafts Council of Ireland, Mairéad McAnallen, organised an exhibition, 'Basketmakers', which showed work

Pl. 9.3—Selection of baskets by Barbara and Irene Kelly, Co. Wexford. Photo courtesy of Barbara and Irene Kelly.

from most of those then making baskets in Ireland. Workshops aimed at both inspiring basketmakers and improving their technical skills were also part of this initiative and tutors included David Drew and Colin Manthorpe. It had also been hoped that Tom Quinlan would have been able to attend but Tom's health had begun to fail by then. Such workshops can have a very positive effect on standards within a craft discipline, particularly as so many of us making baskets have not had the benefit of a traditional apprenticeship. While an apprenticeship system can sometimes become deadening, stifling creativity and joy, an element of it does provide a thorough grounding in the skills of the relevant trade. As Mike Cooley points

Pl. 9.4—Outdoor garden sculptures by Norbert Platz. Photo courtesy of Norbert Platz.

Pl. 9.5—'High Spirits'; willow bottles by Greenmantle (Lynn Kirkham and Paul Finch). Photo courtesy of Lynn Kirkham.

out: 'People often mistake apprenticeships for simply the transmission of manual dexterity, whereas it is actually the transmission of a great culture, of how to organise yourself, how to get materials, how to plan things.'[1]

The conditions for such an ideal apprenticeship certainly have not existed in Irish basketmaking for several years. The continuity of the apprenticeship system pre-supposes a healthy and relatively stable future for a craft. The time spent in training people would have to be paid for by the State or some other outside party for such a system to have any prospect of being revived in the foreseeable future. However, the group of basketmakers at Coolmountain in County Cork are an example of basketmakers supporting each other with sharing of skills and co-operation on many levels.

In the absence of such training, many basketmakers have relied on courses to enable them to learn and then develop their basketmaking skills. The old workshop adage that 'practice makes the basket' reminds us that the aspiring basketmakers must spend many hours making baskets to build up skill and fluency, but with enthusiasm and a good space this can be done at home.

Pl. 9.6—Log baskets by Norbert Platz. Photo courtesy of Norbert Platz.

Basketmakers Linda Scott and Vincent MacCarron got started in this way. Brian Haslett, on the other hand, learned the basics from books and began to attend courses to increase and deepen his knowledge. Lynn Kirkham did the four-year part-time course at the London Guildhall University and developed a strong interest in contemporary basketmaking. Her partner, Paul Finch, a furniture-maker by training, came to Ireland in the mid-1990s and gradually developed a business making unique one-off pieces, many of which are site-specific. Samson Akrinde started basketmaking at Camphill Community, and Mike Kreith and Patsy Cahill relied on a mixture of both courses and learning from books. Only two of the newer generation of basketmakers carry on a direct family tradition. Martin Sinnott, who is the fourth generation of his family to carry on the trade, works part-time in County Laois, and Tom Quinlan's daughter, Veronica O'Keeffe, also works part-time at Lismore, Co. Waterford. Whatever the diverse routes that these people have taken to learn the skills of willow basketmaking, their determination to learn was helped in no small measure by the satisfaction they derive from basketmaking. This satisfaction level is cited by many makers as compensating for the fairly low return that they get for their work, a difficulty that can be even more pronounced in rushwork. Despite this, both Patricia D'Arcy of County Cavan and Patty O'Flaherty of Stokestown have managed to generate a reasonable income from rushwork over the years. For most people, however, rushwork only generates a small, part-time income, and the crafts of rush seating and traditional straw-work are similarly not commercially viable.

Much of the reason for this is due to the low status accorded to basketmaking amongst the crafts in Ireland. Many basketmakers feel rather isolated from the crafts movement, and this is particularly true of crafts shops. It is probably harder for basketmakers to sell their work through crafts shops than it was in the 1980s. The trend since then has been away from small crafts shops that celebrated the local to larger shops with many of the same crafts duplicated in shops throughout the country. In addition to this there is a lack of awareness on the part of many crafts shops about baskets — how else can one explain the fact that the Kilkenny Shop, one of Ireland's most prestigious crafts shops, does not stock any Irish baskets at the time of writing, and indeed uses imported basketware extensively throughout the shop to display other Irish crafts in? Nor is this an isolated case; other large crafts shops with the same policy include Blarney Woollen Mills and Meadows and Byrne. As a result, many basketmakers rely on direct sales to the public, though this can place those who live in very isolated locations at a disadvantage. Some have also developed a mail order business. A selection of crafts shops that currently stock Irish baskets is listed in Appendix 3. It also contains a list of those currently working at basketmaking in Ireland.

Most Irish basketmakers are reasonably optimistic about the future of their craft, and sales today are probably less tourist-oriented than ten years ago, as Irish people themselves are beginning to appreciate baskets more.

Pl. 9.8—
Rectangular log
basket made by the
author.

APPENDIX 1

BASIC TECHNIQUES

Pairing

Most bases are made using pairing weave. In pairing, two rods are woven alternately, the left-hand rod goes into the space that the right-hand rod is coming out of and then comes out the next space so that it becomes the new right-hand rod. See **Pairing 1**, where for clarity the pairing weave is shown on vertical uprights.

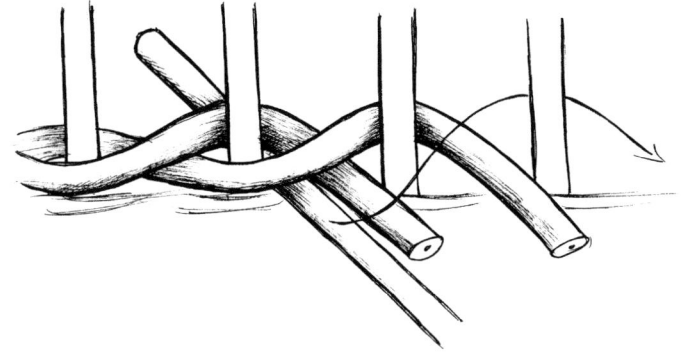

Pairing 1

In professional basketmaking, each time two rods are selected care is taken to ensure that they are both evenly matched in strength and in length, and rods are usually joined tip to tip and butt to butt. Thus when the tip of a rod is within 8–10" (200–250mm) of being spent, the tip of the new rods are inserted underneath it and both the old and the new are woven together for a stroke or two. When the butt of a rod is spent, the butt of a new rod is inserted to replace it. In the earlier stages of a base, the new butt is placed under the spent butt (a simple join), but as the base widens a more secure join known as a lock join (see **Pairing 2**) is used.

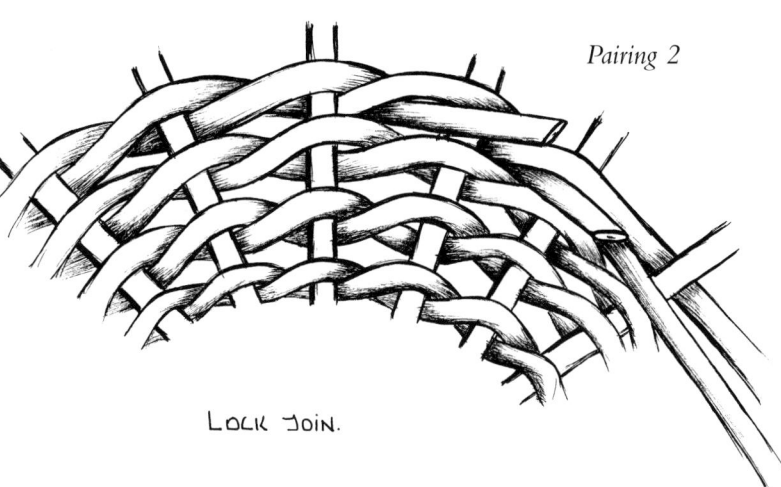

Pairing 2

LOCK JOIN.

241

Country basketmakers often used unsorted material of varying lengths. In this system, when a rod is within 9" (230mm) of being spent at its tip, it is replaced by a new rod, butt first each time. This method of joining was also used when waling with unsorted material. This style of basketmaking is often referred to as hedgerow basketry.

Three-rod waling

Waling can involve the use of four or more rods, but its most common form is three-rod waling. The left-hand rod goes in front of two uprights and behind one, as shown in **Waling 1.**

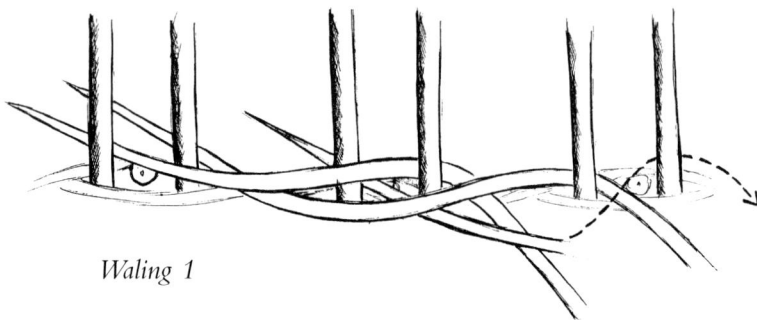

Waling 1

To wale correctly it is necessary to hold the left-hand waling rod with the thumb of the left hand as it passes in front of the upright **(Waling 2)**. This prevents the uprights from being driven sideways by the waling. Because the correct position of the hands makes it difficult to see the uprights, I would prefer to describe waling as the left-hand rod going into the space the right-hand rod is coming out of, and then coming out of the next space.

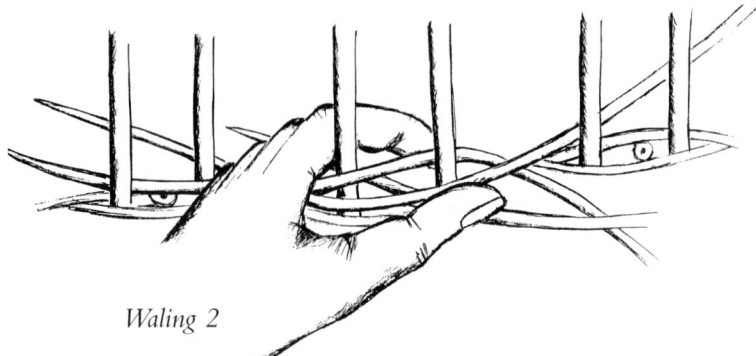

Waling 2

In professional basketmaking, joins are made tip to tip and butt to butt, usually using two sets of weavers that follow each other around without catching up, a system usually referred to as chasing. Rather than working both tips together as described for pairing, the top 12" (300mm) of the waling rod is discarded.

Randing

Randing describes any weave where a single rod is woven in front of one upright and behind the next. The most common form of randing in Ireland was French randing (although it was known simply as randing), as shown in **Randing 1**. This involves selecting the same number of weavers as the uprights in the basket. They should each be about the same length and should be somewhat thinner than the uprights, at least until you have gained experience. Take the first weaver and, having placed the butt behind an upright, go in front, behind and out. Introduce the next and subsequent weavers, one space to the left of the one already worked. The final two weaving rods are inserted by easing up randing rods 1 and 2 so that the final two rods can be woven without crossing over numbers 1 and 2.

Randing 1

Once you have a rod coming out of each space, begin a new round by taking a randing rod in front, behind and out. Take the next randing rod to the left and weave it in the same way and continue this process, ensuring that the final two randing rods are woven without crossing over the initial two that started the round. Many people put tape or clothes pegs on the first two randing rods in order to facilitate learning the weave.

A simpler version of this is mock randing, where the number of weavers is two fewer than the number of uprights. Thus for 24 upright only 22 weavers are used, sparing the necessity of weaving the final two weavers under the initial two. Mock randing looks the same as French randing, but it cannot be used in the creel, as the full number of weavers is needed for the mouthwale.

The randing rods are woven out to the tips, and if more height is desired a new set of randing rods is introduced by laying the butts of the new rods, in turn, on to one of the spent tips. Randing should be beaten occasionally with the iron, particularly while the randing rods are still fairly thick.

Putting on a four-rod wale over outstretched uprights (German wale)

This rim is put on over the outstretched uprights, so having inserted the upright you *don't* kink them. Do ensure that the *underside* of the base is uppermost before starting the German wale rim.

Pl. GW. 1

For this rim you use a four-rod wale. This is similar to the three-rod wale already described except that you are working with four rods. Thus the left-hand rod goes in front of three and behind one. To start, select the first four waling rods and measure them roughly from the butts so that they can comfortably go halfway round the base **(Pl. GW 1)**. Cut off the surplus tips and anchor the rods (on the newly cut 'tip' side) behind four consecutive uprights **(Pl. GW 2)**. Start a four-rod wale. It is a good idea to work at the edge of the lap-board so that you divide the stroke, going in front of three and

Pl. GW. 2

holding it tightly before going behind one and thus ensuring that the wale presses tightly against the base. Join butt to butt when you are halfway round but do not cut the surplus tips off these rods, because the length will be useful for pulling the rods through at the finish.

When you reach the start, the first rod is woven in front of three, behind one and dropped, you could hold it in place with your knee, if necessary. The second is similarly woven in front of three, behind one but is also tucked under the front of the wale, in this case under one rod **(Pl. GW 3)**. The next rod goes in front of three, behind one and is tucked under two, and the final rod is tucked under three.

Turn the base right side up and kink the uprights close to the base and gather into a hoop or tie as normal.

Pl. GW. 3

Five-behind-two border

This border is so named because you will be working with five pairs and each standing stake is initially taken behind two others. Each rod also goes in front of 4 and behind 1 so the border may be known by other names, especially in mainland Europe.

1. Kink five rods using a blunt knife in the same manner in which you kink the uprights at the bottom of the basket. The kinking height should be almost twice the thickness of the rods you are kinking so that when the upright is folded down a rod of similar diameter to the upright will fit comfortably in the gap between the kinked rod and the top of the basket. A sixth rod can be kinked if desired; it will save you having to use your thumb to do so later.

2. Bend down five rods, each one going behind two others; for example, rod 1 goes behind rods 2 and 3, 2 goes behind rods 3 and 4, etc., as shown in **Bor. 1**.

Bor. 1

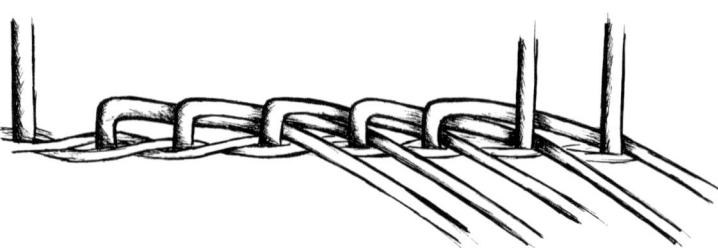

3. Take the left-hand rod (rod 1) and put it with flow (i.e., loosely) in front of two standing stakes and out the next space. Another way to phrase this is that the left-hand rod goes *into* the space that the right-hand rod (5) is coming out of and then comes out the next space. This is shown in **Bor. 2**. (The actual movement is in front of rod 4, behind rod 1, but two of these stakes are bent down. I think it is easier to use the concept of in front of two standing stakes, or alternatively to say that the left-hand rod goes into the space that the right-hand rod comes out of, since these will work for any behind-two border).

Bor. 2

4. As soon as this rod has been worked, you provide it with a partner by bringing the leftmost standing stake (rod 6) down alongside it out the same space as shown in **Bor. 3**. You will notice that this standing stake goes behind two (rods 7 and 8), the initial movement of every upright.

5. Now that you have a pair, repeat the sequence, i.e., take the leftmost of the knocked-down rods (rod 2) and go in front of two standing stakes (rods 7 and 8), into the space that the right-hand pair is coming out of, and out the next space. Provide it with a partner

by kinking the leftmost standing stake (rod 7) off the front of the border, thereby giving it a distinct kink, then releasing it and bringing it behind two (rods 8 and 9) to form a pair with the other rod. You now have two pairs and three singles protruding.

6. Repeat the sequence, taking the leftmost knocked–down rod (rod 3) in front of two standing stakes (rods 8 and 9) and out the next space. Provide it with a partner by knocking down the leftmost standing stake (rod 8) and going behind two stakes with it to give another pair. You now have three pairs and two singles protruding.

7. Repeat the sequence to give four pairs.

8. Repeat to give five pairs.

9. This time when you go to repeat the sequence, there is a pair there rather than the single rod you met each time up to this. Take the right hand rod of the left-hand pair (i.e., the fifth pair counting from right to left) and put it in front of two standing stakes and out the next space as before. This is shown in **Bor. 4**. Provide with partner by knocking down the leftmost standing stake.

10. Count back from the right-hand pair to get the fifth pair back. You will use the right rod of this pair to continue the sequence. (This rod has only gone behind two and has, as yet, not gone in front of two standing stakes. The left-hand rod of the pair is finished with, having gone behind two when worked initially and then subsequently having worked in front of four—two of which were standing, two of which were kinked — and gone behind one.) Give it a partner by bringing the leftmost standing stake behind the next two standing stakes

11. Repeat the sequence until you come back to where you started. It is helpful to count back five pairs each time until you are familiar with the border. Keep the border flat to ensure that you *don't* select the left-hand rod instead of the right-hand rod of the relevant pair.

12. When you come to the starting point, both rods are threaded under the first rod (rod 1) that you kinked. **Bor. 5** shows the border before the relevant pair has been worked. **Bor. 6** shows both rods having been threaded in turn under rod 1.

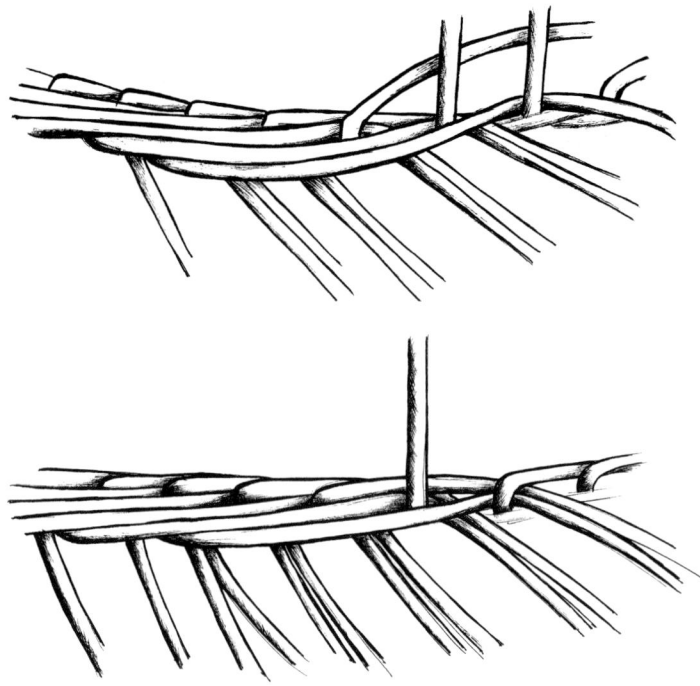

Bor. 5

Bor. 6

13. Look at the next space where your rods have to exit (immediately to the right of the space you have just done) and put your bodkin out under the kinked rod (I usually call it the knuckle). **Bor. 7** shows the bodkin in position. Count back (from the right) five pairs, select the right-hand rod of the fifth pair back and thread

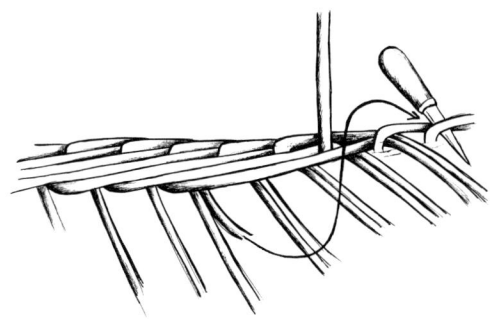

the tip of it out through the space as guided by the bodkin (withdraw the bodkin as soon as you have a grip on the rod). You must now give this rod a partner by bringing the last standing stake out the same space or gap but *remember this standing stake goes out under two* in order to correspond to the other rods, the initial movement of which was to go behind two. **Bor. 8** shows these two rods having been worked.

14. You again have five pairs and all that remains to do is to reduce these to singles by threading the right-hand rod of each out the appropriate space. Find the first space that has to be filled (immediately to the right of the one you have just done), put the bodkin out at a right angle under the kinked rod or 'knuckle'. Then count back (from the right) five pairs, take the right-hand rod of the fifth pair back and thread the tip of it through where the bodkin is showing. Then withdraw the bodkin and pull the rod through, flattening down before finally pulling through. **Bor. 9** shows this rod flattened down and in correct position ready for final tightening. (Notice that this first rod you have worked of the final five pairs goes out under one.)

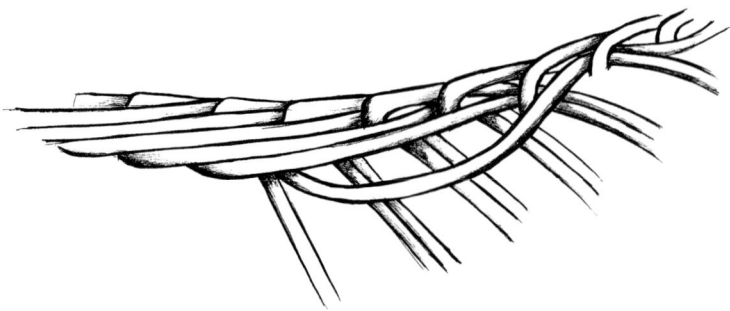

15. Find the next space for a rod to come out (immediately to the right of the previous one) and take your bodkin out at a right angle under the knuckle and whatever is outside it. Each time flatten with your fingers to ensure it has gone in front of four. You will notice the second rod of the five finishing rods has gone out under two.

16. Again find the next space with your bodkin and come out at a right angle under the knuckle and whatever is outside it. In the case of the third rod you deal with, you come out under three, in the case of the fourth rod you come out under four and in the case of the fifth you come out under five **(Bor 10)**. Remember to flatten each rod down to the front as you pull it through and to start the pulling through by catching each rod by the tip and shepherding it through to avoid kinks. When all five have been pulled through, tighten the first few border rods if necessary.

17. Trim the border, remembering to keep the cut-offs either for

Bor. 10

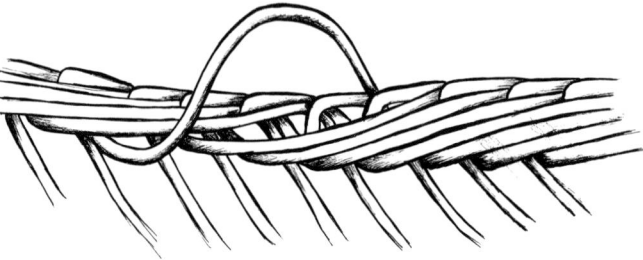

use as a foot (if they are thick enough and the basket does not already have a rim) or for some other purpose.

APPENDIX 2

NOTES ON CURING A RAWHIDE

Obtain a large hide from a slaughterhouse or abattoir. This must first be 'fleshed' to remove all remaining pieces of meat or fat from the inside of the skin. A blunt blade is used for scraping, and if the hide can be obtained in winter or in cool autumn or spring weather, you will avoid the flies that make this job even less pleasant in summer.

When the hide has been fleshed, prepare a salt bath with 4lb (2kg) of salt petre and 3lb (1.5kg) of alum salts dissolved thoroughly in boiling water. Put this into a long (i.e., oval) bath and add further water if needed so you will be able to immerse the hide. Put the hide in with tail at one end, neck at the other and move it around to get the salts dispersed. Leave in the bath for ten days and each day rotate the hide so that one day the hairy side is facing out and the next day the hairy side is inside. Use a waterproof apron and long rubber gauntlet gloves for the job. When you have turned it, get rid of air pockets.

After ten days take the hide out, put it over a rail and give it a good hosing down with fresh water. You may want to use a horse currycomb if you like to comb away any debris. Allow as much water to dry away as possible — the hide should be like a huge moist chamois leather, very pliable but not stiff. Do not leave it out to 'dry' for too long or it will become hard and unworkable. Put it on over the currach framework while it is still moist.

For the Boyne currach one hide should suffice to cover the framework, but it is usually necessary to put a patch where the tail of the hide was. This patch was usually on the stern end where the nets were, rather than at the bow end where the paddler knelt. The Colm Cille currach built at Mayo Abbey took eight hides. Because of the width, two hides — one on either side — were needed along the main body of the boat, with one hide each at the bow and the stern. For joining along the seams, a strip of hide about 3" (75mm) wide was placed between the two faces of hide to give added strength, and this was stitched with a blanket stitch running across the top of the seam and a two-needle stitch underneath, using a flax thread that had been impregnated with tar or lanolin.

Since the rawhide external face is not waterproof it must be waterproofed. For the large currach built at Mayo Abbey, Peter

Faulkner used lanolin that was heated to near boiling point and then rubbed on. Brendan Brennan, who covered two Boyne currachs (one for the Waterways Museum, Ringsend, Dublin, and one for the Heritage Collection of baskets (see Appendix 4), used tanned hide in the same manner as Michael O'Brien (see Chapter 4), and rubbed these with a few coats of beeswax.

APPENDIX 3

RESOURCES

Includes, museums, list of basketmakers, courses and a selection of shops that stock Irish baskets. (For books, films and videos, see Select Bibliography)

Museums

The following is a list of the main museums that have some baskets in their collections (see also Appendix 4 for the Heritage Collection). Large museums are usually closed on Mondays and open for a half day on Sundays instead. The largest collections are at the Museum of Country Life in Castlebar and the Ulster Folk and Transport Museum, Cultra, Co. Down. Remember that these two museums hold much of their collection in reserve so it is best to phone first if you hope to see the complete collection.

Armagh County Museum, The Mall East, Armagh, Co. Armagh.

Bunratty Castle and Folk Park, Bunratty, Co. Clare.

Carraig Craft Visitor Centre and Basketry Museum. April to October, Mon–Fri, 10 a.m. to 6 p.m. Sunday 2 p.m. to 6 p.m.

Craggaunowen Project, Quinn, Co. Clare. (Crannóg dwellings and Brendan boat.)

Glencolumkille Folk Museum, Glencolumkille, Co. Donegal.

The Irish Agricultural Museum, Johnstown Castle, Co. Wexford.

Knock Folk Museum, Knock, Co. Mayo.

The National Museum of Ireland, Museum of Country Life, Turlough Park House, Castlebar, Co. Mayo. Tel: (01) 6777444; lo-call 1890 687386.

The National Museum of Ireland, Collins Barracks, Benburb St., Dublin 7. (Baskets on the top floor.)

Newtowncashel Heritage Centre, Newtowncashel, Athlone, Co. Westmeath.

Riverstown Heritage Centre, Co. Sligo

Ulster American Folk Park, Camphill, Omagh, Co. Tyrone.

The Ulster Folk and Transport Museum, Cultra, Holywood, Co. Down. BT18 0EU. Tel: (01232) 428428.

Basketmakers

Samson Akrinde, River Cottage, Kinsealy Lane, Malahide, Co. Dublin.
Tel: (01) 8460014.
Open: By appointment.

Patsy Cahill, Kylatlea, Mullinahone, Co. Tipperary.
Tel: (051) 647056.
Open: If at home.

Coolmountain Baskets, The Dome, Coolmountain, Co. Cork.
Tel: (026) 49218.
Open: By appointment.

Marie Crean (Rushwork), Moanbeg, Fethard, Co. Tipperary.
Tel: (052) 31467.
Open: Attends Fethard Country Market each Friday morning.
10 a.m.–12.30 p.m.

Patricia D'Arcy, Carraig Craft Visitor Centre and Basketry
Museum, Mountnugent, Co. Cavan.
Tel: (049) 8540179.
Open: April–October, Mon–Fri 10 a.m.–6 p.m.,
Sunday 2 p.m.–6 p.m, closed Saturdays.
Nov–March by appointment.

Alison Fitzgerald, Greenwood Baskets, Unit 9, Armagh Business
Centre, Loughgall Rd., Armagh, BT61 7NJ.
Tel: (04837) 528112. Fax: (04837) 526717.
Open: Usually 9 a.m.–4 p.m. weekdays but best to phone first.

Greenmantle (Lynn Kirkham and Paul Finch),
Bohernarudda, Templemore, Co. Tipperary.
Tel: (0504) 32341.
Open: By appointment only.

Brian Haslett, 23 Lansdowne Crescent, Portrush, Co. Antrim,
BT 56 8AY..
Tel: 0801 265823004
Open: By appointment only.

Joe Hogan, Loch Na Fooey, Finny, Clonbur, Co.Galway.
Tel: (092) 48241.
Open: Usually open Mon–Fri 10 a.m.–5.30 p.m. during July and
August; phone first if travelling specially. Otherwise by appointment.

Barbara and Irene Kelly, Ballyvarogue, Saltmills, New Ross,
Co.Wexford.
Tel: (051) 397618.
Open: Summer. Tue–Sat 10 a.m.–5.00 p.m. but phone first to be
sure someone's there. Otherwise by appointment.

Ted Kelly, Ballintogher, Co. Sligo (straw baskets).
Tel: (071) 64463.
By appointment.

Mike Kreith, Keekill, Headford, Co.Galway.
Tel: (093) 35357.
Open: Mon–Fri. 9 a.m.–4 p.m. but please phone first.

Vincent Mac Árainn, Creig a Chéirín, Inis Mór, Árainn,
Co. Na Gaillimhe.
Tel: (099) 61209.
Open: 9 a.m.–9 p.m. Casual callers welcome.

Hans and Madelon Mathes, Milmorane Basketry, Ballingeary,
Co.Cork.
Tel: (026) 47230.
Open: Shop in Ballingeary Village.
Summer 9 a.m.–5 p.m. each day except Wednesday.
Spring and Autum, 9 a.m.–5 p.m.

James Mulholland, 2 Moss Rd., Gawley's Gate, Craigavon, Co.
Antrim.
Open: 10 a.m.–5 p.m., but since all baskets are made to order
there may not be a variety of baskets to see.

Naomh Padraig Rushbaskets (Patricia O'Flaherty), Cloonshee, Strokestown, Co. Roscommon.
Tel/Fax: (078) 37077.
Open: By appointment.

Martin and Yvon O'Flynn and Family Willow Basketry, Maughanasilly, Kealkil, Bantry, Co. Cork.
Tel: (027) 66111.
Open: More or less seven days a week. When home we're open, but we like to take Sunday afternoon off.

Norbert Platz, Basketcraft, Ballymurphy, Innishannon, Co.Cork.
Tel: (021) 885548.
Open: visitors always welcome by appointment.

Linda Scott, Willowworks, Knockmore, Ballina, Co. Mayo.
Tel: (094) 58284.
Open: Most afternoons but phone first to make someone's there.

Pearl Sheehan, (Rush baskets), Drumacoo, Kilcolgan, Co.Galway.
Tel: (091) 796350.
Open: by appointment.

Martin Sinnott, 115 Hillview Drive, Portlaoise, Co. Laois.
Tel: (0502) 61530.
Not open to visitors.

Gráinne Uí Mhaitiú, Valleymount, Blessington, Co. Wicklow.
Tel: (045) 867332.
Open: Visitors welcome but it would be better to phone beforehand.

Courses
The following basketmakers give courses:

Patsy Cahill
Marie Crean
Patricia D'Arcy
Alison Fitzgerald
Joe Hogan
Lynn Kirkham (Greenmantle)
Martin and Yvon O'Flynn

Linda Scott
Katrin Schwartz (Coolmountain Baskets)

The Centre for Traditional Skills runs courses in basketmaking
(tutor Barbara Kelly).
The Railway Station, Lismore, Co. Waterford.
Tel: (058) 53196. E-Mail: cts.lismore@ireland.com

Selection of shops that sell Irish baskets
The Bay Tree, Holywood, Co. Down.
Commodum, Dingle, Co. Kerry.
Craft Granary, Cahir, Co. Tipperary.
The Doolin Craft Centre, Doolin, Co. Clare.
Joyce's Craft Shop, Recess, Co. Galway.
Kelly's Craft Shop, High Street, Galway.
Kinallen Craft Centre, near Dromore, Co. Down.
Loft Gallery, New Ross, Co. Wexford.
National Museum Shop, Kildare St., Dublin.
Nicholas Mosse Country Shop, Bennettsbridge, Co. Kilkenny.
Power's Woollen Mills, Kilcolgan, Co. Galway.
Skibbereen Arts Centre, Skibbereen, Co. Cork.

Associations
The Irish Basketmakers Association
Aims to promote basketmaking in Ireland through a wide range of
activities. Issues a twice-yearly newsletter.
Secretary: Linda Scott, Willow Works, Knockmore, Co. Mayo.
Tel: (094) 58284.
Membership: Yvon O'Flynn, Maughansilly, Kealkil, Bantry,
Co. Cork.
Tel: (027) 66111.

The Basketmakers' Association
Membership: Secretary, 37 Mendip Rd., Cheltenham,
Gloucestershire, GL 52 5EB, England
Quarterly newsletter, most members are from the UK but the
association also has international membership.

The Irish Coppice Workers Association
c/o Joe Gowran, Drumcliff South, Sligo
Tel/Fax: (071) 45504.

APPENDIX 4

HERITAGE COLLECTION OF BASKETS

This collection, which is the responsibility of the Irish Basketmakers Association, can be borrowed for exhibitions and individual baskets can be borrowed by basketmakers. The collection received an award from the Irish Heritage Council, An Comhairle Oidhreachta. People wishing to access the collection can contact the Secretary of the IBA, Linda Scott, at (094) 58284 or Joe Hogan at (092) 48241. An A4 poster showing certain items in the collection is available from Joe Hogan. Write for details to Joe Hogan, Loch Na Fooey, Finny, Clonbur, Co. Galway.

Creels
Standard (4 x 3) knotted.
Rectangular *pardóg* (hinged-bottomed creel).
Mayo (5 x 4) creel, inward-turned mouthwale.
Fermanagh creel, hump-bottomed, shallow.
Cavan creel, hump-bottomed, deep.
Aran Island creel.
Kerry (oval) creel.
Back creel, single uprights, alternate weaving directions after Co. Tyrone creel in the UFTM.
Sligo creel, maker Johnny Hannon, Monasteraden, Co. Sligo.
Úimeacha, slip-bottomed creels, west Kerry.
D-shaped Tuam *pardóg* in hazel.
Foddering creel with *súgán* ropes (midlands).
Hazel creel (west Clare), maker Johnny Toole, Fanore.
Kish, large hazel basket for slide car.

Potato baskets
Split oak potato basket after one made by Nicholas Hilliard (maker Owen Jones).
Ulster potato harvesting basket (maker Alison Fitzgerald).
Sciath, Waterford scuttle type.
Sciathóg, two-rib start (maker Alison Fitzgerald).
Sciathóg, one-rib start.
Sciathóg, horseshoe-shaped, west Cork.
Ciseóg (skib), four types.
Aran Islands 3 x 3 with bi-stakes.
Mayo 4 x 4.
Joyce country basket.
Skib with inner skib.
Losset (white willow and wood), County Fermanagh.

Fishing baskets
Hazel crab pot, after one by Sammy Gault, Dunservick, Co. Antrim.
Heather lobster pot, County Mayo.
Willow lobster pot, Innishturk, Co. Mayo (maker Pakie O'Toole).
Willow lobster pot, north Connemara, after one made by Festy Mortimer, Rossroe.
Hazel lobster pot, which was also sometimes used for rock fish, south Connemara and formerly Aran Islands.
Willow lobster pot, County Kerry.
Willow eel trap, Carrick-on-Suir, Co. Tipperary (maker Joe Shanahan).
Ribh (Aran longline basket), long type, wooden back (maker Vincent McCarron).
Ribh, woven back, based on one in the National Museum of Ireland collection.
Longline basket based on one made by Sammy Gault, Dunservick, Co. Antrim.

Other willow and hazel baskets
Cradle bird (bird trap).
Aran cradle.
Crandy, Co. Offaly.
Aran kisheen.
Calf muzzles.
Start of skib bases.
Boyne currach, with tanned hide; hide fitted and sewn by Brendan Brennan, Co. Kilkenny.

Straw work
Hen's nest (maker Ted Kelly).
Hen's nest with woven rod door.
Two-storey hen's nest (maker Ted Kelly).
Straddle-mat, hinged (maker Ted Kelly).
Straddle mat with crutch (*coirb*), mat made by Ted Kelly, *coirb* made by Robert and Tommy Staunton, Foxford, Co. Mayo.
Straw egg basket (maker Bernie Winters, Clare Island, Co. Mayo).
Strawboy's hat, skirt and leggings.
Ball of *súgan* rope made from 'bent' grass (maker Patrick Shevlin, Binghamstown, Belmullet, Co. Mayo).
Start of hen's nest and straddle mat.

Rush (field rush)
St Bridget's crosses in various patterns.
Baskets not credited above made by Joe Hogan.

APPENDIX 5

BASKETMAKERS WORKING IN IRELAND *c.* 1945

This list of professional and semi-professional basketmakers working in Ireland around 1945 is largely based on information contained in an unpublished survey of handcraft workers carried out by Chrissie O'Gorman on behalf of the Homespun Society. The County Antrim list is based on information in Patrick Smyth's book *Osier culture and basketmaking.*

COUNTY ANTRIM

(All of the listings for County Antrim are in the south-west of the county near Aghalee or Ballinderry).

Sam Courtney, Aghadalgon; James Crossey, Ballinderry; Samuel McAreavey, Aghadalgon (a few people employed); James Mulholland, Moss Rd., Aghgallon; Mulhollands, Derrymore Rd.

COUNTY CARLOW

Michael Fitzgerald, Brewery Lane, Carlow
A wide range of baskets, had two osier beds and he peeled a lot of the crop for 'fancy' work.

Brigid Coleman, Hackettstown
Made a wide range of baskets. The Carlow potato basket was a frame basket type, 24" (61cm) long, 20" (51cm) wide and 10" (26cm) deep. A lot of her material was stripped willow.

Patrick Barron, The Lock, Borris
Made potato baskets, cutting his rods on the islands along the River Barrow (part-time). Mentions common osier, bitter osier (*S. purpurea*) and timber osier red (*S. alba*).

John Shaw, Rathvinden Lock, Leighlin Bridge
Made baskets and hoops but found hoop-making more profitable and devoted most of his time to this. He made the hoops from four-year-old willow, which he split with a 'fender' (a large cleave) into four before shaving with a draw knife. There were barrel hoops from

6ft (1.8m) to 9ft (2.7m) long and ferkin hoops, about 4' 6"
(1350mm) long. The willow was harvested on the islands on the
River Barrow.

Peter Hughes, Bagenalstown
Potato baskets (part-time).

Patrick Hyson, Carlow.
Potato baskets (part-time).

COUNTY CAVAN

John and James Morgan, Virginia
Made creels, two types of potato baskets (a skib and also a *sciathóg*-
type, locally known as a 'paddock') and calf muzzles, for which the
local name was 'gubbins'. Had a half-acre sally garden but bought a
lot of rods from people in the locality.

James Carberry, Snugboro, Ballyconnell
Made creels and straddle mats during the season. Rods for creels
were usually supplied and people gave him a day's work in return.

James Donoghue, Doogra, P.O. Killeshandra
Made creels and potato baskets. The potato baskets were frame baskets
with an odd number of ribs and he called rods for these 'sally osiers'.

Patrick Gilmartin, Dowra
Part-time creel-maker.

Thomas Mills, Lurton, Cootehill
He and his son made creels and a *sciathóg*-type potato basket which
he called a 'losset'.

COUNTY CLARE

Stephen McNamara, Ardnaculla, Ennistymon
Made creels for potatoes and turf from hazel, and also shoppers and
calf muzzles from willow.

Peter McNamara, Ardnaculla, Ennistymon
Made creels, calf muzzles and the local potato basket. This was a
round frame basket locally known as a 'scuttle'.

Patrick Kelly, Tullyroe, Kilkee
Used to make all sorts of baskets but now only made shoppers. He said that around 1920 there were several basketmakers in the district. He was making *sugán* to thatch his house and it is clear that *sugán* rope-making was a very common skill in County Clare and County Kerry at that time.

Denis McMahon, Carrowduff, Ennistymon
Made plaited straw chairs, which he called *suidhistíní,* hen's nests, which he called *siantán,* and rollers for carrying loads on the head, which he called *pillíní.* He also made strawboy hats and seated *súgán* chairs. He called the oblong roll of *súgán* a *meigeall.*

Michael O'Donoghue, Ballyvaughan
Made creels and lobster pots. The lobster pot has sixteen standards, was 19" (48cm) high and wide and also had a handle. A Doolin fisherman called Patrick O'Brien said every fisherman could make his own pots. Michael O'Donoghue gave the Irish names for the parts of the pot in County Clare as follows: the mouth: *an barrach;* the shoulder*: an clár;* the body*: an cabhal;* the handle*: an iris;* bait sticks*: na biríní.*

Mrs Crowe, Doonbeg
Made straw shopping baskets from a long plait of straw, which was sewn together on a similar principle to a rush log basket.

COUNTY CORK

Thomas Kearney, Church Cross, Skibbereen
Made creels that were known locally as 'kishauns'. They were often carried on the back.

Jeremiah Collins, Drimoleague
Made 'kishauns' as described above but also made lobster pots, chairs and garden seats. He used to make a lot of cradles until people got too 'grand' for them!

Patrick Lynch, Ballingeary
Made a creel known locally as a kish—uprights were hazel with five sets of willow weavers and two knapsack-style handles of hay *súgán*. He also made the west Cork horseshoe-shaped *sciathóg* and he mentioned steaming the hoop over a fire to bend it (seasonal).

Patrick O'Sullivan, Kilgarvan

Made creels and the *sciathóg* in the same style as at Ballingeary but also made shopping baskets (seasonal).

Edward Dixon, Straduff, Fenagh

COUNTY GALWAY

J. O'Reilly, Portumna

Taught basketmaking at night classes but didn't make many baskets for sale.

Michael Rabitte, Lavally, Tuam

Made skibs (seasonal).

John McNamara, Kilconly, Tuam

Made shopping, bicycle and farm baskets (probably creels). Would have worked full-time if he could get enough rods.

COUNTY KERRY

Maurice Joy, Glenbeigh

Made creels and the horseshoe-shaped *sciathóg*. The creels were double-staked (seasonal).

Michael Sullivan, Glenbeigh

Made creels and *sciathógs* as above.

Michael Sugrue, Rosbeigh

Made lobster pots and the *cliabh* (creel), and commented that most people made their own creels and pots.

Patrick John Sullivan, Glenbeigh

Made creels, potato baskets (known locally as a *birdeóg),* muzzles for calves (known as *púicín)* and bicycle baskets. Worked almost full-time, as the County Council were buying creels for turf harvesting.

Neil O'Donnell, Cahirciveen

Made all sorts of baskets, including creels, turf baskets, *sciathógs, birdeógs,* etc.

Timothy Murphy, Annascaul, Dingle
Made the *úimeacha* described in Chapter 2 **(Pl. 2.17)**, and it seems they were also used to draw sand to enrich the land.

John Sullivan, Ballyseedy, Tralee.
Made creels and *sciaths*, also baskets for bicycles and shoppers. Got his rods from Shanahans, Carrick-on-Suir (part-time).

COUNTY KILDARE

Jeremiah Quinn, Athy
Made potato baskets, frame basket type. Mentions a large osier bed near Stradbally in County Laois, but all the rods went to the Blind Institute in Dublin.

Patrick McLoughlin, Ballytore
Potato baskets only (seasonal).

Patrick Kittrick, Kilmeague, Naas
Potato baskets only (seasonal, about 5 dozen a year).

COUNTY KILKENNY

Robert Byrne, Waterford Road, Kilkenny
Learned from his father and later from a German instructor at Castlecomer. Made a wide range of baskets, including furniture. The potato basket of the area was 14" (36cm) high with an 11" (28cm) base and a top width of 20" (51cm).

John Dwyer, Ballycallan
Used unpeeled rods only, made potato harvesting baskets and a straining basket called a *sciach*, which was a circular basket 20" (51cm) wide and 13" (33cm) high.

Alexander Byrne, Castlecomer
Made all sorts of baskets. He used to be employed in the Wandesforde factory in Castlecomer and still got his rods free from the estate.

David Gaule, Inistioge
Made a wide range of baskets and had osier beds of about 5 acres, which were rented from the Tighe estate. The beds were on islands on the Nore River.

Martin Vigors, Inistioge
Made various types of baskets and had up to 9 acres of willow divided into yearling and two- and three-year old sections.

David Fenlon, Graigue-na-Managh
Made potato baskets, frame basket type, oval, about 23" x 20" (59cm x 51cm) and 9" (23cm) high.

Mrs Brophy, Graigue-na-Managh
Coiled straw baskets, mainly bee skeps and egg baskets; the local name of the egg basket was a 'grub'.

Mrs Daly, Brandondale, Graigue-na-Managh
Coiled straw bee hives and market baskets. The bee hives were 14" (36cm) wide and 20" (51cm) high with a handle 6" (15cm) high. The market baskets were like inverted hives.

COUNTY LAOIS

John Walsh, Kilbricken
Made potato baskets known locally as 'skibs'. These were potato harvesting baskets, however, and dimensions were about 14" (36cm) wide at base, 11" (28cm) high and 18" (46cm) wide at top. (seasonal).

John Loughnan, Mountrath
He made 'skibs' on a piece-work basis for Raheen Co-Op at Abbeyleix; they rented an osier bed from Laois County Council and also had one of their own.

John Conroy, Clonad, Portlaoise
Made 'skibs' and shopping baskets (seasonal).

Patrick Cahill, Kilcoran, Rathdowney
Made 'skibs' on a seasonal basis.

Michael and Thomas Murphy, Portarlington
Made potato baskets from sallies and hazel.

Thomas Smith, Portarlington
Made the local potato skibs. Used hazel and willow for handles.

Thomas Brophy, Draspa Bay, Mountrath
Made the local potato skibs, using only willow.

William Callaghan, Castlecuffe, Clonsalee
Made the potato 'skibs' from willow. He also made straw bee skeps and straw seed baskets.

COUNTY LEITRIM

Peter Walsh, Foxfield, Manorhamilton
Made shopping baskets, creels and potato baskets, but for barter rather than for sale. He also made hen's nests (locally known as a *cisín*) and these were two-storey, similar to one of the nests in **Pl. 7.8**. He also had a straw mattress that was made up of two sections. This straw mattress had another mattress placed on top of it.

Patrick Thornton, Faughary, Manorhamilton
Made all kinds of shopping baskets, also bicycle baskets and creels.

Jonathan Dennison, Gortinar, Manorhamilton
Made creels, shoppers and bicycle baskets.

Thomas Rourke, Cloone
Made creels, many of which were sold at St Manachan's fair in Mohill on 25 February. It is clear that the creels have a rounded bottom similar to those in **Pl. 2.13** but the Leitrim creels at that time had double uprights. The wale on the creel, known as a *buinne* in most parts of the west of Ireland at that time, were known as the 'ring' in Leitrim. The Leitrim creel has three rings: the first ring, the eye ring (for the window/*an táis*) and the third ring.

Frank Kilkenny, Tallaghtmore, Mohill
Seasonal creel-maker.

Thomas McGirl, Leitrim, Carrick-on-Shannon.
Creel-maker.

COUNTY LIMERICK

Francis O'Grady, Chapel Street, Limerick
A full-time basketmaker whose father was also a basketmaker. He made cradles, chairs, shopping baskets and bicycle baskets, which he

called 'pushkins'. He harvested about 200 bundles of willow at Ballinacurra on the banks of the Shannon but in all there were 15 acres there, some of it gone wild for want of cutting. Most of their rods were pitted and peeled for white. The best rods were 'reds'; golden rod and English green were the next best. The white rods were sometimes dyed with 'Bismuth Brown' to give them a buff appearance.

Patrick Delaney, Gerald Griffin Street, Limerick
Made a full range of baskets including cradles and wicker chairs. He had one acre of willow rented for cutting with the rest coming from the Shanahans.

Hickey Brothers, Francis Street, Limerick.
Also made a full range of baskets, cutting some willow by the Shannon with the balance coming from Shanahans.

Daniel Wills, Newcastle West
Made potato baskets and shopping baskets. The shoppers were always in peeled willow. Bought his willow from local farmers but didn't have enough for year-round work.

John Tully, Newcastlewest
Made farm baskets, calf muzzles and shoppers (seasonal).

Mrs Heffernan, Rathkeale
Made potato baskets shaped like flower-pots (known locally as 'hampers'). She also made calf muzzles (seasonal).

Patrick Moran, Castlemahon, Newcastle West
Although a thatcher by trade, he made bee skeps from wheaten straw sewn with split briar. The blackberry briar was cut in winter and split and shaved, then soaked for an hour before use. Size of skep was 15" (38cm) diameter at base and 16" (41cm) high.

COUNTY LONGFORD

Hugh Carty, Ballinalee, Co. Longford
Shopping baskets, bicycle baskets and creels.

Mrs Rose Coyle, Granard
Turf baskets (seasonal).

Joseph Keane, Ballynagoshen, Edgeworthstown
Creel–maker (seasonal).

James Farrell, Croshea, Edgeworthstown
Creel maker (seasonal); also a thatcher.

COUNTY LOUTH

Peter McGurk, Baltray, Drogheda
A blind basketmaker specialising in fancy work. Got his rods from a Mr Connolly in Carrick-on-Suir, though he had been unable to get rods in 1946.

James McCawley, Termonfeckin, Drogheda
Made shoppers and bicycle baskets.

COUNTY MAYO

Edward John McNeela, Derrykill, Newport.
Seasonal worker making creels and fancy baskets. He also made straw straddle mats.

John McAndrew, Dereens, Barnatragh, Ballina
Made skibs, which he said were often called round tables, and oval frame baskets called *corracháns* for collecting potatoes. He also made creels and made the handles of these from bog-deal rope (seasonal).

Michael Moran, Slievenagarch, Ballina
Sold baskets to shops in Ballina (seasonal).

John Feeney, Larganboy, near Ballyhaunis
Made straw horse-collars (see Chapter 7).

COUNTY MEATH

George Ogle, Drumconrath
Made shoppers and bicycle baskets from white rods, 'pellocks' from brown rods (seasonal). These are the *peillics* mentioned in Chapter 2. These are also listed among the baskets made in County Monaghan.

COUNTY MONAGHAN

Bernard McConnell, Coolderry, Carrickmacross

Mainly made 'pellocks' (these are the *peillics* mentioned in Chapter 2). Bought rods at £16.10.0 a ton. This quantity would make 14 dozen 'pellocks' and he used 6 tons of rods per year. The price of a dozen 'pellocks' was £3 in 1946. Many sold in Drogheda.

James Lennon, Coolderry, Carrickmacross

Also made 'pellocks' but on a smaller scale.

James Dunbar, Coolderry, Carrickmacross

Made 'pellocks' for local sale.

John McGrory, Leitrim, Silverstream

Worked with his three sons, all making potato baskets, probably the Ulster potato baskets mentioned in Chapter 3. Had 2 acres of willow and bought in rods to supplement this.

Felix Agnew, Leitrim, Silverstream

Made potato baskets only. Had 1? acres of rods.

James Mulligan, Cara Street, Clones

Turf baskets only. Did not have a sally garden; probably part-time.

Edward McPhillips, Rockcorry, Co. Monaghan

Although a carpenter by trade, he also made straw mats, hen's nests and straw mattresses.

COUNTY OFFALY

Michael Dunne, Kiltubber

Crandies of hazel were his main output.

Thomas Slamon, Kilcormac

Maker of hazel crandies with willow handles. These sold at 35/- a dozen. Worked from July until May every year, presumably using semi-green hazel.

James Spencer, Tubrid, Brosna

Potato baskets of hazel for £2 a dozen.

Thomas Treacy, Eden Road, Birr
Potato baskets.

COUNTY ROSCOMMON

John Higgins, Carracastle, Ballaghadereen
Made turf baskets and creels (seasonal).

Martin Gara, Clooncara, Ballaghaderreen
Made straw horse-collars and commented that there was great demand for them. These were similar to the stitched collars described under the heading Rough Plaited Collars, in Chapter 7. Martin Gara used rye straw and he first made a two-ply rope of the straw by twisting it on the fingers. This was then tied onto a willow rod that had been made to the shape of the collar. Subsequent rows were stitched to the first to build up the collar.

COUNTY SLIGO

John Grady, Fauleens, Monasteraden
Made shopping baskets, bread hampers and chairs in peeled rods.

Francis Cryan, Tully, Keash.
Made very high-quality baskets, some examples in National Museum collection.

John Grady, Fauleen, Monasteraden
His output was mainly 'fancy work' using peeled (white) rods (part-time).

COUNTY TIPPERARY

Patrick O'Connor, Connolly Street, Nenagh
He and two brothers, Joe and Martin, were full-time basketmakers and they also employed four or five boys whom they had trained. Made shoppers, bicycle baskets and rough horseshoe-shaped baskets for harvesting potatoes. They also had a contract for covering tea-pot handles in willow skein for the local aluminium factory.

Denis Corbett, Ballinderry, Borrisokane
Made wicker chairs, farm and shopping baskets (part-time).

Joseph and George Reid, Cloughjordan
Potato baskets (seasonal).

Frederick Draper, Dunkerrin, Roscrea

P. O'Shea, Ballylynch

P. Fitzgerald, Carrickbeg

COUNTY WATERFORD

Patrick Quinlan, Owbeg, Lismore
Full-time basketmaker working almost entirely in peeled willow. His osier bed, locally known as a 'twig bog', was rented from a Mrs Chanley, Saltersbridge, Cappoquin.

John Mongan, Bridane, Lismore
Worked full-time with his four sons at basketmaking, harvesting their willow along the River Bride where they had a 'twig bog' of about 20 acres rented.

Tom and Michael Quinlan, Tallow Hill
Worked full-time and had two 'twig bogs', one about 4 acres at Moorehill and one about 6 acres at Jeanville. They peeled most of their rods at that time.

Miss A. Maher, John Street, Waterford
Made shoppers, bicycle baskets and laundry and butchers' hampers. Bought her willow from Shanahans, Carrick-on-Suir.

Thomas Wade, Westown, Tramore
Made shopping, bicycle, fishing and farm baskets and also lobster pots. The farm basket was locally known as a kish and was of the creel type with sixteen uprights. The dimensions were 21" (53cm) long, 15" (38cm) wide and 18" (46cm) high. Lobster pots were circular with a 7" (18cm) neck and about 19" (48cm) high and wide.

William Power, Kilrosanty
Made kishes similar to those made by Thomas Wade (seasonal).

William Duggan, Villierstown, Cappoquin
Made potato baskets, stake and strand type.

Michael Devine, Bishopstown, Lismore

Thomas Foley, Grange, near Youghal
Made potato baskets, oval, frame basket type.

John Drohan, Villierstown, Cappoquin.
Made straw floor mats that were of *súgán* rope woven around rods
nailed onto a frame.

COUNTY WESTMEATH

George McCarthy, Kiltoom, Castlepollard
Potato baskets, shoppers and hampers (seasonal).

Thomas Moore, St Ciaran's Terrace, Athlone
Made lunch baskets and also shoppers and bicycle baskets. Harvested
willow in the countryside and found it difficult to get enough
material to work full-time. Lunch baskets were 10/– or 12/–
depending on size and bicycle baskets were 6/–.

Christopher Giff, Barrack Street, Mullingar
Made shopping, bicycle and potato baskets and also calf muzzles.
Used willow and dogwood but had difficulty sourcing rods.

Patrick Caulfield, Rathowen
Creel-making on an occasional basis.

Patrick Geraghty, Fermore, Streete
Creels and shoppers, occasional basis only. Noted that the only rods
around were strong sallies and there were no fine rods for 'fancy'
work.

Thomas Heavey
Creels and bicycle baskets, seasonal; main occupation was thatching.

Thomas McLoughlin
Creels and potato baskets. These were flat frame baskets that were
used to strain the potatoes in the Westmeath/Longford area.

COUNTY WEXFORD

Stephen Fortune, John's Gate St., Wexford
Shoppers, bicycle baskets, moses baskets and hampers. Bought rods from Shanahans, Carrick-on-Suir. This man was blind and worked full-time.

Christopher Moran, Commercial Quay, Wexford
This man was blind but worked part-time as he couldn't afford the rods. Made hampers and shoppers.

James Butler, Roslare Harbour
A blind basketmaker who made various types of shoppers and a lunch basket which he sold to railway workers. He used imported rods.

Patrick Owens, Monamolin, Gorey
Potato baskets on a seasonal basis.

Timothy Carr, Wells, Gorey
Farm and shopping baskets (seasonal).

Thomas Connolly
Part-time; cut his rods on banks of the River Slaney.

James Sullivan, Eire St., Gorey
Potato baskets, frame basket type (seasonal).

Ellen Holmes, Wellington Bridge
Potato baskets (seasonal).

Laurence Grace, Bannonmore
Potato and shopping baskets, used dogwood as well as willow (seasonal).

John Murphy, Taghmon
Coiled straw-work. He made children's chairs, bee skeps, and, up to 1935, he also made seed baskets (part-time.). The proof of a well-made skep was that it should be able to hold water.

Aidan Carty, Wellington Bridge
Plaited straw-work. Made straw floor mats, childrens' chairs and

hen's nests according to local demand (part-time.). He called each fistful of straw a 'fletch'.

Nellie Casey, Cloneven, Gorey

Plaited straw–work. Made hen's nests that were like a low cyclinder, about 2ft (61cm) wide and 10" (25cm) high.

Thomas Furlong, Kilmore Quay

Lobster pots, three types: (a) cylindrical, (b) French pots, (c) half cylinder. The cylindrical type had formerly been made completely of sally rods but by 1946 standards were of wire, weaving on top and bottom was willow and siding was wire netting.

COUNTY WICKLOW

Nicholas Hilliard, Ballinglen

Made the split oak potato baskets locally known as chip baskets. Also made ones with split oak ribs and willow weavers.

James Hilliard, Carnew

Made potato baskets and shopping baskets. The potato baskets were of split oak like Nicholas Hilliard's and some also had willow weavers. Some ash was also used.

John Marah, Rathnew

Made potato baskets of hazel and willow. While split hazel was used for the ribs, some baskets also seem to have been woven from split hazel. Also made whelk pots, as described in Chapter 5.

Thomas Kelly, Donard

Made potato baskets (frame basket shape) from willow, also occasional shoppers (seasonal).

Patrick Condren, Laragh

Made potato baskets (frame basket shape) from hazel and willows.

NOTES

Chapter 1

1 Research by Dr Olga Soffer, Dr James Adovasio and Dr David Hyland, in *Journal of Current Anthropology* (Spring 2000). See 'Science Time', *New York Times*, 14 December 1999.

2 Frank Mitchell and Michael Ryan, *Reading the Irish landscape*, (Dublin: Town House, 1997), 260.

3 A.T. Lucas, 'Wattle and strawmat doors in Ireland', *Studia Ethnographica Upsaliensia* (Essays presented to Åke Campbell), pp 16–35.

4 *Ibid.*

5 J. Raftery, 'Prehistoric coiled basketry bags', *Journal of the Royal Society of Antiquaries of Ireland* **100** (1970), 167–8.

6 T. Johnson, 'Willow growing', in *Some Irish industries*, (Dublin: Irish Homestead, 1897), 99. This book also has a chapter on the Letterfrack basketmaking factory, written by Miss Eastty (pp. 89–92).

7 T. Johnson, 'Willow growing', op. cit.

Chapter 2

1 James McParlan, *Statistical survey of the County of Mayo* (Dublin: Dublin Society, 1802). Page 70 states: 'Almost every poor man, of ever so small a holding must have his pony.'

2 The correct plural forms are *pardóga* and *liódanna* but I have used the English plural form of an added *s*, thus *pardóg* becomes *pardógs*. This convention is widely accepted when using Irish words in English.

3 Bill Egan in conversation with James Delaney, Irish Folklore Commission, 1976, 53ff., Main Manuscript Collection, Department of Irish Folklore, University College, Dublin.

4 Pádraig Óg Ó Connaire's novel *Giolcach*, quoted in *Conamara agus Árainn* 1880–1980 by Micheál Ó Conghaile (Cló Lar-Chonnachta 1988). (Author's translation).

5 E. Estyn Evans, *Irish folk ways* (London, 1957), 9, 169.

6 Department of Irish Folklore, Dublin, MS 39 (1934).

7 National Museum of Ireland, notes relating to F 1956:43, 'a cleeve made from dock stems'.

8 E. Estyn Evans, *Irish folk ways*, op cit., 173 ff.

9 Department of Irish Folklore; IFC, 1976, 56.

Chapter 3

1 The degree of poverty in pre-Famine Ireland is illustrated by a census by a national schoolteacher, P. McKye, in West Tullaghobegley, Co. Donegal, in 1839. Within a population of 4,000, he records the only furniture as 243 stools, 93 chairs, 8 chaff beds and 2 feather beds. The majority of people lived in one-roomed hovels, often without windows or chimneys, and slept on straw, rushes or even heather spread on the floor. Quoted in E. Estyn Evans, *The personality of Ireland* (1973), 93.

2 More details of this factory in Chapter 8.

3 E. Estyn Evans, *Irish folk ways*, Fig. 71, no. 4, 212.

4 Irish Folklore Commission, 1976: 53, Main Manuscript Collection, Department of Irish Folklore, UCD.

5 See notes accompanying the lossets, in the National Museum of Ireland.

6 Patrick Smyth, *Osier culture and basketmaking: study of the basketmaking craft in the south-west County Antrim* (Published by Patrick Smyth, Marymount, Lurgan, Co. Armagh, 1991).

7 Alfred Grant, quoted in *Osier culture and basketmaking*, op. cit., 39.

8 *Oak swill basketmaking in the Lake District* (Publ. Mary Barrat, Cumbria 1983).

9 There is a good description of the Longford boat skib in James G. Delaney, 'Baskets and their uses in the midlands', in A. Gailey and D. Ó hÓgáin (eds), *Gold under the furze studies in folk tradition* (Dublin, 1982), 215–27.

Chapter 4

1 Some sources give measurements of 6ft (183cm) long by 4ft (122cm) wide. It is possible that this size Boyne currach may have started out being longer and narrower but may have widened somewhat in use. This would certainly be possible if the twisted willow ties that hold the nets are broken, since they also act to hold the boat in shape by their tension.

2 A.E.J. Went, 'County Louth', *Archaeological Journal* **13** (1953), 18–33, quoted in E. Estyn Evans, *Irish folk ways* (Routledge 1988), 236.

3 James Mitchell, who learned to make the Boyne currach from Michael O'Brien, and James Craven were able to make the currach by the time this article was written in 1932, and had made one for the Millmount Museum. (From information supplied by Clive Ó Gibne.)

4 This story is included in P.W. Joyce, *Ancient Celtic romances* (1894; reprint London: Parkgate Books, 1997).

5 A full account of this voyage, including navigational details, can be found in Richard McCullagh, *The Irish currach folk* (Dublin: Wolfhound Press). I recommend this book for anyone interested in currachs and their use.

6 This voyage is documented in *Columba's crossing*, a documentary film by BBC Scotland.

7 Tim Severin, *The Brendan voyage* (Britain: Hutchinson Ltd; USA: McGraw Hil 1976). A concise account of the voyage is found in Seán J. White, 'The impossible voyage', *Ireland of the welcomes* (Nov–Dec 1978), 21–32.

8 A.B. The Rosses in 1753: An Appendix to *Historical memoirs of the Irish bards* by J.C. Walker vol. 2 (2nd Edition, 1818). Quoted in E. Estyn Evans, *Irish folk ways*, op. cit., 237.

9 C.H. Hartshorne, 'Early reminiscences of the great isle of Aran', quoted in Hornell, *British coracles and Irish curraghs* (London, 1938), Section 5 1.

10 *Ibid.*

11 E. Estyn Evans, *Irish folk ways,* op. cit., 238.

12 George Hill, *Facts from Gweedore* (Dublin, 1846), quoted in Hornell, op. cit.

13 John Delargy, Ediphone record taken 16 June 1930 with Michael O'Brien.

Chapter 5

1 Information supplied by Vincent McCarron, a basketmaker based at Bungowla, Innismór, Aran Islands. Vincent worked as a commercial fisherman for many years and also fished for lobster off Innismór, so his advice was invaluable for this chapter.

2 See *The Yarmouth Herring Cran*, a documentary film featuring Colin Manthorpe making a quarter cran basket, issued by the Basketmakers Association (see address in Select Bibliography). The skill needed for making these baskets can be readily appreciated from this video.

3   Brian Haslett, 'The fishermen-basketmakers of north Antrim', *Irish Basketmakers Association Newsletter*, 1999.

4   This photograph was marketed as a postcard 'Irish Fisherman *c.* 1920', by Dark Island, Turagh, Cappamore, Co. Limerick. It may be from the Lawrence Collection.

5   Tomás Ó Crohan, *The Islandman*, translated by Robin Flower (Dublin: Talbot Press 1937; reprint, Oxford University Press, 2000). 'The things I had seen them throwing into the sea were pots to catch lobster. The Blasket people were as strange to that sort of fishing tackle as any bank clerk at that time' (153).

6   Photograph no. B007 68.9 from collection at Béaloideas, Irish Folklife Commission, UCD.

7   Information supplied by Michael Barrett, c/o Pléaráca Conamara, Ros Muc.

8   Radio interview on RTE Radio. This was an interview featured in a selection from archive material, but I have been unable to locate further details of the programme.

9   Notes from card index on baskets at the National Museum of Ireland. Notes relate to F 1947,94, a heather lobster pot made by Richard Walsh, a native on Inishkea, in August 1947 at Doogort, Achill, from heather obtained on Slievemore Mountain. These depressions may also have been for the ropes which secured the pots. More information on heather pots is contained in IFC 1491:4–12.

10 Unpublished report by Chrissie O'Gorman for the Homespun Society. Begun in 1943 as a three-month experiment at the instigation of Muriel Gahan, this report developed into a major survey of the crafts in Ireland. All but one of the 26 counties of Ireland were surveyed, Dublin being omitted only because the Homespun Society was already informed about crafts-people there. Plans to survey the counties of Northern Ireland were not realised. See Geraldine Mitchell, *Deeds not words: the life and work of Muriel Gahan* (Dublin: Townhouse, 1997). The survey is the basis for the list of basketmakers in Appendix 5.

11 Notes supplied to the author by Brian Haslett from an interview with Sammy Gault.

12 My thanks to Aidan O'Sullivan of UCD for allowing me access to a proof copy of his new book for The Discovery Programme, *Foragers, Farmers and Fishers in a coastal landscape*, to be published in Novemebr 2001 by the Royal Irish Academy.

13 Information supplied by Laurence Hutson.

14 *The Porthleven Lobster Pot*, a documentary film featuring George Chambers. Available from Basketmakers Association (see address in Select Bibliography).

Chapter 6

1 E. Estyn Evans, *Irish heritage*, Dundalk: Dúndealgan Press 1942), 127.

2 The terms *murlag, murlainn* and *ciaracháin* are mentioned by Alistair Davidson in a communication to the Scottish Museum. Alistair is a basketmaker on the Isle of Arran in Scotland with a special interest in the Scottish traditional baskets. The word *creelagh* is used for the same basket by Dorothy Wright, *Baskets and basketmaking* (Newton Abbot: David and Charles 1972), 82 and 132. It is probable that this basket was introduced to Northern Ireland by Scottish settlers. A *muirleóg* is described in Ó Donaill's dictionary as 'a narrow-mouthed fish basket'.

3 E. Estyn Evans, *Irish Heritage*, op. cit., 127.

4 Rev J. Hall, *Tour through Ireland, particularly the interior and lesser known parts etc.*, (vol. 1 London 1813), 277, quoted in Claudia Kinmoth, *Irish country furniture 1700–1950* (London: Yale University Press, 1993), 165.

5 Thomas Mason, *The islands of Ireland* (Dublin, 1936; reprint, without photographs, Cork: Mercier Press, 1967), 24.

6 See A.T. Lucas, 'Making Wooden Sieves', *Journal of the Royal Society of Antiquaries of Ireland*, vol. 81 (1951), 148. This gives a comprehensive account of sieve-making. Dr Lucas also wrote further notes on making wooden sieves for the same journal, vol. 84 (1954), 59–67.

7 E. McLysaght, *Irish life in the seventeenth century* (Dublin, 1939).

8 Sue Gabriel and Sally Goymer, *The complete book of basketry techniques* (Newton Abbot, 1991; reprint 1999), 55; Mary Butcher, *Willow work* (London, 1986; reprint, Canterbury, 1995), 36–43.

9 See Gabriel and Goymer, *The complete book of basketry techniques*, op. cit., 134.

Chapter 7

1 For a comprehensive account of the different styles of thatching in Ireland, see E. Estyn Evans, 'The Thatched House', in *Irish folk ways* (Routledge, 1988).

2 Bill Egan in conversation with James Delaney, Irish Folklore Commission, 1976, 46, Department of Irish Folklore, UCD.

3 Thomas Ó Maille, *An Béal Beo* (Baile Átha Cliath: Comhlucht Oideachais Na hÉireann), 44; 'Bíonn fiataíl no tuí shúgáin a' fás ar thalamh bun gharbh'.

4 J.G. Delaney, extract from a letter by Mr Delaney to the National Museum. Extract is recorded in an entry card for a seed-sowing basket from County Offaly.

5 K.M. Harris, 'Plaited straw work', *Ulster Folklife* **9**, (1963), 53.

6 E. Estyn Evans, *Irish heritage*, op. cit., 60.

7 K.M. Harris, 'Plaited straw work', op. cit., 55.

8 E. Estyn Evans, *Irish folk ways*, op. cit., 206 and 207.

9 E. Estyn Evans, *Irish folk ways*, op. cit., 34–8 and 120.

10 K.M. Harris, 'Plaited straw work', op. cit., 57.

11 William Carleton, *Traits and stories of the Irish peasantry* (Dublin, 1830), quoted in K.M. Harris, 'Plaited straw work', op. cit., 54.

12 K.M. Harris, 'Plaited straw work', op. cit., 58.

13 The samples of straw seed-sowing baskets in the National Museum of Ireland that I have seen have all been made using coilwork technique.

14 Jill Dixon, 'Strawboy's costume from County Fermanagh', *Ulster Folk and Transport Museum Yearbook* (1978/1979).

15 From information contained in a letter to the author by Meg McSpirit Jones, Lower Mullinastea, Enniskillen, Co. Fermanagh.

16 Mrs Stevenson, Drumclamph, Co. Tyrone, quoted in K.M. Harris, 'Extracts from the Committee's Collection', *Ulster Folklife* **6** (1960).

17 E. Estyn Evans, *Irish folk ways*, op. cit., 279.

18 Ibid., see illustrations of Halloween caps from County Down and County Kerry, 278.

19 Robert E. Bernen, *More tales from the Blue Stacks* (London: Hamish Hamilton, 1983). The story referred to is called 'Two Lives'.

20 E. Estyn Evans, *Irish folk ways*, op. cit., 164.

21 Ronald H. Buchanan, 'Calendar customs', *Ulster Folklife* **9** (1963), 61.

22 William Lithgow, *The Totall Discourse of Rare Adventures, and Paineful Peregrinations of Long Nineteene Yeares. Trauayles, from Scotland, to the most famous kingdoms in Europe, Asia and Africa* (London: 1622), quoted in A.T. Lucas, 'Irish ploughing practices', *Tools and Tillage* **2** (4) (1975), 195.

23 Thomas Dineley, *Observations on a voyage through the kingdom of Ireland by Thomas Dineley, Gent, in the year 1681* (Dublin 1870), quoted in A.T. Lucas, 'Irish ploughing practices' **2** op. cit., 79.

24 Quoted in A.T. Lucas, 'Irish ploughing practices' **4**, op. cit., 198.

25 Ibid., 198.

26 Michael McGrath, SJ (ed.), *Cinnlae Amhlaoibh Uí Súilleabháin* (London, 1936), quoted in A.T. Lucas, 'Irish ploughing practices', op. cit., 201.

27 J.G. Kohl: *Travels in Ireland, translated from the German* (London 1844), quoted in A.T. Lucas, *Irish ploughing practices*, op. cit., 198.

28 E. Estyn Evan, *Irish folk ways*, op. cit., 207.

29 Jonathan Bell, 'Horse collars in County Donegal', *Ulster Folk and Transport Museum Yearbook*, (1981/1985), 8.

30 Irish Folklore Commission, MS 1319, 197, Department of Irish Folklore, University College, Dublin, quoted in A.T. Lucas, 'Irish ploughing practices', op, cit., 202.

31 Jonathan Bell, 'Straw harness collars in Ireland', *Ulster Folklife* **24**, (1978), 24.

32 Ibid., 27.

33 A.T. Lucas, 'Irish ploughing practices', op. cit., 203.

34 Jonathan Bell, 'Straw harness collars in Ireland', op. cit., 27.

35 (A.W. Hutton (ed.), *Arthur Young's tour in Ireland 1776–1779*, vol. 1 (London, 1892), quoted in A.T. Lucas, 'Irish ploughing practices', op. cit., 204.

36 George Hill (ed.), *The Montgomery Manuscripts* (Belfast, 1869), quoted in A.T. Lucas, 'A hay rope packsaddle from County Louth', *Journal of the County Louth Archaeological Society* **15**, (1) (1961), 14.

37 A.T. Lucas, 'A hay rope packsaddle from County Louth', op. cit., 16.

38 A.T. Lucas, 'An Fhóir: a straw rope granary', (*Gwerin* 1956). This article contains full details of the *síogóg*, 2–20.

39 *Ibid.*, 7.

40 *Ibid.*, 17.

41 Geraldine Mitchell, *Deed not words: the life and work of Muriel Gahan*, (Dublin: Townhouse, 1997), 76.

42 *Ibid.*, 67.

43 E. Estyn Evans, *Irish folk ways*, op. cit., 208.

44 *Ibid.*, 268.

45 *Ibid.*, 268

Chapter 8

1 Alastair Heseltine, *Baskets and basketmaking* (Princes Risborough: Shire Publications Ltd., 1982), 4.

2 See W.R. Hughes, *Sophie Sturge: a memoir* (London: George Allen and Unwin, 1940).

3 Buff is a reddish-brown-coloured willow. The colour is obtained by boiling the willow for about six hours and then peeling it.

4 *Osier culture and basketmaking: a study of the basketmaking craft in south-west County Antrim.* (Marymount, Lurgan, Co. Armagh: Patrick Smyth), 25–26, 30.

5 I'm indebted to Geraldine Mitchell, author of *Deeds not words: the life and work of Muriel Gahan* (Dublin: Townhouse, 1997), for providing me with this survey.

6 Patrick O'Connor was eventually forced out of business by a prohibitive bill for carriage on an order. He had understood that carriage would be based on the weight of the baskets but it was instead calculated by bulk. This information was supplied by Geraldine Mitchell, who interviewed him around 1995.

Chapter 9

1 Mike Cooley quoted in John Quinn, *My education* (Dublin: Townhouse, 1997) 60.

GLOSSARY OF ENGLISH AND IRISH TERMS

Glossary of English terms

Back:
: Outside curve of a willow rod.

Bardock:
: Anglicisation of *bardóg* or *pardóg,* a hinged bottomed creel in Cavan and Monaghan.

Base sticks:
: Thick bottom sticks.

Belly:
: Outside curve of a willow rod.

Boss:
: A straw seat or stool.

Brown:
: Rods that have been dried with the skin on them and which must be soaked before use. The actual colour of the rods need not be brown (see also green).

Bucky briar:
: Wild rose.

Buff:
: Rods that have been peeled and boiled to give a buff (brownish-red) colour.

Butt:
: The thick part of a willow rod.

Chip basket:
: A basket made from split oak or split hazel (see Chapter 3).

Cleeve:
: Anglicisation of *cliabh* (see also creel).

Clew:
: A ball of twisted hay or straw rope known as *sugán* rope.

Coilwork:
: Making a basket using a core of material that is then coiled and sewn.

Coppice:
: A system where trees are cut at or near ground level. The shoots that spring up are cut on a rotation from one to twenty years depending on the thickness of the poles required. Some trees are often allowed to grow to full height while the coppice occupies the understorey in a system known as coppice with standards.

Cram:
: Kinking a stake and pushing it into the work rather than pulling it through. Often used when finishing a border, especially in professional work.

Crandy:
: A basket made by sticking the uprights into the ground, making a creel-like basket, which is then bordered when it is pulled from the ground.

Creel:	A basket made by sticking the uprights into the ground and described in detail in Chapter 2; known as a *cliabh* in Irish.
Currach, curragh:	Anglicised forms of *curach*.
Currags:	Bundles of osiers or sallies tied together and placed outside on the windward side of the door during winter months to prevent draughts, mainly in the north-east of Ulster where some houses had spikes driven into the wall to hold currags.
Fletch:	Small handfuls of straw used in weaving, a term mainly used in the south-east.
Flow:	The angle or slope of the side of a basket.
Frame basket:	A basket made on a frame or a hoop.
Froe:	A tool for splitting large diameter logs to get chips or spale; illustrated in Chapter 3.
Green:	Fresh rods that have been either just cut or have been left lying in grass to keep them fresh. Semi-green rods have partially dried and are often used for creel–making.
Hoop:	A ring of willow, hazel or bucky briar that can be used to make a frame basket hold the uprights at the correct angle when making a stake and strand basket.
Hodson Bay codger:	A round basket made like a creel in the Hodson Bay area near Athlone, Co. Westmeath.
Kish:	A large basket made on the principle of a creel for putting on a slide car; described in detail in Chapter 2.
Osier:	A variety of willow suitable for basketmaking.
Packing:	Extra weaving back and forth to fill a space.
Pairing:	Weave using two alternate rods, which is mostly used on bases. This is explained and illustrated in Appendix 1.
Panel:	A hay packsaddle, for more details see under the heading Straw and hay packsaddles, Chapter 7.
Plain border:	The most common border in willow basketmaking, where the stakes are initially kinked and knocked behind one or two uprights before being taken in front of other rods. Illustrated in Appendix 1.

Picking off:	Trimming the basket with a picking knife.
Randing:	A system of weaving where one weaving rod crosses an upright each time. The most common form used in Ireland was French randing (known simply as randing in Ireland) and this is explained in Appendix 1.
Rive:	To split wood along the grain. This can be done by hand, sometimes using a knife or bill-hook as a lever to help in splitting. One can also use a riving brake for this. This is a hardwood pole tapered to a thin angle on one face.
Sally:	A willow rod, from the Irish *sail* or *saileog*.
Scallom:	Tongues cut on rods to facilitate attachment to a hoop or a rectangular base.
Scuttle:	A County Clare term for a hoop-style potato basket.
Siding:	The weaving on the side of a basket.
Skeins:	Willow rods that have been split with a cleave (see Tools, Chapter 1) and then shaved to give thin, pliable lacing strips.
Skib:	An English form of the word *sciob* (a potato basket).
Skep:	An old word for a basket; usually refers to a straw basket for bees.
Slewing:	Weaving with two or more weavers (see Fig. 8.12).
Slide car:	A horse cart without wheels that was dragged along rough roads. It was usually fitted with a large basket called a kish (see Chapter 2, Fig. 2.26).
Slype:	Slanting cut, usually on the butt of a rod to facilitate insertion into the base.
Spale:	A word used in the UK to describe split oak baskets.
Stake:	Upright or vertical element in a willow basket.
Stake and strand:	A basket where weavers (or strands) are woven over and under rigid stakes, which are usually vertical.
Staking up:	The process of putting the stakes into the base and pricking them up.
Standards:	Another word for stakes.
Stool:	A willow stump from which rods grow.

Straddle:	A curved wooden yoke with pegs for hanging creels. The straddle is pinned to the straddle mats by pins (see Chapter 7, and also *srathair* in list of Irish words).
Straddle mats:	Woven in three-strand plait, these provide protection for a donkey's back.
Strawboy:	An uninvited visitor to a wedding who dressed in straw costume to gain entry and who provided entertainment by dancing or playing music.
Stroke:	A single movement or weave similar to a stitch in knitting.
Suggan:	An anglicised form of *súgán,* which can refer to a twisted straw or hay rope but can also refer to any object or basket made using three-strand plait technique; thus a suggan could be a head cushion of twisted hay or straw (County Roscommon) or a collar used in the classroom (Ulster).
Tate:	A small handful of straw for weaving; can also be referred to as a fletch or a wisp.
Thraw hook:	Used for making *súgán* rope.
Tip:	Thin end of a willow rod.
Twisted rod handle:	Small handle sticking up from the border of the basket. Usually made from two rods that must be twisted to enable them to form a handle (see technique section of Chapter 8).
Underfoot base:	A technique used in professional basketmaking to form a slath without splitting the base sticks (see technique section of Chapter 8).
Uprights:	Another word for stakes.
Upsett:	The foundation rows of weaving on a basket.
Wale:	A stroke using three or more weavers. A wale is strong so is used at the upsett and at the top. The mouthwale (*buinne béil*) is a special wale that is used at the start of the creel.
Weaver:	A weaving rod.
Wheeze:	A straw mat used to protect a thatcher's knee.
Whelper:	A County Roscommon term for a strawboy.
White:	Rods that have been peeled.
Withy:	A willow rod.

Glossary of Irish terms

Liosta foclaí Gaeilge atá baint acu le caoladóireacht.

Áis (an t-áis):   The open section or window of the creel.

Bacach: Term for a strawboy in west Clare and Cork. Also a beggar or lame person.

Baithis: The top of a lobster pot (see illustration of *póta gliomach*/lobster pot.

Barrach: The neck of a lobster pot. This can aso be spelled as *bearrabach* (see IFC 1491: 4–12)

Barrdóg: Variation of *pardóg*, anglicised as bardock in Cavan and Monaghan.

Birdeog: A Kerry frame basket mainly used for potatoes.

Birín: Bait stick used with a wicker lobster pot (diminutive of *bior*, pointed rod.

Bogshifín: Bulrush (*Scirpus lacustris*).

Braighdeán shúgáin: A straw horse-collar.

Brídeog: Straw doll representing St Bridget.

Buinne: A wale.

Buinne béil: The mouthwale or top wale, mostly used to refer to the initial wale used in the creel or *cliabh*.

Buinne cúil: Foundation wale (lit: the back wale) or upsett.

Caisín: Border of a basket.

Caisirnín: Kink, also a hard turn on an over-twisted straw rope.

Caoladóir: Basketmaker.

Caoladóireacht: Basketmaking.

Ceirtlín súgáin: A ball or clew of *súgán* (straw rope).

Cis: Wicker container or basket, also wickerwork sides for a cart (anglicised as kish) (plural: *ciseanna*).

Ciseán: A basket.

Ciseog: A shallow potato basket used for straining and serving potatoes.

Cisín: Diminutive of *cis*, a small food basket (Aran Islands), a hen's nest or laying basket (County Leitrim).

Cléibhín: A little basket, usually a little creel but could also be used to refer to other small baskets.

AN CLIABH

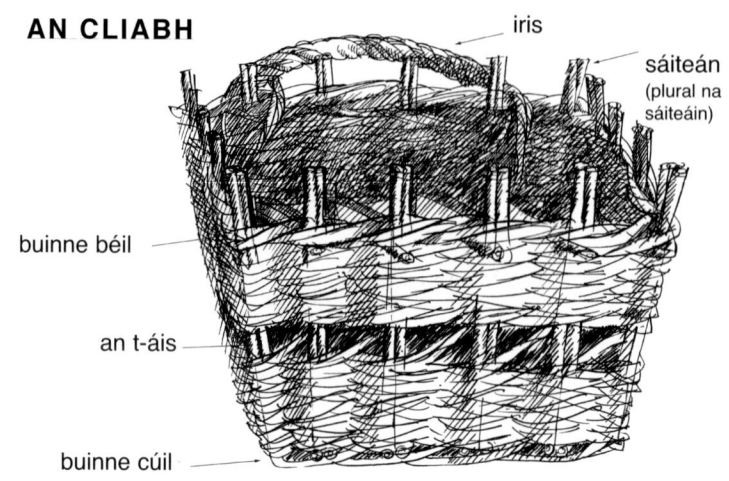

iris

sáiteán
(plural na
sáiteáin)

buinne béil

an t-áis

buinne cúil

Cliabh:	A creel, see illustration by Alex Bury.
Cliabh buana:	A reaping basket or creel.
Cliabh droma:	A back creel.
Cliabhán:	A cradle.
Cliabhán caolaigh:	A wicker cot.
Cliabhán éin:	A bird trap (usually called a cradle bird in English).
Cliath:	A wicker hurdle.
Cliatha caolaigh:	Wattle hurdles, often used to refer to wattle hurdles used in roofing.
Cliath thulca:	A flood raft.
Cluas:	Handle
Criathar:	A fine-meshed sieve.
Coll:	Hazel (*slat coill*: hazel rod).
Coirb:	The yoke or wooden cross-piece of the straddle.
Corr Shúgáin:	Thraw hook or rope twister for making *súgán* rope.
Cosáin iall amuigh:	Depressions on top of a heather lobster pot.
Crompán:	A stump, a block of wood. The plural form *crompáin* was used in Inniskea, Co. Mayo to describe the extra sticks put into the base of a lobster pot, these additional rods were called *scibhéirí* in other districts of west Mayo, (see IFC 1491: 4–12).
Crúbóg:	A low, creel-like basket with two handles used in Ulster; a knot in weaving.

Curach:	Currach, coracle (*currachán:* diminutive of *curach*).
Dallán:	Blind sieve used for winnowing.
Doimhineóg:	A straw rope granary. This word was used in the area around Dunmanway, Co. Cork. In other areas of west Cork the granary was known as a *síogóg, fóir* or *fóirín*.
Easna:	Rib, upright rod of a basket (plural: *easnacha*).
Fiataíl:	Purple moor grass, a grass widely used for making *súgán* ropes and for thatching. This grass is commonly called sedge in Ireland. See also note 3, Chapter 7, where *fiataíl* is equated with *tuí shugáin*.
Fíochán:	**1**; (act of) weaving. **2**; weave.
Fionnán:	Purple moor grass (sedge) that has whitened in late Autumn or Winter; can be used for making *súgán* rope and for thatching..
Fóir:	A straw rope granary, this word was used in the Garrynapeeka area of west Cork, and the diminutive form *fóirín* was used near Macroom.
Gad:	A twisted twig or osier; *gad brollaigh:* a twisted rod used to tie the hames in tackling; *an slat a cruaighann le aois, is deachair é a sníomh 'na gad* (the rod that hardens or ages is hard to twist into a willow tie; *is mithid a bheith ag bogadh na ngad* (it's time to soften the rods, i.e., prepare for tomorrow).
Gadrach:	A withy tie, a tough osier or withy.
Garbhóg:	A sally or wicker; *garbhóg shailí:* a thick sally rod.
Iris:	Handle of a creel, as in *iris cléibh,* also occasionally spelt as *eiris;* see also *muic-iris.*
Lámh:	Handle.
Lód:	A slip-bottomed creel, term mainly used in Galway and south Mayo (see also *pardóg).*
Losaid:	Shallow food basket, a potato basket in County Fermanagh, anglicised as losset. Also a 'kneading trough ot 'dough tray'.
Luachair:	Field rushes; *brobh luachra:* a rush.
Lúbacha:	Small circles of two-ply *súgán* rope used to fetter sheep.

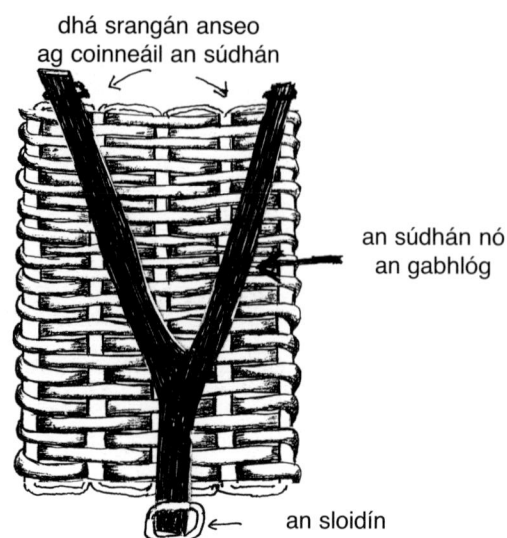

dhá srangán anseo
ag coinneáil an súdhán

an súdhán nó
an gabhlóg

an sloidín

Tóin na pardóige agus an súdhán
Pardóg base and forked stick

Maide Seasta:	A thick upright.
Meathán:	A weaving rod, see also *slat fí.*
Meigeall:	A torpedo-shaped ball of *súgán* rope used for chair seating (from *meigeall;* a goat's beard.
Muic-iris:	A straw rope for a creel; carrying straps of *súgán* rope for carrying a back creel.
Muiríneach:	Bent-grass used for *súgán* ropes and thatching.
Muirleóg:	A murlin or murlan, a round, narrow-mouthed basket used, according to Dineen's Dictionary, by fishers for sand eels; also refers to yarn basket; variations include *murlóg, múrlóg, murlán, múrlan.*
Pardóg:	A hinged-bottomed creel used on a donkey or pony, see illlustration of base: *tón pardóige.*
Peillic:	A wicker basket made similiarly to a creel and used for harvesting potatoes (County Meath area), a straw hen's nesting basket (County Mayo), e.g. *peillic chocáin,* a basket as in *trí peillice gacha tighe, peillic deachmhaide agus peillic míreann agus peillic tuirtín ciricc* (three baskets for each house, the tithe basket, the crumb basket and the wax basket).
Pillín:	Straw roll or pad used to carry loads on the head.

Pota gliomach
(Lobster Pot)

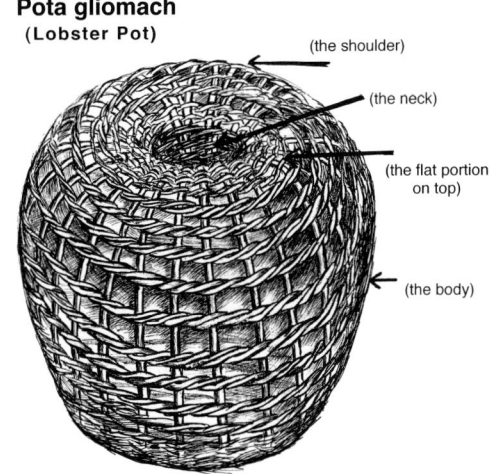

(the shoulder)

(the neck)

(the flat portion
on top)

(the body)

Pota fraoch:	Heather (lobster) pot.
Pota gliomach:	Lobster pot.
Púicín:	Calf muzzle.
Punann:	Sheaf, e.g. *punann coirce,* a sheaf of oats.
Putog:	Thick *súgán* rope impregnated with mud or clay plaster.
Riabh:	An Aran Island longline basket.
Ribh:	Variation of *riabh*.
Rilleán:	A large-meshed riddle for winnowing grain.
Sail:	Willow, anglicised as 'sally'.
Sailchearnach:	Pussy willow, goat willow.
Saileán:	Osier bed, sally garden.
Saileánach:	Osier, usually used in Connemara to refer to reddish-coloured willow used for lobster pots.
Sailearnach:	**1** Sally rods; **2** Sally field or willow bed.
Saileog:	Willow (shrub).
Saileog bhuí:	Common osier with a yellow tinge, usually called golden sally or golden osier.
Saileog dhubh:	Black sally.
Saileog ghlas:	Common osier.
Sáiteán:	Stake; *sáiteáin cléibh:* stakes of a creel; *sáiteáin ciseáin:* stakes of a basket.
Saoiste:	A straw seat.
Saoisteog:	Variation of *saoiste*.
Sciath:	A shield-shaped basket, a wicker-work partition, a frame basket used for harvesting potatoes (Munster).

Sciathóg:	Diminutive of *sciath*, a ribbed frame basket used for straining and then serving potatoes.
Scib:	A basket, usually a potato basket; loosely used it can describe a boat-shaped frame basket (*sciathóg*) or a flat potato tray (*ciseog*); *scib sheileán*: a wicker bee skep.
Seamhnán:	Seed basket
Seastán:	A stand, but this word is sometimes used for an upright; plural: *seastáin*.
Siantán:	A hen's nest (straw basket). This term from County Clare was used in Chrissie O'Gorman's survey (Appendix 5).
Síogóg:	A straw granary (see also *fóir* and *doimhineóg*).
Siomnóg:	A straw hen's nest (east Galway). I got this word from John Michael Larkin of Ballinakill, Co. Galway. Other words for the hen's nest included *síomóg* and *siúnán* in Galway and Clare, *pocóide* in Galway and Sligo, *caiteog* in Leitrim and Roscommon and *fáir* in Donegal and Sligo; other recorded terms include *séideog* and *púcán* in Mayo(quoted in *Tiachóg, peillic and objects of straw and rush* by Ann O'Dowd).
Slat:	Rod.
Slat fí	*Weaving rod.*
Sop:	A wisp, e.g. *sop tuí*, a wisp of straw.
Sop Srathrach:	A straddle mat.
Srathair:	A straddle, a harness pad, a packsaddle; *srathair fhada*: a long straddle. The parts were as follows: **1** *Coirb:* The wooden cross piece. **2** *Scuróg:* The handle or peg from which the creel hung. Also known as *scorán*. **3** *Clár:* The side board. **4** *Srathair:* The mat or pad (although it could also refer to the entire straddle). **5** *Pionna Srathrach:* Straddle pin (also *sáiteán*). **6** *Tiarach:* The crupper or tail band. **7** *Tarrghad:* Belly band, also *fáscadh faoi*.
Starragán	A poaching basket which was illegal to have in ones possession. It could also be used as a

back basket. There were local variations.
Some of these baskets must have been
roughly made since the word came to refer
to any clumsy basket.

Súgán: Straw rope.

Súgán saic: A straw or hay pack saddle.

Súisteog: A variation of *saoisteog*.

Súistín: A variation of *saoistín*.

Táis: A variation of *áis*, the open section of a
creel, as in *an t-áis*.

Tiachóg: The *tiachóg* could be made of either field
rush or straw. The rush *tiachóg* was a type of
bag with a top draw-string of plaited rush
that could be pulled to close the *tiachóg*. The
straw *tiachóg* was a burden basket similar to a
haversack, made using three-strand plait
technique. It was primarily used for carrying
grain and potatoes.

Tóin druidte: The bottom of a rush *tiachóg*.

Tónóg: The base of a *pardóg*.

Tuí: Straw.

Tuí choirce: Oat straw.

Tuí chruithneachta: Wheat straw.

Tuí seagail: Rye straw.

Úim: Donkey pannier in County Kerry; plural
úimeacha; (e.g. *úimeacha móna:* turf panniers).
The twisted rod that connects the panniers
is referred to in Chrissie O'Gorman's survey
(Appendix 5) as the *burlach;* the stout stick
to which the rods are tied is named a *maide
burlaigh*. The hinged-bottom is called a
sciathán and the bottom stick a *ribín*.

SELECT BIBLIOGRAPHY

Irish interest

Basketmakers Association, Newsletter 56, an Irish Issue (Winter 1991).

Bell, J. 1978 'Straw harness collars in Ireland.' *Ulster Folklife* **24**, 23–30.

Bell, J. 1981/85 'Horse collars in County Donegal.' *Ulster Folk and Transport Museum Yearbook,* 7–8.

Bernen, R. E. 1983 *More tales from the Blue Stacks*. London: Hamish Hamilton.

Brody, H. 1973 *Inishkillane: change and decline in the West of Ireland*. London.

Crafts Council of Ireland. 1994 *Basketmakers, May 5th to June 25th 1994*. Exhibition catalogue with illustrations by Ursula Mattenberger and an introduction by David Shaw-Smith. Dublin.

Danaher, K. 1978 *A bibliography of Irish ethnology and folk tradition*. Dublin.

Delaney, J. 1982 'Baskets and their uses in the Midlands.' In A. Gailey and D. Ó hÓgáin (eds.), *Gold under the furze: studies in folk tradition*. Dublin.

Dineen, P. S. 1927 *Foclóir Gaedhilge agus Béarla*. Dublin.

Dixon, J. 1978/79 'Strawboy's costume from County Fermanagh.' *Ulster Folk and Transport Museum Yearbook.*

Evans, E.E. 1957 *Irish folk ways*. London. (Reprinted 1988, Routledge, London.)

Evans, E.E. 1942 *Irish heritage*. Dundalk: Dúndealgan Press.

Evans, E.E. 1981 *The personality of Ireland: habitat, heritage and history*. Belfast.

Gailey, A. 1962 'Ropes and rope twisters.' *Ulster Folklife* **8**, 72.

Hall, J. 1813 *Tour through Ireland, particularly the interior and lesser known parts etc.* vol. 1. Dublin.

Harris, K.M. 1963 'Plaited straw work.' *Ulster Folklife* **9**, 53–60.

Hill M. and Pollock, V. 1993 *Women of Ireland, image and experience, c. 1880–1920*. Belfast.

Hogan, J. 1999 'Prospects for willow growing in Ireland.' *Irish Timber and Forestry* **8**, (8) 16–18.

Hornell, J. 1938 *British coracles and Irish curraghs*. London.

Irish Folklore Commission, *Manuscript Collection,* UCD Library, Dublin.

Kinmoth, C. 1993 *Irish country furniture 1700–1950*. London: Yale University Press.

Lucas, A.T. 1956 '*An Fhóir*. A Straw Rope Granary.' In *Gwerin,* 2–20.

Lucas, A.T. 1961 'A hay rope packsaddle from County Louth.' *Journal of the County Louth Archaeological Society* **15**, (1), 13–16.

Lucas, A.T. 1954 'Bog wood. a study in rural economy.' *Béaloideas* **23** 96–105.

Lucas, A.T 1975 'Irish ploughing practices.' *Tools and Tillage* **2** (2) 67–83; **2** (4) 195–210.

Lucas, A.T 1951 'Making wooden sieves.' *Journal of the Royal Society of Antiquaries of Ireland* **81**, 146–155, and **84** (1954) 59–67.

Lucas, A.T 'Wattle and straw mat doors in Ireland.' *Studia Ethnographica, Upsaliensia* (Essays presented to Åke Campbell).

McCullagh, R. *The Irish currach folk.* Dublin: Wolfhound Press. 1984.

McManus, M. 1986 *Crafted in Ireland.* Ulster Folk and Transport Museum exhibition catalogue.

J. Manners, 1982 *Irish crafts and craftsmen.* Belfast.

Mason, T.H. 1936 *The Islands of Ireland.* Dublin. Reprint without photographs, Cork 1967.

Mitchell, F. and Ryan, M. 1997 *Reading the Irish Landscape.* Dublin: Townhouse.

Mitchell, G. 1997 *Deeds not words: the life and work of Muriel Gahan.* Dublin: Townhouse.

Ó Conghaile, M. 1988 *Conamara agus Árainn, 1880–1980.* Cló Lar-Chonnachta.

Ó Crohan, T. 1937 *The Islandman.* Translated by Robin Flower. Dublin: Reprint Oxford: Oxford University Press, 2000.

Ó Dónaill, N. 1977 *Foclóir Gaeilge-Béarla.* Dublin.

O'Dowd, A. 1984 'Baskets.' In David Shaw-Smith (ed.), *Ireland's traditional crafts.*

O'Dowd, A. 2001 '*Tiachóg, peillic* and objects of straw' in S. Ó Catháin (ed.), *Northern lights—essays in honour of Bo Almqvist.* Dublin.

O'Neill, T. 1977 *Life and tradition in rural Ireland.* London.

Ó Súilleabháin, S. 1942 *A handbook of Irish folklore.* Dublin. Reprint 1963.

O'Sullivan, A. 2001 *Foragers, farmers and fishers in a coastal landscape.* Dublin.

O'Sullivan, J.C. 1971 'Sheep cribs from County Offaly.' *Journal of the Royal Society of Antiquaries of Ireland* **101**, 109–12 and 141–2.

Pollock, V. and Hill M. 1993 *Women of Ireland, image and experience, c. 1880–1920.* Belfast.

Raftery, J. 'Prehistoric coiled basketry bags.' *Journal of the Royal Society of Antiquaries of Ireland* **100**, 167–8.

Sharkey, O. 1985 *Old days, old ways.* Dublin.

Shaw-Smith, D. 1984 *Ireland's traditional crafts.* London.

Smyth, P. 1991 *Osier culture and basketmaking: A study of the basketmaking craft in South West County Antrim:* Marymount, Lurgan, Co. Armagh: Patrick Smyth.

Other books

Barratt, M. 1993 *Oak swill basketmaking in the Lake District*. Cumbria.

Bobart, H. 1936 *Basketwork through the ages*. Oxford. Reprint London 1997.

Boston, E. and Heseltine A. 1986 *David Drew: baskets*. London.

Butcher, M. 1999 *Contemporary international basketmaking*. London.

Butcher, M. 1986 *Willow work*. London. Reprint Canterbury 1995.

Duchesne, R., Ferrand, H., and Thomas, J. 1981 *La vannerie: l'osier*. Paris.

Elton Barrat, O. 1960 *Basketmaking*. London.

Florance, N. 1962 *Rushwork*. London.

Gabriel, S. and Goymer S. 1991 *The complete book of basketry techniques*. Newton Abbot. Reprint 1999.

Heseltine, A. 1982 *Baskets and basketmaking*. Princes Risborough: Shire Publications Ltd.

Law, R.N. and Taylor, C.W. 1991 *Appalachian white oak basketmaking*. Tennessee.

Madsen, S.H. 1994 *Flet Med Pil*. Copenhagen.

National Museums of Scotland. 1998 *Making Weaves*. Exhibition catalogue. Edinburgh,

Nicolson, A. and Sunderland, P. 1987 *Wetland: life in the Somerset levels*. London.

Okey, T. 1912 *An introduction to the art of basketmaking*. London. Reprint Canterbury.

Stephenson, S.H. 1977 *Basketry of the Appalachian Mountains*. New York.

Stott. K.G. 1956 'Cultivation and uses of basket willows.' *Quarterly Journal of Forestry*.

Verdet–Fierz, B.and R. 1993 *Willow basketry*. Colorado.

Wilkinson, J. and Vedmore, A. 2001 *Craft willows in Scotland*. Fife.

Wright, D. 1992 *The complete book of baskets and basketry*. Newton Abbot.

Films, videos etc.

Hands, a series of films made for RTE by David Shaw–Smith. Subjects covered include rushwork, the Shanahan brothers and the basketmakers of Loch Na Fooey. Contact David Shaw–Smith, Film Corporation of Ireland, Rinaneel, Ballyglass, Claremorris, Co. Mayo. Tel: 00353 (0) 94 60370.
Fax: 00353 (0) 94 60371.
E-Mail: filmcorpireland@eircom.net

Hidden Treasures, four films with rich archive footage directed by Ann O'Leary and made for BBC Northern Ireland and RTE by

Loopline Films. Available from Loopline Films, c/o Griffith College, South Circular Rd., Dublin 8.
Tel: (01) 453 5081.
E-Mail: loopline@tinet.ie

Porthleven Lobster Pot and *The Yarmouth Herring Cran,* Documentary videos available from the Basketmakers Association Sales, 216 Walton Road, East Molesey, Surrey, KT8 0H8, UK.

The Irish Basketmakers Association will have videos available from 2002. Contact secretary, Linda Scott, Willow Works, Knockmore, Co. Mayo, .